The Political Economy of the Transition Process in Eastern Europe

The Arne Ryde Foundation

Arne Ryde was an exceptionally promising young student on the doctorate programme at the Department of Economics at the University of Lund. In 1968, at the age of only 23 years, he died after an automobile accident. In his memory his parents Valborg Ryde and pharmacist Sven Ryde established the Arne Ryde Foundation for the advancement of research at our department. We are most grateful to them. The Foundation has made possible important activities to which our ordinary resources are not applicable.

With the agreement of Valborg and Sven Ryde, we have decided to use the funds made available by the Foundation to finance major scientific events, mainly a series of symposia. Our intention is to alternate between pure theory and important applications. The themes of our previous Arne Ryde Symposia have been: Economics of Information (1973), Econometric Methods (1975), The Theoretical Contributions of Knut Wicksell (1977), The Economic Theory of Institutions (1979), Social Insurance (1981), Pharmaceutical Economics (1982), The Role of the Primary Sector in Economic Development (1983), Incentives and Economic Systems (1985), Problems of the Mixed Economy (1987), Nya fält för marknadsekonomin (New Areas for the Market Economy, 1988), Nonlinearities, Disequilibria and Simulation (1990), and Trade, Growth and Development – the Role of Politics and Institutions (1991).

Björn Thalberg

The Political Economy of the Transition Process in Eastern Europe

Proceedings of the 13th Arne Ryde Symposium,
Rungsted Kyst, 11–12 June 1992

Edited by

Laszlo Somogyi

Edward Elgar

Published by

Edward Elgar Publishing Limited
Gower House
Croft Road
Aldershot
Hants GU11 3HR
England

Edward Elgar Publishing Company
Old Post Road
Brookfield
Vermont 05036
USA

British Library Cataloguing in Publication Data

Political Economy of the Transition
Process in Eastern Europe: Proceedings of
the 13th Arne Ryde Symposium, Rungsted
Kyst, 11–12 June 1992
I. Somogyi, Laszlo
330.947

ISBN 1 85278 857 7

Printed and Bound in Great Britain by
Hartnolls Limited, Bodmin, Cornwall.

Contents

Tables and Figures

Abbreviations

AECD	Agency for Economic Coordination and Development
BNB	Bulgarian National Bank
BFTB	Bulgarian Foreign Trade Bank
BTA	Bulgarian Telegraphic Agency
BTPA	Bilateral Trade and Payments Agreement
CEC	Commission of the European Community
CEEC	Central and East European Countries
CEPR	Centre for Economic Policy Research
CIS	Commonwealth of Independent States
CMEA	Council for Mutual Economic Assistance
COMECON	Council for Mutual Economic Assistance
CSCE	Conference on Security and Co-operation in Europe
CSFR	Czech and Slovak Federal Republic
DDR	German Democratic Republic
DM	Deutsche Mark
EC	The European Community
EEC	European Economic Community
EFTA	European Free Trade Area
EIB	European Investment Bank
EPU	European Payments Union
FSU	Former Soviet Union
G-24	Group of Twenty-four
GDP	Gross Domestic Product
GDR	German Democratic Republic
GM	General Motors
GMT	Greenwich Mean Time
IEA	International Energy Agency
IIASA	International Institute for Applied Systems Analysis
IMF	International Monetary Fund
KIME	Kazakhstan Institute of Management and Economics
LPG	Landwirtschaftliche Productions-genossenschaften
MTOE	Metric Tons Oil Equivalent
NBER	National Bureau of Economic Research
NEM	New Economic Mechanism
NEP	New Economic Policy
NIC	Newly Industrialised Countries
NMP	New Material Product
NVA	Negative Value Added
OECD	Organisation for Economic Cooperation and Development
PCSC	Paris Conference of Security and Co-operation in Europe
PET	Planned Economies in Transition

PIT	Personal Income Tax
PPP	Purchasing Power Parity
PPWW	Popiwek
R&D	Research and Development
SAO	State Audit Office
SEI	Socialist Economic Integration
SITC	Standard Industrial Trade Classification
SOE	State-owned Enterprise
SPA	State Property Agency
SPC	State Property Company
SPK	Statens Pris och Konkurrensverk
STS	Soviet Type System
TR	Transferabel Rouble
UA	Unemployment Assistance
UDF	Union of Democratic Forces
UI	Unemployment Insurance
UK	United Kingdom
UNDP	United Nations Development Programme
USD	US Dollar
VAT	Value Added Tax
WIDER	World Institute of Development Economic Research of the United Nations University
ZBE	Zwischenbetriebliche Einheiten

Preface

The 13th Arne Ryde Symposium, which took place on 11–12 June 1992, dealt with the highly complex problems of transforming centrally planned economies into free market economies. The Symposium was held at Rungstedgaard, Rungsted Kyst, Denmark, on the estate that used to belong to the Dinesen family. Back in 1934 one Isak Dinesen, a member of the family, published a book entitled Seven Gothic Tales. The book, which became an instant success in the United States, laid the foundations for the fame of its author, better known under the name of Baroness Karen Blixen.

Old Knudsen is a character of Baroness Blixen's world-famous novel *Out of Africa.* He was one of those visitors from Europe who drifted into Karen's African farm 'like wrecked timber into still waters, turned and rotated, till in the end they were washed out again, or dissolved and sank.' Old Knudsen was a born rebel who 'did not even respect, or believe in, the law of gravitation ... he saw no reason why it should not be – by unprejudiced, enterprising people – changed into the exact reverse.'

The events that have unfolded since 1989 in the East and Central European region sometimes make the worried spectator wonder whether the governments which are desperately trying to lead their tormented countries into the relatively still waters of Western capitalist civilisation, should be in possession of those supernatural powers of which old Knudsen was dreaming. In the meantime, researchers struggle to disentangle the myriad of problems faced by the policy makers of the ex-socialist countries. During their intensive, two-days deliberations, the participants of the 13th Arne Ryde Symposium made considerable intellectual efforts of their own to contribute to the better understanding of these problems. When the proceedings of the Symposium now appear in print, it is hoped that the readers of this volume, scholars, students, or people actively involved in the transition process, will gain some important fresh insights into the utterly complex problems of this process.

Thanks are due to the Arne Ryde Foundation without whose support neither the publication of this volume, nor the Symposium itself would have been possible. The editor also wishes to express his gratitude to Alan Harkess for his efforts and skills for transforming the manuscripts of the majority of us into readable English, to Jörgen Norén for taming our computers, and last but not least, to the indefatigable secretary of the project, Jeanie Petersson who converted the disparate material dumped onto her desk into a nice, camera-ready manuscript.

Lund, February 1993.

Laszlo Somogyi

1

Introduction

*Laszlo Somogyi**

The two and a half years that have passed since the inception of the reform process in Central Europe allow us to pass only a tentative judgement on its success or failure. The transition from planning to market is a largely process of learning by doing, not least because at the outset, there was no clear theoretical blueprint for its design and implementation, nor were there entirely relevant historical experiences to imitate. Thus, it looks timely and appropriate to make a tentative evaluation of the process.

The papers presented at the 13th Arne Ryde Symposium on the Transition Problem covered a large variety of problems and policies in various countries. Most of the authors felt that there was a need for a simultaneous attack on several fronts: transition policies should be seen as a 'big push', although not necessarily a 'big bang'. Therefore, instead of presenting the papers one by one, this introduction will single out the most burning issues and put them into the broader context of the general current of Transition Economics, represented by the ideas of a small but influential group of mainly Western scholars.

First Principles

There is a vast literature on the transition from capitalism to socialism, while that on the movement in the opposite direction hardly existed three years ago. Policy makers and advisors had mainly to rely on first principles (for an inventory see Grosfeld, 1990) and near-relevant historical experiences: neoclas-

* Department of Economics, University of Lund. Helpful comments by Yves Bourdet, Björn Thalberg, and Bodil Thordarson are gratefully acknowledged.

sical synthesis-type theorising, assessment of Ricardian or Heckscher–Ohlin-type comparative advantage, and property rights and transaction cost analysis on the one side; as for history: stabilisation and structural adjustment programmes in third world and semi-industrialized countries in Latin America, and elsewhere as well as growth strategies in Asia. During the last and increasingly senile years of communism, there was still some talk of a socialist market economy, partly as a result of wishful thinking in radical circles in the West, partly as a manifestation of pragmatism (on the side of economists in the East) because, as recently as in the late 1980s, the total collapse of communism was so hard to imagine.

There were exceptions, though. Having scrutinised the attempts at reforming the Hungarian economy, Kornai (1986) reckoned that the limits of reforming a socialist economy were already reached. He also found it unlikely that any government anywhere else could go much further within the traditional socialist framework. One year later, a group of dissident Hungarian economists demanded a far greater role for the private sector and the implementation of outright monetarist macro-policies as well as increased political pluralism in the country (Antal et al., 1987). In Poland Jan Winiecki (1990) came to the conclusion that, as a result of the given distribution of wealth which ensured for members of the *nomenklatura* privileged access to goods in short supply and countless other benefits, party *apparatchiks* and members of the economic bureaucracy had a considerable interest in preserving the *status quo*, with its muddled property rights and ill-functioning markets.

By 1990 the goal was no longer a socialist market economy but a market economy pure and simple, and the question was no longer where to go but how, and how fast. The unfavourable initial conditions and the observed direction of change presented researchers and policy makers with an overwhelming task: low and falling incomes; shortage of essential goods; high and accelerating inflation; environmental degradation; grossly distorted prices; underdeveloped infrastructure; indebtedness; lack of essential services; a multiplicity of irrelevant exchange rates; underdeveloped or non-existent financial markets.

Despite substantial differences in initial conditions, there is in the profession a rather broad consensus on the main elements of the reform:

- macro-economic stability
- liberalisation and restructuring of production and trade
- institutional change
- a social safety net

Most of the papers presented at the symposium were about macro-economic adjustment and institutional change, although liberalisation and restructuring naturally entered the discussion as a result of their potential impact on macro-performance and the inter-relationship with institutional development. To date few attempts have been made to formally model the macro-economics of transition. Instead, attention has been focused on two omnipresent phenomena, *viz.* inflation and balance of payments disequilibria and how to cure them.

Inflation and Budget Deficit

Why is combating inflation of such paramount importance? Back in the 1950s and 1960s it was widely thought to be beneficial to have a moderate inflation as it would facilitate investment and the structural adjustment necessary for growth. Although such tolerance is no longer found in the declared policies of developed industrial countries, bringing down the annual rate of inflation to two digit figures is considered better than merely acceptable in the first phase of transition. In other words, the problem is the high level of inflation, rather than its mere presence.

The main macro-economic consequence of a high rate of inflation is that it renders money less and less useful. It is '... a tremendous disorganising force that will destroy the financial structures that a private enterprise economy requires in order to function efficiently and in order to mobilise the capital for growth.' (Leijonhufvud in this volume). But rapid changes in the price level also have undesirable effects on relative prices: because the speed of adjustment in one market will differ from that in other markets, investment and production decisions will be based on incorrect information.

Anti-inflation policies and recommended devaluations figure prominently in most structural adjustment programmes designed for developing countries. There are important analogies between the disturbances observed in LDCs and those in the ex-socialist countries: in both groups of countries, one of the main causes of inflation is the deficit in the government's budget. Since capital markets are non-existent or underdeveloped, the deficit will be monetised. In addition, repressed inflation and, in some countries, a considerable monetary overhang may exist as a result of decades of price controls and consequential forced savings. Blejer and Szapáry (1989 and references therein; see also McKinnon 1992 and 1991, Chapter 11 and Szapáry in this volume), were among the first to observe that market-oriented reforms in socialist economies tend to lead to inflation for reasons other than the planned and immediately monetised budget deficit. In the traditional socialist economy, taxation of enterprises was implicit in so far as the state, the owner of the enterprise, could extract the latter's profit without reference to any formal system of taxation. With marginal profit taxes amounting to anything up to 100 per cent, managers had no incentives to be efficient. Since one of the very purposes of marketisation was enhanced efficiency, marginal and average enterprise taxes had to be reduced. The change of amortisation rules had the same efficiency-enhancing and tax-reducing effects. With decentralised decision making and the corporatisation of state-owned enterprises, the state has fewer opportunities to collect taxes.

Thus, even without austerity measures, market-oriented reforms tend to weaken the income side of the budget more than they strengthen – if at all – the expenditure side. Such a strengthening would follow from the abolition or gradual reduction of subsidies to enterprises. Current experiences in Central Europe indicate that tax receipts fall for a variety of other reasons as well. As output falls, so do both enterprise and personal incomes and, as a consequence, personal consumption. It follows that revenues from enterprise, personal income, and consumption taxes will also fall. There are negative indirect effects as well: due to widespread inter-enterprise credits, the failure of one enterprise may pull down others as well. The increasing amount of bad debt tends to reduce (or even eliminate) whatever profits the banks may have made, thereby reducing tax payments still further.

The emergence of a host of new private businesses should, in theory, improve the income side of the government's budget, but the combined effects of an underdeveloped tax collection system and the reluctance of people to pay taxes have hitherto given meagre results.

At the same time, the payment of rapidly increasing unemployment benefits weighs heavily on the expenditure side which is also burdened by increased payments for badly needed investments in all kinds of infrastructure – railways, the road network, telecommunications – long neglected in the region.

The immediate abolition – or gradual phasing out – of subsidisation impacts heavily on the budget deficit but, at the same time, it also fuels inflation. The latter effect, however, may be a one-shot affair, provided governments have the nerve to withstand the pressure from labour unions and other interest groups to pay full compensation for price rises. If public policy is successful, price rises will level off.

Macro-Balance, Liberalisation, and Institutional Change

In addition to being a macro-economic policy instrument, scrapping subsidies will also contribute to liberalisation by reducing price distortions. Liberalisation is itself a multidimensional phenomenon. To fulfil its efficiency-enhancing function, it must lead to the elimination of distortions. Subsidisation, however, is not the only source of distortions. It is well known that the industries of the former communist countries are highly concentrated. Increased competition, essential for increased efficiency, can be stimulated in a number of ways: by finding an appropriate exchange rate; by removing all the obstacles to the establishment of new firms, domestic and foreign alike; by splitting existing monopolies; and by allowing foreign goods to compete. At least two of the above measures, the breaking up of companies and opening up the economy to unrestricted foreign competition, are controversial and will be dealt with in subsequent sections.

Liberalisation, in turn, necessitates institutional change. First of all, there is a need for a clear definition of property rights and a legal framework for the enforcement of contracts. This is overwhelmingly the task of the state but, as Rubin (in this volume) argues, there is considerable scope for private initiative in setting up institutions designed to stifle opportunism and thereby reduce the costs of transacting. Legislation on competition is another major element in the reformed institutional structure. Furthermore, there must be rules to deal with bankruptcies. However, one of the major shortcomings of the institutional set-up of most ex-socialist countries is the virtual absence or grossly under-developed state of financial markets. As pointed out (in this volume) by Csaba, this constitutes a serious impediment to rapid and large-scale privatisation.

Simultaneity or Sequencing of Reforms

The exchange rate has also both macro- and micro-economic implications. From the macro-economic point of view, it serves as a means to balance the foreign exchanges. Its micro-economic significance is to determine which goods should be exported and which ones should be imported.

Hence, it is no accident that most reform proposals place a heavy emphasis on comprehensiveness and simultaneity. In grossly distorted economies, with large-scale shifts not only in the terms of exchange but also in macro-economic intervention and institutional adaptation, policy measures will interact far more than in developed market economies where such interventions are most often marginal.

There are a number of highly debated and controversial issues: the pace of change, the strength of corrective measures, the sequence of transition policies. The first and second points will be discussed in some detail in the next two sections. On the third one, not very much was said at the symposium but a brief note here is not out of place, first of all because mainstream economics lets us down on the subject.

To date, McKinnon has provided the most penetrating analysis but other writers are also bothered by the sequencing problem. McKinnon's main concern is with government finance and the state of financial markets. Similar to other analysts, he gives the highest priority to balancing the central government's finances. This is to be achieved by limiting government spending to a small share of GNP, establishing a new system of taxation with a broad tax base that taxes both enterprise and household incomes and, last but not least, by setting up an internal revenue service to collect taxes.

The second stage is the liberalisation of domestic trade and domestic capital markets, a process that should start with charging positive real interest rates and limiting new credit flows until the price level is stabilised. He even argues for the exclusion of liberalised enterprises from formal bank credits –

leaving them to finance their operations by generating their own savings, borrowing on the informal market, or selling bonds and shares – until macro-economic stability is attained.

As to the opening up of external trade and payment flows, this should be done first '[A]fter the (successful) liberalisation of domestic trade and finance ...'(1991, p. 7). The liberalisation of capital accounts transactions should also come much later than that of current account transactions (as should the decentralisation and privatisation of the banking sector). Let us also note that, for McKinnon, the liberalisation of foreign trade is not the same thing as the scrapping of all tariffs at once (more of this below).

In WIDER (1991), the desirable sequence is specified as: 1. the establishment of appropriate price signals (which requires both macro-economic stabilisation and price liberalisation); 2. the creation of an incentive system with the establishment of underdeveloped and missing markets, and the definition and codification of a new structure of property rights; and 3. the setting up of a social safety net. However, they add: 'Some measures [laws, rules, institutions] ... must be implemented right away ...' (p. xxi).

Inspired by the Plan Monnet, Stoléru (1990) strongly emphasises the inter-relation of political and economic decisions. In his view, there should be a political consensus on the main ingredients of the reform and continuous consultations during its implementation. As to sequencing, Stoléru urges currency convertibility and the introduction of market clearing prices, the establishment of financial institutions and the demolition of all obstacles to private enterprise (which is not the same thing, however, as immediate privatisation). Handling the imbalances (unemployment, structural disequilibrium) would come in the second phase, and total liberalisation (doing away with tariffs, relieving the labour and capital markets from restrictions) at the end of the process.

For Newbery (1991), in turn, the main concern is the monopolistic structure of state-owned enterprises. In order to 'keep open desirable options and foreclose undesirable options' monopolies should be broken up before privatisation since 'splitting up enterprises before they are privatized keeps open options for subsequent merger where there are genuine synergies. It will, on the other hand, be much harder to break up monopolies after they have been privatized.' (See also Somogyi and Török in this volume.)

Few would doubt that macro-economic stability is one of the most important preconditions of successful reforms. However, in the papers presented at the symposium, sequencing issues were more implied than explicitly stated, suggesting, perhaps, that researchers are losing interest in the topic. As Nuti puts it (in this volume): 'There is now ... widespread agreement that, whatever the merits of a possibly potentially superior critical path it is much more important to move as fast as possible 'meandering' in the right direction than to make slower progress along a sequentially optimal path, even if it existed.' Looking for the optimal sequence may even prove paralysing: 'In Poland institutional reforms practically came to a standstill in the first half of 1990 for a considerable time, while privatisation was unnecessarily delayed by political arguments and by the pursuit of facile schemes of mass privatisation.' (ibid).

A similar conclusion is reached by the IIASA (1991) group concerning changes in the former Soviet Union: '... the time is short. ... There is no time for half-measures or for carefully planned stages, sequences and steps. Decisive actions must be taken quickly ...' (p. 93), although the members of this group themselves spell out measures to be implemented *before* ('... establishing the infrastructure for the market, stabilizing the budget ...') and *after* D-day, when prices are freed, the economy is opened, and hard budget constraints are imposed on SOEs (ibid., p. 102).

Creative Destruction or Overkill: Dimensions of the Bang

When output falls, is it a result of an ordinary slump in the business cycle or of structural imbalances? This is a question which has been bothering macro-economists, researchers and policy makers alike, for a long time. In a free market economy, firms and industries are born, they prosper, decline, and, when no longer profitable, they die. Schumpeter labelled this process of economic Darwinism as *creative destruction* whereby enterprises in the possession of new products or new production processes smash the demand curves of their technologically less advanced competitors. In the capitalistic world of today agonising companies are sometimes saved and put on a new track by benevolent governments. The major difference between real life capitalist and real life socialist companies is that the latter may never have been viable propositions. Moreover, as a result of a highly distorted price structure, it is hard to tell which industries are profitable and which ones are not, and even harder which enterprises within the latter group have the potential to become competitive at international prices. Creative destruction in the East European context would mean the elimination of actual and potentially unprofitable industrial capacity.

Shock Therapy vs. Gradualism

One of the more controversial issues of transition policies is the shock therapy vs. gradualism problem, the implication being that shock therapy (or big bang) would cause greater hardships – in the form of a greater fall in output and employment – in the short run, but, after some time, it would result in faster recovery and growth. It is hardly possible to give a precise definition of big bang. However, we can describe the concept with reference to the ideas of Sachs, one of the pioneers of this strategy (*The Economist*, 13 January 1990, and 19 January 1991; Sachs, 1990 and 1992). The key words are simultaneity and speed: to establish free and stable market prices by doing away with price controls, subsidies, cheap credits, vertical relationships, the monopoly power of state-owned enterprises, the obstacles to setting up private business, quota restrictions and high tariffs in foreign trade, and, last but not least, by opening up the economy to foreign competition. To ensure macro-economic balance, the government's budget must be balanced or, at least, the budget deficit reduced substantially. To attain currency convertibility the multiple exchange rate system must be replaced by a unified one combined with a massive devaluation.

Looking at some of the country experiences dealt with in this volume we can single out the case of Poland as a big bang benchmark (the former GDR would be even better but its case is atypical because, apart from the policy-delivered shock components, it also had immediate access to all the modern institutions of capitalism as well as to the markets of the EC member countries, a huge influx of capital, and freedom for labour to move). Starting on 1 January 1990, the Polish reform programme had most of the ingredients prescribed by Sachs (Nuti in this volume): prices were liberalised for 90 per cent of transactions; subsidies were reduced from 17 per cent of GNP in 1989 to 4 per cent in 1990; monetary policy became restrictive, average turnover taxes went up from 10 to 20 per cent, a uniform capital tax was introduced, and the state budget was balanced; wage increases in excess of the guidelines were heavily taxed; and, after a somewhat excessive devaluation and with the fixed exchange rate chosen as the nominal anchor, the currency was made convertible for current account transactions (for households a floating rate was applied).

Bulgaria (see Nuti and Wyzan in this volume) adopted a similar programme but with some significant differences. Even here, the bulk of prices (90 per cent) were liberalised (the exceptions mainly being energy prices). Foreign trade was to be liberalised gradually. The nominal anchor would be the money supply, the exchange rate was unified but would float. Wage ceilings in SOEs were chosen as the instrument for incomes policy.

Hungary was the only country to opt for a more gradual approach, probably because of its long history of reforms. Although the reform pendulum was swinging all the time with decentralisation followed by intensified central control and the loosening of the reins again, the last two and a half decades before the reemergence of democracy left important marks in at least three areas which put the country some steps ahead of its socialist neighbours. Agricultural output grew enough to feed the population and generate some export earnings. Small-scale private enterprise managed to take a firm hold despite ideological bashing and even outright harassments. From 1979 and onwards, repeated attempts were made to reform the institutional structure: the establishment of a bond market and of an embryo of a stock exchange, and the reforming of the banking system paved the way for the rebuilding of financial markets. The tax system was also reformed: income taxes and VAT were introduced. Lastly, a new company law together with legislation on bankruptcy and liquidation also contributed to the modernisation of the institutional environment.

With the basic institutional building stones in place, the new government that took office after the March–April 1990 elections embarked on its slow but steady transition path. Three-quarters of consumer prices were liberalised, the budget was almost balanced in 1990. As to the exchange rate, a crawling peg has ensured a relatively stable real effective rate. Foreign trade was liberalised for about 90 percent of goods and services (Ábel and Bonin, 1992).

Where adopted, the big bang-style policy shock was superimposed on another one already present: the external shock that was caused by the collapse of trade within the former socialist bloc. Thus, as a result of external shocks as well as of policy choices, output fell in all of the countries concerned. Although such a development was expected, many observers were surprised by the extent and duration of the recession. In most cases the figures are comparable with those observed in Britain, Germany and the United States in the 1930s. Compared with 1988, GDP in 1991 was some 32 per cent lower in Bulgaria and 19 and 11 per cent lower in Poland and Hungary, respectively (Williamson in this volume).

Avoidable vs. Unavoidable Reform Costs

The question is: to what extent can the policies actually pursued be blamed for the outcome. Williamson (ibid.) offers a taxonomy for analysis according to which the sources of loss in output are classified into a decline in external and internal demand, and in supply.

Let us consider these categories one by one. A fall in external demand may be caused by either an exogeneous decline in the demand for exports or an overvalued currency under a fixed exchange rate regime. A currency overvaluation is self-inflicted thereby causing an avoidable loss. Williamson puts East Germany and tentatively also Poland into this category. The collapse of COMECON-trade is apparently more tricky. Williamson puts it as the cause of an unavoidable welfare loss, while Nuti argues that 'Keenness to undermine Soviet dominance [and other motives] ... have resulted in the otherwise *avoidable costs* of trade collapse within the ex-CMEA' (in this volume; italics added). However, it could be argued – as it was at the symposium – that, since the CMEA was a vehicle for Soviet economic and political dominance, the desire of member countries to gain independence made it quite natural to press on for the dissolution of the organisation. Moreover, despite the formal liquidation of COMECON, some former member countries were making (vain) efforts to sustain past trade relations with (different parts of) the Soviet Union, but Russia's declining ability to produce and thereby its capacity to pay for imports, alongside its apparent inability to honour past financial obligations, have made continued exports increasingly risky.

Among the causes of insufficient internal demand mentioned by Williamson, we single out unnecessarily contractionary monetary and fiscal policies. Williamson believes this was the case in the CSFR and possibly also in Poland where excessive devaluations gave rise to a redistribution of income – from wage and salary earners to entrepreneurs and the state, transfers to the latter showing up as a budget surplus. Nuti's assertion that '... in Poland it was a mistake to let real wages and the real exchange rate float at random with the vagaries of inflation ... to effectively tax old loans by raising their interest rates ...' (ibid.) as well as those of Szapáry (ibid.) and of the WIDER group (ibid.) blaming continued uncertainty and scepticism concerning government policy belong also to this category.

Using a demand-determined model, Brada and King (1992) come to the conclusion that '... macro-economic policy in [the CSFR, Hungary, and Poland] may well have been excessively deflationary and hopes for an economic recovery will require governments to adopt a more expansionary stance than they have been willing to countenance to date.' (p. 51).

Protection for Whom? Infant and Senile Industries

The decline in output may also emanate from the supply side and the entries listed by Williamson under this heading are exogeneous supply shocks, uneconomic output, input dislocation, credit squeeze, and monopoly pricing which, except the first and last types of disturbances, all give rise to avoidable losses. What to do with uneconomic output seems to be the most controversial issue. It is expedient to divide the industries that generate such output into two groups. The first group consists of the 'value subtractors', i.e., those with negative value-added at international prices. In the other group we put industries with positive but very small value-added ('senile industries').

The 'big bang' solution, with world market prices adopted and subsidies scrapped overnight, would (and has in Eastern Germany) result(ed) in the immediate closure of such industries. Sachs (1991) finds the protection of value subtractors unjustified. Williamson and Nuti argue (in this volume) for the temporary protection of senile industries as long as they generate positive value-added, while Brabant (also in this volume) suggests temporary subsidies.

In his recent book on the order of economic liberalisation McKinnon (1991, Chapter 12), hypothesises that present value subtractors may become potentially profitable. The technologies of many industries in the former socialist bloc were chosen in view of the low oil prices set by the Soviet Union. Given time, part of these industries could be made profitable by selecting a less energy-intensive technology. Therefore, McKinnon finds it justified to give temporary protection even to some value subtractors.

It is clear from what has been said above that gradualism (or certain aspects of it) is (are) not entirely out. Temporary protection of some industries has many supporters, albeit with the possible provisions that there ought to be a timetable for phasing out the tariffs and that such a timetable should be credible. An alternative solution is advanced by Nuti who would prefer temporary income transfers to protection.

Experience of the past few years suggests that, amidst political turbulence, it is difficult indeed to stick to a harsh programme. The obvious example is Poland: after a brave start in January 1990, wage rises were outpacing guideline indexes already in the second part of that year. In 1991, the trade surplus fell drastically, the budget deficit took a deep dive, the currency began to crawl, and, last but not least, the government that had engineered the shock therapy programme was swept away by the November 1991 elections (Wilczynski, 1991, and Williamson in this volume).

Privatisation

The question of ownership rights occupies a subordinate place in mainstream micro-economics textbooks. The hegemony of neoclassical economics and Lange's apparent victory over the Austrians over half a century ago gave the long-lasting impression that asset ownership mattered little from the point of view of resource allocation. Non-Marxist Schumpeter, albeit no neoclassical exponent either, even predicted the eventual victory of socialism over private enterprise capitalism. Even though the majority of economists probably believed in the superiority of private enterprise capitalism, the question of private vs. public ownership did not fit into the general analytical framework of traditional theory. As Lindbeck (1973, p. 12) remarked, hard core theory had to give way to critical reflections and common sense, '... fragile instruments to analyse difficult social problems.'

More recently, however, the arguments in defence of capitalism have become less timid as well as more articulated. As the IIASA group puts it: 'Privatisation is necessary ... because only private owners can establish an enduring basis for self-financing and managerial independence. Private owners have a vested interest in the long-run financial success of the firm.' (ibid., p. 150). Furthermore, ownership rights may be held desirable from the democratic point of view, since they increase the independence of the individual from the state. In addition, they may serve the purpose of equity as well as that of mobilising political support, in our case, for the reform programme. However, our attention will be mainly focused on their efficiency-enhancing functions, while comments on the other objectives will be inserted here and there. We should also remember that the objectives of privatisation will have to be attained subject to a variety of constraints: underdeveloped institutions, inexperienced agents, macro-economic disarray, a generally noisy environment for decision making.

There are a few detailed questions to ask about the privatisation process. What should be privatised and what should remain in state ownership? Should priority be given to new private business or to the privatisation of SOEs? What should be the speed of the privatisation process? How to compensate previous owners (if at all)? What forms should privatisation take: free distribution of assets or sales? If sales, should certain groups ('insiders') have preferential access to assets or should everything go to the highest bidder? Even if he is a foreigner? Should companies be sold individually or should they be put under holding companies? What role should be assigned to institutional investors? What should be done with collective and state farms? What ways are there for the state to assert its property rights during the process of transition? What will be the rights of SOEs to markets previously monopolised? How will these rights change when the SOE is sold? The questions are many and we are not going to discuss them all. But surely, the process is bound to be both complex and long.

Theoretical Arguments for Privatisation

Let us shortly recap the theoretical underpinnings of the ideal, private enterprise, competitive economy. Traditional theory holds that, in the absence of externalities and economies of scale, perfect competition and utility and profit maximising behaviour will lead to a Pareto-efficient state. Big business capitalism could violate these conditions on at least two counts because, apart from the externalities issue, monopoly profits may be reaped and, as a result of the separation of ownership and management functions, profits will not necessarily be maximised.

In the following we leave aside the externalities issue, not least because the environmental disasters in the former Soviet Union and the other socialist countries should be evidence enough that the public ownership of productive resources is not a sufficient condition to solve the pollution problem. (Aage, in this volume, discusses the sustainability of transition with respect to the environmental constraint.)

From the debate of the recent past, in this introduction we single out three propositions pertinent to the problem of privatisation:

– when ownership and management functions are separated, private ownership is more conducive to profit maximisation and efficiency than is public ownership;

– the breaking up of state monopolies is necessary for the establishment of competitive markets;

– during the initial phases of the transition process, market signals are bound to be distorted by a noisy environment. This will have consequences for the desirable speed and sequencing of privatisation.

The issue of efficiency decomposes into allocative efficiency, a principal determinant of which is market form, and corporate governance. As McAuley puts it (in this volume): 'The 'case' for privatisation thus involves two implicit assumptions: that both factor and product markets are competitive and that private owners do, indeed, exercise better corporate governance than politicians and civil servants.'

Let us start with the simplest case, *viz.* small-scale enterprises, where agency problems do not arise or are likely to be small (small shops, restaurants, small farms, petrol stations, and the like). By selling such production units to individuals, markets can be made reasonably competitive almost overnight, the financial stakes are fairly small, foreigners need not be involved, etc. Competitiveness basically hinges on the human capital embodied in the owner-manager.

It is no accident that the privatisation process started with this sector all over the region with the added component of the establishment of new businesses. In Poland this second component seems to dominate. Hungary, in turn, made a headstart with small-scale private firms long before the fall of the communist regime. There was also the intermediate alternative of leasing businesses (mainly restaurants) from the state. After 1989, small-scale privatisation, with both new establishments and buyouts, intensified. In Russia, as well, small-scale privatisation is the priority. According to plans, more than half of such establishments will be sold before the end of 1992 (for more details see McAuley in this volume).

The problems are bound to be considerably greater when it comes to privatising large firms. One essential question is: in an economy where ownership and management are separated, how can managers (the agents) be made to act in the long-term interests of owners (the principals)? The answers the profession has come up with have two components (for an overview, see Grosfeld, 1990, McAuley in this volume, and Tirole, 1991): incentive contracts can be used to partially align the interests of managers and owners; and by monitoring specific markets (the stock market, the takeover market, the market for managers) owners may get a fairly good idea about the performance of hired managers. If, for example, the general index of the stock market is increasing while the value of a specific company is falling, the owners of the firm have all the reasons in the world to find out whether the poor performance of their firm depends on adverse market conditions or the incompetence of the company's manager. Similarly, if a takeover bid is placed on the firm, owners might suspect that there are unrealised profits that the actual management of the company is unable or unwilling to coax out. Then dissatisfied owners can, if they wish, sack the manager.

Strong Owners and Competitive Conditions

A caveat, though: if ownership is dispersed, the cost for the typical shareholder of supervising managers could greatly exceed the benefits to him. Thus, as it is widely held, strong owners are more conducive to efficient corporate governance than weak ones.

The state *could* be a sufficiently strong owner. Competent, altruistic, and dedicated civil servants, acting on behalf of the state, *could* wield enough power to minimise opportunism on the part of managers. One problem is: why should they? With the monitoring civil servant, an extra agent is introduced into the decision-making process, an agent who must be monitored and given incentives to act in the interest of the principal, i.e., the politicians, who are the agents of the people, who must be monitored. Another problem is that senior managers and workers' representatives often have political clout, knowledge of which may make the monitoring civil servant think twice before he picks a quarrel with workers, managers and politicians. The absence of the threat of bankruptcy may also be a source of SOE-inefficiency. Despite all the added theoretical complications, empirical studies suggest that, given *competitive conditions,* a public enterprise can be as efficient as a private one. In this view, what really matters is market form, rather than the nature of ownership (for reference see McAuley).

Alas, conditions in East Europe are different. The label *competitive conditions* implicitly assumes a whole gamut of well-functioning institutions that are not yet in place in the transitional economies. SOEs may perform satisfactorily in a competitive *and* predominantly private enterprise environment, but are known to behave differently when all or the majority of large-scale enterprises are publicly owned. Looking at the relationship between ownership forms and coordination mechanisms, Kornai observed strong linkages between state ownership and bureaucratic coordination on the one hand, and private ownership and market coordination on the other, while he found the linkage between state ownership and market coordination weak and unstable (1990b). Add the deep-rooted distrust of the state and one arrives at the tangle of attitudes and malfunctioning institutions which reinforce stagnation and decline, rather than competitive efficiency.

Despite his distrust of the 'ill-operating state' Kornai is no advocate of a swift privatisation programme ('It is impossible to institute private property by cavalry attack', 1990a p. 54). On the contrary, he visualises a step-by-step, organic process towards a full-scale private enterprise economy, assigning a critical role to newly formed small- and medium-sized firms. Similar views are held by several of the contributors to this volume and by McKinnon (1992). Tirole (1991), also, considers continued public ownership of SOEs as one possible option during the noisy phase of the transition process.

Other analysts are more in a hurry. One type of argument focuses on the political desirability of rapid privatisation. The political revolutions of the late

1980s foreshadowed systemic change and in no other area did systemic change appear more natural than in the field of ownership rights. The faster systemic change was taking place, the more credible reform policies would be. Moreover, because in the first months of the post-communist era, a backlash could not be ruled out, a rapid systemic change would possibly make the process irreversible.

Principal-Agent Problems During the Transition Process

Another group of arguments emanate from the principal-agent tangle. A short reference to the events of the second half of the 1980s, especially in Hungary and Poland, will contribute to an understanding of the problem more fully (see also Voszka in this volume, and Sachs, 1992). In these countries, important institutional changes were taking place. Enterprise councils had been formed and given considerable decision-making powers, including the capacity to dispose of assets. Small wonder that employees were increasingly considering themselves as the actual owners of the plants where they worked.

In Hungary, a series of laws permitting the formation of new types of business organisation were promulgated, making it possible for SOEs to set up subsidiary companies. It became especially popular to transform the SOE or, more frequently, parts of it into a joint stock or a limited liability company (-ies) whereby most of the assets were transferred to the subsidiary (-ies) while the parent company, now converted to a holding, would retain the debts. Voszka labels the phenomenon 'escaping from the state' the threefold purpose of which was to 'solve' the liquidity/solvency problem of the SOEs facing gradually hardening budget constraints, realising a long-yearned-for independence from upstream vertical links and, last but not least, to obstruct ministerial plans for privatisation.

In Hungarian parlance the process came to be known as 'spontaneous privatisation', somewhat of a misnomer, because the label is better suited to describe another phenomenon, namely the sale to private persons or companies of heavily underpriced assets. This, of course, is a typical principal-agent problem, where management opportunism is made possible or strengthened by all of a sudden pushing the gates wideopen for the purchases of SOEs by private persons or companies. Another factor which contributed to increased opportunism was the serious reduction of the ability of the state to assert its property rights. This was partly the result of changes in legislation that took place during the latter part of the 1980s and which made the property rights picture more confused, and partly due to the ascendancy of democratically elected but inexperienced political forces.

Two types of outcome proved as unfortunate for the principal as they were profitable for the agent: first, when underpriced assets were sold either to the managers themselves (alternatively to companies owned by them or their relatives) or to foreign interests with the understanding that incumbent managers would be ensured continued employment on favourable terms; the second method of 'ripping off' the owner-state usually took the form of enterprise councils granting management and workers excessive wages and salaries with the predictable result known as decapitalisation or asset subtraction (Török's phrase), leaving previously viable units physically destroyed, psychologically demoralised, and financially bankrupt.

It was such practices that prompted some analysts to urge the immediate renationalisation, or rather restatisation of decentralised firms, others to recommend the speeding up of the privatisation process. As the WIDER group put it: 'If privatisation takes place only as the state-owned firms are steadily but slowly restructured, there will be little left to privatize' (p. 36). Sachs, not only an expert of but also a participant in the Polish transformation process, arrived at a similar conclusion: '... the behavior of workers and managers tends to be exceedingly short-sighted and geared to wage increases, asset-stripping and job protection, rather than long-run restructuring.' (1992, p. 45). In addition, however, he also thinks that the breakdown of the system of enterprise management, which followed in the wake of the demise from power of the communist parties, necessitates organisational changes, the creation of new incentives and, not to be forgotten, the finding of new markets: all these changes would be greatly facilitated by rapid privatisation (ibid., p. 43).

Models for Rapid Privatisation

The next question is: if rapid privatisation is indeed desirable, what are the ways and means of attaining it? Selling enterprises one by one does work but it takes too long. The answer is mass privatisation. One way to do that would be to transfer ownership rights free of charge to the employees, a 'logical' continuation of the decentralisation policies of the 1980s. However, such a solution would be neither equitable nor efficient. It would violate the requirements of equity on at least two counts: first, employees of capital intensive firms would receive a higher portion of the national wealth than others (civil servants would not receive anything); second, since many SOEs are bound to go bankrupt, the shares of those companies would be worth nothing.

The dilemma can be solved by putting all shares into one or a few national pool(s), to be administered by holding companies. This solution, advocated among others by the WIDER group, would ensure both equity and efficiency. Efficiency can be attained because, with a small (but large enough) number of competing holding companies, the owners – any mixture of individual citizens, insiders (workers and managers), institutions as well as the state – will be able to monitor management performance by comparing the movements of share prices in the different holding companies. At the initial stage at least equity can be assured by giving each citizen the same number of equal-risk shares.

Insiders can be given added incentives by allocating them a small proportion of the shares of the company.

Perfect risk-sharing could be attained by allocating each firm's shares equally among the holding companies. In the view of the WIDER group, such a solution has a drawback. Given, as they assume, the objective that holding companies should 'restructure, divest, and sell' rather than become perpetual owners of firms, Blanchard et al. (1991), recommend the one-owner-of-each-firm option in order to make restructuring less complicated.

Up to now mass privatisation by means of the free distribution of shares has not taken off anywhere. In the CSFR Vaclav Klaus, then Minister of Finance, pushed through a special brand of mass privatisation scheme: citizens were offered vouchers worth 1000 points at a nominal price corresponding to approximately one week's earnings of an average worker. With these vouchers, holders would bid for the shares of individual firms, the auction price of the shares being expressed in points rather than koruny. The shares offered for sale do not necessarily comprise the entire share capital, or even the majority of shares in a given firm.

One big advantage of the Klaus model is that there is no need for a valuation of assets before they are auctioned off. This saves much time and much money. However, by bidding for the shares of individual firms, voucher holders have no guarantee that they are buying anything of value. But, those loath to take risks can put their money into some form of private investment fund which emerged spontaneously as a response to risk aversion and lack of pertinent information: once let out of the bottle, the spirit of capitalism begins to work and form its own institutions.

In terms of popular participation the scheme proved to be a success: more than 8.5 million citizens started to use their voucher power in the first auctioning round and the *Financial Times* (3 July 1992) hailed the programme as a model for the rest of the countries in the region (see also *The Economist*, 12 September 1992).

Limitations of Recentralisation

Meanwhile, in all ex-socialist countries the SOEs are in the no-man's-land between state ownership and privatisation. What powers should be given to their managements? It is recognised that market signals are not of much value in the noisy phase of the transition process when it comes to evaluating management performance: distorted labour and capital markets will give the wrong signals on relative costs, monopolistic practices will continue to blur commodity price structures, legal and political uncertainty will impact on the pattern of investment (Tirole, 1991). All this will result in relative share prices that are more accidental than a correct reflection of relative managerial efficiency (although the WIDER group expects the share prices of their proposed *holdings* to provide reasonably accurate information). According to

Tirole (ibid.) noisiness calls for stable ownership and low-powered incentive schemes.

Voszka (in this volume) provides some interesting hints about the limitations of recentralisation. As we saw above, legal changes in the 1980s led to a considerable reorganisation of Hungarian industry including the possibility for enterprise managers to make sweetheart deals with relatives or foreigners. Second thoughts and popular pressure led both the last communist government and the democratically elected one to institute the recentralisation measures called for by so many. However, Voszka argues, although these measures did change management behaviour, they did not essentially enhance the influence of the state over the SOEs: 'The extension of the formal rights of state organisation to an increasing number of questions and a growing number of firms meant a weakening of the opportunities for real control. Hence managers may restore their informal quasi-ownership position (or formalise it in the new construction of asset management), bargaining continuously with state organisations.'

Foreign Investors and Demonopolisation

Let us return for a moment to Tirole's analysis. Two more of his conclusions are also of interest here. One is that monopolies should be broken up before privatisation, a proposition already noted in connection with the sequencing of reforms. Quoting a dissenting view may be appropriate here. McKinnon in particular is worried about the eagerness of economists to speed up the process of demonopolisation because, state monopolies being the main source of central government revenues, the breaking up of monopolies will, without the prior establishment of appropriate institutions for tax collection, lead to growing budget deficits which are likely to upset a precarious macro-economic balance, or worsen an existing imbalance, thereby jeopardising the entire reform programme (1992). Revenue boosting is often revealed to have a higher priority than monopoly busting.

Tirole's next conclusion warns that 'The threat of capture of government decision-making by interest groups is, during the transition period, more serious in E[ast] E[urope] than in western countries' (p. 240). This hypothesis seems to have considerable support from recent experiences in Central Europe where both domestic players and foreign investors are only too eager to ensure continued monopoly rights to their newly acquired companies (investors perceive it as a *right* to inherit protected markets when they acquire a state monopoly).

This is the leitmotiv of the paper by Somogyi and Török (in this volume). They argue that, although governments may be honestly dedicated to the ideals of competition – as is testified, for instance, by the competition laws introduced in Hungary – the felt need for the temporary protection of infant and/or senile industries may induce them to pursue policies that are at variance with the concept of competition. In such cases, governments face the dilemma that, while they badly want the technology, organisation, and marketing skills of the multinational companies, they may endorse agreements that will hurt consumers and jeopardise growth prospects. The problem is further complicated by the fact that, as a result of product differentiation, it is becoming increasingly difficult to determine when competition laws are violated.

Restructuring Socialist Agriculture

The bulk of the literature about privatisation deals with industry. However, in the ex-socialist countries, agriculture is not only a large sector with a considerable share of both employment and GDP. In several of these countries it is also the Achilles' heel of the economy. In a penetrating paper (in this volume) Pryor puts the question: given the weaknesses of collectivised agriculture, why has decollectivisation been so slow, not only in the former Soviet Union but also elsewhere. Comparing experiences from a number of countries – with an emphasis on Eastern Germany – Pryor identifies a number of factors that slow down the process. Indeed, in the former DDR, many old collective farms have been converted into a new type of cooperative which seem to do well in the new institutional and market environment.

Having stressed the significance of initial conditions as well as of macro-economic events, Pryor singles out four essential micro-economic problems of decollectivisation: restructuring of decision-making rights, repartitioning of assets, privatisation, and marketisation. He concludes, firstly, that '... the creation of strong property and marketisation appear to be the logical first steps, while repartitioning and privatisation can be delayed' and secondly, that 'If the first two steps do not occur close to each other in time, several problems arise.' As, for example, developments in the CIS show, price liberalisation without structural change results in chaos.

Let us now turn to some special problems caused by the dissolution of the Soviet Union.

Things Fall Apart

The disintegration of the Soviet Union was yet another major economic shock to the former member republics. Excessive belief in scale economies and neglect of the costs of transportation had given rise to excessive interdependence. The trade flows that had emerged had little to do with specialisation according to comparative advantage. Several of the republics (for example Armenia, Belorussia, the three Baltic states, Moldavia) had total trade flows (exports + imports) whose estimated value exceeded or was almost as high as their respective GDPs (*The Economist*, 1 February 1992). There are, of course, problems with these estimates: because the flows were valued at administered prices, it is difficult to tell what they would be worth at market-clearing prices. There are reasons to believe, however, that a new structure of prices will generate new imbalances which will, unless satisfactory payments arrangements are soon put in place, stifle trade and ultimately lead to considerable reductions in output, possibly mitigated by *ad hoc* barter agreements.

'... how best to maintain some trade flows while restructuring the geographical pattern and commodity composition of trade' is the main concern of the paper by Brabant who would like to see a comprehensive (rather than country-by-country) approach toward the reforming countries, one put into a broader international framework, to take into account the interests of third (world) countries as well. He finds the present piecemeal approach – which too narrowly focuses on the stabilisation of the rouble – deficient on two counts: firstly, because such a project '... does not make sense unless a firm, enforceable commitment to monetary control and structural reform in Russia can be secured and adhered to', and secondly, because '... it would not solve the newly emerging external trading needs of the other republics that can be expected to run sizeable deficits with Russia ...' As a solution, Brabant would like to see some kind of internationally supervised payment facility that would ensure the settlement of trade imbalances. This is largely in tune with the proposal of Havrylyshyn and Williamson (1991) of an Eastern Economic Community making use of the techniques and experiences of the European Payments Union which was instrumental in generating trade – and currency convertibility – in a post-World War II Europe, starved of both hard currency and commodities.

At the country level, experiences from two former Soviet republics were reported at the symposium. 'What in the way of economic reform could be undertaken in Kazakhstan as long as there was stalemate in Moscow?' This very central question is asked in the paper by Leijonhufvud. The external difficulties of that country emanate from two sources. Firstly, having no currency of its own, it cannot pursue independent macro-economic policies. This would not necessarily be a problem had Russia's own macrorelations been anywhere near balance, which they are not. Secondly, as a result of the extreme interdependence with the other former Soviet republics, previously intra-Union trade flows have now become internationalised creating difficulties not only in the form of more awkward payments arrangements (as discussed above) but also because politically motivated delays or cancellations of inter-republican trade flows are generating bottlenecks which create serious problems for whole sectors.

The internal difficulties are those also present in most other PETs (planned economies in transition, Brabant's term): the inherited industrial structure, unclear property rights, underdeveloped institutions, non-existing markets, political taboos, etc.

If macro-economic policies are impossible, what reform policies are possible? For some time, privatisation has been high on the President's reform agenda. Leijonhufvud calls attention to some remarkable complications. Decollectivisation and a return to smallholder farming are anything but simple. In the context of the agriculture of Kazakhstan, where the formation of collective farms meant the destruction not of small farms but a nomadic way of life, such a 'return' is not possible, nor is it yearned for. Yet, it may be surprising for the student of European and Chinese as well as of South-East Asian collectivised agriculture, that even the modest proposal of doubling private household plots was rejected as politically impossible.

Another complication, obviously not restricted to Kazakhstan, is the valuation of manufacturing enterprises. As Leijonhufvud points out, these are parts of a vertically integrated system, and the 'value' of the individual enterprise depends heavily on how the whole 'conveyor belt' of deliveries and outlets perform. Lastly, Leijonhufvud warns that 'destatisation' is not necessarily the same thing as privatisation, because the assets taken out of the command economy are not '... put into the legal and institutional context of a free market economy. Rather, they end up in a legally indeterminate or less than determinate status.'

In contrast to Kazakhstan, the political leaders of Estonia have never hesitated on the two major issues their country was facing: secession from the Soviet Union – and not just 'sovereignty' within the framework of a rejuvenated confederation – and political democracy. Even the introduction of a new currency was an obvious choice, although some interesting discussion has gone on about the currency regime to be chosen (should one opt for a currency board or a central bank?). Using a Coasean brush, Ståhl paints an impressionistic picture of the economy of Estonia where, as in the other countries of the former Soviet bloc, planners had managed to *externalise* most transaction costs to be carried by firms and consumers, where government ownership or just ill-defined property rights have resulted in dilapidated buildings, and where important institutions like brand names, trade marks and '... all the norms of a market economy that are necessary to prevent or limit opportunistic behaviour' are either totally missing or very weak. Like other participants at the symposium, Ståhl believes privatisation will be a slow process and '... the establishment of new domestic firms mainly in the service sectors will be the first step towards the market economy.'

Concluding Remarks

The papers presented at the symposium covered a wide range of topics, looking at key aspects of the transition process from many different angles. No attempt will be made here to make an exhaustive list of the wealth of factual information, observations, insights, warnings, and recommendations found in the papers. Instead, we will content ourselves with a few broad remarks on certain crucial problems.

Firstly, a broad political consensus on the main features of the reform process is highly desirable if delays and slow-downs in the transition are to be avoided.

Secondly, initial conditions do matter a lot. This is true as much of the 'choice' of strategy – i.e., some countries did have a choice between 'big bang' and 'slow but steady' while others did not – as it is of privatisation in general and the decollectivisation of agriculture in particlar.

Thirdly, some costs, in terms of output and employment, are avoidable while others are not. With the taxonomy offered in this book conceptualisation has come a long way. What is needed now is more empirical research that can support the formulation of policies.

Finally, privatisation is going to be a long process and it has to go hand in hand with institutional development. While the creation of institutions is primarily the responsibility of the state, the private sector must also take an active part in the process.

The organisation of the book is as follows: Chapters 2–8 are either macro-economically oriented or take a broad sweep of the problems of the transition process. Chapter 9 discusses possible avenues for private sector contributions to institutional development. Chapter 10 deals with the role of labour market policies in the transition process. Chapters 11–13 tackle the problems of privatisation, while Chapter 14 deals with the transformation of socialist agriculture. Chapter 15 discusses different options to minimise costs emanating from the dissolution of the Soviet Union, while Chapters 16 and 17 take a closer look at developments in two former member republics. Chapter 18 looks into the issue of how authoritarian socialism can set the stage for ethnic collective action, while the final chapter discusses the sustainability of transition.

References

Ábel I. and J. P. Bonin, 1992, "The 'Big Bang' Versus the 'Slow But Steady': A Comparison of the Hungarian and Polish Transformations". CEPR Discussion Paper No. 626. London.

Antal L., L. Bokros, I. Csillag, L. Lengyel and Gy. Matolcsy, 1987, "Fordulat és reform", *Közgazdasági Szemle* XXXIV: 642–663.

Blanchard, O., R. Dornbusch, P. Krugman, R. Layard and L. Summers, 1991, *Reform in Eastern Europe*. Cambridge Mass., and London: MIT Press.

Blejer, M. and Gy. Szapáry, 1989, "The Evolving Role of Fiscal Policy in Centrally Planned Economies under Reform: The Case of China". International Monetary Fund Working Paper, No. 0407. Washington, DC.

Brada, J. C. and A. E. King, 1992, "Is There a J-Curve for the Economic Transition from Socialism to Capitalism?" *Economics of Planning* 25, pp. 37–53.

The Economist, various issues.

Edwards, S., 1990, "The Sequencing of Economic Reform: Analytical Issues and Lessons from Latin American Experiences", *The World Economy*, March 1990.

Grosfeld, I., 1990, "Reform Economics and Western Economic Theory: Unexploited Opportunities", *Economics of Planning* 23, pp. 1–19.

Havrylyshyn, O. and J. Williamson, 1991, *From Soviet disUnion to Eastern Economic Community?* Policy Analyses in International Economics 35 Institute for International Economics, Washington, DC.

IIASA, 1991, *What Is To Be Done? Proposals for the Soviet Transition to the Market*. Peck, M. J. and T. J. Richardson (eds). New Haven and London: Yale University Press.

Kornai J., 1986, "The Hungarian Reform Process: Visions, Hopes, and Reality", *Journal of Economic Literature*, Vol. XXIV, December, pp. 1687–1737.

_____, 1990a, *The Road to a Free Economy*. New York and London: W. W. Norton and Co.

_____, 1990b, "The Affinity Between Ownership Forms and Coordination Mechanisms: The Common Experience of Reform in Socialist Countries", *Journal of Economic Perspectives* 3, Vol. 4.

_____, 1992, "The Postsocialist Transition and the State: Reflections in the Light of Hungarian Fiscal Problems", *American Economic Review*, May.

Lindbeck, A., 1973, "Ekonomiska system – ett mångdimensionellt fenomen", *Ekonomisk Debatt* 1.

McKinnon, R. I., 1991, *The Order of Economic Liberalization. Financial Control in the Transition to a Market Economy*. Baltimore and London: Johns Hopkins University Press.

_____, 1992, Review of "Reform in Eastern Europe" by Blanchard, O. et al., *Journal of Economic Literature*, Vol. XXX , June.

Newbery, D. M., 1991, "Reform in Hungary: Sequencing and Privatization", *European Economic Review*, May.

Prybyla, J. S. (ed.), 1990, "Privatizing and Marketizing Socialism", *The Annals of The American Academy of Political and Social Science*, Vol. 507, January.

Sachs, J. D., 1990, "Charting Poland's Economic Rebirth". Interview with J. D. Sachs, *Challenge*, January–February.

_____, 1991, "Sachs on Poland", *The Economist,* 19 January 1991.

_____, 1992, "The Economic Transformation of Eastern Europe: the Case of Poland", *Economics of Planning* 25, pp. 5–19.

Stoléru, L., 1990, "Un plan monnet pour l'Est", *Le Monde,* 16 février 1990.

Tirole, J., 1991, "Privatization in Eastern Europe: Incentives and the Economics of Transition", *NBER Macroeconomics Annual 1991.*

WIDER, 1991, see Blanchard et al.

Wilczynski, W., 1991, "Polens väg tillbaka till marknadsekonomi", *Ekonomisk Debatt* 7.

Winiecki, J., 1990, "Obstacles to Economic Reform of Socialism: A Property-Rights Approach" in Prybyla (ed.) (1990).

2

Why Did Output Fall in Eastern Europe?

*John Williamson**

One of the most spectacular, most surprising, and most distressing features of the East European transition to the market is the sharp fall in output that has been experienced everywhere. The present paper aims to summarise what is known about the extent of, the reasons for, and the consequences of those declines in output.

The first section of the paper documents the facts. The second section presents a taxonomy of the reasons that have been advanced to explain the collapse of output, together with an assessment of how the welfare consequences of lower output depend upon the reasons for the decline. The final section discusses the implications for policy.

The Collapse of Output

Since all the economies in transition except Czechoslovakia were suffering either open or repressed inflation (or both) when they initiated the transition, they concluded that it was necesary to implement strong stabilisation programmes. They simultaneously freed prices and devalued the currency. This combination of policies was expected to produce a sharp initial increase in prices – a 'corrective inflation' – as prices were liberalised, the monetary overhang was inflated away, and devaluation pulled prices up. But it was hoped that, after the initial steep price increase, inflation would quickly die away, since there would no longer be a monetary overhang, fiscal and monetary discipline would eliminate excess demand, and (in the Central

* Senior Fellow, Institute for International Economics, Washington, DC.

TABLE 2.1 The Decline in GDP in Eastern Europe (1988 = 100)

		1991	*1992 Projection*
Albania		69	55
Bulgaria		68	65
Czechoslovakia		84	80
Eastern Germany		60	66
Hungary		89	90
Poland		81	80
Romania		77	71
Russia		85	68
Ukraine (NMP)		91	65
Memorandum Items: Historical Precedents			
USA	1933/29	70	
UK	1930/28	94	
Germany	1932/28	89	
	1946/39	45	
Japan	1945/39	50	
Finland	1991/90	94	

Sources: Data from IMF and the World Bank; Maddison (1989) and Eichengreen and Uran (1991).

European countries, at least) the fixed exchange rate would act as a nominal anchor.

All countries (except Eastern Germany, which experienced an effective revaluation when monetary unification occurred) did indeed have large initial price increases – in every case substantially larger than anticipated. In one case, Czechoslovakia, this was a one-shot increase as expected, and price stability was achieved within months of the 'big bang'. In other cases inflation did fall back from the months of (and in some cases immediately before) the 'big bang', but nevertheless showed a worrying degree of persistence that has had to be accommodated through a flexible exchange rate policy (a frequently adjusted peg in Hungary, a crawling peg in Poland, floating rates in Bulgaria, Romania, and Russia).

What was even more unexpected than the persistence of inflation was the magnitude of the fall in output. Table 2.1 shows estimates of how far output has fallen since 1988, before the communist system started to unravel. To provide some historical perspective I also provide figures of the output decline in the United States, Britain and Germany during the Great Depression, and in Germany and Japan at the conclusion of World War II. Clearly ouput has in several cases fallen even further in Eastern Europe than it did in the United States during the historic disaster of the 1930s Depression, and in every case it has fallen at least as far as it did in Britain or Germany. The output decline is,

TABLE 2.2 A Taxonomy of the Possible Causes of Output Decline in Developing Countries

External demand:	Exogenous decline (world recession) Overvalued currency (inflation and fixed exchange rate)
Internal demand:	Keynesian demand deficiency – induced by FX-shortage
Supply:	Exogenous shocks (weather)

however, still less drastic than that experienced in Germany and Japan at the end of the war.

It is true that the extent of the fall in output is almost certainly exaggerated by the official figures. The reason is that the collection of statistical data is largely, or in some cases wholly, confined to the state enterprises and largely or wholly ignores the private sector. Since the public sector is declining while the private sector is growing, in most cases at dramatically high rates (although from a small base), the actual situation is somewhat less bleak than portrayed. But the needed correction is probably worth only two or three percentage points of GDP, so the stylised fact of imploding output remains.

Critics of the big bang strategy claim that these output falls provide strong support for their position. In order to assess that contention, it is necessary to examine the causes of the collapse in output.

A Taxonomy of the Sources of Output Decline

When output declines in a developing country, one frequently thinks in terms of the sort of taxonomy displayed in Table 2.2 in order to try and understand why. Output may have fallen either because of demand or supply. Demand factors would be broken down into those stemming from external demand and internal demand respectively. External demand might fall exogenously, because (for example) of a world recession, or it might fall because the country had allowed its currency to become overvalued on the foreign exchanges (typically as a result of holding the exchange rate fixed in nominal terms despite an internal inflation much above the world rate). A fall in internal demand would result in a Keynesian demand deficiency. A special case of the latter arises where the government is forced to deflate domestic demand because of a balance of payments constraint. The supply factors that cause output declines are typically exogenous shocks like bad weather or natural disasters.

The first few entries in this taxonomy can remain unchanged when we turn to analysing what has happened in Eastern Europe. It is certainly still true that a reduction in demand from abroad may cause output to decline. Indeed, if the production facilities were specifically geared to supplying the market that vanished, it will be impossible to restore output through macro-economic policy. This is generally believed to be true of the empirically important case of this phenomenon – the 50 per cent-odd decline in Soviet demand in 1991, which was important in all the other economies in transition. Most of the goods for which demand dried up were 'shoddy goods' that were unsaleable in the West at any price.

Dani Rodrik (1992, Table 5.2) has recently made estimates of the extent of the output loss occasioned in the three Central European countries in 1991 by the collapse in Soviet orders. Excluding the terms of trade cost of the change in the CMEA trade regime, which enters at a later stage of the taxonomy, the direct cost amounted to 1.6 per cent of GDP in Poland, 2.2 per cent in Czechoslovakia, and 4.5 per cent in Hungary. Eastern Germany and Romania also suffered, though perhaps to a more modest extent, while the impact on Bulgaria was presumably massive in view of Bulgaria's former dependence on the Soviet market (around 65 per cent of its exports were shipped there). The order in which the countries are listed in Table 2.3 gives my guess of the relative magnitude of the impact of this factor on the various countries.

Those direct costs exclude multiplier effects, which one might expect would roughly double the impact. In fact, the experience of Finland – the one Western country that was dependent on the Soviet market to a comparable extent, exporting nearly 3 per cent of its GDP there in recent years[1] – suggests that this may be conservative, for Finland suffered a 6 per cent decline in GDP in 1991 following the collapse of Soviet orders.

The final column of Table 2.3 presents a concise summary of the welfare significance of each source of output decline. An exogenous decline in foreign demand confronts a country with an unavoidable welfare loss, which is greater the more difficult it is to transfer the resources formerly used to produce exports into alternative uses. The losses stemming from the disappearance of the Soviet market were undoubtedly severe.

The second heading is currency overvaluation. An overvalued currency can destroy the tradable-goods industries and thus damage output. So far this seems to have been important only in Eastern Germany, where the 1:1 exchange rate chosen at the time of German monetary union made East German costs hopelessly uncompetitive. I am not claiming that matters could have been materially alleviated by choosing a different nominal exchange rate at the time of unification: on the contrary, the fact that East German wages rose sharply after unification suggests that the competitive benefits would have been inflated away very quickly. Exchange rate policy was impotent because of the high degree of labour mobility combined with the willingness of West-

1. By way of comparison, in 1989 Hungary exported around 9 per cent of its GDP to the Soviet market and Poland around 7 per cent. (1989 data are not available for Czechoslovakia, but in 1987 as much as 14 per cent of GDP consisted of exports to the Soviet Union.)

TABLE 2.3 Possible Causes of Output Collapse in the Economies in Transition

Cause	*Countries involved*	*Welfare implications*
External demand:		
Exogenous decline	Bulg, Hung, CS, Pol, Rom, EG	Unavoidable loss
Overvalued currency	E Germany; Poland?	Avoidable loss when excessive (unavoidable in EG)
Internal demand:		
Keynesian	CS; Poland?	Avoidable loss when excessive
– FX shortage	Bulg, Rom, SU, successor states	Avoidable/unavoidable loss[a]
Demand-shift	CS, Poland	Slow: investment Excessive: avoidable social loss
– Unwanted goods	Russia, all	Benefit
Supply:		
Exogenous shocks	Russian oil	Unavoidable loss
Uneconomic output	Widespread	NVA: benefit LVA: avoidable loss when excessive
Input dislocation	Russia, CIS	Avoidable loss
Credit squeeze	Poland?	Avoidable loss
Monopoly pricing	All?	Difficult-to-avoid loss

Note: *a* Depending on whether transitional protection can buy more expenditure-switching per unit of inflationary pressure than devaluation.

ern Germany to pay almost unlimited sums to curtail the migration of workers to the West. It nonetheless remains true that the uncompetitive exchange rate led to the collapse of output in Eastern Germany.[2]

The other candidate for this category is Poland, which originally picked an undervalued exchange rate at the time of the big bang but then clung to the fixed exchange rate despite the failure to stop inflation afterwards (an attempt motivated by the usual unrealistic longing to turn a fixed exchange rate into a nominal anchor). It looked last year as though the Polish zloty was in danger of becoming seriously overvalued, but Poland began to crawl last October, perhaps just in time, and has subsequently undertaken a medium-sized step devaluation as well. Thus I enter Poland with a query under this head in Table 2.3.

In general I would classify currency overvaluation as a social loss due to policy error (an 'avoidable loss'), although a modest and temporary overvaluation may be a rational part of a programme of combating inflation and therefore be classified as an investment in stability. (The phrase 'avoidable loss when excessive' in Table 2.3 is intended to convey the notion that some output

2. Akerlof et al. (1991) argued that the output costs could have been diminished by a well-designed labour subsidy.

loss from this cause may be a rational investment, but that when carried to excess it involves social waste.) But in the particular case of Eastern Germany I think it is fair to classify the overvaluation as exogenous, because of Western Germany's willingness to pay subsidies of over 100 per cent of Eastern German GDP to curtail migration.

The third heading is Keynesian demand deficiency. Fiscal and monetary policy may be tightened with a view to controlling inflation or correcting the balance of payments, and the consequent reduction in nominal demand may cause a fall in output for Keynesian reasons. We know that in principle a totally credible stabilisation programme might not have any output cost at all in the presence of rational expectations, but we also know that stabilisation typically does have a temporary cost in terms of lost output, perhaps because of the need to build credibility, perhaps because not all expectations are rational, and perhaps because of the structure of contracts. Such output losses are in the nature of an investment if they are no larger than is necessary to achieve stabilisation, and a social waste if demand deflation overshoots.

There has been vigorous debate, perhaps especially in Poland, as to whether demand deflation was responsible for the magnitude of the fall in output. The fact that output fell abruptly after the big bang at the beginning of 1990, and that evidence to be reviewed subsequently suggests that this was not due to a sudden change on the supply side, implies that this was due to a decline in demand. At first many of us assumed that this resulted from a fall in real balances, as an excessive devaluation of the zloty at the beginning of 1990 replaced monetary overhang by monetary stringency. However, in an interesting paper Stanislaw Gomulka (1992 forthcoming) points out that the bulk of the Polish money supply at the end of 1989 was in the form of dollars rather than zlotys, and therefore its internal purchasing power tended to be increased rather than decreased by devaluation. It nevertheless seems likely that the devaluation was responsible, since it forced prices up, which had two effects. The first is that it redistributed income from wages to profits. The second is that it created paper profits on which enterprises were taxed: the budget actually moved into surplus for a period in early 1990.

Czechoslovakia provides an even clearer case of a country where recession was primarily due to an excessively contractionary macro-economic policy. This is a shame because the micro-economics of the transition were handled better there than anywhere else: the government took a year to prepare its plans and then moved with a broad-ranging and well-conceived package of measures, very much in line with the consensus of recommendations by the profession. Until the end of 1990 the economy remained in macro-balance: output had fallen only marginally, inflation was low, there was no appreciable monetary overhang or external deficit, the budget was balanced, and the foreign debt remained modest. This situation provided no convincing rationale for pursuing a strongly deflationary policy (a devaluation too close to the black market rate,[3] which again resulted in contractionary distribution effects and a temporary fiscal surplus as a result of the taxes that enterprises had to pay on the paper profits resulting from inventory revaluation, and a real interest rate of around 20 per cent a year). That looks like deflationary overkill to me. Moreover, Czechoslovakia did not have Poland's excuse of being in a situation with no precedents; it – and certainly the IMF – should have learnt from the mistake in Poland.

I am not sufficiently familiar with the situation in other countries to judge whether the declines in output experienced there have also had a strong Keynesian element. I hope that light will be shed on this during the conference.

The fourth reason for output loss can be considered a special case of the preceding one,[4] when a demand deficiency is dictated by a shortage of foreign exchange. When I was a student we took it as axiomatic that inadequate foreign exchange could force a country into deflationary policies, but since this seems to be doubted nowadays by those whose training is too narrowly neoclassical it may be worth spelling out why a freely floating exchange rate does not make this a non-problem. Consider a country whose exports are less than its full-employment imports at a competitive exchange rate, defined as an exchange rate such as to induce balanced trade[5] at full employment in the medium term. But suppose that exports have not yet built up to their steady-state level, so that there is a trade deficit at full employment. Does it follow that devaluation could necessarily reconcile internal and external balance in the short run? No. The short-run effect of devaluation in switching expenditure toward domestic goods is minimal, and capital inflows require national creditworthiness that is currently lacking in Eastern Europe. Thus the mechanism that will achieve external balance with a floating exchange rate is a downward float until domestic inflation has deflated real money balances (and/or redistributed income and/or inflated real tax bills) sufficiently to achieve trade balance, at the cost of the level of output. Internal balance is sacrificed.

It may be possible to limit that output loss by restricting imports, which is what Western Europe did during the years of post-war reconstruction. This can be efficient if protection that is confined to imports that compete with domestic production can buy more expenditure-switching per unit of inflationary pressure than can be achieved by devaluation, which seems likely although not quite tautological. Where this alternative exists, to tolerate a loss of output because of the foreign exchange constraint is another case of social waste: transitional tariffs – though not quantitative restrictions – are much to be

3. The objection to going too near the black market rate is that, since black markets are marginal markets driven by attempted capital flight prior to stabilisation, there is a strong presumption that the exchange rate established there will be too weak to sustain a desirable macro-economic equilibrium after stabilisation.

4. Special cases are indicated in Table 2.3 by a dash preceding them in the first column.

5. Strictly speaking one should refer to a trade deficit that can be safely financed on a sustainable basis rather than implying that only trade balance is acceptable in the medium term.

preferred (Williamson, 1991, especially the paper of McKinnon and my own discussion on pp. 389–400). Where it does not exist, a foreign exchange shortage has to be classified as imposing an unavoidable loss. Of course, output losses imposed by the foreign exchange constraint provide a classic case for international aid.

Several East European countries seem to have been foreign-exchange constrained in the past couple of years; at least Bulgaria, Romania, and in 1991 the Soviet Union. All the successor states of the Soviet Union face a foreign exchange constraint in the future, although Russia has the best prospect of overcoming that constraint relatively rapidly (because of its supplies of exportable energy and raw materials). These constraints are probably more severe than can be dealt with solely by transitional tariffs, although it still seems sensible to seek what relief can be obtained from that source.

There is no obvious evidence that the Central European countries have also suffered from a foreign exchange shortage. This implies that the deterioration in their terms of trade consequent on the demise of CMEA[6] cannot be blamed for their recessions. Of course, they have suffered a loss of real income, but that is another matter.

At this point it is necessary to extend the taxonomy that we hijacked from the developing countries, because there are at least two other demand-side effects that have been blamed for reducing output in Eastern Europe. The first of these is *demand-shift*.[7] When demand shifts from one type of good to another, resources have to be redeployed from production of the former to production of the latter. There is typically a delay between their release and their reabsorption in a different activity, and in the meantime they produce nothing and in consequence output declines. For example, in Czechoslovakia last year government spending fell by an estimated 12 per cent of GDP (OECD, 1991): most of that was offset by tax cuts so that in due course the main effect will be on the composition rather than the level of output, but because this redeployment takes time the short-run effect is to decrease output.

An important cause of demand-shift in an economy integrating itself into the world economy is from the production of import substitutes to that of exports. This shift is in the nature of an investment – an immediate cost that will bear fruit in the future as redeployment into higher-productivity activities occurs. But it is nevertheless inefficient to have large pools of resources that are made idle years before they can be reabsorbed elsewhere. This provides the justification for transitional 'senile industry' protection: it is better that, until they can be reabsorbed elsewhere, resources should produce goods of low value-added than that they should not add any value at all. Hence I divide my

6. These were estimated by Dani Rodrik as amounting to 2.9 per cent of GDP in Poland, 3.7 per cent of GDP in Hungary and 5.4 per cent of GDP in Czechoslovakia (Rodrik, 1992, Table 5.2).

7. This has sometimes been classified as a supply-side effect.

entry in column 3 into a 'slow demand-shift' that is an investment and an 'excessive demand-shift' that goes into the category of avoidable social loss.

A special form of demand-shift occurs when goods that were formerly produced are no longer wanted. Unwanted goods in Eastern Europe are not only military supplies but also inventories that were accumulated as a store of value in the absence of financial assets capable of fulfilling that role and investment goods whose only purpose was to produce unwanted goods, including more investment goods with no end use (steel to build steelworks to build more steelworks...). Production of fewer unwanted goods is a benefit and not a cost.

This is a particularly potent factor in the former Soviet Union, especially Russia, where the military-industrial complex was vast, perhaps as much as 25 per cent of GDP. The surplus inventories and pointless investment activities were also extensive. It is remarkable, and unfortunate, that there are no serious estimates of just how large the benefits of stopping producing unwanted goods may prove to be or have already been, but they were probably significant in all the countries of the region, except perhaps Hungary.

Let us now turn to the supply side of the equation. We can again start with the sort of exogenous shocks that figured in the previous taxonomy, though there is not much reason to attribute the decline in East European production to that source, except possibly for part of the fall in output of petroleum in the former Soviet Union.

Of vastly more importance is the fact that price changes make some part of former output uneconomic. The extreme case is where the production of a good requires inputs with a higher value (at world prices) than the value of the output – the case of negative value-added (NVA).[8] Hughes and Hare (1991) calculated that between 19 per cent and 24 per cent of industrial production in the three Central European countries resulted in negative value-added. That may be an over-estimate inasmuch as it assumes zero ability to substitute inputs, but on the other hand it makes no allowance for the costs of pollution. (Some observers also question the plausibility of their finding that the food processing industries of Central Europe all seem to have negative value-added.)

In general an end to the production of goods with negative value-added is another benefit almost as great as ending the production of bads. It is true that Ronald McKinnon (1991) has argued that industries producing negative value-added should be given time to adjust to the new vector of input prices confronting them, on infant-industry grounds. Clearly it is conceivable that some enterprises that presently produce negative value-added might be driven out of business by a precipitate move to world prices despite having the

8. The most famous anecdote of negative value-added is of Polish production of semi-tropical flowers, which absorbed energy resources of far greater foreign-exchange value than the value of the flowers.

potential to adjust and become viable, but I must say that I would want to see evidence that the present value of saving an activity was likely to be positive before I went out of my way to defend value subtraction. In the absence of evidence we should cheer the demise of such activities.

Activities may also be forced to close down where value-added is positive but too low to support conventional levels of payments to the factors of production involved. Modest output losses as such activities are closed gradually and the resources are absorbed in other, more profitable, activities are an investment. But in excess we come again to the case for senile industry protection – a far more promising cause in Eastern Europe than infant industry protection *à la* McKinnon.

Another supply-side reason for output declines has been the dislocation of input supplies. As enterprises stop supplying intermediate goods through the traditional channels formerly dictated by the planners, their customers may have difficulty in arranging alternative sources of supply. Similarly, there are fears in the former Soviet Union that the new international boundaries between the sovereign states may result in disruption of input supplies. The output lost through such dislocation of input supplies is pure social loss.

What is not clear is whether this is a cost that can legitimately be attributed to liberalisation, rather than to the collapse of the old regime. Consider the Soviet case, which is where the disruption of input supplies has certainly been a major factor. As Soviet central planning broke down, more and more enterprises began to neglect their duty to fulfill their state orders before selling some of their output at free-market prices through the commercial exchanges. These exchanges are still only two years old, but there are now over 400 of them dealing in everything from primary commodities to used steel rails to consumer goods. Their rapid emergence is a standing refutation of the charge that Russians lack entrepreneurial instincts. At first blush one would assume that a market that provided a mechanism for enterprises to relieve their bottlenecks by buying critical missing inputs could hardly fail to be welfare-enhancing; but diversion of supplies to the exchanges has also been responsible for *creating* bottlenecks. In an environment where there is no mechanism that enables managers to know which state orders are supplying critical needs and which are dispensable (even if there were an incentive for them to respect such priorities, which was in fact also lacking), it is at least possible that a part of the reason for the collapse in output is that input supplies have been arbitrarily disrupted in order to earn the much higher prices available from sales on the commercial exchanges. Presumably one benefit of liberalisation will be to make the more conservative enterprises willing to trade on the exchanges (or bid the market price), thus diminishing the danger that supplies will be diverted from high-priority to low-priority uses. That gives ground to hope that, after the current initial period of chaos as supply relationships are changed, liberalisation should decrease rather than increase output losses from this source.

Another possible supply-side effect might come from a credit squeeze. Calvo and Coricelli (1992) have suggested that this effect was important at least in Poland. The argument is that the withdrawal of subsidies coupled with massive devaluation and severe limits on credit expansion meant that enterprises no longer commanded the credit to buy the inputs needed to continue producing the former level of output. The enterprises resorted to increased levels of inter-enterprise credit to try and circumvent the shortage of bank credit – a circumvention that the authorities also tried to limit. Calvo and Coricelli argue that this can explain a number of the apparent paradoxes of the Polish stabilisation programme: the coexistence in labour-controlled enterprises of high profitability and wages less than the ceiling allowed by the incomes policy, and the coexistence of continuing inflationary pressures with the fall in output and rise in unemployment.

While the Calvo–Coricelli hypothesis can explain some of the macroeconomic paradoxes, it appears to be strongly inconsistent with microeconomic data on inventories and output (Berg and Blanchard, 1992). Specifically, the data show that inventories tended to accumulate where the declines in output were largest. Admittedly the inventories in question were of finished goods rather than of inputs or intermediate goods, but the implication is still that the output decline was due to a fall in demand, which was resisted by allowing inventories of final goods to accumulate. Had a credit squeeze limited supply, one would have expected to see the inventories of finished goods being drawn down where the squeeze was pinching and in consequence ouput was being cut back. This evidence thus makes it difficult to accept the case for a credit crunch as having been a cause of output decline in Poland, and *a fortiori* I doubt also whether the build-up of inter-enterprise credit in other countries (like Czechoslovakia and Hungary) can be interpreted as a symptom of a credit crunch that curtailed supply.

A credit squeeze beyond what is necessary to control demand and to impose hard budget constraints on enterprises would be counterproductive, and accordingly I describe it as imposing an avoidable loss.

A final possible explanation for the output decline is that it results from the exploitation of monopoly power after price liberalisation. Berg and Blanchard (1992) find no indication that output has declined more where production is more concentrated, which they take to be evidence against this hypothesis. Nevertheless, the notion that the prevalence of monopoly that was bequeathed by the planners is a source of the problem has a certain appeal, especially to those who find Mancur Olson's (1982) view of the world persuasive, and at least in the sense that this would make it difficult to reconcile price stability with a high level of activity. Since the avoidance of this social loss requires the difficult and time-consuming process of demonopolisation, plus import liberalisation and an exchange rate that exposes domestic producers to more foreign competition than it may be wise to risk in the early stages of the transition, I describe the welfare implications of monopolistic behaviour as a difficult-to-avoid loss.

Assessing the Conventional Wisdom

Does the above assessment of the factors that have led to the collapse in output in the economies in transition suggest that the sort of advice we economists have been giving is seriously flawed?

Note first that Table 2.3 suggests there are a lot of reasons why output might have been expected to decline. Unfortunately, apart from Rodrik's estimates of the impact of the Soviet demand shock and the Hughes and Hare attempt to measure the prevalence of negative value-added, we have no quantitative estimates that would help decompose output declines among the various possible causes. I am not sure that my taxonomy is perfect, i.e. mutually exclusive and collectively exhaustive, but I would like to hope that it might help stimulate effort into decomposing the sources of the collapse. Until we have a reasonably convincing decomposition of the causes of output decline all policy recommendations have to rest on an act of faith.

Second, some output losses were positively desirable, others were unavoidable, and others were in the nature of an investment. I do not doubt that some waste of resources remains, but its magnitude is less, perhaps substantially less, than suggested by the magnitude of the decline in output.

Third, excessive demand deflation has played some role in explaining the fall in output, but it is far from clear that this was the dominant factor. Even in Czechoslovakia, where the evidence for over-restrictive policy is clearest, there were other factors at work – notably the collapse in exports to the Soviet Union and important shifts in demand.

The table suggests two areas where policy may have erred. One is in not providing substantial transitional protection to buffer the adjustment process. In early 1991 I heard a high Polish official boast that Poland's trade regime was as liberal as that of Hong Kong. He may have exaggerated slightly, but one cannot doubt that several countries did make a dash for world prices. It is one thing to argue in favour of starting off adjustment quickly on a broad front, it is another to demand that the system go straight to free trade prices. The problems of adjustment in response to demand shift, of a foreign-exchange shortage and of low value-added at world prices all call for transitional protection. This is one of the issues that remains controversial among economists interested in the East European transition, but I am increasingly convinced that economists did those countries a disservice by urging an immediate jump to minimal protection.[9]

9. Note that Poland no longer has a particularly open trade regime. There would be no reason for concern if its present tariffs had resulted from it being in year two of a process of

The other policy error consisted of the decision to inflate away the monetary overhang and compensate for the resulting burst of inflation by large devaluations. As it turned out, most of the devaluations were larger than was necessary for that purpose (as a result of the decision to follow the misleading guide provided by the exchange rate set in the black market prior to liberalisation of the economy). These devaluations gave enterprises headroom to raise prices and wages without the hard budget constraint biting, and presumably a degree of inflationary momentum built up from what was supposed to be a one-shot price increase. The fact that the exchange rate was fixed subsequent to its devaluation was described as 'providing a nominal anchor'; since the exchange rate was so devalued as to pull prices up, however, it would have been more accurate to describe it as providing a nominal balloon. The resulting price increases deflated output, by a varying combination of the real balance effect, distribution effects, and fiscal effects. Stagflation rules.

The alternative policy would have involved a monetary reform designed to absorb the monetary overhang without large price increases, on the model of what was widely done in Western Europe after World War II (Dornbusch, 1991; Newbery, 1991; Sturzenegger, 1991). This would have needed to be accompanied by an initial wage freeze and an exchange rate that was fixed so as to validate the existing wage level. The idea of monetary reform was rejected out of hand in the Soviet Union, one case where it was at least considered, as a result of the bitter public reaction to Pavlov's 'monetary reform' of January 1991. That was surely a mistake. Inflating away the overhang results in its confiscation just as much as any monetary reform does. Moreover, confiscating money balances in excess of some threshold is not the only possible form of monetary reform. Indeed, it seems a very silly form in countries that have a vast stock of assets needing to be privatised and virtually no non-monetary savings that the public can call on in order to buy those assets. It is not practicable to mop up the overhang directly by selling assets because privatisation takes time if it is to be done properly. But it would have been possible to issue vouchers that could have been used in due course to purchase assets in exchange for money holdings in excess of whatever threshold was allowed to be converted into the new money.

Two other complaints about the reform programmes are often voiced, though neither emerges from the preceding review. Both argue that the programmes err in concentrating overwhelmingly on the demand side, when in fact the real problems of the ex-socialist economies lie on the supply side. One is the complaint that privatisation has been too delayed. I imagine most of us would have liked to see small privatisation move faster, which suggests it

gradually phasing out, according to international commitments, substantial transitional protection that had been introduced at the time of the big bang. Unfortunately its present tariffs are the result of piecemeal surrenders to pressure groups as the results of the free trade ideology were found politically nonviable. This makes the prospects of an ultimate liberal regime much less favourable than they might have been.

would have been wise to skip restitution. However, the idea that privatisation of large enterprises would have provided some sort of panacea strikes me as naive, though this is not the place to justify that assertion.

The other complaint, voiced in a recent paper of Tad Rybczynski (1991), is that banking reform (including bank recapitalisation) needed to precede or accompany price liberalisation, so that the financial system would have been in a position to carry out its function of intermediating funds to those enterprises able to make a supply-side response. Once again, this is something that one would surely have liked to see happen sooner, although there is a question as to how much a reconstruction of balance sheets could do before the banks acquire personnel trained in the art of loan appraisal. Despite this caveat, there is a case for wiping the slate clean of debt inherited from the past so as to permit a real hardening of budget constraints – a sort of equivalent to monetary reform so far as the enterprise and banking sectors are concerned.

What does this diagnosis of the policy errors that have been made in designing the transition imply about the issue on which most attention has been focused, namely the relative merits of gradualism versus a big bang? There is no unambiguous message. Transitional protection and smaller initial devaluations would have made bangs smaller, while monetary reform and the sanitisation of the balance sheets of banks and enterprises would have made them bigger. (I am not clear what the absence of restitution would have done to the size of bang.) Hungarian experience has shown that gradualism is feasible, so I reject as misleading the analogy of transition as a chasm that has to be crossed in a single leap or it will not be crossed at all. (The moral is that we should stop substituting analogies for analysis.)

The fact that the output decline has been smallest in Hungary (Table 2.1), and the consideration that Finnish experience suggests that most of that decline can be attributed to the loss of Soviet orders, obviously argues in favour of gradualism. There nonetheless remain two considerations pointing in the opposite direction. One is that there was really no alternative where the previous system had already collapsed (as in Bulgaria, Poland, Romania, and Russia). The other is the lack of a theory explaining how a gradual transition should be sequenced, in comparison to the reasonably convincing story of why it is desirable to do a number of mutually supporting things in a single package. If Czechoslovakia had not spoilt its micro-reform package by ill-considered macro-measures, its output decline might have been even smaller than that in Hungary. Thus my own judgement is that the trouble has been less in the size of the bangs than in some of the measures that went into them.

The primary advice that we should address to Eastern Europe at the present stage must be to hang tough where a bang has already happened and to grit their teeth and take the plunge in those places where it has still not occurred. There are no demons whose ouster will take the pain out of the transition, and no panaceas whose implementation will guarantee a rapid turnround. To say this is not to claim that policy has been perfect or that we should stop searching for improvements, such as summarised above. But it is to assert that there is a far greater danger of the transition being aborted because of a surrender to populist pressures than because some desirable policy modification remains unmade.

References

Akerlof, G., A. Rose, J. Yellen and H. Hessenius, 1991, "East Germany in from the Cold: The Economic Aftermath of Currency Union", *Brookings Papers on Economic Activity*.

Berg, A. and O. Blanchard, 1992, "Stabilization and Transition: Poland 1990–91". Paper presented to a conference of the National Bureau of Economic Research, February 1991.

Calvo, G. and F. Coricelli, 1992, "Stagflationary Effects of Stabilization Programs in Reforming Socialist Countries: Enterprise-Side and Household-Side Factors", *World Bank Economic Review,* January 1992.

Dornbusch, R., 1991, "Money, Trade, and Debt: Reform Options for the Soviet Union". Mimeo.

Eichengreen, B. and M. Uzan, 1991, "The Marshall Plan: Economic Effects and Implications for Eastern Europe and the Soviet Union". Paper presented to the CEPR Economic Policy panel, Prague, October.

Gomulka, S., 1992, "Polish Economic Reform 1990–91: Principles, Policies and Outcomes", *Cambridge Journal of Economics*. Forthcoming.

Hughes, G. and P. Hare, 1991, "Competitiveness and Industrial Restructuring in Czechoslovakia, Hungary and Poland", *European Economy* 2.

Maddison, A., 1989, *The World Economy in the Twentieth Century*. Paris: OECD.

McKinnon, R. I., 1991, *The Order of Financial Liberalization: Financial Control in the Transition to a Market Economy*. Baltimore: Johns Hopkins University Press.

Newbery, D., 1991, *Sequencing the Transition*. CEPR Discussion Paper No. 575.

Olson, M., 1982, *The Rise and Decline of Nations*. London: Yale University Press.

Organisation for Economic Cooperation and Development, 1991, *OECD Economic Surveys: Czech and Slovak Federal Republic*. Paris: OECD.

Rodrik, D., 1992, "Making Sense of the Soviet Trade Shock in Eastern Europe: A Framework and Some Estimates". Mimeo.

Rybczynski, T. M., 1991, "The Sequencing of Reform", *Oxford Review of Economic Policy* 4.

Sturzenegger, F., 1991, "Financial Adaptation and the Optimal Timing of Financial Liberalization in Eastern Europe", in O'Brien, R. (ed.), *Finance and the International Economy* 5, Amex Bank, London.

Williamson, J. (ed.), 1991, *Currency Convertibility in Eastern Europe*. Washington: Institute for International Economics.

3

Lessons from the Stabilisation Programmes of Central and Eastern European Countries, 1989–1991

Domenico Mario Nuti[*]

Introduction

For a number of years before 1989 Central Eastern European countries had been facing, to various extents, severe domestic and external imbalances, economic slowdown or decline and the need to restructure production capacity, while attempting to reform their traditional central planning system (see Nuti, 1988). These problems were less intensely felt in Hungary and Yugoslavia, both early starters on the road to reform, relatively free from endemic shortages and more open to trade with the West; but even there the same underlying trends were present. In the first half of 1989 Gorbachev's *perestroika* and Soviet economic debacle led to Soviet acquiescence to the demise of the communist party in Poland; this in turn triggered off a cascade of political revolutions in the other Central-Eastern European countries in the second half of the year.

The 1989 revolutions had three immediate economic effects:

– the target model of economic reform switched from the search for a market-oriented version of socialism back to the restoration of a capitalist economy, with dominant private ownership and enterprise;

[*] University of Rome 'La Sapienza' and Commission of European Communities, DG-II, Bruxelles 1.

– the new governments, unlike their communist predecessors, enjoyed the kind of political legitimacy and popular support necessary to undertake unpopular measures of stabilisation;

– the end of Soviet rule throughout the bloc led to the speedy collapse of CMEA trade arrangements (with formal CMEA dissolution in September 1991), which greatly opened up Central and Eastern European economies, and the reorientation of their trade towards the West.

The new political conditions and the precarious state of these economies required urgent stabilisation plans, to put an end to shortages, open inflationary pressures and impending debt crisis. Radical institutional reforms were required including for the first time large-scale privatisation. The economies would also have to be opened up to international trade and finance. These were also preconditions for effective restructuring of productive capacity. Former political obstacles to these measures were no longer present. Thus a wave of stabilisation and reform programmes, supported by loans and grants from international organisations and Western countries, were introduced in rapid succession in 1989–91. The exceptions were Hungary, which was able to continue with a gradualist approach because of a much earlier start; the ex-GDR, which rapidly achieved the same targets by virtue of German reunification; the Soviet Union, because of disastrous procrastination.

When, in the autumn of 1989, the first non-communist government in Poland started preparing its plan there was no precedent for the simultaneous undertaking of stabilisation, systemic transition and capacity restructuring, and on such a large scale. Therefore it was natural to proceed from first principles and to examine – because of the underlying hyperinflation – the experience of Latin American stabilisation plans in spite of their extremely poor record. Today, however, when exploring desirable economic strategies for the further progress of transition in the whole area, there is no justification for ignoring the performance of stabilisation plans to date, the experience of transitional economies which for one reason or another have not undertaken such plans (Hungary, ex-GDR, the Soviet Union before its disintegration at the end of 1991), as well as that of economies further east, such as those of Vietnam, China and the more successful South-East Asian countries. This paper is an attempt to draw certain lessons from the experience of Central Eastern European countries in 1989–91 (on Vietnam see Kolodko, 1990a, Kolodko et al., 1992; on China, Chen, Jefferson and Singh, 1990; on South-East Asian economies, Fry and Nuti, 1992).

Gradualism Versus Speedy Transition: Hungary and the ex-GDR

Hungary and the ex-GDR represent unique, extreme, opposite patterns respectively of gradual and instantaneous 'transition', which could not be followed by other countries.

Hungary, by virtue of its early start with the 1968 New Economic Mechanism (NEM) and better economic conditions, was able to avoid a drastic programme in 1989–91 and continued its gradualist strategy, now redirected towards the new target model. Its earlier achievements provided a model for the other countries in a number of areas: the transformation of the monolithic monetary and banking system into a multi-level, competitive and pluralist system; the liberalisation of trade and foreign investment; the development of an articulated tax system, replacing diversified (*ad hoc* and often enterprise-specific) tax and subsidy rates with uniform rates of income and value-added taxes; the development of financial markets first for bonds then for shares. The option of gradual transformation, however, by 1989–91 was no longer open to the other countries: their domestic and (except for Romania) external imbalances had cumulated to unsustainable levels, the CMEA had disintegrated cutting them off from cheap Soviet supplies of oil and materials, and less favourable conditions prevailed in international trade and financial markets, with respect to Hungary's position in the first years of the NEM.

The ex-GDR achieved all the desired goals (stabilisation, systemic transition, opening of the economy) at once, by virtue of accelerated reunification with Federal Germany, first *de facto* then *de jure* in under a year (see Siebert, 1990a and b; Jackson, 1991a and b). The Ostmark overhang was partly confiscated, partly made good by instant replacement with a convertible currency. At a stroke, a complete new price system, body of legislation, and set of financial institutions were imported into the ex-GDR. The economy was not only opened but also joined to the European Community. All these factors facilitated privatisation.

The ex-GDR transition incurred additional costs, with respect to other countries, because of the rapid growth in real wages, which caused large-scale unemployment. This was not due to the one-to-one DM/Ostmark rate of conversion for wages and for part of the liquid assets of the population, as is often believed. The conversion of a limited amount of liquid assets at a favourable rate had only a once-and-for-all wealth effect which actually sustained demand and employment. DM wages in the Eastern region were bound to move towards the Western level regardless of the rate of conversion applied to wages, simply due to labour mobility, which started first with migration through Hungary then through the gaps in the Wall, and became totally free after unification. The additional costs of the consequent real wage rise, as well as the general costs of such a speedy transition and restructuring, were mostly borne by the Federal budget and German financial markets, rather than by the ex-GDR population. While some aspects of the German experience are potentially repeatable in other countries (for instance, rapid privatisation through Treuhandanstalt), neither the ex-GDR transition model nor the speed of its implementation are repeatable anywhere else.

Stabilisation and Reform Plans, 1989–1991

The first stabilisation plan of 1989–90 was introduced by Yugoslavia (1 December 1989; see Coricelli and Rocha, 1990). This was, however, a fairly conventional plan (see Table 3.1), which could not provide a model for the other countries. At that time Yugoslavia had virtually no overhang, and already had a considerable degree of economic decentralisation, fairly free trade and a nearly convertible currency, experience with restructuring and a sizeable pool of labour unemployment. Moreover the Yugoslav programme was rapidly aborted in mid-1990, because of republican failure to comply with federal wage guidelines and resulting monetary indiscipline and pressure on the exchange rate; convertibility was suspended *de facto* in late 1990; the country precipitated into civil war in 1991.

The first comprehensive and innovative programme for stabilisation and reform was the Polish plan of 1 January 1990, associated with the name of Finance Minister Leszek Balcerowicz. It included broad price and trade liberalisation, nominal anchoring of the programme to money wages and the nominal exchange rate, targeting the real money supply and real interest rates, monetary and fiscal austerity, large devaluations and internal convertibility, extreme fiscal pressure on the state sector, taxes on excess wage increases and, in the longer run, privatisation and capacity restructuring. The Polish stabilisation plan has provided a prototype for other transitional countries: in 1990–91, similar plans were introduced in Romania (1 September 1990), Czechoslovakia (now known as CSFR, or Czech and Slovak Federal Republic, 1 January 1991), Bulgaria (1 February1991).

Meanwhile, in 1989–91 the Soviet Union continued its inexorable march towards repressed and open hyperinflation, economic disorganisation and supply disruption, republican disintegration and associated drastic falls in consumption and output. The end of the Soviet Union, accomplished by the August 1991 *putsch* failure, was formalised by the creation of a smaller and looser Commonwealth of 11 Independent States (CIS; SNG from the Russian initials), established by the Alma Ata and Minsk treaties of December 1991 and excluding Estonia, Latvia, Lithuania and Georgia. This paved the way for the unilateral introduction by Russia of a stabilisation and reform programme on 2 January 1992. The programme had been announced by Boris Yeltsin on 28 October 1991 but would have been incompatible with the Draft Economic

Union Treaty, which was then still under discussion, and excluded unilateral price increases by individual republics. Implementation was originally due in mid-December but was postponed at the request of other republics, notably Ukraine; further and more coherent rounds of measures followed in April and in June 1992.

Russian price liberalisation forced all the other ex-Soviet republics to follow, because of the continued use of roubles as legal tender not only within the CIS but also in the rest of the former Union. However the other republics, including Ukraine, are very much behind on their way to a new system. The Russian package has a great deal in common with the Polish prototype of January 1990, on which it is modelled. However, in view of the speed of developments, the special features of the ex-Soviet area (such as size, the persistence of a rouble area and the introduction of republican currencies, inter-republican trade and payments regime) and of the Russian programme, and its implementation failures in 1992, we shall leave it out of this paper (see Nuti and Pisani-Ferry, 1992).

The Polish Prototype

The Balcerowicz plan envisaged the following steps (see Kolodko, 1990a and b; Nuti, 1990a; Rosati, 1991a and b):

i) Instantaneous price liberalisation of 90 per cent of transactions and a reduction of government subsidies (from 17 per cent of national income in 1989 to 4 per cent in 1991); initially some budgetary support was retained for coal, electricity, gas, state housing rents, heating and hot water, transport and telecommunications, pharmaceuticals; support was reduced for energy in June 1990.

ii) A balanced state budget for 1990, accompanied by a restrictive monetary policy aimed at restoring a positive real interest rate; interest rates were raised on old as well as new credit contracts. State enterprises assets were revalued on average by a factor of 14 (and again in 1991), at rates differing by type of assets but uniform throughout the economy, with a uniform capital tax (called a 'dividend', improperly because it bore no relation to either current profits nor reinvestment requirements of enterprises) levied on revalued state assets. Average turnover tax was raised from 10 to 20 per cent.

iii) Wages policy; money wages were set for January on the basis of an expected monthly rate of inflation of 45 per cent in January, with maximum wage guidelines indexed to prices at a monthly pre-fixed rate for 1990: 20 per cent of price inflation in January, 30 per cent in February to April, 60 per cent in the rest of the year except for June (when energy prices would be raised) when wage indexation was at 100 per cent. A tax on wage increases over these guidelines (PPWW or 'popiwek') was levied, at progressive rates of between

200 to 500 per cent of excess wages, exclusively on enterprises with state majority capital.

iv) Unilateral suspension of debt service from 1 January 1990, soon followed by formal rescheduling of foreign debt, with interest and debt amortisation due in 1990 postponed to 1991; large-scale debt relief was granted by official creditors in April 1991.

v) Zloty convertibility for residents and for current account transactions; following the devaluations of 22 and 28 December, a further devaluation of the zloty by 31.6 per cent (43 per cent in ten days) on 1 January 1990 lifted the US dollar to 9,500 zlotys, i.e. practically to the end-year free market rate (the black market for foreign exchange had been legalised already since March 1989). Domestic enterprises could buy freely at this rate to finance current imports; households could buy dollars for current purposes (i.e. not to invest in foreign assets) from licensed foreign exchange 'counters', at a floating rate which was maintained very close to the official rate. A $US1 bn loan was made available by the G-24 to support convertibility, in addition to a $US700 mn IMF standby, a $US300 mn structural adjustment loan from the World Bank (plus additional project loans totalling $US780 mn in 1990) and a substantial package of aid and loans from the EIB, the European Community, its member states and other members of G-24; there was an informal commitment to maintain the rate of exchange constant until May 1990, but this was not taken as a performance criterion. In the event the rate of exchange was maintained until mid-May 1991, when the zloty was devalued by 17.4 per cent and linked to a basket of currencies instead of the dollar; in October 1991 a crawling peg regime was introduced, with a maximum monthly devaluation of 1.8 per cent; further devaluations in October 1991 and February 1992 restored some of the competitiveness lost through inflation.

vi) Trade liberalisation, with a new tariff system whose average incidence was 12 per cent, followed for most goods by a tariff reduction to 5 per cent (April) or outright suspension (July); the elimination of export quotas (in January and in October 1990) except for coal and a small number of items (though 20 commodities were still subject to licences at the end of 1991), and automatic authorisation to trade for all registered firms whether state or private.

vii) An undertaking to implement further institutional reform in the direction of a private market economy, including the development of banking and credit institutions, competition, privatisation and the introduction of financial markets, accompanied by capacity restructuring in the medium term. A spate of new legislation was introduced in 1990–91 to implement this part of the programme. Following extensive debates on privatisation, a new Law was adopted in June 1991 (Nuti, 1990b); small-scale privatisation (housing, retail and catering establishments, land) was to be followed by large-scale privatisation of state enterprises; however this side of the programme was delayed mostly because of the technical difficulties of implementing mass privatisation (Grosfeld and Hare, 1991). This was to take place through the free distribution to the whole adult population of entitlements to certificates in foreign-managed investment funds, but their establishment was postponed to late 1992; there were also delays due to the complexities of property restitution to old owners (so-called 're-privatisation', first introduced by Germany and followed throughout the area except by Yugoslavia).

Other Polish-Style Plans, 1990–1991

Table 3.1 summarises the main features of the Polish plan and the main differences with respect to the plans subsequently adopted by other countries.

Romania adopted a more gradual price liberalisation in three stages, beginning on 15 November 1990, 1 April and 1 July 1991; price increases were subject to three months advance notice to be given to central authorities. The nominal anchor was fixed as a 15 per cent increase of the nominal money supply. A special fund financed out of a 10 per cent tax on enterprise profits was set up for the purpose of liquidating inter-enterprise arrears (400 bn Leu). There were no provisions for wages policy. Convertibility was supposed to be introduced on 27 September 1991 but was postponed in the absence of a government and implemented on 11 November under a 'managed float' regime (*Romania Economic Newsletter* 1, 2, 3, 1991).

In 1990, ahead of the stabilisation plan, the CSFR took preparatory measures that in Poland had followed the plan, such as major legislative changes, price increases, tax changes (Hrncir and Klacek, 1991); announcements of price increases forced a devaluation already in September 1990. With the 1991 plan, convertibility was granted to enterprises, excluding households; even for enterprises access to foreign currency was subject in practice to considerable delays. Small-scale privatisation proceeded fast but large-scale privatisation, much more reliant on free distribution of assets to the population, was delayed until 1992. Inter-republican conflicts between the Czech and the Slovak Republics have characterised the CSFR experience, with the creation of duplicate Ministries and Agencies at the federal and the republican level, and the difficulties of coordinating fiscal policy, privatisation, and other aspects of stabilisation and reform. Inter-republican conflict, though not as sharp as in the Soviet Union/CIS, the Russian Federation or Yugoslavia, has put a brake on transition progress. A split now appears inevitable, only its form and modalities are under discussion.

The Bulgarian plan was perhaps the one closest to the Polish prototype, however with more gradual trade liberalisation, nominal anchoring to the money supply, slower privatisation of state assets (even small scale, except for land, where quick progress was made). The lower real wage reached after price liberalisation was stabilised and strongly indexed, unlike the Polish real wage

TABLE 3.1 Stabilisation and Reform Programmes in Central-Eastern Europe

Feature *Start*	*Yugoslavia* *1.12.89*	*Poland* *1.1.90*	*Romania* *1.8.90*	*CSFR* *1.1.91*	*Bulgaria* *1.2.91*
Price liberalisation	instant 90%	instant 90%	3 stages	instant 85%	gradual
Subsidy reduction 1989/1991	yes	17.4–4%	partial	16.1–4.6%	16.7–3%
Fiscal squeeze	temporary	yes	no	yes	limited
Monetary restraint	temporary	yes	no	yes	limited
Currency devaluation	yes	yes	yes	yes	yes
Foreign trade liberalisation	extensive	extensive	v.limited	extensive	v.limited
Internal convertibility for firms	yes;aborted	yes	end–1991	yes;delayed	yes
Internal convertibilty for households	yes;aborted	yes	no	no	no
Wages policy	yes;ignored	fiscal	no	yes	yes
Small-scale privatisation	yes	yes	yes	yes	slow
Sale of state enterprises	some	some	mostly land	slow	slow
Property restitution	no	yes	yes	yes	yes
Mass privatisation through vouchers	no	delayed	delayed	delayed	delayed
Capacity restructuring	no	little	no	little	no
Real anchoring		M,r		M,r	
Nominal anchoring	W,i	W,e		W,e	M

Note: M=Money, r=real interest rates, W=wages, i=nominal interest rate, e=exchange rate

guideline which was indexed much more weakly but was linked to the pre-stabilisation level (Angelov, 1991).

Economic Performance

The main indicators of macro-economic performance in the five Central Eastern European countries under consideration, immediately before and after the stabilisation plans, are summarised in Table 3.2, Yugoslavia is atypical, because of both plan abortion and civil war.

The programmes succeeded in establishing market-clearing prices, except of course for Romania during the intermediate stages of price liberalisation. Inflation predictably rose at first (Romania and Bulgaria are still at that stage) but was brought down fairly fast in Poland and even faster in the CSFR (price stability was reached already in the summer 1991) although it is still subject to sudden revamping. Fiscal deficits in 1991 (not shown in the table) have been higher than expected because of a lower tax basis for the state sector, lower tax rates and lower collection rate for the private sector, higher welfare expendi-

TABLE 3.2 Key Macro-Economic Variables in Central-Eastern European Economies (percentages)

	(1) Rate of GNP growth		*(2) Overall government balance/GNP*		*(3) Inflation rate*		*(4) Rate of unemploy-ment*		*(5) Current account balance/GNP 1990*	*(6) Monetary overhang*		*(7) Net foreign debt/hard currency exports*	*(8) Foreign exchange reserves/imports*
	1989	*1990*	*1991*	*1990*	*1990*	*1991*	*1990*	*1991*	*1990*	*January 1990*	*June 1991*	*1990*	*1990*
Bulgaria	–0.4	–11.8	–22.9	–12.7	19.3	574	1.0	12.0	–2.8	small	zero	497	31
CSFR	–0.7	–4.1	–15.9	0.2	10.0	45.3	1.0	6.6	–2.9	small	zero	116	26
Hungary	–0.2	–3.3	–11.0	0.1	28.9	35	1.6	8.0	0.4	zero	zero	328	19
Poland	–0.2	–11.6	–7.5	0.4	585	70.3	6.1	11.4	1.1	significant	zero	408	53
Romania	–5.8	–8.4	–13.0	1.2	40.2	222.8	1.5	4–5	–4.4	small	small	35	27
Yugoslavia	–6.6	–8.0	–20	n.a.	583	235	17.0	20.1	–7.1	small	significant	75	34

Note: This table has been compiled from official statistical sources and the *ECE-UN Economic Bulletin for Europe* 43, 1991. Inflation rates are point-to-point rates of change.

tures made necessary by higher unemployment and poverty.

With the exception of Yugoslavia, the degrees of convertibility introduced with the stabilisation plans were maintained. Exports in convertible currencies rose, mostly because of diversion to trade to Western countries; imports were often cut drastically.

Everywhere the recession of 1989 accelerated in 1990 and continued in 1991 and 1992. The collapse of CMEA trade exacerbated the recession; this is generally regarded as an exogenous shock but was actually the result of a deliberate, concerted action on the part of Soviet trade partners, seeking economic independence in spite of the cost, and refusing to maintain CMEA even in a modified form, or to establish multilateral clearing arrangements among former members. Soviet economic decline was another contributory factor; indeed it is now clear that this would have led to trade collapse within the former CMEA area regardless of attempts to maintain a trade area. Thus persistent recession was at least partly unrelated to the presence or the intensity of the stabilisation effort.

There are ongoing debates on whether the depth of recession has been perhaps overestimated, due to the under-recording of the growth of private activities, including a 'black' or 'grey' sector. However, while under-recording may underestimate the current *level* of private activity, it must have surely decreased in the new conditions, thus actually *overstating the growth* of the private sector. In any case, given the initial low weight of the private sector, no plausible allowance for a possible underestimate of private activities is bound to make a difference to trends.

Unemployment, virtually unknown before the start of the plans (except for Yugoslavia), rose rapidly although not nearly as fast as output reduction but faster relatively to output than in Western countries at times of recession.

Prospects for 1992 are poor everywhere in the area: further output decline or stagnation, and further unemployment, is expected. According to the OECD the average GNP decline in the area was about 10 per cent in 1991 and is expected to continue at 2 per cent in 1992; in the autumn of 1992, this expectation appears to be over-optimistic.

A number of political and economic lessons can be drawn from these experiences to date.

Political Lessons

Economic austerity requires political legitimacy, and a formal or informal social pact. Under a communist government in Poland, a modest real wage cut of 8 per cent in early 1988 was followed by successful street protests and over-compensatory wage claims, ending up with the resignation of the Minister who had taken the initiative, Zdzislaw Sadowski, and an increase in the (statistical) real wage of 17 per cent; Balcerowicz got away with a real wage cut of one-third. In Bulgaria the stabilisation plan could only be introduced under a coalition government and a non-communist President, with a social pact with the Trade Unions, succeeding where the former government had failed. Hungarian stabilisation, though slower, also relies on a social accord through its Council for the Reconciliation of Conflicts, though its implementation leaves something to be desired. Romania, where the government lacks the necessary popular support, is lagging behind. The best contribution that a communist government can make to stabilisation is to follow Mieczyslaw Rakowski's example (August 1989) and to take unpopular decisions before resigning.

Political legitimacy needs a local (regional, republican) foundation. The 1989 revolutions were not only anti-communist but also anti-centralist. Centralisation of economic policy decisions, even in conditions of political pluralism and free elections, is no longer acceptable. This is demonstrated not only by Yugoslav, Soviet, Russian and Czech/Slovak separatist movements but also by the autonomy acquired *de facto* by large cities and small regions especially in the ex-Soviet Union.

Economic crisis is necessary – up to a point – to impose a consensus on drastic measures. Protracted and endemic shortages, inflation and hyper-inflation are a great problem but also mollify the population and reduce popular resistance to the shock therapy of an austere stabilisation plan; thus governments should not be so reluctant to free prices even before a proper stabilisation plan. This is also confirmed by the Yugoslav experience; in the ex-USSR outside Russia, and perhaps in Romania, things may have to get worse before a Polish-style stabilisation plan can be fully implemented.

Popular support for austerity, even when undertaken by a legitimate government, is short-lived. Unpopular measures should not be spread over time but taken as quickly as possible. The population should soon be able to perceive a degree of improvement in living standards after the fall; if a positive supply response is too slow or too weak to allow an early reversal in consumption trends then one should deliberately induce a worse squeeze than strictly necessary in order to be able to deliver the expected and pre-announced improvement within the honeymoon period, after which the population will stop being cooperative. In Poland this period lasted roughly 200 days and in other countries the honeymoon is unlikely to last longer. The improvement has to be sustainable; 'double-dips' in consumption have adverse effects on expectations.

There is a great danger of populism in the course of stabilisation. Populist temptations should not be tolerated; on the contrary they should be discussed, identified, publicised and specifically rejected. For a start, the costs and risks of speeding up transition and especially trade liberalisation and convertibility should be recognised by the government. In particular, unemployment should not be underestimated and appropriate provisions should be made for it: belittling the costs of stabilisation, as was done in Poland, is as populist a practice as the making of impossible promises.

Domestic Macro-Economic Balance

Shock therapy stabilisation can bring an instant end to shortages, through a large but tolerable hike in prices, after which the rate of inflation can be brought down.[1] This may now seem obvious but at the time was not at all clear in Poland at the end of 1989, in view of the unprecedented features of that stabilisation: disequilibrium relative prices and the unknown size of repressed inflation, which might have generated prolonged chaos instead of a relatively orderly bout of inflation; the combination of supply rigidities and the possible recreation of soft budget constraints, a potential recipe for protracted hyperinflation. Purely administrative price increases, below the market-clearing level, of the kind introduced by the Romanian government, and in the Soviet Union by Premier Valentin Pavlov on 2 April 1991, aroused popular resistance and discontent without eliminating shortages. They may have had some positive effect by inducing some supply response from farmers, reducing shortages, bringing down the ratio between black and official exchange rates, but otherwise are counterproductive in that they generate hostility against market reform.

There is another reason why all price increases (and compensatory payments) should be made all at one go: if price increases are diluted over time (as they were in Romania, through three stages of price liberalisation; to a smaller extent in Poland) the consequences are inflationary expectations, forward-looking inflationary wage settlements, and a secondary wave of inflation that may set in motion an inflationary spiral.

Stabilisation needs prior or simultaneous monetary and fiscal restraint. Budgetary and monetary discipline is indispensable, otherwise the round of price increases involved by stabilisation is wasted, and inflationary pressures are continually recreated. Again, this may seem obvious enough but it is a lesson which was lost, for instance, on Soviet or Romanian leaders. In this respect Janos Kornai has been proven both right and wrong: wrong in that state enterprise budget constraints can be hardened, right in that it requires a non-communist government aiming at restoring a private market economy.

1. Shock therapy stabilisation should be distinguished from global shock therapy *à la* Dornbusch (1990), which would also include instant privatisation through free handouts of capital to citizens, debt for equity swaps, instant total liberalisation of trade and capital movements, and more; and from the actual global shock therapy followed in Polish-type programmes which include free trade and convertibility as well as stabilisation.

An incomes policy, especially for workers and for farmers, is a necessity. In view of the underdeveloped monetary and financial system, monetary policy is not sufficient to sustain a stabilisation programme; an incomes policy is also needed. Unusually this was also recognised for Poland by the IMF; the same principle was accepted in the CSFR, Bulgaria and – although not implemented – in Yugoslavia (December 1989) and Hungary (1991). The Romanian and (until the Russian 1992 attempt) Soviet exceptions are a further confirmation of this principle.[2]

Contrary to the policy followed by Poland, *farmers' incomes should not be penalised but protected* on the grounds that everybody else does it. Their loans should not be taxed (see below) but subsidised; they should not be charged international prices for their inputs when they face trade obstacles in selling their output at international prices and face the competition from subsidised imports.[3] Paradoxically in Poland farmers' supply response was impeded by competition with food aid granted by the European Community and other donors in early 1990.

Monetary Policy

Anchoring a programme to real money supply can be inflationary; anchoring it to nominal money supply can be severely recessionary. Some programmes have avoided this dilemma through drastic reductions in the real money supply (Poland) or through ambiguity about whether money targets were nominal or real (as in the CSFR, and in earlier Soviet programmes which were not implemented).

Real interest rates should be raised but not necessarily to positive levels during stabilisation. It is preferable to hold down interest rates initially, introducing some credit rationing instead. In a growing economy in conditions of tranquillity, the real interest rate equilibrium has to match the positive rate of return on investment. But in the turbulent times of transition a positive real rate of interest is highly recessionary, raises the burden of government debt service, and is probably unnecessary, as even a negative real rate may be sufficient to induce the public to hold voluntarily liquid monetary assets, especially in a situation where interest differentials between domestic and hard currency deposits are greatly in excess of differential inflation or likely domestic de-

2. On the importance of incomes policy in the stabilisation of transitional economies see Coricelli and Rocha (1990).

3. I was once asked (by Gerhard Fink): why should farmers be protected and not, say, barbers? This is a good question, but has several very good answers: because it is easier to grow longer hair and beard than to go without food; because haircuts are non-tradable and do not require tradables for their production; because haircuts are not capital-intensive services both in terms of capital/output and capital/labour ratios.

valuations. If the government expects to get inflation down during the year, it should underpin that expectation by lending over the medium term at interest rates which embody that expectation of lower inflation and therefore lower subsequent monthly rates of interest, instead of lending mostly on variable monthly rates as was done in Poland; (on possible perverse real interest effects, see Kolodko, 1990b and 1991).

In no circumstances should interest rates be raised on old, long-term credit contracts stipulated at fixed rates. Retroactive high interest rates are a tax on liabilities, a very bad tax which nobody has ever suggested. Assets, not liabilities, should be subject to tax. The increase in net wealth due to a drastic fall in the present value of liabilities may be subject to a capital gains tax, along with all kinds of other capital gains – not liabilities as such. Retroactive interest rises on long-term loans are also unfair and arguably unconstitutional; they were disastrous for Polish farmers and literally stopped their supply response.

The same mistake might be repeated in Bulgaria, where raising interest on old contracts has been seriously considered. Hungarians have had a much better idea, namely raising the interest rate on enterprise payment arrears *vis-à-vis* other enterprises and the banking system, up to twice the 22 per cent basic bank rate. However in Hungary in mid–1991 the marginal cost of borrowing to enterprises was of the order 30–40 per cent and therefore automatic borrowing at 44 per cent through cumulating arrears could still be preferred to negotiated borrowing at 40 per cent; twice the actual borrowing rate would be a preferable penal stipulation.

A real wage level lower than actual (theoretical) levels, and consistent with the consumption available during stabilisation, should be strongly indexed. This is the policy which was followed in Bulgaria. A weak indexation of the actual wage level – as was done in Poland for the determination of wage norms – produces the kind of U-shaped time pattern of real wages that occurred in Poland in 1990. The reversal of an excessive decline in real wages requires that money wages rise faster than prices, but punitive taxation of excess wages above government guidelines can amplify the resulting wage inflationary shocks by inducing a more than proportional rise in enterprise labour costs. By itself, wage indexation is neither good nor bad; its effect depends on what wage level is being protected (which should not exceed what is allowed by sustainable consumption and its distribution), on the coefficient of elasticity of money wages with respect to prices, on the lag between price and wage adjustments, on the interval between wage negotiations (when real wage protection ceases to be automatic and money wages become entirely subject to renegotiation anyway).

International Aspects

Trade liberalisation makes an important contribution to stabilisation and reform: it conveys signals of opportunities for a more efficient pattern of imports and exports; it 'imports' a system of relative prices for tradables which otherwise may be hard to settle at an equilibrium level following domestic liberalisation of prices; it enhances competition in an over-concentrated industrial system during the time it takes to partition it into smaller and competing units; it is a guarantee of decentralisation of enterprise decisions. Free trade leads to the overdue elimination of activities which would have a negative value-added at world prices (which according to recent empirical studies may be as much as one-fifth or one-quarter of industrial activities in transitional economies), and therefore facilitates the restructuring process. *However, free trade also destroys domestic activities which are unprofitable at world prices but still produce a positive value-added and make a positive contribution to national income, employment, exports and consumption.* This cost should not be neglected when deciding the degree of openness of the national economy during the process of stabilisation and transition to the market economy. Gradualism in stabilisation is not economically justified; gradualism in convertibility and trade opening until some progress is made in capacity restructuring is not necessarily unfounded – as long as the reform impetus is not lost on the way, as might happen in Hungary.

There is a contradiction between the pursuit of generalised free trade and the will to join a trading bloc such as the European Community. Inexplicably this contradiction was little understood by Central-Eastern European governments and impeded rapid progress in the negotiation of association agreements with the EC, finally concluded in November 1991 by the CSFR, Hungary and Poland. Paradoxically these countries have had to reimpose tariffs in order to be able to negotiate their reduction in trade with the EC.

Internal convertibility for current transactions is within closer reach than previously thought. One of the reasons for Polish success in this area is the pre-existence of hard currency-denominated assets and banknotes, mostly dollars, in the hands of households and firms on a scale which was unique in Eastern Europe (at 1 January 1990 of the order of $US4.5 bn for household deposits plus $US2.5 bn for enterprises, plus cash estimated at between $US4 bn to $US8 bn). The possibility of early convertibility had not been at all clear in Poland at the time; indeed many economists had warned of the dangers of capital flight and loss of reserves, whereas the opposite happened. This does not imply that, in the words of the CSFR Minister of Finance Vaclav Klaus, 'The only problem with convertibility is to declare it'; obviously there is no point in any exchange rate manoeuvre unless there are market-clearing prices, subsidies have been eliminated or very substantially reduced on tradable goods and services, and there is significant elasticity of demand and supply with respect to prices (Nuti, 1991a; none of these conditions were present in Russia in early 1992). In Poland the simultaneous price liberalisation and reduction of subsidies, and the presence of a significant private sector and the hardening of budget constraints in the state sector, ensured that these preconditions were satisfied (as they were in the CSFR on 1 January 1991 when limited convertibility was also introduced, without a private sector and therefore with more limitations than in Poland).

In heavily indebted countries, the rescheduling of debt and capitalisation of interest, whether de jure or de facto, are a clear precondition for establishing convertibility. Convertibility is immensely facilitated by the lack of externally-held balances in domestic currencies (such as the sterling balances which marred British early attempts to return to convertibility). However convertibility is impossible without the freezing, or funding, or outright relief, of externally-held debt denominated in hard currencies. Poland first rescheduled unilaterally, then came to agreed rescheduling, then benefited from debt relief. Hungarians, pursuing convertibility under the burden of debt service, have faced great difficulties and have not yet established it fully.

Debt rescheduling and relief should be requested before and not after stabilisation. In the interest of the stabilising country, in order to bargain from a position of strength, the easing of the burden of debt should be made a negotiated condition for the introduction of convertibility and trade liberalisation; even after a very successful stabilisation such negotiations are held from a position of weakness. This is demonstrated by Poland's delay in obtaining debt relief and its uneven treatment by different creditors.

Exchange Rate Policy

Some undervaluation of the domestic currency and a commitment to initially support a fixed rate are necessary to establish credibility of convertibility. In Poland, through inflation continuously revaluing a nominally constant, initially undervalued zloty rate of exchange for the dollar, the real price of the dollar started high and was continuously reduced in a kind of repeated Dutch auction until it found its own equilibrium level, signalled by the nominal rate of exchange coming under pressure. Credibility of convertibility with respect to domestic holders of dollars as well as foreign and domestic firms is initially low, but grows as convertibility is maintained. This gradual credibility enhancement allowed real appreciation of the zloty in 1990–91, which would not have occurred if the zloty had been initially set at a higher rate. Then the equilibrium rate can rise over time because of increasing confidence – up to the limits set by trade competitiveness. Yugoslavia fixed a realistic rate of exchange which however could not be maintained – among other reasons –

because it was not undervalued;[4] there is no point in introducing a convertibility which cannot be maintained, especially if there is a misguided commitment to fixed rates. An initial commitment to a fixed rate also enhances credibility (Aghevli et al., 1991).

Undervaluation of the domestic currency has to be fixed well below Purchasing Power Parities. PPP is not a good guidance to initial rate for three reasons: the equilibrium rate is affected by stock equilibrium, which in Polish-type conditions may require a lower rate than flow equilibrium; PPP includes non-tradables; more importantly, PPP is an average concept whereas competitiveness is a marginal one, i.e. what counts are the elasticities of supply of and demand for tradables. This is why Russian attempts in 1992 at fixing an exchange rate close to the PPP rate have floundered.

Notwithstanding the need for some undervaluation of the domestic currency for the sake of credibility, the price of hard currencies should not be pitched as high as the level prevailing in the free market. The free price in a two-tier free/controlled market is always higher than the single price which would prevail in a completely free market (due to the income effect of raising the single level above the lower-tier level). Some undervaluation is necessary but excessive undervaluation is expensive because it leads to distress exports and it worsens the terms of trade. Excessive undervaluation, such as is necessarily involved in officially adopting the free market rate, unnecessarily raises domestic inflation and, under the kind of wages policy followed in Poland, unnecessarily reduces real wages;[5] thus it is to be avoided.

The nominal exchange rate, in any case, is a bad anchor if further inflation is expected and moreover cannot be controlled. This is what happened in Poland; the ensuing progressive revaluation to the point of gross overvaluation – partly the result of inflation generated by undervaluation itself – was as unfounded as the initial excessive undervaluation and required further (still inadequate) corrections. The later then a new devaluation occurs, as it eventually must, the larger it has to be, probably raising inflation and inflationary expectations more than a series of smaller adjustments. A combination of real wage policy and floating exchange rate (as in the Bulgarian programme of

---

4. In addition, of course, Yugoslavia was forced to suspend convertibility *de facto* in the autumn of 1990 because by mid-1990 it had lost control of money wages, of monetary expansion and of republican contributions to the federal budget.

5. Gomulka (1991b) rejects the notion that the January devaluation was excessive on the ground that in December 1989 in Poland nearly 60 per cent of the total money supply was dollar-denominated, and therefore devaluation did not amount to a contractionary monetary policy. However he neglects that wages were not dollar-denominated, and that the inflationary implications of the January devaluation unduly depressed real demand through real incomes if not through real balances.

February 1991) or, better, some kind of crawling peg, appears to be preferable.[6]

It is absurd to pre-announce devaluations. This was done in the CSFR in mid–1990 for 1 January 1991 thus forcing an earlier devaluation in September 1990, in Romania for August 1991 and in a way also in Hungary with the January 1990 devaluation which had been openly called for by government members; but prior indication of general exchange rate policy is far better than maintaining an overvalued currency until a crisis occurs.

Privatisation

Privatisation takes a great deal of time to be implemented and/or to become effective. We already know from the privatisation experience of Western countries that the preparation of state enterprises for sale and the issue of shares to the public is a lengthy process (see for instance the British experience). The transfer of ownership titles can be speeded up by the free distribution of claims to state assets to the population, as envisaged everywhere except the ex-GDR and Hungary. This in fact may eliminate or at least reduce the need for prior financial and capacity restructuring, capital valuation and share issue pricing. However the organisation of even such 'free' transfers has proven inordinately time-consuming in practice, and by mid-1992 has not yet been implemented in any of the transitional economies in spite of earlier commitments. In any case the simple transfer of ownership titles has no effect whatever – other than an undesirable inflationary wealth effect on demand – in the absence of properly functioning financial markets: for managers to be subject to stockmarket discipline it is necessary for them to feel the threat of takeover in case of poor performance. Restrictions on voting and on early resale of shares, and the pulverisation of shareholdings, are actually a guarantee that financial markets will not be able to exercise a function of corporate control for a long time to come.

---

6. Aghevli et al. (1991) discuss the relative merits of fixed and flexible exchange rate regimes in developing countries. On the one hand a commitment to manage the exchange rate flexibly may provide helpful assurances to producers of traded goods and thereby support external adjustment; on the other hand, it may undermine the credibility of the government in adopting restrictive demand policies and thus make it more difficult to lower inflation without imposing an output cost. On balance, they recommend a nominal exchange rate rule, under which the rate of crawl of the nominal exchange rate is fixed. Following this line of reasoning it was effective for Poland to maintain a fixed nominal rate for an initial extended period, to establish credibility, but the continuation of such a policy after credibility had been established will have had advantages outweighed by disadvantages with respect to exchange rate flexibility.

Privatisation, because of its necessary slowness, should not be relied upon as a means of easing the task of stabilisation. 'Small-scale' privatisation (housing, catering and trade establishments, land) can be much quicker than the privatisation of state enterprises, but even that cannot soften the blow of instant price liberalisation, unless it starts beforehand and its progress is clearly and credibly announced in all its details. It follows that the Shatalin–Yavlinsky Plan of September 1990 for Soviet stabilisation in 500 days was not credible, because of its attempt to reduce the overhang through front-loaded privatisation. Soviet reform attempts of end-1990/early 1991 failed not because privatisation *per se* was not introduced, as Jeffrey Sachs argues (*Repubblica*, 8 March 1991), but because privatisation was relied upon as an instrument of stabilisation – already a tall order – and was not replaced by other stabilisation measures such as higher prices or taxes.

Property restitution to old owners is a respectable political objective but is economically costly. Restitution, introduced everywhere (except Yugoslavia) following the ex-GDR lead, is not economically necessary to build up confidence in the new institutions, since there is no expectation of policy reversals in the target system. It slows down further the process of privatisation because of the time needed to allow and process claims, especially if restitution in kind is contemplated. It also absorbs precious time to settle a large number of issues: the eligibility of nationals versus expatriates (and from what date), the fixing of ceilings and progressive scales for compensation (always confiscatory on a progressive scale – a residual of socialist egalitarianism); the fixing of arbitrary dates from which nationalised property is to be returned to old owners, and often of specific nationalising laws and types of property. Restitution to old owners, including aristocrats and the Churches, at a time when considerable sacrifices are asked of ordinary citizens and workers, is politically divisive. These economic costs may be regarded by the governments involved as worth paying (in Hungary, restitution was a condition of the Smallholders' Partys essential participation in the government coalition), but they should not be ignored.

During the inevitable delays of privatisation the state sector, which continues to exist and to provide the bulk of productive capacity, should not be ignored, neglected and penalised. Central-Eastern European governments, particularly the Polish government, confuse their potential ability to privatise with the realisation of that potential and simply pretend that the state sector does not exist.[7] Worse, state enterprises in Poland are subject to distortionary and discriminatory taxation with respect to the private sector, such as the tax on wage payments above statutory guidelines (the so-called PPWW) and a

7. In this the new governments display the same kind of attitude that the old regime had with respect to inflation, confusing their potential ability to implement price stability with the realisation of that potential, and ignoring the cumulative build-up of the large monetary overhang which played such a great part in systemic failure.

payment of a so-called 'dividend' to the state budget calculated not on profits but on a revalued historical capital value; similar policies are followed, to a lesser extent, in the other countries. It is inappropriate to enforce incomes policy only in the state sector; a generalised progressive income tax is preferable. The argument of lack of owners' control over wage expenditures in the state enterprises is used in support of excess wage tax in Poland and Hungary but this is a case for privatisation and for the overhauling of managerial incentives in the state enterprise sector, not for tax exemption of the private sector.[8]

On the rebound from former 'soft budgets' state enterprises are indiscriminately starved of resources, whether from the reinvestment of profits or access to credit, regardless of the viability of potential investment. Under the prospect of a rapid privatisation which does not however materialise, there is hardly any reorganisation, redeployment of productive assets within the state sector, or revision of methods of assessing and rewarding managerial performance. Managerial uncertainty about the prospect, timing and terms of their enterprises' privatisation leads at best to paralysis, at worst to de-capitalisation, anarchy and rapid decline. This kind of policy is not necessarily an improvement on the former central tutelage.[9] The only incentive for efficient managerial behaviour is the prospect of finding a foreign buyer or partner, and this is not sufficiently widespread or, apart from a few exceptions, strong enough to vitalise state enterprises.

Under the old system state enterprises were basically administrative units executing central instructions and rewarded or penalised according to the degree of fulfillment of such instructions. This, however, does not necessarily imply lack of 'entrepreneurship' on the part of managers; indeed it has been argued that the task of running a state enterprise in the face of continuous unpredictable changes in often conflicting central instructions, in conditions of endemic shortages of labour and means of production and uncertain supplies, is a much harder challenge than that faced by Western managers running a private enterprise in a market economy. The problem is not the absence of entrepreneurship but the misdirection of whatever entrepreneurship is there. There are signs that state enterprises have actually responded to some extent to the new conditions; a pilot study of Polish state enterprises conducted by the World Bank (Jorgensen et al., 1990) concludes that 'in the light of the immense and continued uncertainty and the time necessary for adjustment, the degree of response observed was high, and in most cases in the right direction'.

8. Polish government documents (for instance the Government Memorandum of 25 March 1991, section IV.1) candidly recognise that the 'popiwek' tax is 'expected to provide a significant incentive' for privatisation. Surely this kind of incentive should not be needed, or less distortionary incentives could be provided.

9. On the negative perception of the Polish stabilisation programme by managers, from a sample of 70 state enterprises, see Maj (1991).

However, some of this response had negative side-effects (for instance, the growth of inter-firm payments arrears, which firms expected to be somehow guaranteed by the state); excess wage tax proved to be constraining output and generating distortions; firms suffered from a 'vacuum of ownership'; 'the best-placed firms are probably those with previous exposure to selling on Western markets'. It is urgent to provide new indicators of enterprise performance, budgetary constraints (e.g. cash limits) and an appropriate system of managerial incentives (rewards and penalties geared to market success).

Especially in the state sector some capacity restructuring should be effected from the start, following the kind of industrial policy which is usually formulated and implemented in all other market economies. When, as in Poland in January–March 1991, enterprise profits are subject to 87 per cent taxation and access to credit is restricted in principle, there can be no supply response from any stabilisation programme.

Sequencing, Announcements, Contingencies

Speedy action is better than orderly procrastination. In recent literature there has been considerable discussion of the question of appropriate sequencing of reform and stabilisation steps: some have pointed out the high degree of interdependence of tasks and therefore the need to do everything at once (e.g. Dornbusch, 1990); others have attempted to draw a desirable sequential critical path (e.g. Nuti, 1991b). There is now, however, widespread agreement that, whatever the merits of a possibly potentially superior critical path, it is much more important to move as fast as possible, 'meandering' in the right direction than to make slower progress along a sequentially optimal path, even if it existed. Clearly stabilisation must come first, as market-clearing prices without excessive inflationary pressures are a precondition of viability of any system where markets are used at all, even if only for the distribution of resources in place of their allocation as in the traditional centrally-planned economy. Currency convertibility without price liberalisation (even solely for the tourist rate, as it was done in the Soviet Union in November 1991) unloads the monetary overhang on to that one market and leads to costly and absurd results (such as a Soviet average wage of the order of $US3 per month in the second half of 1991). It is essential that Central-Eastern European governments should not stop after stabilisation wondering what would be best to do next, but should keep going. In Poland institutional reforms practically came to a standstill in the first half of 1990 for a considerable time, while privatisation was unnecessarily delayed by political arguments and by the pursuit of facile schemes of mass privatisation. Without such gaps and delays the expected supply response might have been stronger. Of course complex and unprecedented systemic reform is bound to take time; but, confronted with such delays, it may be better to follow the line of least resistance and implement what is immediately feasible, rather than follow a rigid ideal pattern of reform sequencing: bad sequencing is costly, but may be better than no change.

Even incomplete and unsuccessful attempts at reform may have positive effects. It has been claimed that such attempts have brought about 'reform fatigue'; certainly the repeated pre-1989 aborted attempts at constructing a market socialist model must have worn out all those involved. However even failed attempts are not necessarily a waste of time. It helps stabilisation to have, beforehand, a private sector in agriculture and in manufacturing; some free trade in foreign currency, currency retentions by exporters and currency auctions (admittedly distortionary, but a powerful instrument of decentralisation and an incentive to trade); a previous banking reform, legislation of the kind already passed in Poland under Jaruzelski, even under Martial Law.

In the delay of implementation the effects of time-consuming measures can be approximated by making credible and detailed announcements. Thus, for instance, the effects of a necessarily slow privatisation programme – on saving behaviour, on incentives – can be accelerated by announcing the exact terms, schedule and procedures of the entire programme. However, this presumes that the path to be followed is clear and widely agreed, and that the government enjoys credibility when it announces what it intends to undertake next. Policy reversals or even continuous piecemeal alterations within the same general policies undermine such credibility.

Instead of adopting a single package of stabilisation measures, the government should make contingent commitments to cover possible undershooting or overshooting, and some of the possible additional external shocks. A single package could not possibly be 'robust' enough with respect to exogenous factors and to unpredictable behavioural responses. Once a package is announced, if external or domestic conditions change in an expected direction the government is paralysed, for fear of destabilising expectations by taking necessary action. For instance the Polish government could not react to the recessionary overshooting of its stabilisation plan in 1990, fearing that reflationary measures would signal the abandonment of its commitment to austerity. Only the prior announcement of contingent measures, at the same time as the stabilisation was announced, could have avoided Keynesian unemployment, which is not as justified as the unemployment generated by capacity restructuring.

System-Specific Features of Stabilisation

Post-communist countries are different from ordinary underdeveloped countries; high costs can derive from neglecting such differences. In the elation of the 1989 revolutions the prospect of an early transition to capitalism induced new rulers, international agencies, Western governments and their advisors to forget the heavy burden of the former regime's legacies. Not only were older historical legacies initially neglected – nationalist and ethnic conflicts, to name only the ones which most spectacularly manifested themselves soon afterwards – but also the more recent but deeply ingrained economic legacies of habits, institutions and expectations.

By and large, Central-Eastern European economies have been treated like ordinary developing countries, facing familiar tasks of de-regulation of economic activities, privatisation of state assets, coping with a large external debt, trying to bring down inflation and hyperinflation, opening their economies to trade, attracting new foreign investments. The skills of area studies specialists and of economists expert in centrally-planned economies and their long path to reform were, wrongly, regarded as obsolete. Knowledge of the target model was regarded as the only necessary qualification to manage the transition to that model, whereas a successful organ transplant across different species obviously requires deep knowledge of both donor and recipient.

Qualitatively the tasks of transition are the same as, or similar to, those familiar from the experience of underdeveloped countries. But one might be forgiven for quoting Engels' proposition (in Anti-Düring) that quantitative differences can become qualitative: the sheer scale of these tasks, as well as their simultaneous presence, reduces very greatly the relevance of the stabilisation and reform programmes of underdeveloped countries to Central-Eastern Europe. Moreover, the ultimate difference between the two groups was neglected or underestimated: namely, the extraordinary economic inertia of a centrally-planned economy no longer subject to central control but not yet fully subject or responsive to full market stimuli.

There is an inordinate difference between reducing the size of the state sector, say from 60 to 30 per cent, and reducing it from 100 to 50 per cent; for a start, one has to introduce from scratch property legislation, joint stock companies, commercial banking, financial markets, price competition, liquidation and bankruptcy; if legislation takes time, jurisprudence takes a much longer time. There is the same difference between raising unemployment, say, from 5 to 10 per cent and raising it from zero to over 10 per cent; between liberalising some price controls, and replacing with market-clearing prices a historical stratification of multiple prices varying according to agents and type of transactions; between introducing convertibility for a domestic currency and introducing a true domestic currency in place of what was essentially a unit of account or, at best, a lottery ticket. The list could go on. The neglect of these differences has led to a serious underestimation of the time-scale of transition and of the costs of a transitional economic non-system, and to a serious overestimation of the supply response that could be elicited through familiar policy instruments in an inert economy.[10]

Costs and Benefits

The benefits expected of stabilisation and reform do not have to be emphasised: the viability of markets, which for consumers means a return to 'normal life' (a theme which has frequently recurred in electoral campaigns) and for firms the elimination of the most glaring inefficiencies; the de-politicisation of economic activities; the establishment of market discipline for enterprises and personal incentives for individuals; a return to the world economy and in particular to Europe; the expectation of better standards of living.

The list of expected benefits is long but, when there is no alternative target available the benefits of such a target do not even need to be mentioned, let alone quantified. There remains however a problem of cost-effectiveness of alternative ways of reaching that target (i.e. not a question of what to do but of how to do it).

The stabilisation and reform plans of Central-Eastern European countries have been accompanied by inordinately high costs, in terms of employment, output, consumption, distribution of income and wealth.

Some of those costs have nothing to do with the transition to market but are simply the open manifestation of the hidden costs of the earlier system: hidden unemployment and inflation, environmental disaster, inappropriate capacity; such costs would have been openly incurred, sooner or later, whatever the target model selected.

Some of the costs have been the result of the uncoordinated nature of stabilisation and reform plans undertaken in the whole area, which have resulted in the collapse of trade within the ex-CMEA. These costs could have been at least alleviated if the countries concerned had been able to agree on establishing free trade areas or on setting up schemes for automatic trade clearing and mutual payments of the type adopted through the European Payments Union (EPU) in post-war Europe (which would have attracted Western aid just as EPU attracted Marshall aid). Keenness to undermine Soviet dominance, to make a clean break with the past, as well as fear of delaying the more desirable course of joining the European Community, have resulted in the otherwise avoidable costs of trade collapse within the ex-CMEA (although, with the benefit of hindsight, trade within the ex-CMEA would have shrunk regardless of such attempts due to the drastic decline in the Soviet or ex-Soviet area). Similar costs now are bound to be incurred if the ex-Soviet republics fail

10. The specific features of stabilisation in post-communist economies, however, are well understood in Kolodko (1990a and 1991; see also Nuti, 1991b).

to establish a trade and payments regime capable of handling their interdependence and preserving viable trade flows.

Some of the costs of 'transition' have been the result of the sudden opening of national economies, due to i) the lack of protection of those activities which – again, with the benefit of hindsight – we now know should not have been undertaken in the past but, being there, were still making a positive contribution to national income; ii) the related costs of a speedy convertibility. Of course there were also benefits from opening the economy, like the expected gains in trade, competition and foreign investment, listed above; but we should not take for granted that the net result is necessarily positive, let alone positive and large.

Partly, some non-negligible costs of stabilisation and reform plans undertaken in Central-Eastern European countries have been the results of true and predictable mistakes, in the narrow sense of decisions which can be proved wrong under any circumstances, rather than plausible 'quasi-mistakes' in the sense of decisions which proved to have been inappropriate only with the benefit of hindsight and therefore can generate 'surprises'.[11] Using President Bush's language, these are 'the wrong kind of mistakes'.[12]

Thus, for instance, in Poland it was a mistake to let real wages and the real exchange rate float at random with the vagaries of inflation, to excessively over-devalue the zloty only to let it steadily overvalue, to effectively tax old loans by raising their interest rates, to neglect farmers' incomes and supply response, to neglect the state sector, to postpone further institutional changes, not to make clear announcements about further developments, and to make no provision for possible overshooting.

The inability to recognise mistakes and to learn from them, which was a main drawback of the old system, seems another legacy inherited by the new system. What is worse, Central-Eastern European governments often fail to learn not only from the mistakes of others, which is true wisdom, but even from their own.

---

11. Recently there has been a tendency in official circles to recognise Polish overshooting and the negative phenomena associated with it, but to claim that these had been 'surprises' (Gomulka, 1991a and b) and to dub economic decline and unemployment with the dubious euphemisms of 'creative destruction' (Gomulka, 1991b). Moreover Gomulka also admits that 'some of the forecasts, e.g. on prices and output, were made under the pressure of policy convenience' (1991a), i.e. were actually fabricated. One might have been 'surprised', perhaps, by the results of the stabilisation plan in January 1990, but not in February 1990 (when I actually had the privilege of making these same points to Minister Balcerowicz), let alone in April–May 1991.

12. 'As Yogi Berra used to say, I do not want to make the wrong kind of mistake.' (President George Bush discussing with journalists his cautious attitude to Soviet crackdown in Lithuania, in January 1991).

References

Aghevli, B. B., M. S. Khan and P. J. Montiel, 1991, "Exchange Rate Policy in Developing Countries: Some Analytical Issues". IMF Occasional Paper 78. Washington.

Angelov, I., 1991, "One Year Monetary Reform in Bulgaria", Institute of Economics, Bulgarian Academy of Sciences. Sofia.

Chen, K., G. H. Jefferson and I. Singh, 1990, "Lessons from China's Economic Reform", World Bank, December.

Coricelli, F. and R. Rocha, 1990, "Stabilisation Programs in Eastern Europe: A Comparative Analysis of the Polish and the Yugoslav Programs of 1990". Conference Paper, World Bank, Poltusk (Poland), October.

Dornbusch, R., 1990, "Transition to a Market Economy in Central and Eastern Europe". OECD Conference Paper. Paris.

ECE-UN, 1991, *Economic Bulletin for Europe* 43.

Fry, M. J. and D. M. Nuti, 1992, "Monetary and Exchange Rate Policies during Eastern Europe's Transition: Some Lessons from Further East", *Oxford Review of Economic Policy*. (Forthcoming.)

Gomulka, S., 1991a, "Polish Economic Reform: Principles, Policies and Surprises". Conference paper, Jerusalem, April.

_____ ,1991b, "Tworcza destrukcja", *Zycie Gospodarcze* 18, 5 May, pp.1, 6–7.

Government of Poland, 1991, "Memorandum on Economic Reform and Medium Term Policies, 1991–1993", Warsaw, 25 March.

Grosfeld, I. and P. Hare, 1991, "Privatisation in Hungary, Poland and Czechoslovakia", *European Economy* 48.

Hrncir, M. and J. Klacek, 1991, "Stabilization Policies and Currency Convertibility in Czechoslovakia", *European Economy*, Special Issue 2, pp. 19–39.

Jackson, M., 1991a, "One Year After German Economic Union: The Impact on the German Economy". Report on Eastern Europe, 28 June, Munich, pp. 38–43.

_____ , 1991b, "One Year After German Economic Union: Are There Lessons to be learned?", Report on Eastern Europe, 28 June, Munich, pp. 43–48.

Jorgensen, E. A., A. Gelb and I. Singh, 1990, "Life for Polish Firms under the 'Big Bang': Preliminary Findings from a Field Trip". Conference Paper, World Bank, Poltusk (Poland), October.

Kolodko, G. W., 1990a, *Inflacja – reforma – stabilizacja*. Warsaw: Alma Press.

_____ , 1990b, "Polish Hyperinflation and Stabilisation 1989–1990", Working Papers of the Institute of Finance 10, Warsaw; also in *Most- Moct: Economic Journal of Eastern Europe and the Soviet Union* 1, 1991, pp. 9–36.

_____ , 1991, "Polish Hyperinflation and Stabilisation. A Year After", *Rivista di Politica Economica*, June, pp. 289–330.

Kolodko, G. W., D. Gotz-Kozierkiewicz and E. Skrzeszewska-Paczek, 1992, *Hyperinflation and Stabilisation in Postsocialist Economies*. Boston, London and Dortrecht: Kluwer.

Maj, H., 1991, "Proces dostowan mikroekonomicznych. Reakcje przedsiebiorstw w warunkach polityki stabilizacyjnej", in Kolodko, G. W. (ed.), *Polityka finansowa-stabilizacja-transformacja*. Warsaw: Instytut Finansow.

Nuti, D. M., 1988, "Perestroika: Transition Between Central Planning and Market Socialism", *Economic Policy* 7, pp. 353–389

_____, 1990a, "Internal and International Implications of Monetary Disequilibrium in Poland", *European Economy* 43, pp. 169–182.

_____, 1990b, "Privatisation of Socialist Economies: General Issues and the Polish Case", in Bloomenstein, H. and M. Marrese (eds), *The Transformation of Planned Economies*. Paris: OECD.

_____, 1991a, "How Fast Should Convertibility Be Introduced? A Comment on F. Levcik and J. J. Polak", in Williamson, J. (ed.), *Currency Convertibility in Eastern Europe*. Washington DC: IIE, pp. 48– 55.

_____, 1991b, "Sequencing and Credibility in Economic Reform"; in Atkinson, A. B. and R. Brunetta (eds), *Economics for the New Europe*. London: MacMillan, pp. 126–139.

_____, 1992, "Le conseguenze economiche della rivoluzione russa d'agosto e le risposte occidentali", *Rivista di Politica Economica*, LXXXII 2, February, pp. 109–119.

Nuti D. M. and J. Pisani-Ferry, 1992, "Post-Soviet Issues: Stabilisation, Trade and Money", Conference on the economic consequences of the East, CEPR and Deutsche Bundesbank, March, Frankfurt, and Economic Papers 93, May 1992. Brussels: CEC-DGII.

Rosati, D. K., 1991a, "Institutional and Policy Framework for Foreign Economic Relations in Poland", in UN-ECE, Reforms in Foreign Economic Relations of Eastern Europe and the Soviet Union, New York.

_____, 1991b, "The Polish Road to Capitalism: A Critical Appraisal of the Balcerowicz Plan", *Thames Polytechnic Papers in Political Economy*, New Series 2.

Siebert, H., 1990a, "The Economic Integration of Germany". Discussion Paper 160. Kiel Institute of World Economics.

_____, 1990b, "The Economic Integration of Germany – An Update". Discussion Paper 160a. Kiel Institute of World Economics.

4

Output Gains from Economic Liberalisation: A Simple Formula

*Thorvaldur Gylfason**

Introduction

The state of macro-economics as an applied social science concerned with the structure, functioning, and interaction of national economies should be of paramount interest to economists and policy makers in Central and Eastern Europe as they strive to establish a well-functioning market system on the ruins of central planning. The persistence of unresolved controversies and unanswered questions in macro-economics may not inspire confidence among those who are new to the subject and need to design an effective programme of action. It would be unwise, however, to sweep macro-economic theory aside on these grounds. On the contrary, its many weaknesses notwithstanding, macro-economic theory can provide useful guidance to the architects of economic reforms in Central and Eastern Europe.

The main purpose of this paper is to attempt to provide a glimpse of the potential usefulness of macro-economic analysis for assessing the effects of economic liberalisation on national income and output. Specifically, the paper is intended:

– to show how the removal of relative price distortions through trade liberalisation ultimately increases aggregate output in a macro-economic general-equilibrium context, even though output may fall in the short run;

---

* University of Iceland; Institute for International Economic Studies, University of Stockholm; and CEPR. This paper was prepared for the Arne Ryde Symposium on the Transition Problem, Rungsted Kyst, Denmark, 11–12 June 1992. The author is indebted to the organisers of the Symposium and other participants.

– to derive an explicit formula for the potential output gain from economic liberalisation and to relate it to similar expressions for welfare gains from tax reforms in the literature on public finance and foreign trade; and

– to provide a rudimentary quantitative assessment of the potential output gain from adjustment by numerical examples.

In short, the main point of the present paper is that the government can play a constructive role in structural adjustment and stabilisation, in Central and Eastern Europe and elsewhere, regardless of most current controversies about the effectiveness of systematic macro-economic policy.

From Demand to Supply: A Brief Review

Let us begin by laying out a simple aggregate-supply-and-demand framework for the analysis to follow. But first, to set the stage, a glance at recent history is offered.

About twenty years ago, macro-economics was commonly considered to be fairly easy. By and large, the main body of macro-economic theory seemed adequate. Policy prescriptions based on the theory seemed to work quite well. National output and employment were widely viewed as being determined essentially by aggregate demand for goods and services; demand created supply. Aggregate demand was considered to be fairly well understood: an inverse relationship between output and the general price level for given money supply and income velocity followed directly from the quantity theory of money. Macro-economic theories of later times, including Keynes' *General Theory*, incorporated more variables into the analysis of aggregate demand, including private consumption, investment, interest rates, assets, government expenditure, taxes, exports, imports, and exchange rates, but the inclusion of these variables left the essential inverse relationship between aggregate demand for output and the general price level intact. This meant, of course, that an exogenous increase in aggregate potential output could result in higher actual output *and* a lower price level, other things being equal (see Figure 4.1), but this was not considered important during the long period of steadily increasing output and stable prices in the industrial countries following World War II. However, this period came to an end with the oil price hikes in the early 1970s.

After the oil shocks, high unemployment and inflation directed the attention of many macro-economists to the crucial importance of aggregate supply. One should not forget, however, that the Keynesian revolution was really a supply-side revolution in the sense that aggregate supply was shown to be responsive, temporarily at least, to changes in aggregate demand, including changes in government spending and in private investment through monetary policy. As is well known, this point has been contested by adherents of the

FIGURE 4.1 Stabilisation

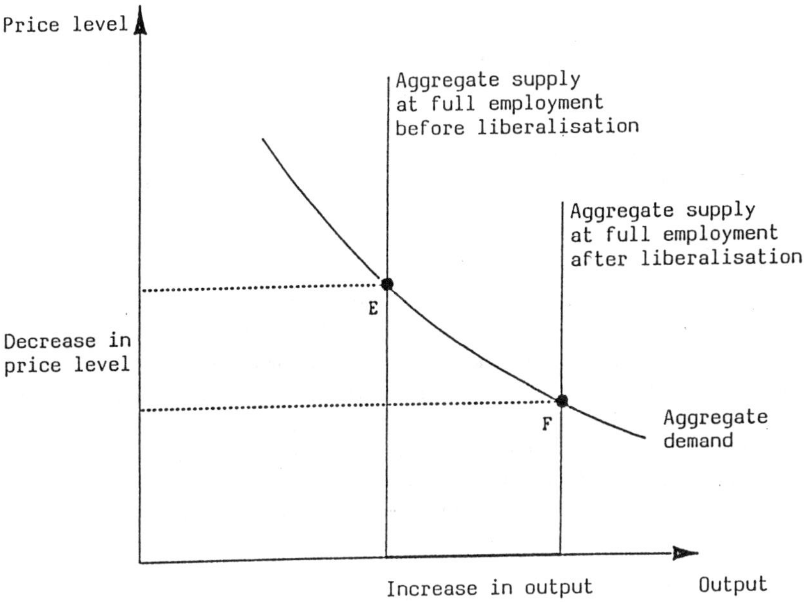

classical school, old and new. To this day, economists are not universally agreed whether the aggregate supply of output is positively related to the general price level in the short run or not, primarily because they have different views of the extent and speed of the adjustment of money wages and price expectations to actual price developments. To be sure, the possibility of a permanently vertical aggregate supply schedule has potentially important implications. It implies, for example, that fiscal policy influences only the composition but not the level of aggregate demand, with or without 'Ricardian equivalence'.[1] However, this possibility appears remote. History abounds in well-documented episodes of increased exports and output following devaluation (Vietnam, of all places, is a recent example, and so is India) and of increased unemployment in the wake of monetary restraint (compare, for

1. Curiously, economic hypotheses sometimes derive their names from those who have refuted them. The 'Ricardian equivalence' hypothesis that it makes no difference whether government spending is financed by levying taxes or by issuing bonds was rejected by David Ricardo. Also, the 'Fisher relation' by which increased inflation raises nominal interest rates point for point was rejected by Irving Fisher.

instance, the United States in the early 1980s). Neither would be possible if aggregate supply were completely unresponsive to changes in aggregate demand. But this need not concern us further here: we shall assume for the sake of the argument that aggregate supply is independent of the price level.

Another point of contention revolves around the extent to which aggregate supply can be influenced by economic policy. If the government knew how to increase aggregate supply, unemployment and unused production capacity could be reduced or even eliminated ultimately without raising prices and jeopardising exchange rate stability or the balance of payments. The persistence of high unemployment and economic slack in the world economy since the early 1980s bears witness to the prevailing lack of confidence in effective aggregate supply management among economists and policy makers. The main problem is not that there is no way to increase aggregate supply, but rather that most measures that would increase supply would also have important effects on aggregate demand, and are probably sufficient to destabilise prices and exchange rates or the balance of payments in many cases. For example, fiscal policy measures aimed at stimulating aggregate supply would inevitably entail changes in government expenditures or receipts that would impinge on aggregate demand. Thus, a bond-financed increase in public employment, increased government subsidies of private employment, or a reduction of payroll taxes in order to reduce wage costs and raise output from the supply side would also increase aggregate demand (in the absence of 'Ricardian equivalence'), other things being equal. A reduction of income taxes in order to stimulate work effort and aggregate supply would also boost aggregate demand. Increased government investment or private investment tax credits would inevitably increase aggregate demand as well as supply, and so on. This is the main reason why persistently high unemployment has been tolerated in Europe since the early 1980s. Governments have not wanted to risk a relapse into high inflation in the belief that sustained price stability is a prerequisite for a return to permanent high employment and a resumption of rapid economic growth.

At the same time, important new developments in theoretical and applied supply-side macro-economics have opened interesting possibilities in recent years. The theory of economic growth has been extended in a new direction by incorporating external effects and scale economies in a way that makes economic growth in the long run an endogenous variable in contrast to the neoclassical model in which the rate of growth of output per head is determined exogenously by technological progress (Solow, 1956). A potentially important upshot of this is that long-run growth performance may be responsive to economic policy after all, including subsidies to research and development (Grossman and Helpman, 1991), fiscal policies (Barro, 1990; Barro and Sala-i-Martin, 1992), redistribution of income and wealth (Persson and Tabellini, 1991), and financial policies (Fischer, 1991).[2]

Moreover, macro-economic policy analysis over the last 10–15 years has emphasised structural adjustment as an essential complement to stabilisation in order to increase economic efficiency and to promote *intensive* rather than *extensive* growth by using existing resources more efficiently as opposed to increasing the use of resources. Such measures include, among other things, the elimination of major economic distortions (e.g., excessive subsidies and tariffs and other trade barriers); the restoration of adequate incentives to work, save, and invest (e.g., by tax reform and by maintaining positive real interest rates); the restructuring or privatisation of public-sector enterprises, including banks in some cases; and various institutional reforms (e.g., by introducing profit-sharing in labour markets (Weitzman, 1986) or by improving the efficiency of credit markets (Stiglitz, 1992). Indeed, the market unification of Western Europe to be completed by the end of 1992 involves structural adjustment on a large scale: increased competition and specialisation are intended to increase output, income, and employment in Europe *and* to reduce prices at the same time (again, see Figure 4.1).

These developments present great challenges to economists and policy makers in Central and Eastern Europe, for, even if reasonable men do not all agree whether monetary and fiscal stimulus can be used safely to counter declining output and increasing unemployment from the demand side of the economy without destabilising prices, there is hardly any question that important opportunities remain to be exploited on the supply side. In this spirit an attempt is made in the next section to build a bridge from structural adjustment to stabilisation by showing how, and how much, the elimination of relative price distortions increases potential and, ultimately, actual output at full employment and efficiency without raising prices. The following analysis of the long-run effects of economic liberalisation on output is mostly conducted within a neoclassical general-equilibrium framework in an attempt to bypass most of the controversies in modern macro-economic analysis reviewed above.

The Effects of Economic Liberalisation on Output

Consider an economy characterised initially by full employment of all available resources and excess aggregate demand (denoted by the horizontal distance EG in Figure 4.2), repressed inflation, and a general shortage of

2. The new and rapidly expanding literature on endogenous growth is not without noteworthy precedents in development economics. For example, Lewis (1954) shows how a redistribution of income to entrepreneurs can stimulate saving and hence economic growth. The effect of increased saving on growth can only be temporary, however, in the neoclassical exogenous-growth model of Solow (1956) with constant returns to scale, but this effect can be permanent in endogenous-growth models with constant returns to capital as, for example, in Romer (1986).

FIGURE 4.2 Temporary Loss Versus Permanent Gain

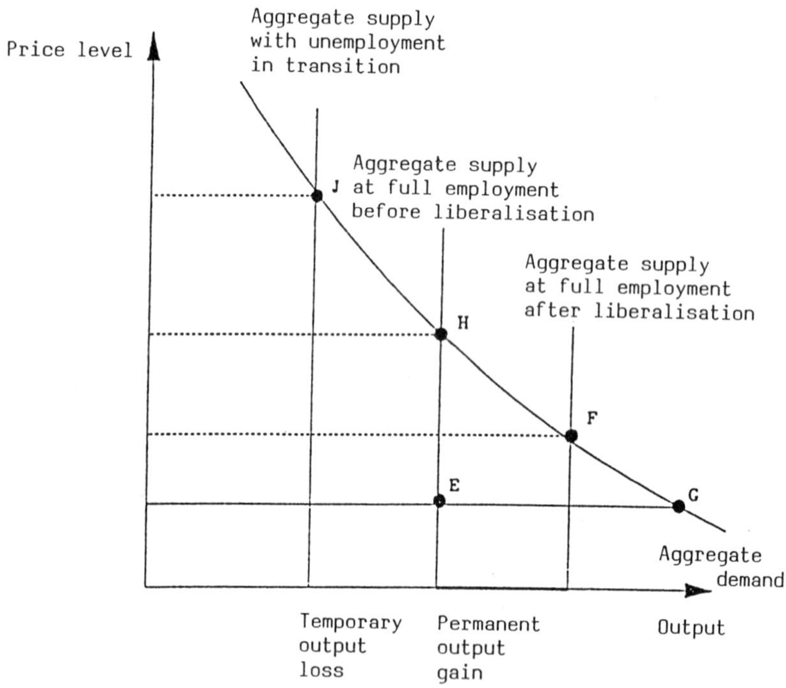

goods and services. All factors of production (labour, capital, land, raw materials, and technical know-how) are held fixed throughout by assumption.

Temporary Loss Versus Permanent Gain

When prices are liberalised, the general price level rises in response to market forces towards point H in the figure. This general price increase is accompanied by a change in relative prices because some prices rise more rapidly than others. Specifically, prices tend to increase most in those sectors where the initial excess demand was largest. At first, output contracts and unemployment emerges as inefficient firms go bankrupt in those parts of the economy where relative prices have fallen. The resulting contraction of aggregate supply increases the pressure on the price level which moves towards point J in the figure.[3] The slump in aggregate demand may reduce output and employment temporarily also in those markets where relative prices have risen, due to the spillover effects of bankruptcies across sectors. With or without such chain reactions triggered by 'Keynesian' demand deficiency, this process continues until the new profit opportunities and incentives arising in markets where relative prices have increased begin to be exploited by entrepreneurs. When this occurs, resources that have become redundant in the contracting sectors of the economy are drawn into more productive employment than before in the expanding sectors and the decline of aggregate output, represented by the horizontal distance between points E and J in the figure, is gradually reversed. The speed at which idle resources are thus absorbed into gainful employment elsewhere depends on many factors, including local infrastructure and institutions and the costs of adjustment or installation of new productive capacity. At any rate, the economy ends up at point F where all profit opportunities have been exploited in full and full employment has been restored. The ultimate output gain is indicated by the thick segment of the horizontal axis.

Even though the output loss from E to J is temporary and the ultimate output gain from J to F is permanent, the adjustment from E to F *via* J may or may not increase the present discounted value of output because the output loss is suffered before the gain materialises. The cure may conceivably be worse than the disease.

To see this clearly, suppose that output falls short of its initial level by ΔY from time $t = 0$ to $t = T$, and then exceeds its original level by $\theta\Delta Y$ from $t = T$ to infinity where θ is some positive constant. Then the present value of the output loss during the adjustment period is

$$(1) \qquad \int_0^T \Delta Y e^{-\rho t} dt = \Delta Y(1 - e^{-\rho T})/\rho$$

where ρ is the annual discount rate. The present value of the output gain thereafter is

$$(2) \qquad \int_T^\infty \theta\Delta Y e^{-\rho t} dt = \theta\Delta Y e^{-\rho T}/\rho.$$

The net gain is found by subtracting equation (1) from equation (2):

$$(3) \qquad \Delta Y[(1+\theta)e^{-\rho T} - 1]/\rho$$

3. Consumers would not necessarily be worse off at J than at E, however, because the adjustment from E towards J may involve the reduction of 'forced' consumption through the removal of unwanted low-quality goods from the consumption basket (in addition to the evaporation of virtually worthless money holdings through inflation).

which is positive as long as

(4) $T < \ln(1+\theta)/\rho$.

If, for example, the temporary output loss equals half the ultimate gain ($\theta = 2$) and the discount rate is 5 per cent per year ($\rho = 0.05$), the structural adjustment would yield a positive net gain as long as it took 22 years or less. A less favourable gain/loss ratio (say, $\theta = 1$) and less patience (e.g., $\rho = 0.1$) would shorten the relevant time horizon considerably: in this case, the output reversal would have to take place within 7 years for the structural adjustment to be worthwhile from an economic point of view.

These simple examples do not, of course, tell the whole story. If the structural adjustment raises not only the level of output once and for all but also its long-run rate of growth through some of the mechanisms emphasised in the new theory of endogenous growth, the present value of the temporary output loss will be overshadowed by the long-term output gain sooner than otherwise if at all. Put differently, the temporary slump can then be tolerated longer.[4] On the other hand, the current generation bears a disproportionate part of the burden of the adjustment. This may reduce public support for the transition as unborn generations that would be the prime beneficiaries of a more efficient allocation of resources have no direct influence on the current generation's choice between structural adjustment and *status quo*. Even so, the examples indicate the importance of attempting a quantitative assessment of the entire adjustment path of output following economic liberalisation. The short-run reaction of output is difficult to deal with, however, because it depends on the complex and controversial interaction between aggregate demand and supply and between different sectors of the economy. In what follows, therefore, we shall concentrate on the long-run effects of liberalisation.

Output Gain: A Simple Formula

What is the exact relationship between the ultimate increase in output and the extent of the initial disequilibrium?

Let us now reconsider the long-run response of aggregate output to economic liberalisation of the type described above within a general-equilibrium framework. To set the stage, think of two sectors, agriculture (the 'traditional' sector) and industry (the 'modern' sector, i.e., manufacturing, trade, and services). Suppose that productive resources are fully, but inefficiently, employed initially and that the relative price of industrial goods in terms of

4. For example, if the structural transformation increases the annual rate of growth of output by 1 percentage point, it yields a positive net gain as long as it takes 29 years or less when $\theta = 2$ and $\rho = 0.05$, and 8 years or less when $\theta = 1$ and $\rho = 0.1$. If the growth rate rises by 2 percentage points, the critical time extends further to 44 and 9 years in the two examples.

FIGURE 4.3 Output Gain from Liberalisation

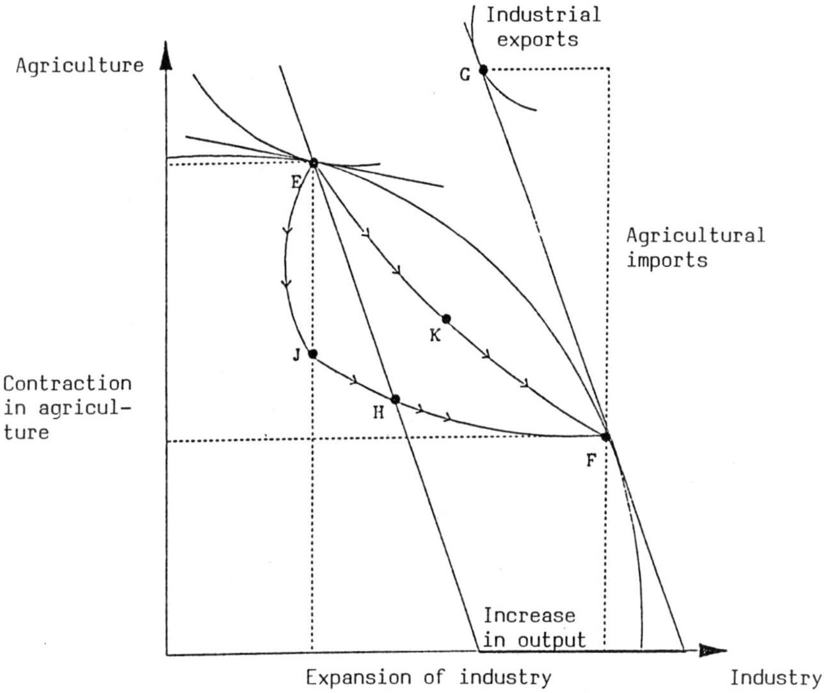

agricultural goods is lower at home than in world markets. This means that more resources are devoted to agricultural production at prevailing domestic prices than would be the case under free trade at world market prices.

In Figure 4.3, the initial full-employment equilibrium position is described by point E where the domestic relative price line, with the slope $-\pi = -p_I/p_A$, is tangential to the production possibility frontier. (This point corresponds to its namesakes in Figures 4.1 and 4.2.) At point E, domestic production equals domestic consumption and no trade takes place. The steeper line, with the slope $-\pi^* = -(p_I/p_A)^*$ where $\pi^* > \pi$, describes the ratio of the prices of the two goods in world markets.[5] The intersection of this line through point E and

5. To keep Figure 4.3 as uncluttered as possible, no distinction has been made between domestic consumer and producer prices. However, in conformity with Figure 4.2, this distinction could be introduced in Figure 4.3 by drawing an intermediate relative consumer price line with the slope π_c (where $\pi < \pi_c < \pi^*$) through point E. The tangency between that line and a higher social indifference curve at a point somewhere above and to the left of E,

the horizontal axis gives total national output Y (i.e., GNP) measured in terms of industrial goods:

$$(5) \qquad Y = I + (1/\pi^*)A.$$

If the factors of production were not fully employed, the economy would be placed inside the production possibility frontier – for example, somewhere below or to the left of point E. Output would then be lower than at E by equation (5).

Suppose now that the economy is liberalised and trade begins at world market prices. Inefficient collective farms are driven out of business. Agricultural output falls. The economy moves downwards from point E in Figure 4.3 to a point such as J inside the production possibility frontier. Unemployment emerges. If the contraction of agricultural production spread to industry, i.e., if the decline in purchasing power in agriculture reduced the demand for industrial goods as well, industrial production would first fall and then rise again on the way from E to J. In any case, aggregate output is lower at J than at E by equation (5). Sooner or later, however, the business opportunities created by the increase in the relative price of industrial goods will begin to be exploited by profit-seeking entrepreneurs. As resources are transferred from agriculture and idleness to industry, the economy begins to move to the right from the interior point J towards point F on the production possibility frontier.

One possible adjustment path is described by the locus EJHF. Along the segment EJ, output is lower than initially in both agriculture and industry. At J, industrial output is restored to its original level, but national output is still lower than initially. At H, national output has returned to its initial level, but full employment is not restored until the new equilibrium point F is reached. Another possible path is represented by the locus EKF where, along the segment EK, both national output and unemployment rise in tandem; here output and unemployment are inversely related by Okun's law only along the segment KF. Gradual adjustment trajectories of this type involving unemployment of labour and other factors of production during the process of transformation can be derived from optimal producer behaviour if the adjustment itself is costly.[6]

---

and hence outside the production possibility frontier, would then reflect a state of excess demand for output as in Figure 4.2.

6. Consider, for example, an industry that seeks to minimize a quadratic cost function:

$$C_t = (I_t - I^*)^2 + \lambda(I_t - I_{t-1})^2$$

where I* is the industrial production target corresponding to point F in Figure 4.3 and the constant parameter $\lambda \geq 0$ reflects the cost of adjustment. It follows that the optimal path of adjustment of I_t towards I* can be described by

$$\Delta I_t = [1/(1+\lambda)](I^* - I_{t-1})$$

which has the solution

Anyway, when point F on the production possibility frontier is reached, aggregate output has increased by an amount indicated by the thick segment of the horizontal axis in Figure 4.3 (and in Figures 4.1 and 4.2). Domestic production of agricultural and industrial goods in the new equilibrium is described by point F in the figure, and domestic consumption, by point G. Industrial goods are now exported in exchange for agricultural imports. The current account is balanced at world market prices.

The welfare cost of *status quo* is somewhat different. This cost is measured by the external transfer of resources that would be required at domestic prices without trade to lift the economy to the same level of social welfare as could be achieved by structural adjustment through free trade. In Figure 4.3, the welfare cost in terms of industrial production is indicated by the horizontal distance between the domestic relative price line tangential to the production possibility frontier at point E and the parallel price line (not shown) tangential to the upper social indifference curve that goes through point G. In general, this hypothetical welfare cost of *status quo* is different from the output gain from structural adjustment denoted by the thick segment of the horizontal axis, and will not concern us further here.

Now the question is the following: how large an increase in output can be attained by eliminating the initial relative-price distortion through liberalisation and structural adjustment?

Clearly, the output gain from moving from E to F in Figure 4.3 depends on the magnitude of the initial distortion and the curvature of the production possibility frontier. Suppose that the relationship between domestic and world market prices is given by

(6) $$\pi = (1-\delta)\pi^*$$

where δ is a constant parameter that reflects the extent of the initial distortion and lies between 0 and 1.

Moreover, suppose that the production possibility frontier is described by the function

(7) $$A = F(I)$$

where $F' < 0$ and $F'' < 0$ as implied by the convexity of the frontier shown in Figure 4. 3. It then follows that

(8) $$F'(I) = -\pi^*$$

at point F in the figure and, correspondingly, $F'(I) = -\pi$ at point E.

The increase in industrial production from E to F is therefore approxi-

---

$$I_t = I^* + (I_0 - I^*)e^{-(1/\lambda)t}$$

where I_0 is the initial level of industrial production corresponding to point E in Figure 4.3. Thus, industrial output is adjusted gradually from I_0 to I^*. The speed of adjustment is inversely related to the cost of adjustment through λ.

mately

(9) $\Delta I = -F''^{-1}(I)(\pi^*-\pi) = -F''^{-1}(I)\delta\pi^*$.

The approximate reduction in agricultural production is obtained by evaluating a second-order Taylor expansion of equation (7) around point F in the figure:

(10) $\Delta A = F'(I)\Delta I - \frac{1}{2}F''(I)(\Delta I)^2$.

The approximate increase in total output from E to F is found by substituting from equations (9) and (10) into

(11) $\Delta Y = \Delta I + (1/\pi^*)\Delta A$,

which is obtained by taking first differences on both sides of equation (5) at given world market prices. With some algebra equations (9), (10), and (11) can be shown to entail

(12) $\Delta Y = \frac{1}{2}(F'/F'')\delta^2 > 0$.

In words, the expansion of output is approximately proportional to the square of the initial distortion. The factor of proportionality, $\frac{1}{2}(F'/F'')$, depends solely on the shape of the production possibility frontier. Alternatively, equation (12) can be expressed as

(13) $\Delta Y = \frac{1}{2}I\phi\delta^2 > 0$

where $\phi \equiv F'/(F''I)$ is the elasticity of industrial production with respect to relative prices. Some readers may find this formula easier to remember if the expansion of output is denoted by e, the multiple $\frac{1}{2}I\phi$ by m, and the constant proportional price distortion by c, for then we have $e = mc^2$.

These simple formulae can be extended to an economy with many sectors if the production possibility function is rewritten as

(14) $A = \Sigma_i[F_i(I_i)]$

where the subscripts i denote different sectors (manufacturing, trade, services, etc.), and if the third and higher derivatives and cross-derivatives of F_i are set equal to zero. In this case, the increase in output can be shown to be a weighted average of the squared distortions of the relative prices of the products of different sectors *vis-à-vis* the numeraire (agriculture):

(15) $\Delta Y = \frac{1}{2}\Sigma_i(F'_i/F''_i)\delta_i^2$.

The quadratic formula (12) or, equivalently, (13) can be illustrated by simple geometry. Consider Figure 4.4 where the expansion of industrial production is represented by the horizontal distance KF and the increase in national output is denoted by the shorter distance MF which equals the thick segment of the horizontal axis because the two relative price lines are parallel. The difference, KM, is the contraction of agricultural production, indicated by the

FIGURE 4.4 Geometric Illustration of Output Gain

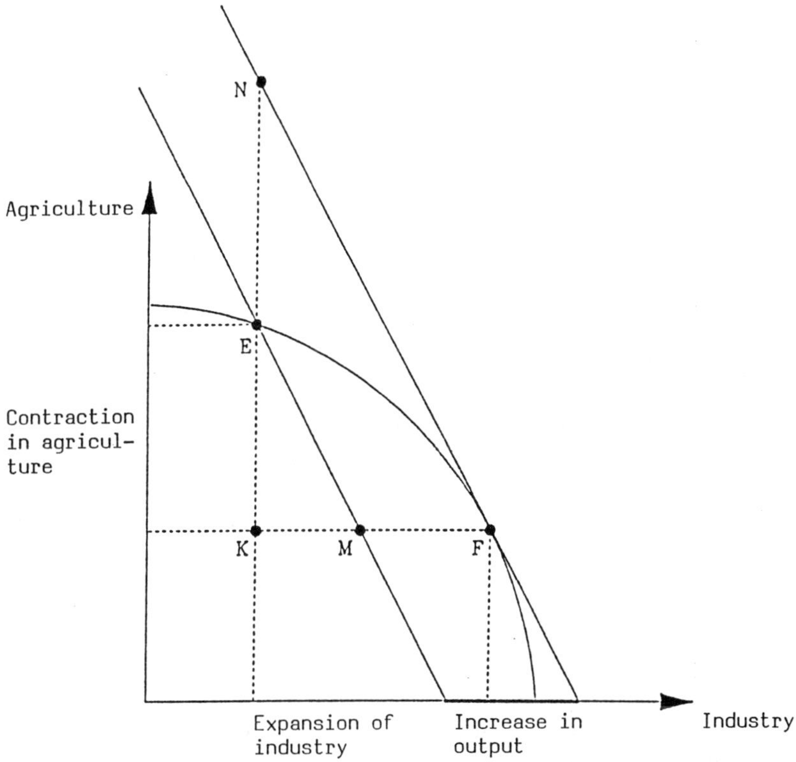

vertical distance EK, measured horizontally in terms of industrial goods. The slope of the two price lines, EM and FN, is $-\pi^*$ as in Figure 4.3. The decrease in agricultural output, EK, is the difference between NK, which equals $F'\Delta I$ by construction, and NE, which equals $\frac{1}{2}F''(\Delta I)^2$ by the usual logic of the Taylor expansion, compare equation (10). Because the slope of the (outer) price line is $-\pi^* = F'$ at the new equilibrium point F, we have $NE/MF = F'$. Therefore, the expansion of output, MF, equals NE/F', so that $\Delta Y = \frac{1}{2}(F''/F')(\Delta I)^2$. But $(\Delta I)^2 = F''^{-2}\delta^2\pi^{*2} = F''^{-2}\delta^2 F'^2$ approximately by equations (8) and (9). Therefore, $\Delta Y = \frac{1}{2}(F'/F'')\delta^2$ as in equation (12).

Examples of Production Possibilities

To make the formula in (12) or (13) operational as a rough guide to the potential magnitude of the responsiveness of output to economic liberalisation, it is necessary to assume the production possibility equation (7) to take a particular functional form.

Consider, as an example, the following quadratic function:

(16) $$A = a - (1/2b)I^2$$

where a and b are positive constants. The slope of the production possibility frontier at point F is

(17) $$\partial A/\partial I = F'(I) = -(1/b)I = -\pi^*.$$

This means that

(18) $$I = b\pi^*.$$

The change in industrial production following liberalisation can now be written as

(19) $$\Delta I = b(\pi^* - \pi) = b\delta\pi^* = \delta I.$$

Similarly, the change in agricultural production can now be written as

(20) $$\Delta A = -(1/b)I\Delta I + ½(1/b)(\Delta I)^2 = -(1/b)\delta I^2 + ½(1/b)\delta^2 I^2.$$

The change in total output is found by substituting from equations (19) and (20) into equation (11) like before. This gives

(21) $$g/(1+g) = ½(I/Y)\delta^2$$

where $g \equiv \Delta Y/Y$ is the proportional increase in output from E to F in Figure 4.3 (with initial output as a base) and I/Y is the share of industry in total output after the structural adjustment has been completed. The elasticity of industrial production with respect to relative prices, $\phi \equiv F'/(F''I)$, equals 1 in this case (compare equation (18)), and is therefore invisible on the right-hand side of equation (21). This simple formula makes it possible to map g as a function of I/Y and δ; more on this below.

To take another example, consider an economy where labour is the sole factor of production and one of the two sectors, say, industry, is characterised by decreasing returns to scale. Then

(22) $$I = bL_I^{\phi/(1+\phi)}$$

where L_I is employment in industry, b is a positive coefficient, and $\phi > 0$ and finite, so that $\phi/(1+\phi)$, the exponent of L_I, lies between 0 and 1.

On the other hand, there are constant returns to scale in agriculture by assumption:[7]

(23) $$A = aL_A$$

7. Assuming decreasing returns also in agriculture would complicate the example without enriching it substantially.

where L_A is employment in agriculture and the output-input coefficient a is a positive constant.

At full employment, the exogenously-given labour force L is divided between industry and agriculture:

$$(24) \qquad L = L_I + L_A.$$

By combining equations (22), (23), and (24) we get the following expression for the production possibility frontier:

$$(25) \qquad A = a[L - (I/b)^{(1+\phi)/\phi}].$$

The convexity of the frontier is ensured by the assumption of decreasing returns to scale in industry, i.e., by $0 < \phi < \infty$.[8]

By similar arithmetic as before, the optimal amount of industrial output can be shown to be

$$(26) \qquad I = c\pi^{*\phi}$$

where $c \equiv a^{-\phi}b^{1+\phi}[\phi/(1+\phi)]^{\phi}$ is a constant and ϕ is the relative price elasticity of industrial production as before. If $\phi = 1$, the production possibility equation (25) is quadratic as in the first example, compare equation (16), and I is proportional to π^* as in equation (18).

Equation (26) implies that the output gain from liberalisation can now be expressed as

$$(27) \qquad g/(1+g) = \tfrac{1}{2}(I/Y)\phi\delta^2.$$

If multiplied through by Y, this equation is identical to equation (13).[9] Also, if $\phi = 1$, equation (27) simplifies to equation (21). Either way, equation (27) or (21) can be used to assess the potential strength of the empirical link between economic liberalisation and the ensuing expansion of aggregate output g for given estimates of I/Y, ϕ, and δ. But first we need to put these results into perspective.

---

8. If ϕ tends to infinity so that constant returns to scale prevail also in industry, the production possibility frontier is linear by equation (25) and liberalisation results in complete specialisation in industry and the demise of agriculture, an unrealistic prospect. With a linear production possibility frontier the formula for the proportional output gain can be shown to be

$$g = [(1/\pi^*)A/Y)]\delta/(1-\delta)$$

where $(1/\pi^*)A/Y$ is the initial share of agriculture in national output. Like equation (21), this formula implies increasing returns to economic liberalisation.

9. But note that $\phi \equiv F'(I)/(F''(I)I)$ is a function of I in equation (13), whereas in equation (27) ϕ is a constant by construction.

Precedents

The simplicity of the formulae developed above should not surprise the reader unduly, for they are a variation on a well-known theme in welfare economics. The welfare gain from removing a single distortion (a tax or a tariff, for instance) is proportional to the square of the initial distortion (Harberger, 1964). For example, by using standard partial-equilibrium analysis of labour supply the replacement of a tax of t percent on labour income L by a neutral lump-sum levy can be shown to result in the following welfare gain ΔW in proportion to labour income:

$$(28) \qquad \Delta W/L = \tfrac{1}{2}\sigma t^2.$$

Here σ is the compensated elasticity of labour supply with respect to the real disposable wage (see also Browning, 1976).

The square of the tax rate enters the formula because the welfare gain is measured by an area enclosed by a right triangle whose short sides are both proportional to the tax rate.[10] Taken at face value, the formula indicates that a country with a marginal income tax rate of 50 per cent and a labour supply elasticity of 0.2 would reap a welfare gain equivalent to 2.5 per cent of labour income by replacing the income tax by a neutral lump-sum tax, other things being equal.[11] As a practical matter, however, this analysis is incomplete – not because of the partial-equilibrium nature of the illustration (it can be extended, somewhat tediously, to general equilibrium as shown by Harberger (1971)), but rather because there is no such thing as a neutral tax system.

In a similar way, the removal of a general import tariff of t per cent can be shown to increase welfare W as a proportion of output Y by the formula

$$(29) \qquad \Delta W/Y = \tfrac{1}{2}(X/Y)[\alpha + \beta(1+\gamma)]t^2.$$

Here X/Y is the ratio of exports to output, α and β are the relative price elasticities of exports and imports, and γ is the initial current account deficit in proportion to export earnings. The expression within the brackets is the left-hand

---

10. This formula can also be derived explicitly from the following experiment: if a tax on labour income is abolished and a lump-sum tax is levied in its place to keep wage earners as well off (i.e., on the same indifference curve) as before, then by how much does the requisite lump-sum levy fall short of the income tax that would have had to be paid in the new equilibrium under the old tax system? The answer is given by equation (28), if the income effect of changes in real disposable wages on labour supply is assumed to be zero. The derivation follows exactly the same logic as the derivation of equations (12) and (13). The curvature of the wage earner's indifference curve in the tax example, captured by the compensated elasticity of the supply of labour in equation (28), plays the role of the convexity of the production possibility frontier in equation (12). Formally, the two problems are identical.

11. This is not a small amount: it is equivalent to $1,500 per year for each family of four if GNP per head is $20,000 and labor income amounts to three-quarters of GNP.

side of the Marshall–Lerner inequality, $\alpha + \beta(1+\gamma) > 1+\gamma$, when the current account of the balance of payments is not in equilibrium initially (i.e., $\gamma \neq 0$).

Again, the square of the distortion enters the formula because the welfare gain is found by adding Harberger triangles. To get a feel for the magnitudes involved in this case, consider a country with (a) unitary relative price elasticities of exports and imports (i.e., $\alpha = \beta = 1$); (b) an export sector that constitutes a third of GNP ($X/Y = 0.33$); (c) a current account deficit that amounts initially to 5 per cent of GNP and hence 15 per cent of exports ($\gamma = 0.15$); and (d) an initial tariff rate of 25 per cent ($t = 0.25$). Given these parameter values, the formula suggests that the replacement of the tariff by neutral revenue would produce a welfare gain equivalent to 2.2 per cent of output once and for all, other things being equal.[12] If both exports and imports were insensitive to relative prices, i.e., if $\alpha = \beta = 0$, the welfare gain would vanish just as in the income tax example above when $\sigma = 0$. Moreover, the tariff example is complicated by the fact that the real and financial ramifications of the current account deficit that would presumably result from replacing tariffs by neutral taxes are not taken into account explicitly, in contrast to the general-equilibrium analysis of the consequences of economic liberalisation illustrated in Figure 4.3 where the current account is in equilibrium and full employment prevails before and after the liberalisation.

Excellent reviews of the theory of optimal taxation are provided by Atkinson and Stiglitz (1980), Tresch (1981), and Dixit (1985, Chapter 6) among others. However, in these surveys the aggregate output gains from improved allocation of resources are not linked to the theory and measurement of deadweight welfare loss from inefficient taxation. This brings us to our final topic: measurement of the potential output gains from economic liberalisation.

Numerical Examples

To appreciate the possible macro-economic and empirical significance of increased efficiency in the allocation of resources, we need numbers. We shall now proceed to plug various parameter values into our formula for the proportional expansion of national output g in reaction to the elimination of the relative price distortion δ,[13]

$$(30) \qquad g/(1+g) = \tfrac{1}{2}(I/Y)\phi\delta^2,$$

in an attempt to convey a rough impression of the possible magnitudes involved for illustrative purposes. This is inevitably a highly speculative exercise in consideration of the simplicity of the formula and the unavailability of

12. The amount involved is of a similar order of magnitude as in the tax example, compare the preceding footnote.

13. Equation (27) is repeated here for ease of reference.

hard evidence about the explanatory parameters. Therefore, our strategy will be to think of countries such as Poland or Russia (or of any other country where domestic prices have been far out of line with world market prices and where the allocation of resources has been biased accordingly towards the 'traditional' sector), assume a wide range of values for the three right-hand side parameters in equation (30), and investigate the sensitivity of the expansion of output to variations in the numerical values assumed.

In the first place, we assume domestic relative prices to be out of line with world market prices initially by a factor of 2, 3, 4, or 5, so that δ takes the values 0.5, 0.67, 0.75, and 0.8. This seems reasonable as the prices of many commodities have risen manyfold following selective price liberalisation in Poland at the beginning of 1990 and in Russia two years later. Second, we assume the relative price elasticity of industrial production ϕ to be 0.5, 1, or 1.5. Relative price elasticities tend to be in this range in general; perhaps the assumption of a unitary elasticity is as good as any. Finally, we assume the share of the industrial (or 'modern') sector in aggregate output following liberalisation to be either 0.6 or 0.9. The latter number corresponds roughly to the current situation in Western Europe where agriculture and other related activity that is similarly shielded from foreign competition to a large extent accounts for about 10 per cent of GNP.

The amounts of the proportional output gains that follow from these assumptions are shown in Tables 4.1 and 4.2.

These numbers speak for themselves. They indicate, for example, that the proportional output gains from economic liberalisation can span the range from 8 per cent to 40 per cent when the relative price elasticity of industrial production is set equal to one (see the third column in Tables 4.1 and 4.2). These gains are permanent, other things being equal. A higher price elasticity implies even greater gains. Given a discount rate of 5 per cent per year, the present value of these gains amounts to 1.6 to 8 times annual national output once and for all. For comparison, the lowest figure in the tables ($g = 0.04$) exceeds the rough estimates of the welfare gains from the abolition of income taxes or tariffs based on equations (28) and (29). Furthermore, estimates of the permanent output gains expected from the market unification of Europe in 1992 range from 2 per cent to 6 per cent according to Cecchini (1988).

If the numbers reviewed above are indicative of the results that would emerge from detailed empirical case studies of the economies of Central and Eastern Europe, it seems reasonable to conclude that abstaining from structural adjustment may be an expensive affair indeed, provided that the initial slump in output is not too deep and enduring. Moreover, the output gain from economic liberalisation is probably a prerequisite for price stability. Indicative or not, however, these numbers and the underlying analysis are obviously not intended to throw light on but a small part of a much larger problem. For one thing, we do not yet have a good theory of the process of adjustment from one

TABLE 4.1 Output Gain as a Function of δ and φ for I/Y = 0.6

I/Y = 0.6	φ = 0.5	φ = 1.0	φ = 1.5
δ = 0.5	g = 0.04	g = 0.08	g = 0.13
δ = 0.67	g = 0.07	g = 0.16	g = 0.25
δ = 0.75	g = 0.09	g = 0.20	g = 0.34
δ = 0.8	g = 0.11	g = 0.24	g = 0.40

TABLE 4.2 Output Gain as a Function of δ and φ for I/Y = 0.9

I/Y = 0.9	φ = 0.5	φ = 1.0	φ = 1.5
δ = 0.5	g = 0.06	g = 0.13	g = 0.20
δ = 0.67	g = 0.11	g = 0.25	g = 0.43
δ = 0.75	g = 0.14	g = 0.34	g = 0.61
δ = 0.8	g = 0.17	g = 0.40	g = 0.76

point to another, neither in the transition from plan to market in practice nor from one competitive equilibrium to another in economic theory in general for that matter. Furthermore, it is not clear how we should characterise the point of departure and the destination, E and F in Figure 4.3; in the 'real' world, they may be better described by fuzzy areas than by points.

This applies in particular to the point of departure because relative price distortions are only one of several causes of macro-economic inefficiency in the former command economies. Other causes include: (a) the absence of appropriate labour and capital market institutions; (b) shortages of capital goods and services and associated technical bottlenecks (compare oil-drilling facilities that lie idle because of missing spare parts, for example); (c) infrastructural deterioration due to inadequate upkeep or outright neglect; (d) overexploitation of natural resources and pollution of the environment; (e) general passivity ('learned helplessness') in the labour force; (f) the absence of initiative and entrepreneurial drive in the existing managerial class; and (g) an excessive and inept bureaucracy inherited from the old regime.

These aspects of inefficiency are difficult to quantify, but they are almost surely of great importance in Central and Eastern Europe at present. Moreover, a successful structural transformation may release economic forces that shift the production possibility frontiers shown in Figures 4.3 and 4.4 farther out once and for all or even repeatedly. The numbers presented in Tables 4.1 and 4.2 are, therefore, likely to reflect only a part of the potential gains to be made from a successful transition to a market economy.

Summary and Conclusion

The purpose of this paper has been to attempt to clarify the contribution of economic liberalisation to the current transition from plan to market in Central and Eastern Europe. Three main points have been made:

– The controversy surrounding macro-economic theory and policy in recent years does not preclude effective aggregate supply management by means of structural adjustment. On the contrary, national output can clearly and indisputably be increased by removing relative price distortions in the form of internal and external trade barriers, for example. This is true even in a classical world where full employment prevails through continuous market clearing and the government has no way of influencing the level of national output through aggregate demand.

– The output gains from economic liberalisation can be modelled simply in a way that allows them to be incorporated into the standard aggregate-demand-and-supply apparatus that macro-economists use to study the interaction of output and the price level. The output gain from removing a single relative price distortion in a two-sector general-equilibrium model with full employment is captured in a simple formula in which the gain is proportional to the square of the original distortion. This formula is analytically equivalent to Harberger's (1964) triangular measure of the deadweight welfare loss from inefficient taxation.

– Substitution of plausible parameter values into the simple formula indicates that the aggregate output gain from economic liberalisation may be quite substantial, other things being equal. For example, if (a) relative prices are out of line with world market prices initially by a factor of 4; (b) the relative price elasticity of industrial output is 1; and (c) the industrial (or 'modern') sector approaches a 90 per cent share of national output after the structural adjustment has been completed, then national output at full employment rises by 34 per cent once and for all (see Table 4.2). The present value of this gain is equivalent to almost seven years' output, given a discount rate of 5 per cent per year.

These points apply not only to Central and Eastern Europe. On the contrary, it seems clear that significant opportunities for increased efficiency and output remain to be exploited also in Western Europe, even after the completion of the single market by the end of 1992. The Common Agricultural Policy of the European Community is a case in point. Many other examples could be cited. It is important to view these opportunities in a macro-economic perspective. A boost to aggregate supply is a potent way to improve living standards and to greater price stability and growth in a world where political authorities are under relentless pressure from powerful groups that plead for a better deal.

References

Atkinson, A. B. and J. E. Stiglitz, 1980, *Lectures on Public Economics*. London: McGraw-Hill.

Barro, R. J., 1990, "Government Spending in a Simple Model of Endogenous Growth", *Journal of Political Economy* 98, pp. S103–S125.

Barro, R. J. and X. Sala-i-Martin, 1992, "Public Finance in Models of Economic Growth", CEPR Discussion Paper No. 630.

Browning, E. K., 1976, "The Marginal Costs of Public Funds", *Journal of Political Economy* 84, pp. 283–298.

Cecchini, P., 1988, *The European Challenge 1992*. Aldershot: Gower.

Dixit, A., 1985, "Tax Policy in Open Economies", in *Handbook of Public Economics* 1. Amsterdam: North-Holland.

Fischer, S., 1991, "Growth, Macro-Economics, and Development", NBER *Macroeconomics Annual* 1991, pp. 329–364.

Grossman, G. and E. Helpman, 1991, *Innovation and Growth in the Global Economy*. Cambridge, Mass. and London: MIT Press.

Harberger, A. C., 1964, "Taxation, Resource Allocation, and Welfare", in *The Role of Direct and Indirect Taxes in the Federal Revenue System*, The National Bureau of Economic Research and The Brookings Institution, Princeton. NJ: Princeton University Press.

_____, 1971, "Three Basic Postulates for Basic Welfare Economics: An Interpretive Essay", *Journal of Economic Literature* 9, pp. 785–797.

Lewis, W. A., 1954, "Economic Development with Unlimited Supplies of Labor", *The Manchester School* 22, No. 2, May, pp. 139–191.

Persson, T. and G. Tabellini, 1991, "Is Inequality Harmful for Growth?" NBER Working Paper No. 3599.

Romer, P. M., 1986, "Increasing Returns and Long-run Growth", *Journal of Political Economy* 94, pp. 1002–1037.

Solow, R. M., 1956, "A Contribution to the Theory of Economic Growth", *Quarterly Journal of Economics* 70, No. 1, 65–94.

Stiglitz, J., 1992, "Capital Markets and Economic Fluctuations in Capitalist Economies", *European Economic Review* 36, No. 2/3, pp. 269–306.

Tresch, R. W., 1981, *Public Finance: A Normative Theory*. Plano, Texas: Business Publications.

Weitzman, M. L., 1986, "Macroeconomic Implications of Profit Sharing", NBER *Macroeconomics Annual* 1986, pp. 291–351.

5

After the Shock. Some Lessons from Transition Policies in Eastern Europe

László Csaba[*]

Introduction

In the third year following the collapse of state socialism, a market economy and sustainable economic growth are still a long way off in the countries which used to belong to 'Eastern Europe' in the post-Yalta parlance. In other words, the 'jump into the market' has proved to be a rather long jump, which will provide food for thought for a fair number of analysts for quite some time to come.

The intellectual challenge posed by systemic transformation is best described by the following paradoxes. On the one hand, the West has won the Cold War, but traditional Sovietology has lost the battle. Whereas its leftist-radical wing was taken by surprise by the collapse of what it postulated to have been a peculiar case for modernisation, the conservative right wing was equally astonished that its apocalyptic prophecies have suddenly come true. For this latter group, it was rather embarrassing to answer the question: why just in 1989 and not at some earlier point did that system collapse, a system which it considered to be unworkable from the very outset?

Therefore, understandably, area studies have been pushed to the background in policy making. Mainstream economics and theoretical economists of some famous universities, as well as officials with the international organisa-

[*] The author is Research Director at Kopint-Datorg, Inc.; Vice-President of the European Association for Comparative Economic Studies; and Professor of International Economics at the College of Foreign Trade (Budapest). He also serves as personal adviser to the Hungarian Minister of Finance.

tions, have taken over. Similar to many developing countries, but especially to Latin America in the 1980s, the universal panacea was prescribed, but is functioning somewhat differently from the way it is postulated. In both Latin America and Eastern Europe, real world economies react differently to the medicines than in the laboratories of abstract modelling. Stabilisation has not been fully mastered, and economic recovery has not taken place in the time frame originally envisaged. This is hardly a surprise to anyone who considers institutional, motivational, historic, and social factors to be relevant explanatory variables for understanding real world economies and economic development.

To put it differently, what we are experiencing in Eastern Europe is anything but a textbook case, for which solutions are easily available provided decision makers show sufficient diligence in studying advanced courses at better universities. Developments – no matter how controversial they are – have not invalidated economic theory or area studies, even less the experience of international organisations in coping with non-market systems. However, they have presented a new challenge to all three areas of activity. The challenge is there both in the theoretical and policy context, requiring fresh approaches and an interdisciplinary effort to attain a better understanding and a better performance alike.

What is the issue? In a nutshell: a fairly large number of countries, from Albania to Lithuania, have decided to give up tinkering with socialist reforms, and instead have opted to jump into the market by way of what is conventionally termed shock therapy and mass privatisation. In fact, Hungary and the Ukraine seem to be the only exceptions to the general rule. Now, the problem is that in all the countries concerned, including the one-time GDR, economic performance is well below targets, whereas the social and direct economic costs are much higher than envisaged. Moreover, the evolution of the salient features of a market order is substantially more sluggish than the majority of analysts and the general public would have expected. This gloomy picture – documented by a vast database assembled by the *Economic Survey of Europe 1991/92* – is that of a depression comparable to that of 1929–33.

This might not be a problem *per se*, at least in economic terms, since a complete overhaul of the development model, specialisation pattern, economic system, and international finances would hardly have been feasible without major sacrifices. The problem lies in the socio-political acceptance of such a protracted hardship, which seems to be quite narrow in the countries which do not enjoy the capital injections and other transfers making the East German economic miracle work. The Polish election results of 1991, the stalemate in Bulgaria, the very thin power base – and the resultant zig-zags in the economic course – of the Gaidar and the Stolojan teams exemplify how the socio-political feedback of recessionary strains restrict the ability to implement given transition policies.

For the time being, the relevant issue is no longer whether or not a shock treatment could have been avoided, as this issue has been settled by history. The immediate policy is that of recovery, and the tasks the states/governments in the region can undertake to foster it. The answer to this is rooted in our reading and interpretation of the events of the last 3–4 years. Is it really the overemphasis on the quantity theory of money against the theory of effective demand which is at the heart of the great recession, as a recent impressive analysis by Laski (1992) concludes? Should we really go so far as to maintain that shock therapy is a road to de-industrialisation and lasting underdevelopment? (Lösch, 1992, pp. 48–53). Is is really the contraction of output which is the major 'failure indicator' of the shock therapies applied all across the region? (Köves, 1992). The answer depends on our reading of the events. Thus, without attempting to be comprehensive, I try to summarise in a thesis-like manner what in my view we have learned in the last few years from transition policies. Then, I shall offer my answer to the policy question. What follows below is anything but an exhaustive catalogue of possible theoretical conclusions, but these seem to me to be the most policy-relevant lessons from empirical evidence.

Life Is Not Like in Books

Policy Making

One of the early experiences in policy making was that no matter how serious theoretical controversies prevailed in the economics profession – both domestically and internationally – there was precious little difference in the policy-relevant propositions made by serious academic economists and professionals in the state administration. It is not only that the relative successes with gradualism have produced a near-consensus in favour of continuing this line in Hungary, whereas the absolute failure with gradualism has created a broad consensus behind shock treatment in Russia and Poland. Alternatively, the collapse of the state administration and the entire political context left no alternative to the ex-GDR, Albania, and Bulgaria. Yet, the similarities are even more striking.

On the one hand, continuity in the institutional and organisational structure, in human capital and also in the overall economic environment for companies *grosso modo*, have contributed to a fair degree of continuity in the behaviour of economic agents. This was most palpable in the typical monopolitisic behaviour of large companies trying to produce less and sell their output for a highly inflated price, which in most countries counted as a prime cause of recession. On the other hand, it proved to be premature to call this a fundamental barrier to transformation (Egger, Kappel and Melzer, 1992, pp. 28–29). The same economic agents have proven to be immensely flexible if the possibility and pressure of economic adjustment forced them to do so. People selling on the streets of cities is but one example; the Russian military-industrial complex deeply involved in privatisation and even in organising the entire economy of the Far East of the country is another; numerous Hungarian firms redirecting their sales from East to West might well be a third.

Thus, if for no other reason than inertia, a combination of continuity and change prevails in all Eastern European economies. On top of this, an element of shock was not missing from any of these countries. For one, the collapse of COMECON delivered a blow, at least on the micro-economic level, to even the most gradualist and non-reforming economies (such as the Serbia or Bulgaria of the day). The collapse of the internal Soviet empire had immediate repercussions for what used to be an integrated economic complex. The logic of history, of the national *renaissance*, superimposed its logic over the meticulous cost-benefit calculation pertaining to secession: Empires rarely disintegrate on the grounds of direct micro-economic calculus. Therefore, it can be taken for granted that the shock implicit in cutting the umbilical cord of imperial division of labour applies to all successor states of the CIS. Moreover, given the unresolved – and probably insoluble – problems of sharing internal and external debt and of sterilising the ever growing rouble overhang, the room for anything other than a version of a shock therapy is extremely restricted indeed.

Since the theory of implicit subsidies failed to explain why Eastern Europe survived the collapse of COMECON, calculations based on historical plan-prices – or their 'recalculation to world prices' – fail to discourage the successor states from seceding from the CIS. However, the micro-economic and also the structural shock remains for them as a given.

No matter how serious these problems are, the heaviest blow in the economic sense was delivered to the economy of the ex-GDR. The economic and monetary union of July 1990 has solved the stabilisation problem in one day. By the same token, the previously highly-protected East German economy was opened up to world market competition at a grossly overvalued rate of exchange. With the five *länder* joining the Federal Republic, the entire legislative infrastructure and institutional infrastructure has been taken over. Despite its shortcomings (see below), this short cut has solved the basic problems of institution-building that other Eastern Europeans will face for quite some time.

German unification is in theory a showcase for what constitutes a jump into the market. However, in policy terms, it is far from being so. On the one hand, East Germany received more in two-and-a-half years in transfers than the Soviet Union would have received under 'the Grand Bargain'. Second, not only institutions, but also human capital have been infused; new rules and institutions have been provided to the 'Eastern brothers'. Third, unification and the concomitant liberties produced an historically unprecedented legitimacy and social acceptance for whatever the Western uncle was about to do. Therefore, if recent analysis (Welfens, 1992) indicates that following the initial euphoria – and subsequent historically unprecedented contraction – East Germany is heading for a 'modest economic miracle' during the rest of the century, the same analysis discloses the inherent barriers to emulation of this laboratory/exercise by any other fellow-traveller. Lacking the five major factors ameliorating the social and, indeed, the economic costs of German shock therapy, anybody following such a route would undertake surgery not only without anaesthesia, but also without medical tools and medicines. To turn the same point around: in policy terms, East Germany has not experienced a classical shock therapy, but rather some much milder version of transition, where the costs were borne to a large extent by others. As large-scale Western involvement in the affairs of the region is rather implausible, the adaptability constraints are equally trivial.

In sum, there was no real 'shock': a combination of radical measures and counteracting factors characterise each and every case. If among the shock therapy adherents a certain delay in institution-building and privatisation is rather conspicuous, gradualists also have some shocks of their own: for the Ukraine, secession from the single Soviet economic space, and for Hungary, the collapse of COMECON coupled with a 25 per cent real appreciation of the national currency (Obláth, 1992). In both countries, these developments constituted a blow to inherited economic structures.

Sustainable Growth

The shock has been delivered. Still, countries of the region are a long way from a full-fledged market economy, and signs for sustainable growth are mixed at best: recovery does not follow immediately after the treatment, as some seem to have expected. In fact, neither development should have taken us by surprise. First, stabilising an economy and building up market institutions are two different tasks of different quality. Second, as the countries in question have been undergoing not only a cyclical or a balance of payments crisis, but also a fundamental, systemic and structural one, medicines devised for curing short-term imbalances obviously fall short of overcoming more basic difficulties. This, however, is not their fault. Finally, though any conventional econometric exercise is able to pinpoint the very sizeable growth potential of the Eastern European countries, experiences of other regions caution us to avoid accepting such an exercise at face value. In Latin America, achieving sustainable growth took a long time. Most of the delays resulted from slow response of private investment. Stability, clarity in tax and property rights rules, and a low but positive rate of interest are the key elements to recovery, but it takes time for these measures to take effect (Corbo, 1992, p. 414). These conditions are known to exist in the majority of post-communist economies.

Again, like Latin America, stabilising and reform policies have continuously been criticised by representatives of vested interests, as well as by those segments of the academic community who consider output growth and increases in GDP as appropriate success indicators of positive economic performance, even in times of structural and systemic change. Experience of West European adjustment following both oil price hikes, as well as the theoretical analysis of several observers (Winiecki, 1991a; Gomulka, 1991), have advanced a large number of factors responsible for a protracted fall in output. Nevertheless, political public opinion, and reliance on Keynesian traditions, have prompted many authors to advocate an expansionist, inflationary line. Industrial circles in Hungary, Poland, and Russia began to fight 'fiscal dictatorship' from the very outset. With some delay, agribusiness also has intensified its lobbying for debt forgiveness, fresh money, and market protection. Within just 3–6 months of the initiation of these policies, pressures to correct the line, and to grant exceptional preferences to certain powerful interest groups, have also made gains in the verbally most radical governments (in Poland, the Czech and Slovak Federal Republic (CSFR), and Russia) (Dabrowski, 1992; Charap, et al., 1992; Csaba, 1992). In Serbia, Bulgaria, and Romania, industrial conflict and political power struggles resulted in the same. In Hungary, first in November 1990, and later in May 1992, an alternative, 'supply-side approach' began to gain momentum within the Government. The real surprise in the latter case is how little these much-publicised political controversies actually influenced decision making, which has something to do with the rather strong institutional independence of the National Bank of Hungary, and with the dominant power position of the Ministry of Finance (which, in fact, is a legacy of socialist reforms).

Should we really follow this line and pass an overall negative judgement on transition policies on the grounds that in two or three years it has failed to produce sustainable growth? I would hesitate to subscribe to this theoretical proposition. For one thing, in Latin America, where only one of the many crises of Eastern Europe (fiscal chaos) surfaced, this length of time was not sufficient for mastering that single problem. Stabilisation and reform policies: a) are of a dimension which is difficult to measure against the time horizon of conjecture; and b) by definition cannot be interpreted in a narrow technocratic sense, i.e., as a means of promoting overall economic growth. Transforming the post-communist economic systems into a liberal market order does have a value of its own at least on two levels: it enhances individual liberties, and rolls back the worst-case scenario, the open and irreversible secular crisis. The latter point is rather obvious in the case of the South-East European countries, notably Yugoslavia, but also in terms of what constitutes the CIS at the time of writing. My own country, Hungary, is a prime example that on occasion avoiding the worst things acquires a value of its own. Thus all policies in the region should be seen as exercises in acute and belated crisis-management.

Having delayed the reforms between 1956–89, the *anciens régimes* of the region created a burdensome legacy. The internationally non-competitive economic structures, the grave indebtedness, and the widespread public misconception of the actual level of development of these countries – not to mention the expectational and motivational structures and value systems which hinder rather than support economic adjustment – cannot simply be overcome by way of a miracle. There is a price to be paid, and the story of East Germany is indicative of the actual cost. If financial structures and public priorities in Western countries are anything but conducive to a new Marshall Plan, which can be taken for granted, it seems obvious that the only way open to the region's governments is that of a lower-cost, slower-pace option. There is no one else but the population of these countries who can pay for adjustment, in terms of recession, unemployment, restructuring, and inflation.

This is not to imply that there is no way out or that the policies of the new governments have been irrelevant. On the contrary, avoidance of socialist obsession with state investment and growth rates is one of the major pieces of advice that should be heeded in the longer run. It can be demonstrated in detail that overcoming the allocative inefficiency of the socialist system means by definition more growth with less investment; however, savings, especially private savings, will be more difficult to accumulate in the transition period (Borensztein and Montiel, 1992, p. 153). Therefore, private investment and the propensity to save deserve special treatment during this period, as do incentives encouraging these factors.

In sum, admittance of the limitations of the stabilising shock does not invalidate the reasons for its being delivered. Stabilisation is a precondition for new institutional arrangements to make sense, even if they are slow and piecemeal in their evolution. Thus, the efficiency gains to be expected from these arrangements are also bound to be gradual, though mutually reinforcing. Further, they help to move the process along in a shorter period of time. (Winiecki, 1991b, p. 10). However, this time has to be taken, and not only because tens of thousands of economic actors must become familiar with the new rules and opportunities. Investment is by definition a matter of confidence, which can of course be taken for granted in a model, but cannot be in an economy in transition. As Corbo (1992, p. 414) notes, the major danger here is uncertainty pertaining to the rules of the game and the overall policy line: in Latin America, 'when the risk of policy reversal was reduced, investment and growth started to emerge – but it took a while'.

Allocative Efficiency

It follows from what has been said above that the major technical economic question for transition policies is not the ideologically inspired issue of privatisation (see below), but rather ways and means of dramatically improving allocative efficiency. Price liberation and formation of a marginal rate of exchange can be expected from stabilisation – or, in the case of Hungary, as a legacy of the past reforms – as given. This encompasses three major elements: a) creation of an independent monetary authority concerned with protecting the purchasing power of the national currency; alternatively, if we are sceptical about this step, joining the national currency to an international currency board (Hanke and Schuler, 1991): b) restucturing and rolling back the budget's almighty role in the economy – discussed in greater detail below: c) evolution of a truly independent, partly foreign and privately-owned commercial banking system.

Seen historically, capitalism has never started to emerge with the stock market and other refined forms of financial intermediation. If one has to start 'from scratch', there appears to be no realistic alternative to starting markets in areas like labour, housing, retail business, small-scale industry, etc. In this case, as Steinherr (1992) notes correctly, there is neither the need nor the possibility of eschewing the step of creating a large number of small but competing commercial banks offering financial services to their clients. The nature of this market is such that it works through trial and error, and neither the capital nor the special knowledge of refined financial markets are really necessary. This argumentation is well substantiated by what one observes across the region. In Hungary, for example, where the stock market already has several years of history, only 0.2–0.3 per cent of capital transactions ever show up. In the case of Russia, simple money transfers may pose a problem for many banks. In the Czech and Slovak Federal Republic, monopolistic structures must rely on a large number of administrative measures in the banking sector, such as dictated rates of interest, credit ceilings, etc. (Charap, et al., 1992, p. 14). In Poland, all through the reform process, large enterprises with considerable bargaining power have remained 'creditworthy' for the banks (Winiecki, 1992). All in all, less significant problems than the evaluation of large companies on competitive capital markets remain to be addressed. This might pose a problem for the concept of mass privatisation, but for the national economies, the immediate problem lies elswhere.

The major problem of the commercial banks is that while in theory they could substitute for capital markets, in practice they are a major source of misallocation and of allocative rigidity. This is because they embody either implicit fiscal subsidisation, or present sectoral priorities of the State, or carry the weight of investment decisions previously made by governmental authorities at different times (Tanzi, 1992, p. 24). As long as they continue to crowd out private ventures from the market and continue to distort the interest rate structure, these banks positively contribute to the structural rigidity of post-communist economies, since they fail to channel scarce savings in the right direction. In this way, they also have a share in watering down the allocative effects of price liberalisation.

How can this deadlock be overcome? First and foremost, credit liberalisation has led in many developing countries to emergence of a parallel private money market where both the incentive to save and the function of channelling funds to efficient use are given. Further, banks should be gradually freed from state tutelage by selling their shares to non-state agents (who should not be their clients). This is privatisation. Further, the inherited sectoral and territorial segmentation should be overcome, thus producing real competition for clients. Last, but not least, a large number of banks is a commendable but hardly sufficient condition for meeting the challenge. Without a major infusion of capital and technology, which can only be imported from abroad, financial intermediation will hardly be able to break out of its present role as 'the underdeveloped nerve structure of a dinosaur, unable to coordinate the body of a large and comprehensive economic structure' (Dietz, 1991). This is not to deny the need for a capital market. Countries of East Asia, where high growth rates could be attained for decades without relying on capital markets, have completely different social, cultural and even economic endowments, including the population's high propensity to save coupled with the low articulation of organised vested interests. This experience can hardly be replicated in the context of emerging pluralism and a European cultural setting. Moreover, these countries have been undergoing reforms reducing the role of government and increasing the role of the market in many areas, including allocative decisions (Jung, 1991; Kim, 1991; Chu and Lin, 1991; Hsiao, 1991; and Pascha, 1990).

In other words, given the European and pluralist context, the role of capital markets is fundamental in enhancing allocative efficiency. However, this is a step whose place in the sequence will hardly precede the introduction of the low but positive rate of interest, of competition among banks, and even their privatisation. With the emergence and expansion of private property for buildings, land, small shops and workshops, the valuation of various items of capital assets evolves organically. Thus, if financial reform creates the appropriate institutions, these will be continuously filled with substance. The important point is to have regulation based on the norms and experience of advanced countries, i.e., one protecting the interest of the small investor, prohibiting and sanctioning insider deals, securing the personal responsibility of agents, and precluding financial adventurism. These are the arrangements which seem to have received the least attention by from the playful architects of the CSFR's voucher scheme. Promises of unrealistic returns may end up in major financial scandals, and the need for the State to step in to compensate cheated small investors. This might become both very costly and harmful to the credibility of all financial institutions, especially outside the banking sphere, (i.e., it may backfire).

As we have seen above, the major issue in improving allocative efficiency is removing the sectoral ministries from investment decisions. In the CSFR, the role of sectoral organs is anything but nominal: they have to approve the privatisation project of the company (in addition to the privatisation agency, Kupka, 1992, p. 308). Thus, two governmental bodies have discretionary rights. This is bound to enforce a structure conserving influence, and opens the door wide for bureaucratic interference. The newly proliferating investment funds also may be underinformed about firms and future returns, which might be costly (*NZZ*, 4 February 1992). All in all, at the end of the day, the appropriate legal and institutional arrangements needed for business practices accepted in civilised nations might be more important for the speed, not to speak of the sustainability, of the entire exercise than the actual time required for capital markets to develop in an orderly, organic manner. In this way, merger controls and other antitrust activities can avoid dangerous and random concentration of power in the hands of a few interests of dubious responsibility and legitimacy. These considerations usually play a role in governmental decisions in major industrial powers, including the USA, Japan, and the EC countries, in addition to the previously cited NICs. However, they might not be included in all textbooks devoted to game theory.

Social Security

A further fundamental element in deciding the success of transition is the *reform of the social security system.* The relevance of this particular issue has been revealed by Hungarian development, where many institutional arrangements already have a relatively long history of existence. For one, direct subsidies to production fell from 19 to 5 per cent of the GDP between 1989 and 1992. VAT and PIT, as well as an effective system of customs duties and a realistic exchange rate, have been around for years. State investments have contracted so much that many consider them to be below minimum, e.g., no flats are being built by the State for social purposes.

It has been a sobering lesson for Hungarian authorities to find that the rolling back of the direct economic involvement of the State has not resulted in a fundamental improvement in the budget's balance. In fact, the structural imbalance has become more obvious than before. Since two-thirds of the outlays are related to the social security system and welfare payments, Hungary has found itself to be an early-born welfare state. This implies that more services are being provided to fulfill citizens' rights than the actual level of economic development of the country can support.

The fundamental paradox in this area is that the need to act is most urgent, whereas the possibilities for a sizeable change are the least feasible, especially in political terms. On the one hand, there are no resources in a contracting economy to maintain social services. These have been granted as if the level of development actually corresponded to the figures disclosed by official statistics and as if the economy were already on the path of 'uninterrupted growth'.

Furthermore, the practice of West European welfare states and their demonstration effect make it nearly impossible for the Hungarian Government to adopt a 'wild West' type of early capitalist approach since it had already formally joined the EC Social Charter in December 1991.

It is not only the misconceived approach of those responsible (i.e., the desire to emulate practices of much more advanced economies without having attained their economic performance) which poses a problem. Development policies of the previous decades partly wasted and partly failed to accumulate the wealth which could serve these purposes. Meanwhile, a contraction in economic activity implies a growth in the number of people who are in need of the support of a social safety net. It is difficut to roll back involvement by the State in times of a protracted depression.

In other words, practices of previous decades have extended rights to many people, especially between the second and sixth decile of the income layer. The actions are not economically well-founded, but they constitute a pillar of the socio-political equilibrium. The affected people constitute the social strata most likely to lose in the newly emerging market redistribution of previous income positions and wealth: civil servants, pensioners, manual workers, the rural unskilled population, and state-employed intelligentsia. Thus, it is politically difficult to follow technocratic advice extended by international organisations to introduce more free market measures – through the insurance principle – than is customary in most West European countries (even though this would be justified on economic grounds).

There is no easy solution or trivial outcome. The ideal policies would entail a gradual, though resolute, reform of the social security system through the introduction of pay-as-you-go schemes and private insurance, beginning with incremental levels of service supply. Various mixed-up functions of the same system, i.e., health care, care for the elderly, support for the poor, etc., should be separated. In a transitory period, the introduction of non-prohibitive fees seems to be inevitable for many of the formerly free services, thus in fact institutionalising existing practice, while securing funds being reinvested in the given services. This does not, however, lead to 'self-financing' in any of the areas. Still, it could limit the exploding outlays of the State.

Early retirement is one of the ways of fighting unemployment, though it has proved to be a very costly one. Increases in the retirement age seem to be inevitable. Many other unpopular measures may become necessary even in the knowledge that they are safeguards against a budgetary explosion, not solutions to the problems faced by the respective services.

Combining high social security contributions with the concomitant low level of services is known to be the best incentive to evade taxes and depress legal economic activity in many developing countries. In Hungary, the 45 per cent contribution paid by the employer, and the additional 10 per cent paid by the employee, is a good indicator of the size of the problem. This contribution can hardly be lowered without some withdrawal of the State from financing other activities, whose limits we have seen above.

An alternative element is broadening the tax base and drastic tightening of its collection rules along Italian and American lines. Hungarian experience, but also Polish (Dabrowski, 1992; Winiecki, 1992), Russian, and developing country experience (Tanzi, 1992, pp. 33–35), is indicative of the crucial role played by tax collection in overcoming budgetary crises, and securing social acceptance of growing income differentials. To put it briefly, the only economically sensible way of reducing the crippling size of social security contributions is the extension of taxation to areas where previously no excises existed, primarily in the sphere of the private economy. As the limits to cutting fiscal spending are more or less given, revenues have to be collected in an acceptable manner. It is hardly a sustainable situation in which governmental revenues derive primarily from the ailing and contracting public sector, whilst the booming private sector does not pay taxes to any significant degree. In addition to collection, *lower rates, simple tax rules and heavier reliance on indirect taxes* are necessary to change this situation.

Representatives of the business community would probably protest against these measures, but one should not be very serious about their outcry. All international evidence shows that reliance on indirect taxes, and low rates of corporate tax and social security contribution can, and actually in many cases do, coexist with collection rules without paralysing the propensity to invest. The latter is more inhibited by unclear property rights; proliferating, nontransparent, and inconsequent regulation, and the insecurity of wealth and income. Security of wealth and income – together with the freedom of contract and of economic activity – should be constitutionally guaranteed. Under these conditions, the above-sketched measures would certainly filter out some of the 'mafia economy' currently flourishing on the ruins of socialism all across the region. However, this would contribute to more civilised economic relations, and to improvement of the social balance of capitalist development.

Privatisation

It is hardly by chance that the ideologically dominated, fashionable issue of *privatisation* comes at the end of our policy-relevant list of problems. The experience of 1989–92 from Russia to Hungary, from Romania to the CSFR and Poland, are indicative of the following: though private activities are not slow in gaining a share in the total economy, this has more to do with the 'contraction of the cake' than with their (unquestionable) expansion. Moreover, the choice fruits already have been picked. Consequently, for what is left – loss-making large state-owned enterprises; mismanaged agricultural co-operatives: and worn-down large state-owned hotels and department stores –

there is only lukewarm interest by foreign and domestic investors alike. In other words, the exponential growth of private activities is not really the most probable scenario for the coming years. This situation might change somewhat if 'we get the prices right', i.e., ridiculously low, which might be perfectly right micro-economics, but hardly sustainable as a governmental strategy. We might dislike the nationalist wave in the region, and might be justified in our judgement, but we are certainly wrong to remove it from sight just because we talk economics.

Most economic theories – except for Marxism and its inverted variant, the property-rights school – consider ownership relations important, but not of overwhelming importance. This holds *a fortiori* for the policy perspective, since in real world economies – unlike in textbooks – we more often than not find mixed rather than other economies, especially at the lower and middle levels of development.

As we have seen above, in order to get the State out of business, there are several inter-related tasks to be mastered, and privatisation is only one of them. Given the appropriate mix of policies and institutions, public companies perform pretty well in many countries of the world (Newbery, 1992). At the same time, privatisation has brought about mixed results in different areas and countries. For instance, in Korea, one-third of companies privatised in the second half of the 1980s and early 1990s improved their performance substantially, and one-third of them maintained their efficiency level. However, some of them have gone bankrupt (Kang, 1992). In France, in most cases, major efficiency gains have been achieved *before* rather than after privatisation (Andreff, 1992). This is also in line with Hungarian experience, where a change in ownership has not always resulted in improved performance. On the other hand, in 1991, the pressure of the market forced many state enterprises to behave like private firms, i.e., to care about liquidity, sack superfluous personnel, and change the market for their product. Meanwhile, foreign investors have tended to create monopoly positions in areas where they did not exist previously, as in the sugar industry or in the production of portable gas-fillers. Reference to the shortcomings of Hungarian competition policy hardly invalidates our point, since this is what we are driving at: many things other than ownership shape the behaviour and performance of firms in the real world economy.

This is not to say that privatisation is irrelevant, but from our perspective it is by definition a longer-term process, which gains its rationale in the context of overall *Ordnungspolitik*.

What have we learned from the last few years' experience? First of all, ownership change does not seem to accompany the radical political statements of whatever colour. On the one hand, there is the CSFR's privatisation programme. However, Polish and Russian practice is much behind the self-set schedule at the time of this writing. In analysing the Polish experience, an adherent of mass privatisation notes (Bandyk, 1992, pp. 435–436) that the implementation of the law of July 1991 proved to be a showcase for all the contradictions inherent in the scheme, primarily the conflict among its objectives. The idea of wide dispersion of ownership conflicts with the need for efficient and strong management at the stage of restructuring. The objective of obtaining a fair price is in conflict with the idea of accelerating the process. Finally, the large number of technical and political considerations that can be abstracted away while explaining a scheme on paper have risen to the surface as actual companies are prepared for sale in the form of foreign and employee ownership issues, valuation of assets, control over management, guarantees for invested money, etc. Therefore, the speed of the process is about half of that envisaged.

In Russia, as well as Hungary, spontaneous privatisation, i.e., sales on the initiative of management, continues on its way. Although a substantial number of politicians and the public have been showing animosity towards what they perceive as a conversion of political into economic power, this – and only this – process is well under way. Both in Poland and in Hungary, and to an even greater extent in Russia, governmental projects of privatisation and 'corporatisation' of firms have not yielded any result. Meanwhile, persecuted, criticised, and condemned managerial privatisations proceed. This is understandable and probably unavoidable, given the subtantial edge provided by information, and the strong motivation of managers. Most of the social apprehension comes from the knowledge that neither the last socialist governments, nor the first 'new' authorities, seem to have learned the lesson from socialist reforms. Namely, it is not sufficient for the State to withdraw, since lacking the appropriate market infrastructure and rules, egoistic special interests may prevail and create chaotic situations (Frydman and Rapaczynski, 1992, p. 267).

This implies – besides the earlier mentioned situation of an inadequate competition policy – a very shortsighted handling of labour issues; and disregard for the budget, municipalities, environmental norms, varied public concerns (insider deals sometimes in plain view), and outright theft. Given that the taxation of private activities is unresolved, and that recession implies worsening living conditions for the vast majority, it is next to impossible to find social acceptance of this kind of enrichment, which has little to do with efficiency considerations. This condition is exacerbated by cases in which it was hard to find sound economics in the privatisation and a long-term acquaintance or 'the first foreigner', etc. was the buyer.

These paradoxes underline the need for transparency, supervision, and provision of legal and institutional frameworks for what is commonly seen as fair trade. Anything which goes beyond, i.e., a sectoral policy on privatisation or the attempt to select 'appropriate' owners, is doomed to failure. Numerous articles producing one or two cases have been the result in both countries.

Turning to Russia, the situation is different inasmuch as no legal framework for privatisation was at hand until January 1992. Since then, there is a new project every month. Thus, something that the Germans would include in *Wirtschaftsverfassung* has hardly come about. Still, the army especially, but other power institutions as well, have proved to be quite successful in turning public property into private hands. This is hardly by chance, since the security of private property is not at all secured at the constitutional level. Further private property for land continues to be prohibited by the April 1992 decisions by the Russian supra-Parliament. Meanwhile, old laws persecuting speculation and profiteering are still in force, with thousands of people still being imprisoned on those charges. The Russian Parliament adopted new anti-speculation laws in March 1992. All in all, security of property is anything but certain.

It is no coincidence that with such a legal and political framework, and under the collapse of state authority and public security, the only type of private business which survives is the mafia business, in addition to various companies of the armed forces. Various mafias wage armed fights in broad daylight in major cities, and their domination of private business is one of the public secrets in Moscow. One wonders what kind of development this might lead to. Some analysts (Szilágyi, 1991) are of the opinion that this kind of intertwining is the major obstacle to the evolution of a normal market economy. Others, including this author, believe that a conceivable – though by no means forecasted – consolidation of state authority, coupled with a liberalisation of domestic and foreign competition, may well undermine the monopoly situation of present suppliers, while making the reliance on the services of informal armed groups superfluous, as we have seen in the USA and in Singapore. But only time will tell what constellation of the many 'ifs' will come true: the game is definitely open-ended.

In summation, there seems to be a modicum of truth in the somewhat cynical statement seeing an inverse relationship between privatisation projects and reality in the actual changes in ownership structures (Mizsei, 1992, p. 296). It is certainly true that illiquid and rudimentary capital markets suffering from undermanning and overregulation, with limited skills and experiences of the participants, are not very useful tools for mass privatisation projects. This would imply an equally slow pace for transformation with radical shock therapy and gradualist approaches. Moreover, the changes in governmental policies might only exert a minor influence over the actual course of events. It seems from the commonalities of the the CSFR, Polish, Hungarian and Russian developments that there may be something of a *natural rate of ownership change* which is fairly difficult not only to bypass, but also to prevent from happening. This might not be such a great problem if recognised and taken into account properly in the framework of a longer-term transformation strategy.

Concluding Remarks

What has been stated here does not support the optimism of the early years of transition, but also qualifies the present gloom stemming from the socially unpleasant repercussions of the inevitably protracted recession. In other words, the short-term perspective is basically to blame both for the unfounded euphoria following the revolutions, and for the spread of gloom and loss of perspective after only the second year of transformation.

Experience of many countries at various times has proven the possibility of stabilising an economy in just a year or two. However, if we try to list the more important measures contributing to a policy line which deserves the name 'transformation strategy', we tend to find tasks which are medium to long term in nature. Banking reform, evolution of capital markets, tax and budgetary reform, overhaul of the social security system, reform of the financing and management of public companies, and general institution-building is a time-consuming job. It is not only about an optimal blueprint and legislation; it also is about tens of thousands, indeed millions of economic agents learning, practising, and internalising the rules and their outcomes. It is a societal, self-corrective 'learning by doing' process. Even if we concede that not each and every society has to rediscover hot water in the modern world, East German experiences are clearly indicative of the limits to what can be absorbed and adopted in a short period of time, even under ideal conditions (like capital affluence, injection of human capital, and cultural/linguistic commonality).

Experiences of the reforming countries are also promising, inasmuch as the time required for transformation to be completed is certainly not measured in terms of 50–200 years. In our understanding, most countries in the world do not need a 95 per cent share of private property to have a functioning market economy, provided it is sufficiently open. If the exchange rate is right and FDI is not persecuted, realistic evaluation of capital on the one hand, and the growth of domestic savings on the other, close the gap between supply and demand for assets. Banking, taxation and social security reforms, and the evolving capital markets, ensure a sizeable increase in allocative efficiency. Thus, the organic strategy does seem to work.

What are the policy implications of all this? First and foremost, stability of the transition strategy, and avoidance of policy zig-zags and messianistic projects of whatever sort. Vacic (1992, p. 5) might be right in underscoring one of the reasons for the historical success of Western nations. This meant avoidance of major discontinuities in their socio-economic fabric, as any radical push in any direction *per se* increases the probability of counter-reaction, thus of a stop-go policy of the worst sort. Therefore, the inflationary strategy for recovery, advocated by some of the authors quoted at the beginning of this paper, seems to pose the most serious policy mistakes in terms of *conjonture*, as it would undermine fiscal stabilisation and profit perspectives.

As seen before, the present recession has roots other than insufficient domestic demand, thus a Keynesian recipe seems to be unfit for the given set of conditions.

As seen above, following the organic line requires far-sighted strategies, patience, and considerable self-restraint on the side of policy-makers. This needs to be supplemented by conceptually well-founded and technically elaborate major reforms and institution-building. For this, a broad consensus regarding the aims and means of transition is needed, otherwise excellent economic schemes will either not be translated to legislation, or worse, they will suffer from serious flaws in this course. More advanced countries with a more developed civil society and more emancipated economy might be better suited for these types of transition policies, since the reform constituency cuts across the political spectrum. Less-advanced countries with more uncertainty, less knowledge, and less information-processing ability, aggravated by a weak reform consituency, will probably experience wider movements of the political shuttle, as Daianu (1992) correctly observes. Conversely, in the latter group, the transition strategy is more contingent on the competent policy options of the ruling elite, thus the probability of a successful transition strategy under a sort of enlightened absolutism seems to be higher. This finding seems to receive indirect support from the dynamics of change in Russia as well as from the Newly Industrialised Countries. The above-sketched alternative is, of course, not policy advice or a forecast, but one of the rather plausible options one can speculate about. The problem, as we all know, is that there is no guarantee of enlightenment. Yet our policy preferences should not necessarily overshadow the lessons of development economics.

In sum, there are a growing number of signs that transition to the market will be a long journey full of trials and errors. Societies may or may not want to follow a given route, and the end result is not given by historic necessity or political wisdom. The stakes are great, international competition is stiff. The consequences for those lagging behind are evidenced by a large number of underdeveloped nations. But the chances for reintegration into the historic mainstream of economic and human development have not yet been completely missed: several candidates may well qualify.

References

Andreff, W., 1992, "French Privatization Techniques and Policies – A Model for Central and Eastern Europe?" in Dallago, B. and F. Targetti (eds), *Privatisation and the Role of the Public Sector in East and West.* Aldershot and Brookfield: Dartmouth Publishing Co.

Bandyk, Ch., 1992, "Privatisierung in Polen 1990/91", *Osteuropa*, No. 5.

Bofinger, P. (ed.), 1992, *The Economic Consequences of the East.* London and

Frankfurt: Centre for Economic Policy Research and Deutsche Bundesbank.

Borensztein, E. and P. Montiel, 1992, "Savings, Investment and Growth in Eastern Europe" in Winckler, G. (moderator) *Central and Eastern Europe – Roads to Growth.* International Monetary Fund – Austrian National Bank, Washington, DC, pp. 153–187.

Cassel, D. (Hrsg), 1990, "Wistschaftssysteme im Umbruch". München: Verlag Vahlen.

Charap, J., K. Dyba and M. Kupka, 1992, "The Reform Process in Czechoslovakia: An Assessment of Recent Developments and Prospects for the Future", *Communist Economies and Economic Transformation* 1.

Chu, Y.–P. and Ch.–Ch. Lin, 1991, "Economic and Social Reforms Confronting Taiwan" in Kim et al.

Corbo, V., 1992, "Economic Transformation in Latin America – Lessons for Eastern Europe", *European Economic Review* 2–3.

Csaba, L., 1992, "Russia Beyond Perestroika", *Communist Economies and Economic Transformation* 3.

Dabrowski, M., 1992, "The Polish Stabilization, 1990–1991", *The Journal of International and Comparative Economics* 4.

Daianu, D., 1992, "Transformation and the Legacy of Backwardness – Thoughts from a Romanian Perspective", *Economies et Sociétés, Série des économies planifiées* 51.

Dietz, R., 1991, "The Role of Western Capital in the Transition to the Market – a System's Theoretical Perspective" in Csaba L. (ed.), *Systemic Change and Stabilization in Eastern Europe.* Aldershot and Brookfield: Dartmouth Publishing Co., pp. 103–124.

Egger, U., R. Kappel and A. Melzer, 1992, "Osteuropa auf dem Weg zur Marktwirtschaft: Gedanken zur Unterstützung des Überganges", *Osteuropa Wirtschaft* 1.

Frydman, R. and A. Rapaczynski, 1992, "Privatization and Corporate Governance in Eastern Europe: Can a Market Economy be Designed?" in Winckler, G. (moderator) *op.cit.,* pp. 255–285.

Gomulka, S., 1991, "The Causes of Recession Following Stabilization", *Comparative Economic Studies* 2.

Hanke, S. and K. Schuler, 1991, "Ruble Reform: A Lesson from Keynes", *The CATO Journal* 3.

Hsiao, H.–H. M., 1991, "Explaining the Taiwan Development Model: Lessons to be Learned" in Kim et al., pp. 109–126.

Jung, K.–H.,1991, "Economic Reforms in Korea: In Search of a New Role for the Government, Business and the Market" in Kim et al., pp. 91–108.

Kang, S.–I., 1992, Privatization of Corporations in Korea: Case Studies. Paper presented to the Third Central Europe – East Asia Round Table Conference, Budapest, 23–24 April, 1992.

Kim, D., 1991, "Economic Reforms Confronting Korea" in Kim, et al., pp. 267–296.

Kim, D., K–H. Jung, and K. Y. Jeong (eds), *The Role of Market and the State: Economic and Social Reforms in East Asia and East-Central Europe.* Seoul: Shin Jung Printing Co. for the Institute of East and West Studies at Yonsei University.

Köves, A., 1992,"Shock Therapy Versus Gradual Change", *Acta Oeconomica* 1–2.

Kupka, M., 1992, "Transformation of Ownership in Czechoslovakia", *Soviet Studies* 2.

Laski, K., 1992, "Transition from Command to Market Economies in Central and Eastern Europe: First Experiences and Questions", *WIIW Forschungsbericht* 181, p. 24. Vienna.

Lösch, D., 1992, "Das 'Timing' als Zentrales Problem der Systemtransformation" *HWWA Report* 99, p. 76. Hamburg.

Mizsei, K., 1992, "Privatization in Eastern Europe: A Comparative Study of Poland and Hungary", *Soviet Studies* 2.

Newbery, D., 1992, "The Role of Public Enterprises in the National Economy", *Asian Development Bank Survey.* (Forthcoming.)

Neue Zürcher Zeitung, 4 February 1992, "Ein Volk von Aktionären in der CSFR?"

Obláth, G., 1992, "Veszélyes vizeken". (On Troubled Waters). *Figyelö* 19.

Pascha, W., 1990, "Dritte Welt im Aufbruch: Ostasiatische Schwellenländer als Neue Weltwirtschaftliche Entwicklungspole?" in Cassel, D. (Hrsg.) *Wirtschaftssysteme im Umbruch.* München: Verlag Vahlen, pp. 92–120.

Siebert, H. (ed.), 1992, *The Transformation of Socialist Economies.* Tübingen: J. C. B. Mohr (Paul Siebeck).

Steinherr, A., 1992, "Comments on Tanzi", in Bofinger, P. (ed.) *The Economic Consequences of the East.* London and Frankfurt: Centre for Economic Policy Research and Deutsche Bundesbank.

Szilágyi, Á., 1991, "Vázlat a bandokráciáról" (An Essay on Criminal Bureaucracy), *Társadalmi Szemle* 10.

Tanzi, V., 1992, "Financial Markets and Public Finance in the Transformation Process", in Bofinger, P. (ed.) *The Economic Consequences of the East.* London and Frankfurt: Centre for Economic Policy Research and Deutsche Bundesbank.

Vacic, A., 1992,"Systemic Transformation in Central and Eastern Europe: General Framework, Specific Features and Prospects", *Osteuropa Wirtschaft* 1.

Welfens, P., 1992, "German Unification and Systemic Transition Towards a New German Economic Miracle?" *Acta Oeconomica* 1–2.

Winiecki, J., 1991a, "The Inevitability of a Fall in Output in the Early Stages of Transition to the Market", *Soviet Studies* 4.

_____, 1991b, "Shaping the Institutional Infrastructure" in Siebert, H. (ed.), *The Transformation of Socialist Economies*. Tübingen: J. C. B. Mohr (Paul Siebeck).

_____, 1992, "Polish Transition Programme: Stabilisation Under Threat", *Communist Economies and Economic Transformation* 2.

6

Transition Issues as Seen Through the Experience of Hungary: There is No Cookbook to Go By

*György Szapáry**

Introduction

When Central and Eastern Europe embarked upon the transition two years ago, it was often said that they were entering uncharted waters: that the attempt to move from a centrally-planned economy to a market economy was unprecedented and that the transition would be a process of learning by doing. After two years of experience, it is clear that these statements were not the mere expression of commonplaces but recognition that, while the starting point and the final destination were known, there were great uncertainties about the obstacles and difficulties that would be encountered on the road to a market economy. The transition has already presented some surprises, events that may have been anticipated – and were in fact anticipated by many – but whose magnitude and impact were greatly underestimated.

This paper focuses on a few of these events and the problems that they have created for the process of transformation. Drawing on the experience of Hungary, the paper attempts to highlight those issues which seem to be of particular importance for the success of reforms. Although the discussion is

* Assistant Director at the International Monetary Fund. The views expressed in this paper are those of the author and do not necessarily reflect the views of the International Monetary Fund. An earlier version of this paper was presented at the Arne Ryde Symposium organised by the School of Economics and Management of Lund University in Rungsted Kyst, Denmark 11–12 June 1992.

based on the Hungarian experience, the issues are common to all reform economies.

The Collapse of Output: The Reform Supply Shock

There was general consensus among economists and policy makers at the start of the reforms that there will be a temporary decline in output as the liberalisation of imports, the reduction or elimination of producer subsidies, and the general hardening of budget constraints facing enterprises will affect the production of those companies which could not compete in the new, more open and competitive environment. Furthermore, it was recognised that the transition countries will face inflationary and balance of payments pressures. As regards inflation, the transformation process involved an initial upward pressure on prices due to the elimination of subsidies; the freeing of prices coupled with the existence of a liquidity overhang and monopolistic structures; and the opening up of the economy to international competition and the consequent 'importation' of international prices. On the external side, in addition to the contraction of Eastern markets, there was a need to build up reserves to levels commensurate with the higher degree of openness of the economy and the switch to convertible currency settlement in trade with former CMEA partners. The move to world prices in trade among former CMEA members entailed a terms of trade loss for the non-Soviet members which, although varying among countries, was significant for all of them. All these called for tight financial policies which were also expected to have a negative impact on domestic demand and output.

While these factors were foreseen, the extent and duration of the fall in output were more serious than anticipated. In each of the Eastern European countries, real GDP declined in both 1990 and 1991 for a cumulative decline of about 32 per cent in Bulgaria, 19 per cent in Romania, 18 per cent in Poland, 16 per cent in the Czech and Slovak Republic and 14 per cent in Hungary. In most countries, the prospect is for a further, albeit smaller decline in 1992. It is clear now that the extent of the contraction in Eastern trade has been greatly underestimated, particularly the collapse of solvent import demand in the states of the former Soviet Union, which has had a ripple effect on output and demand in the whole region. Although a reduction in Eastern European exports to the former Soviet Union states had been projected, the collapse of the Soviet market as a result of the break-up of the Soviet Union was not fully anticipated two years ago. In Hungary, for example, the fall in GDP was revised downward several times in the course of 1991, largely because of a continuous downward revision in exports to the former Soviet Union states as it became clear with each passing month that the fall in Soviet demand would be much sharper than had been expected earlier. A similar process of revision of exports to the former Soviet Union states took place in several of the other countries as well. At the same time, it seems that it has not been fully recognised that the negative forces on domestic demand and output associated with the reforms will work simultaneously in the whole region, exacerbating each country's output fall through the shrinkage of trade among former CMEA countries, which previously formed an integrated and largely closed trading area.

There may have been other factors whose impact on production has been underestimated, such as the importance of the reduction in hoarding, a typical phenomenon in a shortage economy. It can also be argued that in some of the countries there may have been a more than intended tightening of credit, as for instance in Poland, due to an overshooting of inflation following a large initial devaluation. It is also true that the actual declines in production are likely to have been smaller than shown in the official GDP statistics because the latter do not yet fully capture the newly emerging private sector. None of this, however, changes the fact that the magnitude of the reduction in Eastern trade has not been anticipated, compounding each country's fall in domestic output associated with the implementation of reforms.[1]

An interesting question to ask with hindsight is whether something could have been done to prevent the sudden collapse of trade. The answer is probably no. First, there is little that could have been done to prevent the sharp fall in solvent import demand in the states of the former Soviet Union. The collapse in output and import demand in the former Soviet Union states has been the result of political events which, although not directly linked to economic reforms, are not independent from the social-political developments that have permitted reforms in Central and Eastern Europe to take place in the first place. Second, trade among Central and Eastern European countries fell largely because, with trade liberalisation, goods produced in the East could not compete with those produced in the West, not always necessarily in terms of price and quality, but often also because of the general appeal of Western goods.[2] Under such circumstances, trade could have been maintained only with a slower speed of trade liberalisation. However, there was little public support in these countries for a slow trade liberalisation, since the latter was regarded as an integral part of the policy to end the decades-long isolation from the West. Whatever the merits of a more gradual liberalisation may have been, it ran against the aspirations of the people at that time. While pressure is mounting to tighten protection, it would be a mistake to reverse course as it would undermine credibility in the reforms.

Taking these factors into consideration, it can be argued that the sharp fall in output in the transition countries should be regarded as an 'exogenous'

1. Calculations in Rodrik (1992) indicate that the Soviet trade shock (including both the market loss and the terms of trade loss effect) explains a substantial part of the GDP loss in 1990–91 in Hungary, the Czech and Slovak Republic and Poland.

2. The greater availability of export credits in Western countries has, to a certain degree, also contributed to a crowding out of Eastern trade.

reform supply shock, in the sense that it has been as much a consequence of the conditions which have led to the reforms, i.e. the break-up of the former USSR,[3] as it has been the result of the reforms themselves and the necessary tightening of financial policies to harden budget constraints and to promote liberalisation and restructuring. This said, the much deeper and more prolonged than expected fall in output has rendered the task of implementing the reforms more complex and difficult. In the following sections, some of these difficulties are reviewed in the areas of fiscal and monetary policy, and privatisation.

Fiscal Policy: Shrinking Tax Base and Sustainability

The fall in output and the implementation of reforms have led to a shrinkage of the tax base which complicate the task of maintaining macro-economic stability and restructuring government expenditure. Revenue in real terms has been declining from all the major sources: the enterprise profit tax, consumption taxes, and the personal income tax (as employment has been reduced). In addition, with a growing number of enterprises facing bankruptcies, the need for banks to provision for bad debt has risen, reducing also the taxable profits of financial institutions. Furthermore, as domestic demand has fallen, the structure of production has shifted toward exports. While this shift is a desirable development from a long-term point of view, in the short run it has the effect of reducing the revenue from the value added tax since exports are not subject to this tax.

Privatisation is also having a negative impact on revenue in the short term, as the sudden multiplication of firms has caught the tax administration unprepared for enforcing tax collection. It will take several years to build up an administration which is capable of collecting taxes from smaller and a much larger number of companies than before. The change in the amortisation rules is also going to affect future revenue developments in Hungary. Until 1992, the amortisation rates in Hungary were below internationally accepted standards and the replacement values were not adjusted for inflation. As a result, when inflation started to accelerate in the 1980s, the resources set aside for amortisation fell far short of the cost of replacement. Figure 6.1 shows that amortisation as a ratio of GDP declined from about 13 per cent in 1980 to 7 per cent in 1991. The insufficient provisioning for amortisation artificially boosted the resources of the enterprises, part of which was distributed in the form of wages and benefits and part of which was transferred to the budget in

3. The drop in Soviet output resulting from the break-up of the former USSR can be considered as a supply shock in the states of the former Soviet Union which has translated into a drop in foreign demand for the other members of the former COMECON.

FIGURE 6.1 Hungary: Enterprise Amortisation, 1975–1991
(in per cent of GDP)

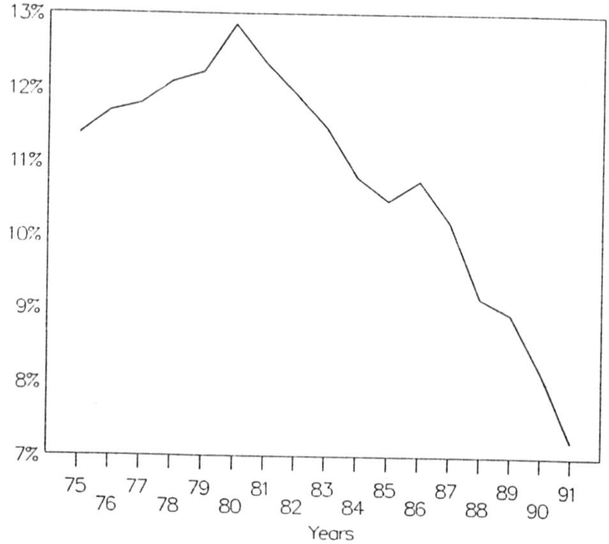

Source: Data provided by the Hungarian authorities.

FIGURE 6.2 Hungary: Government Capital Expenditure, 1981–1991
(in per cent of GDP)

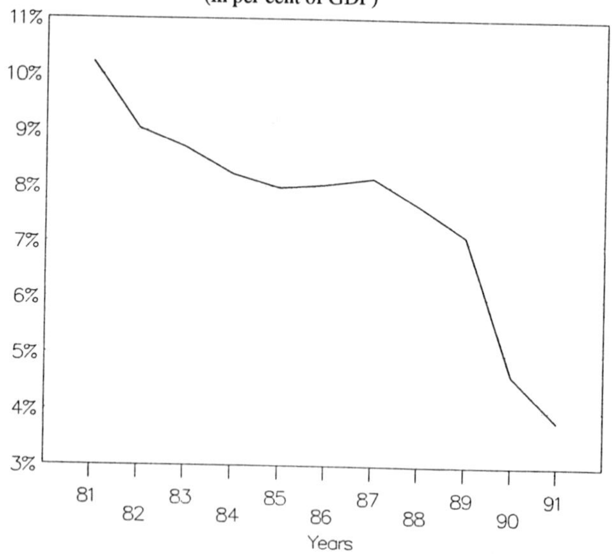

Source: Data provided by the Hungarian authorities.

the form of taxes.[4] It is estimated that in 1990, about one-third of the true replacement value was distributed by the enterprises and one-third was taxed away.[5] Since capital expenditures financed through the government budget also declined sharply as a ratio of GDP during this period (Figure 6. 2), it cannot be argued that the replacement value which was taxed away helped to increase investment through the budget; it simply served to boost the general resources of the budget.

Starting with 1992, the amortisation rates for new investment have been raised to conform with international standards. This was a necessary change from the point of view of promoting investment, but it will affect revenue from the enterprise sector as new firms are being set up and old ones get modernised through privatisation. Consequently, revenue from the enterprise sector is likely to grow more slowly than output for the next several years, underscoring the need to expand the revenue base elsewhere, especially by widening the basis of the VAT and eliminating tax exemptions.

Revenue and expenditure as a ratio of GDP are still significantly higher in Hungary than in the developed market economies or in countries with a similar level of per capita income. A further downsizing of the government is needed to increase the efficiency of resource allocation and prepare the way for Hungary's integration into the European Community. While the factors affecting revenue discussed above are resulting in a decline in the revenue/GDP ratio,[6] a similar scaling back of expenditure is proving difficult – despite the substantial cut-backs in subsidies – when output is shrinking and new reform-driven needs are emerging.[7] On the one hand, it is necessary to channel resources toward social expenditures to support a growing number of unemployed and those segments of the population that are the hardest hit by inflation and the elimination of subsidies, such as those to low-income pensioners. On the other hand, a bigger portion of the shrinking pie has to be channelled toward investment to ensure that the pie is going to grow. This should be carried out in the form of both increasing government expenditure on infrastructure development and allowing the tax burden on enterprises to

4. The initial ideology behind the taxing of amortisation was that enterprise amortisation should cover only investment necessary to maintain the current rate of output growth. Investment needed to increase the growth of output should be decided on and financed by the central government budget.

5. See Matolcsy (1991).

6. A similar reform-induced decline in government revenue has been observed in China since the start of market-oriented economic reforms in 1978. See Blejer and Szapary (1990).

7. General government revenue as a ratio of GDP declined in Hungary from 58.9 per cent in 1989 to 55.7 per cent in 1991, while government expenditure remained at about 60 per cent. The EC weighted average is 43.6 per cent for revenue and 46.5 per cent for expenditure (1989 data, excluding Greece and Luxembourg). Since the GDP data in Hungary do not capture the important and growing 'gray' private economy, the revenue and expenditure ratios are exaggerated to some extent in Hungary.

diminish. The latter is in part taking place through the introduction of higher amortisation rates and also the application of more realistic provisions for losses. However, enterprises in Hungary have to pay social security and unemployment taxes totalling 49 per cent of wages. Such high burden encourages tax evasion and inhibits investors, particularly small entrepreneurs, from expanding their businesses or starting new ones. The tax wedge, i.e. the difference between the net take-home pay of a worker and the wage cost to the enterprise is about 100 per cent in Hungary, substantially higher than in the industrialised countries. This is a reflection of the large income redistribution system inherited from the socialist past, which involves low wages and relatively high social benefits. It would be more desirable to pay higher salaries and reduce redistribution through the budget, since not everybody needs the same services to the same extent and some services are provided more efficiently by the private sector.

One of the main difficulties facing the reform economies is that the socialist redistribution system was not meant to meet the requirements of a market economy. In market economies, the role of social benefits is to mitigate income inequalities: the differentiating factor is the income and the equalising factor is the redistribution system. In the socialist systems, it was the other way around: official incomes were fairly undifferentiated, but the benefits, such as the possibility of getting good housing, medical care, or recreation at subsidised prices were quite differentiated. Even pensions were more differentiated than salaries.[8] This situation has changed over time in Hungary under the impact of reforms, but it has remained dominant in countries such as the states of the former Soviet Union where a complex system of benefits and privileges has prevailed which has dwarfed the inequalities in wages and salaries.

What makes the reform of the redistribution system in former socialist countries particularly difficult is that – unlike in market economies where safety nets were built up, so to say, from scratch – in the transition economies the existing safety mechanisms have to be transformed into a system which is targeted to the most needy, at a time when living standards are falling, the revenue to be redistributed through the budget is shrinking, and every segment of society tries to preserve the benefits it already has. In Western countries the social benefit systems have been expanded and improved gradually over time in line with the increased production capacity of the economies. In Eastern Europe, the governments have inherited a social benefit system which absorbs an excessive proportion of the resources given the requirements for investment and the restructuring of the economy. The aim should be to reduce the overall size of the redistribution system while making it better targeted. One problem that the introduction of a need-based policy must face is the relatively large proportion of hidden incomes not captured by the current tax information system which makes it difficult to determine who are the truly needy.

8. Illés (1992).

The success of the reforms requires the maintenance of macro-economic stability. An issue which is often debated in Hungary is the level of fiscal balance that is compatible with such stability. It is not inconsistent with the reforms that, in the early stages of the transition, the negative macro-economic consequences of fiscal deficits may be offset by an increase in the willingness of households to save. In Hungary, for example, the net financial savings of households increased from an average of less than one per cent of GDP in the 1980s to about 11 per cent in 1991,[9] which was reflected in a rise in the demand for money, allowing the government to collect seigniorage and finance a higher deficit without placing additional pressure on domestic demand. Several factors have contributed to the increase in household savings. First, the reforms have created new uncertainties, such as the risk of unemployment and the possible erosion of social benefits, which have encouraged people to be more thrifty. Second, following the liberalisation of interest rates, the return on financial savings has improved, and savings instruments have become more diversified. Third, income differentiation has widened, with the emergence of a rich class with a high propensity to save. Fourth, investment opportunities have increased, including the possibility of buying the apartments which people have been renting from the state. Finally, the greater availability of imported durable consumer goods, together with the dearth and high cost of consumer credit have provided additional incentives to save.[10]

Although there are factors which will continue to promote savings as the reforms proceed, such as a further differentiation of incomes and greater reliance on private pensions, the higher level of saving observed in the early years of the reform may not represent the desired level in the medium term. For instance, once people have purchased their rented apartments, have adjusted to the uncertainties, and consumer credit becomes more available, the willingness to save may diminish. At the same time, privatisation and the development of the capital markets are likely to induce a portfolio shift away from bank deposit instruments toward shares. Both of these developments may lead to a reduction in the demand for money and the possibility for seigniorage revenue. In addition, the reduction of inflation will also result in a loss of seigniorage revenue in all transition economies.[11] Taking these factors into

9. To the extent that the GDP statistics do not capture the informal economy, the savings ratio is overestimated.

10. A large part of the growth in household bank deposits occurred in foreign currency deposits which were legalised in September 1989. To some extent, therefore, the growth in household deposits may reflect the repatriation of savings held abroad or the recording in the statistics of savings previously held in the form of foreign currency notes. In addition, household deposits include the working capital deposits of small private enterprises. In part, therefore, the growth in household deposits may reflect an increase in the transactions demand for money of enterprises.

11. In Hungary, for example, it has been estimated that reducing inflation from 35 per cent in 1991 to 10 per cent in 1993 will result in a loss of seigniorage revenue equivalent to 2 per cent of GDP. See Dervis and Condon (1992).

consideration, great caution is needed in order to avoid setting expenditures in the early stages of reform at a level which may not be sustainable in later years.[12]

Monetary Policy: The Uncertainty Trap

A major factor complicating the formulation and implementation of monetary policy in transition economies is the unpredictability of expectations. Having learned not to trust government policies under the communist regime and remembering the stop–go reform policies of the past, people remain sceptical about the durability of the reforms now being implemented. Given such historical background, it will take time to gain people's confidence in government policies, even if these policies strive to be consistent and predictable. For example, although inflation has been declining continuously since June 1991 in Hungary, inflationary expectations are slow to change and many people even question the veracity of the data published.[13] There is a lag in the adjustment of expectations in every economy, but the longer the period characterised by the lack of confidence has been, the longer the initial lag of adjustment is likely to be. The slowness of inflationary expectations to adjust downward in line with the decline in the rate of inflation has made it more difficult to bring down real interest rates in Hungary, which is hindering investment and could delay the resumption of growth.

Another area where the 'confidence gap' has implications for policy is in regard of the introduction of currency convertibility for households. Many people in Hungary believe that if such convertibility is introduced, individuals will convert their local currency balances into foreign currency, simply because they do not trust the government, even though domestic interest rates measured against the exchange risk are attractive. The fear of sparking a capital flight weighs heavily on the mind of the Hungarian authorities when considering the timing of the introduction of convertibility for households. This example goes to show that the lack of confidence is a practical problem which policy makers have to face in transition economies. The issue is to find the optimal policies which will minimise the costs arising from the confidence gap.

The implementation of monetary policy is also hampered by the uncertainty about developments in the real economy. With the emergence of a growing private 'gray' economy which is not yet captured in the information

---

12. There is an interesting and detailed discussion in Kornai (1992) of the factors which tend to slow down the downsizing of the government.

13. It should be noted that the official price statistics do not fully reflect the actual situation to the extent that they do not capture price developments in the growing informal economy. This is particularly true for the service sector in such areas as house repairs, rents, car service, etc.

system, the official statistics do not reflect accurately the developments in output, making it hard to predict the demand for money and thus complicating the task of judging the appropriateness of the stance of monetary policy. The difficulty of predicting developments in the demand for money is increased when the economy and the institutions are undergoing fundamental transformation. As discussed above, households' demand for money has increased considerably over the past two years, but there are factors which could reverse the trend in the later stages of reforms. There is uncertainty also about the demand for money of enterprises. There has been an increase in such demand in Hungary as a result of the break-up of large state-owned enterprises into smaller private firms and in response to the gradual hardening of budget constraints, including tighter conditions for credit. While this process is likely to continue, it is less clear how the demand for money of an enterprise facing the prospect of bankruptcy will behave; it may well be that such an enterprise will use up its bank deposit balances to avoid confiscation. If this were the case, the demand for money of the enterprise sector could decline, given the large number of enterprises that are facing bankruptcy.

A further complicating factor is the uncertainty about the functioning of the transmission mechanism of monetary policy in an economy where the banking system is undergoing a fundamental reform. After the establishment of a two-tier banking system with an independent central bank and commercial banks in 1987, the portfolio of Hungarian state enterprises has been distributed among the large state-owned banks. The distribution had a heavy sectoral concentration: for example, the bulk of the mining sector portfolio equal was given to one bank and a large part of the agricultural sector portfolio to another. Such initial sectoral concentration has thwarted competition among banks and has made it difficult for them to diversify their portfolios. Furthermore, because of the concentration of production in the hands of a few firms, a bank's decision to cut off credit from an enterprise may have wide-ranging social and economic consequences. Such heavy, largely inherited responsibility intimidates banks to take the tough decisions.[14] All this makes it difficult to ensure that when credit is tight, it is cut off to those for whom the return is lowest.[15] As a result, when monetary policy needs to be restrictive to control inflation, the cost in terms of output loss may be larger. The inadequacies of the financial intermediation by the banking system are exacerbated by the underdevelopment of the capital markets. Firms that are 'crowded out' from bank credit cannot turn to the capital market, thereby further increasing the bias against output of a restrictive monetary policy.

Finally, there is the need to tackle the issue of the bad debts accumulated

---

14. It seems that banks are risk averse toward the emerging private sector, but risk takers toward the big state firms.

15. There is a discussion of the various aspects of financial sector reform in transition economies in Stiglitz (1991).

by banks. Part of the bad debt portfolio of the banks in Hungary has been inherited from the time of the monobank system prior to 1987, but there has been a very substantial growth in the bad debt portfolio over the past two years as a result of the collapse of markets and output. A 'cleaning' of the books might appear to be an attractive approach to delink the fortunes of bad enterprises from the fortunes of banks.[16] However, such an approach raises two issues. One is the issue of moral hazard: cleaning of the books always carries the risk that after the cleaning operation banks would continue to take unwise risks in the expectation that the Government will bail them out once again. The probability of this happening is less if hard budget constraints already prevail in the whole economy, but if the banks and the bulk of enterprises are still state-owned, budget constraints are likely to remain soft and the danger of the books being 'dirtied' again is considerable. The second issue concerns the task of restructuring or liquidating the enterprises which cannot service their debts. In the case of a book-cleaning operation, the banks would be relieved from this responsibility and the task would have to be given to a separate institution. It is doubtful that the restructuring of hundreds of enterprises could be efficiently carried out by a new central institution which will first have to acquire the information and expertise which already exist at the commercial banks. A more pragmatic solution would be to require the banks to provision for the bad loans (allowing them to do so gradually over a number of years if necessary) and provide them with incentives to play an active role in the restructuring-cum-privatisation of enterprises. Such incentive could take the form of loan guarantees by the Government or the swap of government bonds for the doubtful loan portfolio. However, such incentives should be given on a case-by-case basis and conditioned on the restructuring programme for the enterprise.

Privatisation: Too Many Moving Targets

Privatisation has encountered a wide range of largely unanticipated factors that tend to slow its process. Hungary, which had started with privatisation a few years ahead of the others, has used several approaches: a centralised privatisation programme under which major state enterprises are offered for sale by the State Property Agency (SPA); 'spontaneous' privatisation when the enterprises themselves initiate the privatisation under SPA supervision; and a decentralised programme where buyers approach the SPA with proposals and the SPA may also force enterprises into privatisation. The Czech and Slovak Republic has recently initiated a mass privatisation programme through the distribution of vouchers to financial institutions. The main idea behind this scheme is that financial institutions, such as banks, insurance companies,

16. See Calvo and Frenkel (1991).

pension funds and newly established mutual funds would end up with enough shares in their hands – either through direct distribution or through acquisitions from citizens – to be able to exercise supervision over the management of firms. Since it is too early to judge the success of the voucher system, only the case-by-case approach adopted by the Hungarian Government is discussed here. Whatever the success of the mass privatisation programmes, the case-by-case approach will remain one of the main avenues of privatisation and the lessons of the Hungarian experience are thus not irrelevant for the other countries.

One factor which has slowed privatisation has been the time-consuming process of valuation of enterprise assets, due in part to the lack of adequate accounting. The difficulties have been compounded by the unfamiliarity of the foreign advisory firms selected to carry out the privatisation with the socialist system of accounting. More importantly, however, valuation has been rendered difficult – and subject to more challenge – by the lack of an active industrial assets and real estate market and the fact that the past track record of an enterprise is not a good indicator of its future performance because of the fundamental structural changes in the economy and the markets. For instance, the privatisation hopes of many Hungarian companies have been dashed with the collapse of the USSR economy: investor interest in companies producing mostly for the Soviet markets has simply vanished in the face of the changed market prospects. The prospects of companies producing primarily for the Hungarian market have also changed with the sharp decline in domestic demand.

Paradoxically, just as the market prospects have weakened, the political pressure to obtain the highest possible price for the privatised enterprises has increased. Since the government budget has come under heavy strains in the face of a shrinking tax base and new needs such as in the areas of infrastructural development, restructuring of enterprises, environmental clean-up, and the setting up of new institutions, the desire to use privatisation as a means to raise additional resources for the budget or for different special funds has increased. This has led at times to protracted negotiations over the price – and a long search for the investor who can afford it – in order to get the 'best deal' for the Government. There has always been a trade-off between the best-deal and the speed of privatisation, but as the pressure on the public finances grows and the value of enterprises is eroding, the calls against a 'sell-out' are getting louder and the 'best-deal' attitude gains importance.[17]

As time passes, privatisation gets entangled in politics. People are afraid that if the Government leads the privatisation, only those loyal to the Government will get management positions. Confronted with this fear, many

17. This observation does not apply to the privatisation of small shops and restaurants under the so-called pre-privatisation programme in Hungary, where there hes been a move toward lowering the sales prices in the interests of speeding up the privatisation.

managers are either attempting to privatise quickly in the hope that they can thus preserve their position, or are simply adopting a wait-and-see attitude while living off the firm's assets. Such 'internal looting' is similar to the attitude adopted by private companies before nationalisation. In these circumstances, it becomes increasingly difficult for the Government to resist the political pressure to appoint its own candidates as managers, with the mandate to prevent a 'sell-out' or stop the dilapidation of the firm's capital.

The change in management tends to slow down the privatisation as the new managers have to acquaint themselves with the firms. The temptation to put the enterprise 'back on its feet' and make it 'ready' for privatisation also increases with the change in management. While restructuring the firm before putting it up for sale can be the right course of action in certain cases, it also carries the danger of preventing the phasing out of unviable activities and of maintaining the pressure for subsidies, tax preferences, preferential credit, government guarantees – in short, the soft budget constraint.

There are often conflicts of interest among those responsible for privatisation. Many private investors are interested in majority shareholding while managers who feel secure in their new government-appointed jobs may be reluctant to give up a government majority from fear of losing their position. Local authorities eager to look good to their constituents are often pushing for a higher sales price than the central government; quite a number of privatisation deals have been held up because of the lack of agreement over the price and the distribution of the sales proceeds between the central and the local governments. Also, local authorities seem to be less interested than the central government in full privatisation because they are more eager to share in the profits.

All these have led to frequent shifts in priorities. At times within the same project, the emphasis has shifted, for example, between employment maintenance, minimum Hungarian participation and the best possible price. One complaint often voiced by investors is that there have been too many moving targets which have become an obstacle to speedy privatisation. Delays in the privatisation represent a serious problem because during the 'waiting-for-privatisation' period, enterprises are in a state of limbo when practically all strategic activity, such as investment, search for new markets, conclusion of long-term contracts, etc., come to a halt.

Last but not least, privatisation is seriously hampered by the lack of domestic capital. It would be unrealistic to expect that foreign investors will buy more than a limited portion of the state assets to be sold. As of April 1992, foreign investment accounted for 75 per cent of the accumulative privatisation receipts in Hungary, but this share has declined from 83 per cent in 1990 to 68 per cent in the first four months of 1992 and is expected to decline further as the best ventures are being sold off. Despite the relatively large share of foreign capital in the privatisation receipts so far, foreign ownership through privatisation represented only about 3 per cent of total state enterprise assets as at the end of 1991.[18] Although this share is going to rise, foreign investors are often more interested in launching green field projects than in buying existing companies with outmoded equipment. Therefore, a large portion of the state-owned companies will have to be sold to domestic investors. However, apart from a few individual success stories, there has not yet been enough accumulation of capital in the hands of domestic investors. At the same time, potential domestic investors have difficulties in obtaining bank credit because of the lack of adequate collateral and a long enough track record. The high level of real interest rates is another discouraging factor. An approach which could help to overcome these difficulties would be to offer to potential investors the possibility of leasing the companies with the option to buy.

While it is too early yet to judge the relative merits of the various approaches to privatisation in the region, it is becoming increasingly evident that privatisation will be a slow process. It must also be recognised that politically it is impossible to close down all uneconomic enterprises at once. This raises the issue of what role the government should play in managing the restructuring and phasing out those enterprises which are not yet or cannot be privatised. It seems that governments will unavoidably have to play a more active role lest there will be a greater destruction of wealth and employment then necessary. This would call for the formulation of a national industrial policy to determine which are the 'good' industries to be reorganised and the 'bad' ones to be phased out. Unfortunately the record is not very encouraging in this area, since experience has shown that governments have not been particularly successful in pricing the winners and losers. Restructuring is also costly and, in view of the tight budgetary situation, it becomes increasingly difficult to find funding for the restructuring. It is probable, therefore, that privatisation and restructuring will proceed by trial and error and that the results will be less satisfactory than they would be if optimal solutions could be applied.

Concluding Remarks

The transformation of centrally-planned state-owned economies to market economies in which the private sector becomes the dominant force is a longer and more difficult task than many had expected in Eastern Europe. The establishment of new institutions, the preparation and enactment of new legislation, the reordering of ownership structures, and the reorganisation of

18. See Giday (1992). Note that the total capital over which foreign investors exercise management control is larger than their ownership share, since in many ventures the foreign partner has only a 51 per cent controlling interest. There are also cases where even a smaller share gives control over management to the foreign investor through *ad hoc* arrangements such as 'golden' shares.

production along the lines of new comparative advantages dictated by opening up to the world economy require time, determination, and innovation. The transformation is a process of learning by doing for which there is no cook-book to follow. It has to be recognised that it is often not possible to apply first-best solutions and that one has to settle for less. In conclusion, let me list the three principal factors which are making the transformation particularly complex and difficult:

– Firstly, the break-up of the former USSR coupled with the opening of the economies of Eastern and Central Europe resulted in a collapse of trade among former CMEA countries which has increased the depth and duration of the recession, complicating the implementation of reforms in virtually all areas. The collapse of Eastern markets dictates a much more drastic restructuring of production and trade than was thought necessary at the outset of the reforms. This underscores the necessity of coordinating the policies with respect to privatisation, enterprise restructuring, and the banks' bad debt portfolio into an integrated industrial strategy.

– Secondly, the costly and elaborate social safety net built up under the socialist system is proving to be difficult to transform into a system which meets the requirements of a market economy. The old system places a heavy burden on the budget, which slows the downsizing of the government and poses a continuous threat to the maintenance of fiscal balance, especially at a time when revenue is affected by the recession and the reforms. While the increase in household saving induced by the reforms provides some breathing space, care is needed not to crowd out the private sector by excessive government spending; the large investment needs necessary to ensure sustained growth require a strict limitation on the government's claims on resources. At the same time, the tax base needs to be broadened and the tax enforcement improved to ensure that government revenue grows in line with the expansion of economic activity.

– Finally, privatisation is being hindered by the emergence of a series of factors not foreseen at the start of the reforms. To keep the process moving, it will take not only determination in designing new approaches to overcome the emerging obstacles. Governments should keep privatisation out of politics as much as possible.

References

Blejer, M. I. and G. Szapary, 1990, "The Evolving Role of Tax Policy in China", *Journal of Comparative Economics*, September, pp. 452–472.

Calvo, G. A. and J. A. Frenkel, 1991, "Transformation of Centrally-Planned Economies, Credit Markets and Sustainable Growth". Paper presented at a seminar on "Central and Eastern Europe: Roads to Growth", Baden

Austria, 15–18 April.

Dervis, K. and T. Condon, 1992, "Hungary: An Emerging Gradualist Success Story?" Paper prepared for the 1992 National Bureau of Economic Reasearch Conference, Cambridge, Mass., 26–29 February.

Giday, A., 1992, *A Privatizáció Elmúlt Két Éve.* (The Past Two Years of Privatization), Tulajdon Alapitvány – Privatizációs Kutatóintézet, Budapest.

Illés, I., 1992, "A Társadalmi Átalakulás és Szociális Rendszerek" (Transformation and Social Systems). Paper prepared for a conference on "Transformation and Social Challenges", organised by the University of Economics of Budapest, 22 May.

Kornai, J., 1992, "The Postsocialist Transition and the State: Reflections in the Light of Hungarian Fiscal Problems", *American Economic Review* 2, Vol. 82.

Matolcsy, G. (ed.), 1991, *Lábadozásunk Évei*, (The Years of Convalescence), Tulajdon Alapítvány – Privatizációs Kutatóintezet. Budapest.

Rodrik, D., 1992, "Making Sense of the Soviet Trade Shock in Eastern Europe: A Framework and Some Estimates". Paper prepared for the World Bank/IMF conference on the macro-economic situation in Eastern Europe. Washington DC, June.

Stiglitz, J. E., 1991, "Remarks on the Design of Financial Systems for the Newly Emerging Democracies of Eastern Europe". Paper prepared for the IPR-IRS conference "The Transistion to a Market Economy – Institutional Aspects", Prague, 24–27 March.

7

Stabilisation Policy in Post-Communist Bulgaria

*Michael L. Wyzan**

Introduction

As part of its transition to a democratic political system and a market economy, Bulgaria has since February 1991 been undergoing a bold exercise in economic stabilisation. Few would dispute the need for tough stabilisation measures in the face of the highly inflationary – often hyperinflationary – conditions that prevail in many East European[1] countries. However, in the absence of reliable data for a sufficiently long period to permit estimation of conventional macro-economic models,[2] and of any historical parallel to the transition process, it is

---

* Stockholm Institute of East European Economics. I wish to thank Mark Allen, Rumen Avramov, Rumen Dobrinski, Svetoslav. Gavriiski, Rumen Gechev, Emil Hursev, JJohn Kunstadter, Sten Luthman, Jan Mujzel, Mieczyslaw Nasilovski, Mario Nuti, Georgi Panaiotov, Dimitur Radev, Rosita Rangelova, Georgi Stoev, John Williamson, and Emmanuel Zervoudakis. The assistance and support of the US Embassy in Sofia and of the Centre for Bulgaristika are gratefully acknowledged. None of the above is responsible for the methods employed or conclusions reached herein, or for any statements attributed to them.

1. In this paper I refer to all European former CMEA members (including former Soviet republics) plus Albania and former Yugoslav republics as 'Eastern Europe'. The CSFR, Hungary, and Poland are termed the 'Northern Three', rather than 'Central Europe', as has become fashionable.

2. This is not to say that macro-economic modelling aimed at examining issues relevant to the transition to capitalism has not been attempted. Brada and King (1992) estimate consumption functions for the Northern Three in an effort to discern whether macro-policy has been overly restrictive, by which they mean whether the decline in production exceeded that engendered by exogenous shocks. Charemza (1992) investigates the causes of the stagflation in Poland after February 1990, focusing on whether market uncertainty engendered market failure. Although no attempt has been made to carry out such studies for Bulgaria,

all but impossible to ascertain *a priori* just how contractionary the policy should be.

A debate has emerged as to whether macro-economic policy has been 'too' restrictive in Eastern Europe. Gomulka (1991, p. 85), for example, concludes that 'with a more refined set of policies, a fall in industrial GDP [in Poland] could have been smaller, limited perhaps to 15 per cent instead of the actual 20 per cent'. Although Gomulka (1991, p. 85) adds that the 'right policies are much easier to define with the benefit of hindsight', Brada and King (1992, p. 51) argue more broadly that 'macroeconomic policy in the [Northern T]hree ... may well have been excessively deflationary'.

Such concerns may be especially relevant in the Bulgarian context, where the fall in production, at least as officially measured, has been extraordinarily large. Indeed, apart from Albania, the country has displayed the weakest economic performance in the region in the last two years, at least as officially measured. However, before one blames this situation entirely on mistakes by inexperienced and perhaps overzealous policy makers, it must be remembered that Bulgaria has also been beset by Eastern Europe's worst exogenous shocks. Moreover, Bulgaria's first two post-war non-communist governments inherited the most severe foreign-debt crisis in the region, and along with it the hostility of Western bankers engendered by the unilateral payments moratorium perpetrated by an earlier government in March 1990.[3]

With these factors in mind, this paper provides an examination of the stabilisation measures undertaken in Bulgaria, along with an early assessment of the degree of success of these measures. The first task is to describe the environment within which the Bulgarian stabilisation programme has been implemented, the measures that characterise it, and progress that has been achieved so far. The third section contains a comparison of Bulgaria's stabilisation efforts with those of Poland at the equivalent stage. I conclude with a brief discussion of whether there have been any avoidable policy mistakes.

---

one might mention Hughes (1991), who uses the 1988 Bulgarian input–output table to model the impact of structural reforms on the movement of prices.

3. A brief review of recent Bulgarian political history may be in order. Lawyer Filip Dimitrov formed a new government consisting entirely of members of his anti-communist Union of Democratic Forces (UDF) in November 1991, on the heels of the UDF's 'victory' in the October general elections (it had won 36 per cent vs. 33 per cent for the Bulgarian Socialist Party, i.e. the former communists). Until the autumn of 1992 the UDF and a party representing ethnic Turks had a narrow majority in the National Assembly. Dimitrov took over from Dimitur Popov, an independent but traditional-minded lawyer who had become Prime Minister at the head of a coalition government in December 1990, after the resignation of Andrei Lukanov, the last Bulgarian Socialist Party Prime Minister.

The Bulgarian Stabilisation Programme

Conditions Under Which the Programme was Implemented

The stabilisation programme described below had to be implemented under the worst imaginable peacetime economic conditions. The economy in 1990 was characterised by

> the worst fall in production in memory ..., full isolation from world financial markets, a moratorium on repayment on the foreign debt and the resultant hostile relations with private and official creditors, growing open inflation, enormous inflationary expectations and deficits, headlong dollarisation of the economy, an unnaturally low velocity of money, energy and resource shortages, and the collapse of traditional foreign economic ties (AECD, 1991, p. 2).

Note also that the switch to hard currency trading within the CMEA on 1 January 1991 had brought about a sharp fall in the terms of trade in an economy dependent on cheap Soviet oil for domestic usage (and for reexportation against hard currency).

Table 7.1 describes the domestic economic situation in 1990 in comparison with previous years. As can be seen from the table, all indicators deteriorated considerably in 1990. As they had over the 1986–89 period, nominal wages increased much faster than prices; serious open inflation emerged for the first time. Table 7.2 reveals the country's difficult hard currency balance of payments situation. The improved export performance over the period 1986–88 was largely the result of government subsidisation of exports, particularly of agricultural products. Such subsidisation, plus special investment credits, led to the large 1988 budget deficit evident in Table 7.1. The budget deficit had been cut in 1989 by reducing such credits. However, the deficit increased greatly as a share of GDP during 1990, as a result of a jump in interest payments on foreign debt, increased expenditure on social security and price subsidies, and a decline in profit tax collections as the economy deteriorated (Hughes, 1991, p. 161).[4]

Turning to the foreign sector, note from Table 7.2 that although in 1990 the current account deficit fell, this was due largely to a 22.2 per cent decline in hard currency imports, as compared with 'only' a 16.7 per cent decline in such exports. The capital account took a serious turn for the worse as amortis-

4. Another difficult aspect of the Bulgarian economic situation is the high ratio of pensioners to active population. In 1990 the ratio of the number of women over 55 plus the number of men over 60 – corresponding to the respective current retirement ages – to the number of women 15–54 plus the number of men 15–59 was almost 0.4. Moreover, the ratio of pensioners to the number employed is 0.63 (OECD 1992, pp. 19–20). However, the figures appear far less alarming if a retirement age of 65 is used for both sexes.

TABLE 7.1 The Bulgarian Domestic Economy 1986–1992

	1986	1987	1988	1989	1990	1991	1992
Aggregate Economic Indicators (unless stated otherwise, per cent increase from preceding year; constant prices)							
Net Material Product	5.3	5.1	2.4	-0.3	–17.5	–19.5	–20.0[a]
Gross Domestic Product	n.a.	5.3	5.4	2.4	–0.3	–9.1	–16.7
Gross Industrial Production	4.0	4.2	5.1	–2.6	–12.5	–21.7	–23.0[a]
Gross Agricultural Production	11.7	–5.1	0.1	–4.8	–3.7	–12.5	n.a.
Gross Fixed Investment	n.a.	n.a.	n.a.	–11.2[b]	–18.5	–48.6	n.a.
Retail Trade Turnover	3.5	4.0	1.9	0.8	–8.7	n.a.	n.a.
Retail Price Inflation[c]	2.7	2.7	2.4	6.4	26.3	480	44.8
Average Wages and Salaries	5.2	4.3	7.6	8.8	31.5	150	n.a.
Unemployment (1000s)[d]	n.a.	n.a.	n.a.	n.a.	65	419	507
Central Government Sector(% of GDP)							
Revenue	58.8	60.2	58.0	60.1	54.5	42.7	36.3
Expenditure	61.4	59.0	63.7	61.6	63.7	58.5	49.6
Deficit	–2.6	1.2	–5.7	–1.5	–9.2	–15.8	–13.3
Unpaid Interest on For. Debt	n.a.	n.a.	n.a.	n.a.	4.3	11.9	9.0
'Cash Deficit'[f]	n.a.	n.a.	n.a.	n.a.	–4.9	–3.9	–4.3

Notes: a. First six months of year.
b. Net fixed investment.
c. Annual average except 1992, which is for first seven months of year.
d. For 1990 and 1991, figures are for end of year; for 1992 it is as of 17 August.
e. Deficit less unpaid interest on foreign debt.

Sources: BNB *News Bulletin*, various issues; Grosser (1992); RFE/RL (1992, p. 91); *Demokratsiia*, 9 May 1992, p. 2; NSI, (1991);*Vecherni novini*, 30 May 1991, p. 1; *168 Hours BBN*, 1–23 August 1992; Gulubov (1992); OECD (1992).

ation due on foreign loans jumped from $2,330 million to $3,110 million and disbursements received by the Bulgarian Foreign Trade Bank (BFTB) and the country's commercial banks fell from $3,040 million to $125 million. A financing gap was avoided only by running down $888 million in reserves, an increase in arrears of $378 million, and deferral of maturities to the tune of $2,240 million.

Particularly troubling was the $10,000 million hard currency debt, which had more than doubled since 1986, while over the same period hard currency reserves had fallen from $1,180 million to a pitiful $125 million (IMF sources), and the debt-service ratio had risen to 145 per cent (see Table 7.2).[5]

5. During the late 1980s, Bulgaria switched from a net debtor to a net creditor in its transferable rouble dealings. Hughes (1991, p. 163) notes the 'extent to which the country was borrowing convertible currencies in order to sustain exports to other CMEA countries funded by matching loans.'

TABLE 7.2 Bulgarian Foreign Economic Activity, 1986 –1992

(unless stated otherwise, thousands of millions of US dollars)	1986	1987	1988	1989	1990	1991	1992
			Balance of Payments				
Convertible Currency[a] Exports	2.70	3.30	3.54	3.14	2.62	3.74	2.29[c]
Convertible Currency Imports	3.50	4.20	4.51	4.34	3.37	3.78	1.86[c]
Trade Balance	–0.80	–0.90	–0.97	–1.20	–0.75	–0.04	0.43[c]
Current Account Balance	n.a.	–0.70	–0.80	–0.84	–1.31	–1.15	–0.89
Capital Account Balance	n.a.	n.a.	1.88	0.60	–2.68	–1.12	n.a.
Financing Gap	n.a.	n.a.	n.a.	n.a.	n.a.	–1.98	n.a.
			Other Statistics				
Gross Debt	4.70	6.10	8.20	9.20	10.0	11.60	n.a.
Gross Official Reserves	1.18	0.85	1.46	1.01	0.13	0.75[b]	n.a.
Net Interest Payment	0.30	0.40	0.34	0.56	0.69	0.83	n.a.
Debt Service Ratio (%) [d]	n.a.	n.a.	69	92	145	83	n.a.
Exchange Rate (leva/$) [e]							
Basic	0.90	0.83	0.83	0.81	2.77	n.a.	n.a.
Commercial	1.15	1.24	1.64	2.02	7.00	n.a.	n.a.
Non-commercial	1.62	1.24	1.64	2.02	9.80	n.a.	n.a.
Unified	n.a.	n.a.	n.a.	n.a.	n.a.	21.72	22.23

Notes: a. Including transactions in convertible currencies within CMEA.

b. Result of adding to $125 million, hard currency reserves at end of 1990, $358 million increase in Bulgarian National Bank reserves and $266 million increase in reserves at Bulgarian Foreign Trade Bank and commercial banks, in 1991.

c. First six months of year.

d. Sum of net interest payments plus amortisation due (including unpaid amount), as per cent of exports of goods and services for convertible currency. For 1991 $1,072.1 million in exports under dollar clearing agreements is excluded from the denominator; if such exports are included the 1991 figure is 61 per cent.

e. For 1986–91: exchange rates are for end of year; for 1992: for 28 August.

Sources: BNB (1992a); *Otechestven vestnik*, 28 August 1992; *24 Chasa*, 1–2 August 1992.

The structure of the debt was unfavourable, with 85 per cent of it owed to the London Club of commercial lenders (Letter of Intent, 1992a, paragraph 40), largely in the form of short-term credits; in 1990 alone $3,106 million was owed in amortisation (BNB, 1992, p. 23). At the same time, Bulgaria was owed a total of $2,357 million by such countries as Iraq, Libya, and Syria, which were unlikely ever to repay their loans (Pishev, 1991, p. 109). Under these circumstances, a unilateral moratorium on principal repayments was called in late March 1990, with similar action taken on interest payments three months later.

The Content of the Stabilisation Programme

After Bulgaria joined the IMF and the World Bank in September 1990, the Lukanov government began the country's first Article IV consultations with the former, which were continued by the Popov regime in January 1991. In February the country's first Letter of Intent was filed; it requested a twelve-month stand-by arrangement worth $394 million in five tranches (Letter of Intent, 1992a); the request was approved in March. Since Bulgaria was bereft of hard currency reserves at the time, the 'use of IMF resources was the only possibility for partial recovery of [those] reserves ... [a] possibility [that] could certainly be used only under specific conditions required by the IMF' (Andonov, 1992, p. 1).

The original Letter of Intent from Finance Minister Ivan Kostov and BNB Chairman Todor Vulchev to the IMF laid out the priorities of the stabilisation programme. The overall goals for 1991 were to arrest the decline in production so that recovery would begin by the second half of the year; to reduce inflation to 1–2 per cent monthly by the second half of 1991; and to limit the 1991 current account deficit to $2,000 million. The two nominal anchors were domestic credit and incomes policies; note that the exchange rate was not charged with such a role, due to the lack of reserves and of access to external financing. The elements of the stabilisation programme were as follows:

– price reform to eliminate the monetary overhang and to correct distorted relative prices;

– creation of a unified, flexible and market based exchange rate and liberalisation of most current account transactions;

– limited growth of nominal wages, so that real wages decline at the beginning of the programme and domestic demand is kept in check;

– adherence to strict nominal targets for the budget deficit and restructuring of revenues and expenditures to reduce the economic weight of the state; and

– tight credit via steep increases in nominal interest rates, to be relaxed in the second half of 1991 to 'support a cautious recovery in output [in] the second half of the year' (Letter of Intent, 1992a, paragraph 8).

The programme's assumptions for various aggregate magnitudes are listed in Table 7.3. Many targets, even ignoring for the moment the 'Result' column, were ridiculously optimistic. For example, that 'recovery' would occur by the second half of 1991 is highly implausible, given that under Poland's similar stabilisation programme in 1990 GDP fell by 12 per cent, vs. an expected 3.1 per cent (Laski, 1992, p. 8); it fell by a further 8–10 per cent in 1991 (Laski, 1992, p. 2). The expectation that inflation would be 1–2 per cent monthly by the second half of the year was also unjustified. While in Poland a monthly inflation rate of 1.5 per cent was expected for the fourth quarter of 1990, the

TABLE 7.3 The Bulgarian Stabilisation Programme for 1991: Assumptions and Results

	Assumption	Result
GDP growth	–11%	–22.9%
Retail price inflation	200%	480%
Real income (pub. sector) growth	–35%	–48%
Unemployment	5% (annual average)	10.5%(end of period)
		6.4% (annual average)
M2 growth	25.5%	24%
Income velocity of money	2.3	1.8
Budget deficit as share of GDP	3.5%	7.0%
Exchange rate (leva/$)	7–10	15–22
Convertible currency exports (% change)	–28%	42.9% (incl. clearing with former USSR) 1.9% (not incl. clearing with former USSR)
Convertible currency imports (% change)	25%	12.1% (incl. clearing with former USSR) –16.6% (not incl. clearing with former USSR)
Addition to foreign exchange reserves	$500 million	$624 million ($358 at BNB; $266 at BFTB[a] and commercial banks)
Current account deficit	–$2,000 million	–$886.9 million
External finance	$1,600 million	$600 million

Note: a. Bulgarian Foreign Trade Bank.

Sources: BNB (1992, pp. 23–25); Grosser (1992); Hristov (1992); Letter of Intent (1992a); PlanEcon (1992a); WIIW (1992, pp. 15–23).

actual rate was 5.5 per cent (Laski, 1992, p. 8), and the monthly average for 1991 was 4.1 per cent (WIIW, 1992, p. 20).[6]

6. None of this implies that a reforming former centrally-planned economy must have a high level of inflation. For example, in Czechoslovakia after prices were liberalised on 1 January 1991, retail price inflation was down to 2 per cent monthly by April (WIIW 1992, p. 16). In the Czechoslovak case, however, the economy was undoubtedly relatively well balanced when communism fell.

As elsewhere in Eastern Europe, the programme called for radical *price liberalisation*. Only the prices on goods accounting for 10 per cent of total retail and wholesale trade turnover in 1989 were subject to state administration, namely electricity, heating, petroleum, butane and propane gas and coal. In order to bring the prices of these energy products into line with world level, however, they were increased enormously for industrial (household) users: 222–270 (50–108) per cent for petroleum, 308 per cent for propane and butane gas, 420 (339) per cent for electricity, 1,325 (650) per cent for coal, and 817 (400) per cent for heating. For vital foods – flour, bread, meat and meat products, vegetable oil and sugar – and passenger transport fares, which together made up 18 per cent of retail turnover, prices were increased administratively by an average of fivefold, and subsidies were eliminated.[7] Government intervention would be indirect and rely on market instruments (except for flour, bread, and transport fares, where direct control would continue) and occur in sectors characterised by monopoly power (Letter of Intent, 1992a, paragraphs 10 and 46).[8]

Turning to the *external sector*, a 'major deterioration' of the country's current account was anticipated. The combined effects of the worsening of the terms of trade due to the new payments arrangements in the former CMEA, loss of market share in the CMEA and the Middle East crisis were put at $3,500 million. In view of the expected trade deficit and the need to replenish the reserves and service the debt, the importance of 'the assistance and cooperation of ... private creditors, multilateral institutions, and foreign governments' was stressed. Declines in exports and imports of 28 and 25 per cent, respectively, and a widening of the current account deficit to $2,000 million, were anticipated (Letter of Intent, 1992a, paragraphs 35–36).[9]

An increase in the country's gross official reserves of $500 million was targeted. It was anticipated that Bulgaria would be able to reschedule all of its debt service obligations to official creditors; it would seek to defer all service on its debt to commercial banks. Even with such debt relief, however, $1,600 million would be needed in new foreign credit. The government would not seek to reschedule short-term trade credits guaranteed by export credit agencies. A willingness was expressed to honour 'in due course' the demand of the London Club for a sovereign guarantee of the Club's portion (85 per cent)

7. Despite the attempt to maintain a degree of control over the prices of essential items, during January 1991–February 1992 the prices of the 14 such items went up by 150–200 points more than the overall retail price index (BNB, 1992, p. 44).

8. An anti-monopoly bill, similar to such statutes elsewhere in Eastern Europe, was passed in May 1991. By winter 1992, 137 large enterprises under the (since split up) Ministry of Trade and Industry were broken into 1,121 smaller ones (Andonov, 1992, p. 9). Unfortunately, the splitting up of national monopolies in food processing seems to have created a set of regional monopolies.

9. Presumably, the Letter of Intent is referring here to total convertible currency exports and imports, including trade with the former USSR, as of 1991 on a dollar-clearing basis.

of the debt, although it would be requested that the payments moratorium be extended at least to the end of 1991 (Letter of Intent, 1992a, paragraphs 37–40).

On 1 February 1991, a unified exchange rate was introduced, as was a decentralised system of foreign exchange allocation based on an inter-bank market. Lacking foreign exchange reserves, it was decided to let the exchange rate float. The programme pledged to eliminate gradually the remaining restrictions on current account convertibility. Enterprises were authorised freely to purchase foreign exchange from commercial banks, although full repatriation of foreign exchange receipts was required within a month of delivery of exports. Restrictions on the allocation of foreign exchange to Bulgarians travelling abroad were reduced but not eliminated (Letter of Intent, 1992a, paragraphs 12–15).[10]

All quantitative import restrictions were abolished and the granting of import licences was made automatic, except for a restricted set of products.[11] Enterprises were free to trade directly with foreign partners without the intercession of foreign trade organisations (Letter of Intent, 1992a, paragraphs 16–17). Formal registration of foreign trade transactions was eliminated, so that only the filing of customs declarations was required (Andonov, 1992, p. 7).

The Lukanov government's attempt to run an *incomes policy* having been an abysmal failure (see Table 7.1), wage indexation and a Polish style excess wage tax (see, e.g. Dabrowski, 1991, p. 122) were foresworn in favour of limits on state enterprise wage bills. On 1 February 1991, wages were raised by an average of 65 per cent. All workers received an addition to their monthly wages of 270 leva, reflecting the increase in the cost of a minimum basket of commodities engendered by the price increases for the items in the basket. It was hoped that a recovery in real wages might take place later in the year, provided that inflation had been brought under control. Beginning on 1 July 1991, individual wages would be determined by negotiations between workers and employers at the enterprise level (Letter of Intent, 1992a, paragraphs 18–19).

There were three *fiscal policy* goals: (1) to reduce the budget deficit to 3.5 per cent of GDP (from almost 13 per cent);[12] (2) sharply to reduce government debt to the banking system; and (3) significantly to reduce the shares of GDP accounted for by both government expenditure and revenue, largely by a 'reduction of the redistributive role of the state budget' (Letter of Intent,

10. As of January 1992 Bulgarian citizens can buy up to 10,000 leva worth of foreign currency when they travel abroad (Andonov, 1992, p. 8).

11. However, a special export tax was placed on 26 goods (mostly industrial raw materials and clothing), and an import surcharge of 15 per cent was levied on most imports. The export taxes were eliminated in June 1991 and the import surcharges were removed in May 1992 (OECD, 1992, p. 40).

12. The figures in Table 7.1 are more recent ones from Gulubov (1992) and do not match those contained in the Letter of Intent.

1992a, paragraphs 21–22). Price liberalisation would make possible a reduction in subsidies from 16 per cent to 3 per cent of GDP: retail price subsidies were eliminated, except for heating; subsidisation of enterprise losses would fall from 7.7 per cent to 2 per cent of GDP; and export subsidies to former CMEA states would be limited to those under a recent trade agreement with the USSR. Further savings would be realised by limiting the government wage bill, dismissing 22,000 government employees, and cutting the period of service for military inductees. Defence spending would fall from 5 to 4 per cent of GDP (Letter of Intent, 1992a, paragraph 26). The profit tax was reduced to 40 per cent and the turnover tax streamlined in preparation for the introduction of a value-added tax.

In the sphere of *credit and monetary policy*, a number of steps would be taken in order to eliminate the monetary overhang. These included a privatisation programme for small establishments, sales to the public of long term government bonds, a reduction in bank credit to the government, early repayment of housing and consumer loans at concessional interest rates and price liberalisation. To prevent the establishment of expectations of high inflation, tight credit and high nominal interest rates – from 4.5 per cent at the end of 1990, the BNB's refinance rate hit 45 per cent in early February – were to be applied (Letter of Intent, 1992a, paragraph 30), which stirred the wrath of owners of private firms (see, e.g. *Duma*, 11 March 1991, pp. 1–2).[13] It was expected that the income velocity of money would rise to a level in line with that in developed market economies.

As regards the *social safety net*, the Letter of Intent notes that expenditure on unemployment compensation would increase from 22 million leva in 1990 to 768 million leva in 1991, sufficient to support an average annual unemployment rate of 5.5 per cent. Such compensation was to be financed by enterprise contributions to the already existing unemployment fund. Benefits would be payable over nine months, but taper off over time to provide an incentive to find new work. Child allowances were nearly tripled, the minimum old-age pension more than doubled and indexed to inflation, and other categories of assistance (e.g. to the disabled) increased commensurately (Letter of Intent, 1992a, paragraph 42).[14]

The Results of the Stabilisation Programme

The economic situation has turned out to be far worse than anticipated over the year and a half that has elapsed since the programme was introduced. As a glance at Table 7.3 shows, inflation has been much stronger, the decline in

13. All references of this type are to Bulgarian newspapers or radio broadcasts.

14. Additional paragraphs of the Letter dealt with energy, privatisation and enterprise restructuring, agrarian reform and financial sector reform. In the interest of space, these matters are not dealt with here.

output far more severe and prolonged, unemployment rather higher, the budget deficit larger, the lev weaker, and the supply of external finance smaller, than expected. During 1991, aggregate output generally ran at about 80 per cent of the figure for the equivalent month of 1990; during 1992, the figure has fallen to around 75 per cent. During both 1991 and the first half of 1992, aggregate output (as measured by Net Material Product, a mainstay of Marxian accounting) fell by about 20 per cent and industrial production by 22–23 per cent. Unemployment has risen inexorably, from slightly over 100,000 (a rate of about 2.5 per cent) at the start of the programme to slightly over 500,000 (12.5 per cent) by August 1992.

Although the retail price index rose by only 2.5 per cent in April 1991, inflation took off again with a vengeance in June 1991 (5.9 per cent) as a result of energy price hikes, and was not below 3 per cent again until July 1992. May 1992 was a particularly bad month, as electricity and heating prices were raised by 35 per cent and coal prices by 25 per cent (OECD, 1992, p. 39). A further jump in inflation is likely due to the increase in July in the average trade weighted tariff from 8 to 17 per cent (OECD, 1992, p. 42).

In the realm of *fiscal policy*, the output decline, fall in real incomes, and disappointing supply of external finance had obvious implications for the budget deficit and for domestic interest rates. Moreover, the weaker than anticipated lev necessitated unexpectedly large energy subsidies and foreign interest payments.[15] Mention should also be made of the following factors: the practice of covering the bad loans of enterprises; expenses related to agricultural reform and property restitution; larger than anticipated operating losses in electricity generation; delays in putting in place the new energy prices; and increased social insurance spending due to growing unemployment (interview with Dimitur Radev of the Ministry of Finance, 23 March 1992; Hristov, 1992, p. 5; Letter of Intent, 1992c, paragraphs 3–5).

As can be seen from Table 7.1, the 'cash deficit', that is, the deficit excluding unpaid interest on foreign debt, was 4.2 per cent of GDP in 1991: despite a substantial fall in expenditures as a share of GDP, revenue fell even more. 1992 will be similar to 1991: a cash deficit of below 10 per cent of GDP, with substantially reduced expenditures and revenues. At mid-year, the 1992 budget projections seemed on target, with 41.2 per cent of the year's projected revenue received, and 41 per cent of the year's projected expenditures made (Bulgarian Telegraphic Agency (BTA), 13 July 1992, 17:38 GMT). Tax reform was to be one of the highest legislative priorities in the second half of 1992: laws on tax administration and tax procedures and on personal income,

15. Steps taken during 1991 to contain the budget deficit included doubling the ceiling prices for petroleum and liquid fuels and raising the prices of electricity and coal by 70 per cent, leaving home heating as the only subsidised form of energy (Letter of Intent, 1992b, paragraphs 5 and 6). In addition, a number of administrative measures were taken to increase tax rates and improve the efficiency of tax collection (Letter of Intent, 1992c, paragraph 6).

profit, value added and excise taxation – all effective from 1 January 1993 – were expected to be passed (*Demokratsiia,* 25 August 1992, p. 1).

A particularly challenging aspect of budget policy has been attempting to maintain sufficiently high spending on the social safety net to keep the affected individuals above subsistence without making the fiscal imbalance any worse than it already is. Due among other things to the high old-age dependency burden (see note 4), pensions account for 70 per cent of total social security expenditures. Overall, social security spending in 1991 reached 24 per cent of total government expenditures, up from 19.4 per cent in 1990, contradicting to a degree the effects of reducing subsidies from 24 per cent to 7.4 per cent of such expenditures (OECD, 1992, p. 18). By mid-year there was considerable popular concern, fanned by the former communists, among whose supporters the elderly are especially well represented, that pensions were falling too dramatically in real terms. Although the government denied that pensioners were suffering disproportionately, in July pensions were adjusted upwards so that their average level was brought closer to the average wage, and their differentiation was increased (*Demokratsiia,* 7 August 1992, pp. 1–2)

Monetary policy remained tight: the BNB raised its refinance rate from 45 per cent to 52 per cent in June (Letter of Intent, 1992b, paragraph 14) and to 63 per cent at the beginning of 1992 (Andonov, 1992, p. 5). The other tool of monetary policy was tight credit ceilings imposed on banks, especially during the first two quarters of 1991. These ceilings are set individually for each bank taking into account the share that bank had in overall credit at the end of the previous year (AECD, 1992, p. 7).

Early in 1991 most aggregate monetary targets showed an extraordinary tightening of monetary policy. During the first quarter, there was a fivefold drop in real credit, and it was not until June that the nominal value of credit reached its December 1990 level. Over the year net domestic credit in real terms fell by 78 per cent, while M2 declined by 66 per cent, and the income velocity of M1 rose from 2 to 3.6 and that of M2 from unity to 1.8 (Hristov, 1992, p. 4). Moreover, there is evidence that real interest rates have been positive since March 1991, especially for long-term investors who face high intermediation costs (Letter of Intent, 1992d, paragraph 23). As it turns out, however, the BNB has been reducing its refinance rate over the course of 1992, from 54 per cent to 49 per cent in July, and to 45 per cent in August (*168 Hours BBN,* 10–16 August 1992, p. 3). The reason for this apparent policy shift is said to be the desire to give privatisation an 'early start' and to revive productive investment (Letter of Intent, 1992d, paragraph 23).[16]

16. Two related issues that are somewhat beyond the scope of this paper, but none the less extremely important, are financial sector reform and consolidation of the banking system. Bulgaria at the moment has over 80 'commercial' banks, many of which have balance sheets full of non-performing loans to insolvent enterprises; the value of such loans has been put as high as 20 per cent of 1991 GDP. The government's strategy for financial

As for the state of *labour relations*, during the first six months of the stabilisation programme, 'the social consensus held ... despite [the great compression of real incomes, which is] a testimony to the patience of the population' (Letter of Intent, 1992b, paragraph 12). Under the January 1991 Tripartite Agreement between the trade union confederations (Podkrepa and the Confederation of Independent Trade Unions of Bulgaria), the government and representatives of management and the private sector (the Tripartite Commission), there was to have been no industrial action for six months.

By early June, however, the first of several Podkrepa walk-outs at Tripartite Commission meetings occurred, as it demanded wage guarantees and higher minimum wages. That same month the confederations reached an agreement with the government – but not with management – that called for the state to turn the wage setting process over to negotiations between management and labour by 1 July (in fact such bargaining only began in November (Andonov, 1992, p. 4)), and raised the minimum wage, while the unions agreed not to hold general strikes (BTA, 13 June 1991, 20:34 GMT). New principles of wage-setting were to go into effect, combining free bargaining at the enterprise level over wages beyond the minimum level and strict financial discipline. Wage differentials were to widen somewhat after their initial sharp reduction at the onset of the stabilisation programme (Letter of Intent, 1992b, paragraph 13).

The government of Filip Dimitrov started off on the wrong foot with the trade unions by announcing that it would negotiate with organised labour over only traditional trade union concerns. Stating that the 'trade unions will never participate in executive power', Dimitrov discontinued the regular meetings of the Tripartite Commission (*Vek* 21, 4 February 1992, pp. 1, 5). Podkrepa soon began to demand the resignations of cabinet members, partly in connection with the disbandment of the Commission; it withdrew from the Tripartite Agreement in February (*Podkrepa,* 19 February 1992, p. 1). As part of a cabinet reshuffle in late May, the position of deputy prime minister in charge of relations with the trade unions was created, as was a National Council for Social Partnership, a new version of the Tripartite Commission (BTA, 25 May 1992, 15:54 GMT).

In the realm of *foreign trade and payments*, by the late summer of 1991 the first notice was made of a 'structural shift in trade towards competitive international markets, although at a much reduced level of trade' (Letter of Intent, 1992c, paragraph 10). Any attempt to compare Bulgarian foreign trade flows between 1991 and earlier years is extremely difficult due to the shift in payments methods with countries from the former CMEA, the existence of a

---

sector reform involves merging the banks so that their numbers reach about ten, recapitalising them by writing off non-performing loans and guaranteeing them principal and interest payments on loans made before January 1991 (OECD, 1992, p. 25).

number of rouble/dollar cross exchange rates and the wide discrepancies between trade flows reported on a customs basis and on a payments basis.[17]

None the less, it is clear that Bulgarian foreign trade suffered the worst collapse in the region. PlanEcon (1992b, p. 1) estimates that in 1991 on a payments basis exports dropped by 48 per cent and imports fell by 62 per cent, whereas on a customs basis the declines are 60 per cent and 74 per cent, respectively.[18] Since there is reason to believe that the custom-based statistics substantially understate trade flows, PlanEcon (Report, 1992b, p. 6) holds that the payments based ones are more reliable. There was also a considerable re-orientation of trade away from the former USSR; officially exports to that destination fell from 64 per cent to 50 per cent of total exports (OECD, 1992, p. 43). On the other hand, the author's contacts in the Bulgarian private business community insist that an enormous amount of trade, especially with the former USSR, is going unreported.

Bulgaria is said to be the only reforming former CMEA member that has a completely floating exchange rate. It is true that at the start of the stabilisation programme the country was so bereft of hard currency reserves that central bank intervention in the foreign exchange market was impossible. It is also the case that the country's foreign advisers failed to stress early on the need for a stabilisation fund for the lev and that foreign lenders did not offer to help create one. It is not widely appreciated, however, that the BNB has been tenaciously buying dollars in order to add them to the country's hard currency reserves, which have gone from $125 million at the start of the stabilisation programme to $952 million (*Otechestven vestnik,* 24 August 1992, p. 2). This has, of course, had the effect of keeping the lev weak, which is a desirable for exporters but makes balancing the budget more difficult. In August 1992, Kostov and Vulchev publicly aired a difference of opinion as to whether the BNB should intervene in the foreign exchange market in this fashion (see, e.g. *Demokratsiia,* 21 August 1992, p. 1).

Turning to Bulgaria's relations with its *foreign creditors*, the country reached a ten-year rescheduling agreement with the Paris Club of official creditors, which, it will be recalled, holds 15 per cent of the debt, in April

---

17. Out of concern over the rising trade surplus with the former USSR it was decided in June 1991 to float the clearing dollar, which depreciated between August and December by 40 per cent (OECD, 1992, p. 78). According to presidential economic adviser Boian Slavenkov, the former USSR owes Bulgaria about $500 million (*Otechestven vestnik,* 6 August 1992, p. 2).

18. The figures in Table 7.3 on exports and imports reflect the fact that beginning in 1991 much of Bulgaria's trade with the former USSR (and other former CMEA states) is denominated in convertible currency. Thus, for example, convertible currency exports were actually up by almost 43 per cent if one includes clearing trade with the USSR and, even if one does not, such exports increased by almost 2 per cent. Such measured increases should not be seen as contradicting the enormous declines in overall trade flows described by PlanEcon.

1991. This agreement provided only a broad framework within which Bulgaria was to strike agreements with individual foreign governments by the end of March 1992. The process of reaching these individual agreements proved very cumbersome during 1991, when the Assembly had to approve them; however, a law was subsequently passed allowing the Council of Ministers to lead all discussions as it saw fit. Agreements have recently been reached with a number of nations, including one in May with the German government for the rescheduling of its 136 million D-Mark worth of the debt (*Demokratsiia,* 9 May 1992, p. 1).

The remaining $8,500 million debt that is owed to 308 commercial banks remains one of the country's most severe economic problems. For example, since the March 1990 payments moratorium, foreign banks have been unwilling to guarantee trade credits and investments in the country. Meanwhile, Bulgaria has been deferring payment via a series of three month roll-overs for the past two years. The major bone of contention has been the London Club's demand that the Bulgarian government and the BNB guarantee the debt, which was borrowed by the formally independent BFTB. In December 1991, Deutschebank, which has been heading the bank advisory committee dealing with Bulgaria, threatened to quit the committee if such a guarantee were not forthcoming (*Demokratsiia,* 6 December 1991, p. 1). The government responded by stating that it 'will seek to provide such guarantees when the creditor banks specify the conditions for rescheduling and converting Bulgaria's foreign debt' (BTA, 9 December 1991, 19:43 GMT).

Although this crisis seems to have blown over, matters are far from settled. Negotiations have been held in the spring and summer, with each side advancing its own proposal; IMF and the World Bank representatives, whom the Bulgarians have taken to be supportive of Bulgaria's position, have been in attendance (*Demokratsiia,* 15 May 1992, p. 2). The heart of the banks' proposal is that Bulgaria immediately begin repayment of the interest on its debt and only at a later stage deal with the overall debt problem in the context of a solution to the country's overall economic problems. Bulgaria, on the other hand, holds quite reasonably that it cannot extricate itself from its current economic predicament unless the debt dilemma is resolved.[19] Meanwhile, even with the expected receipt of $197 million in structural adjustment assistance from the World Bank, a further restructuring of Paris Club obligation and the receipt of funds committed by, but not obtained from, the G-24 during 1991, a $500 million financing gap will remain for 1992 (Letter of Intent, 1992d, paragraph 9).

19. This material is based on an interview with Svetoslav Gavriiski of the Ministry of Finance in Sofia, 22 June 1992. Bulgaria's preferred solution to its debt problems includes buying back some of the debt with funds borrowed from international financial organisations.

Finally, there is the matter of *assistance from international bodies*, both bilateral and multilateral.[20] As noted above, Bulgaria has received considerably less such assistance than it had expected: out of $1,600 million that it had expected to obtain during 1991, only $600 million materialised. Bulgaria received $394 million from the IMF in stand-by assistance under the March 1991 agreement, and another $131 million under the IMF's Compensatory and Contingency Financing Facility. In August 1991 the World Bank granted a structural adjustment loan worth $250 million in two tranches of $150 million and $100 million; the Bank has also provided $17 million in technical assistance. The European Bank for Reconstruction and Development made its first loan to Bulgaria in March 1992: about $50 million for the energy sector. One source of disappointment was the fact that the non-EC members of the G-24 (above all Japan and the USA) failed to come up with the matching funds for the $400 million offered by the EC members under an agreement of early 1991. In October the EC states decided to grant the $400 million that they had promised even though only $186 million had been paid by the non-EC states.

More recently, the IMF and the World Bank have made the granting of additional resources to Bulgaria conditional on various actions on the country's part. For example, in March the Fund stated that a second twelve-month $212 million stand-by credit would be made available if by mid-April the privatisation and budget laws had passed and if the government had come up with a mechanism to control the growth of wages (*Otechestven vestnik,* 16 March 1992, p. 1). The funds were indeed granted in April. The World Bank has been holding up the release of the second tranche of its $250 million credit out of disappointment with the lack of progress in land restoration, the absence of a privatisation law, the failure to implement new banking regulations and the lack of a legal mechanism for regulating the social insurance system (*Demokratsiia,* 26 May 1992, p. 2).

A Comparison with Poland

The Polish experience with economic stabilisation, which began almost exactly a year before its Bulgarian counterpart, is in many ways rather similar. Both countries continue to be beset by unacceptably high inflation and, at least until very recently in the Polish case, declining production. They have had smimilar unemployment rates (between 10 and 20 per cent). Both have re-oriented their trade away from their erstwhile CMEA partners, although Poland so far has done more successfully. Both have exchange rates that, although considerably devalued, have moved downward since the start of stabilisation by less than their respective country's rates of inflation would suggest. Both are at present

20. I am indebted to Sten Luthman for much of the information on foreign assistance given here.

running budget deficits that are similar shares of GDP, although, of course, one of the hallmarks of 1990 in Poland was the virtual attainment of a balanced budget.

What of the content of the two programmes? One difference is that in Poland there were three nominal anchors – a wage freeze, limited monetary expansion, and a fixed exchange rate (Gomulka, 1991, p. 73) – vs. Bulgaria's two – domestic credit and incomes policy. Moreover, the famous Polish 'popiwek' progressive tax on wage increases (see, e.g. Dabrowski, 1991, p. 122) was eschewed in Bulgaria in favour of direct controls on the wage bills at state enterprises.

More significantly, as discussed above, Bulgaria alone among the East European countries opted for a floating exchange rate. The ostensible reason for doing so, of course, was the absence of convertible currency reserves. As noted by Hughes (1991, p. 174), however, this 'is not a very convincing objection since the foreign exchange market is relatively thin, so that the scale of any intervention need not be large'. In any case, it is interesting to examine the extent to which the Polish and Bulgarian currencies have depreciated since the start of the countries' respective stabilisation programmes. The zloty was set at 9,500 to the dollar in January 1990 (Lipton and Sachs, 1990, p. 113); the average figure for July 1991 was identical. The lev went from 15,205 to the dollar in February 1991 to 22,230 in August 1992 (i.e. over the equivalent time period since the inauguration of stabilisation), a depreciation of 31.6 per cent.

Thus, if the movement of the value of the currency over the first twenty months of stabilisation is examined, Poland has had a more stable currency and probably avoided the additional inflationary impetus from currency depreciation. However, by July 1992 the zloty has depreciated to 13,525 or by 29.8 per cent. Accordingly, a slightly longer term perspective suggests that the degree of depreciation may be similar in the two countries.

Another difference between the countries, one impossible to quantify, is that overall systemic change, especially in the sphere of privatisation, has gone much further in Poland. Indeed, the economy of Poland has always been far more market oriented, as indicated, for example, by the dominance of private agriculture there. Moreover, Poland already resembles a capitalist country, in that political instability is apparently not sufficient to chase away foreign investors, whereas in Bulgaria political stability has to date not been sufficient to attract them. Still, the implications for economic stabilisation of having, say, a 25 per cent privatised formerly socialist economy rather than a 10 per cent privatised one are not entirely clear. On the whole, therefore, one wonders whether there really is all that much difference between the experiences of Bulgaria and Poland to date in the realm of stabilisation.

Conclusions

Have there been any avoidable mistakes? One candidate for the distinction of 'avoidable mistake' is the failure to create a stabilisation fund for the lev. Indeed, as discussed above, the BNB seems recently to have been doing what it can to keep the lev as weak as possible. There seems to be a consensus among informed observers (see, e.g. Hughes, 1991) that a significant part of Bulgaria's particularly high inflation has been the result of its undervalued currency. As it turns out, a stabilisation fund for the lev is scheduled to be created by 1993.[21]

Another debatable aspect of the Bulgarian programme is the failure fully to liberalise the setting of energy prices, which are periodically raised to reflect international market conditions. Such prices continue to have the potential to cause significant inflationary shocks. Moreover, when and if the exchange rate reacts to the increased inflation in May and June 1992, further inflationary impulses will be generated by increases in the prices of imported energy and in interest payments on the foreign debt. To be fair, however, one must acknowledge the difficulty of attempting to force domestic consumers to face changes in international energy prices while keeping the standard of living from falling to unacceptably low levels.

What of the Bulgarian foreign trade regime, which observers agree is almost completely liberalised? There are those who argue that going directly to free trade prices without any 'transitional protection' was a mistake on Poland's part, one that it has subsequently been forced to undo (see, e.g. Williamson, 1992). Bulgaria did not go as quickly to a completely liberalised regime, but by now has come close to achieving one. Some observers wonder whether an economy like Bulgaria's, undergoing a very slow privatisation and restructuring without significant foreign investment, should not offer its enterprises more transitional protection than it has. However, the collapse of Bulgarian foreign trade and of overall production during 1991 are consistent with extremely severe external shocks and with a contractionary macro-policy, but not with an 'overly' open economy. One would expect such an economy to be characterised by surging imports and declining production in sectors producing for the domestic market. The former is certainly nowhere to be found, even taking into account the slight improvement in the foreign trade sphere in the first half of 1992.

Another debatable feature of the management of the macro-economy was the initially hostile attitude of the Dimitrov regime toward the trade unions. Without their cooperation in ensuring social peace no lasting stabilisation programme will be possible. Finally, the continuing large budget deficits raise

---

21. In the negotiations with the London Club the banks have insisted that Bulgaria use its reserves in any debt buy-back schemes. This fact and the one in the text about the creation of a stabilisation fund are from the 24 March interview with Svetoslav Gavriiski of the Finance Ministry.

eyebrows. None the less, given the enormous fall in revenues that has occurred, it is probably unrealistic to expect the government to be able to balance the budget. If Bulgaria has a bigger budget deficit than certain other East European states, it may well be because the collapse of its economy has been more pronounced.

At a broader level, doubts are often expressed concerning the content of the conventional IMF-type stabilisation programme. As mentioned above, high nominal interest rates have been a very unpopular feature of the programme, especially with entrepreneurs. Some Western economists argue that high interest rates lead to perverse incentives and adverse selection. More specifically, such rates favour investments with short pay-back periods and high profit margins, while discouraging borrowing by enterprises with positive net worth and encouraging it by insolvent ones, which often borrow to repay the interest on older loans. This phenomenon is undeniably a factor in the collapse of productive investment in the last two years. On the other hand, it is difficult to see how banks could have attracted deposits with interest rates much below what they actually were.

Has economic activity been contracted 'excessively' by the authorities, as other authors have asserted has happened in the Northern Three (Gomulka, 1991; Brada and King, 1992)? Bulgarian data do not allow a precise answer to this question, especially so short a time after the inauguration of the stabilisation programme. Demand-side factors that have contributed to the decline in production include the loss of markets in the CMEA, the terms of trade loss engendered by the shift within the CMEA to trade at world prices, the collapse of investment and the draw-down of inventories. Of course, the last two factors are to a large extent the result of conscious policy on the part of the authorities. Supply-side factors, also related to policy, include the effects of price liberalisation on relative prices and a sharp fall in imports.

It is clear, therefore, that the economy is more depressed than it would be simply on the basis of exogenous shocks. However, the country's continuing severe inflationary tendencies, budget problems, tight external financing constraint and growing inter-enterprise credit (as a substitute for bank finance) all militate against the authorities distracting their attention from economic stabilisation. In any case, at least another year or so of observing macroeconomic data will be required before one can say anything definitive about the appropriate degree of fiscal and monetary restrictiveness.

Of more enduring concern, perhaps, is how to manage the macro-economy over the long period during which a high proportion of major enterprises will remain in state hands (even if they have formally been 'commercialised' or 'corporatised'). Must macro-policy keep the economy in recession for several years in order to fight the hyperinflationary tendencies inherent in a transitional economy? The supporters of the 'shock therapy' approach argue that trying to reflate the economy along Keynesian lines will not work in such an economy because of the low or zero supply elasticities characterising state enterprises (see, e.g. Dabrowski, 1991; 1992; for a dissenting view, see Mujzel, 1992). In any case, recent encouraging news on the production front from the Northern Three suggests that there is nothing that militates that a reforming economy must experience a long period of negative economic growth.

On the other hand, the economies of Balkan states like Bulgaria, generally poorer and more isolated from Western markets – due to product mix and quality and to the physical barriers raised by the wars of Yugoslav succession – than those of the Northern Three, may experience at least four or five years of officially-measured decline. This is not necessarily as catastrophic as it seems. Bulgaria's relatively high unemployment suggests that structural change is occurring, even in the absence of significant privatisation and even of functional bankruptcy procedures. Moreover, since the ability of a country's statistical authorities to measure private sector activities, both domestic and foreign, is closely related to the extent of economic reform before communism fell, Bulgarian data must be viewed especially sceptically. For example, according to the OECD (1992, p. 52), trade partner data show that Bulgarian foreign trade statistics miss a third of the country's exports and almost half of its imports.

All things considered, economic stabilisation in Bulgaria has probably been managed about as well as one could have hoped, given the country's dreadful external environment and lack of experience in running a market economy. What is needed now is significant progress on structural reform and a little compassion and flexibility on the part of the country's commercial creditors. The country's continuing political stability and the commitment of its leaders to far-reaching reform provide some grounds for optimism.

References

AECD, 1991, "V Godinata na Zheliaznata Ovtsa", Agency for Economic Co-ordination and Development, Sofia, December.

_____, 1992, *Monthly Business Survey*, Agency for Economic Coordination and Development, Sofia, May.

Andonov, A., 1992, "Managing the Transition from the Centrally-Planned Economy: The Case of Bulgaria". Paper presented at the Conference on Management Development of Centrally-planned Economies in a New Global Environment, Overseas Development Institute, London, 1–3 April.

BNB, 1992b, "Statistics and Analyses", *News Bulletin*, Bulgarian National Bank, 1–15 February, pp. 23–25.

_____, 1992a, "Statistics and Analyses", *News Bulletin*, Bulgarian National Bank, 16–29 February, pp. 44–45.

Brada, J. C. and A. E. King, 1992, "Is There a *J-curve* for the Economic Transition from Socialism to Capitalism?", *Economics of Planning* 25, pp. 37–54.

Charemza, W. W., 1992, "Market Failure and Stagflation: Some Aspects of Privatisation in Poland", *Economics of Planning* 25, pp. 21–36.

Dabrowski, M., 1991, "The Polish Stabilisation Programme: Accomplishments and Prospects", *Communist Economics and Economic Transformation* 3, pp. 121–133.

_____, 1992, "Interventionist Pressures on a Policy Maker During the Transition to Economic Freedom (Personal Experience)", *Communist Economies and Economic Transformation* 4, pp. 59–73.

Gomulka, S., 1991, "The Causes of Recession Following Stabilization", *Comparative Economic Studies* 33, pp. 71–89.

Grosser, I., 1992, "Falling into Slumpflation", Mitgliederinformation, Wiener Institut für internationale Wirtschaftsvergleiche 3, pp. 12–16.

Gulubov, N., 1992, "Biudzhetnata politika na Bulgariia kato chast ot stabilizatsionnata programa". Unpublished manuscript.

Hristov, L., 1992, "Bulgarian Stabilization Program and Performance in 1991". Paper presented at the Conference on The Future of Democracy in Bulgaria and the Transition to Market Economy. US Chamber of Commerce, Washington, DC, 4 March.

Hughes, G., 1991, "Foreign Exchange, Prices and Economic Activity in Bulgaria", *European Economy*, pp. 157–17.5 (Special Edition No. 2).

Laski, K., 1992, "Transition from Command to Market Economies in Central and Eastern Europe: First Experiences and Questions", Wiener Institut für internationale Wirtschaftsvergleiche, Forschungsberichte 181, March.

Letter of Intent, 1992a, "Letter of Intent of the Bulgarian Government to the IMF" (of 14 February 1991), *News Bulletin*, Bulgarian National Bank, 16–29 February 1992, pp. 2–34.

Letter of Intent, 1992b, "Letter of Intent of the Bulgarian Government to the IMF" (of 9 May 1991), *News Bulletin*, Bulgarian National Bank, 1–15 March 1992, pp. 7–15.

Letter of Intent, 1992c, "Letter of Intent of the Bulgarian Government to the IMF" (of 14 August 1991), *News Bulletin*, Bulgarian National Bank, 16–31 March 1992, pp. 1–10.

Letter of Intent, 1992d, "Letter of Intent of the Bulgarian Government to the IMF" (of 11 March 1992), *News Bulletin*, Bulgarian National Bank, 16–30 April 1992, pp. 1–17.

Lipton, D. and J. Sachs, 1990, "Creating a Market Economy in Eastern Europe: The Case of Poland", *Brookings Papers on Economic Activity*, pp. 75–147.

Mujzel, J., 1992, "Two Years of Poland's Economic Transformation and the Problems of Recession". Mimeo.

NSI, 1991, *Statisticheski godishnik na Republika Bulgariia 1991*. Sofia: Natsionalen Statisticheski Institut.

OECD, 1992, *Bulgaria: An Economic Assessment.* Paris: Organisation for Economic Co-operation and Development.

Pishev, O., 1991, "The Bulgarian Economy: Transition or Turmoil", in Sjöberg, Ö. and M. L. Wyzan (eds), *Economic Change in the Balkan States: Albania, Bulgaria, Romania and Yugoslavia.* London: Pinter Publishers, pp. 101–114.

PlanEcon, 1992a, "Bulgarian Monthly Economic Monitor", *PlanEcon Report* 8, May.

_____, 1992b, "Bulgarian Foreign Trade Performance in 1991: Trade Collapses to Less than One-Half the 1990 Level", *PlanEcon Report* 8, August.

RFE/RL, 1992, "Economic and Business Notes, 8–13 April 1992", *RFE/RL Research Report* 1, April, pp. 91–93.

Sjöberg, Ö. and M. L. Wyzan, 1991, "The Balkan States: Struggling Along the Road to the Market from Europe's Periphery", in Sjöberg, Ö. and M. L. Wyzan (eds), *Economic Change in the Balkan States: Albania, Bulgaria, Romania and Yugoslavia.* London: Pinter Publishers, pp. 1–15.

WIIW, 1992, Mitgleiderinformation, Wiener Institut für internationale Wirtschaftsvergleiche 4, pp. 15–23.

Williamson, J., 1992, "Why Did Output Fall in Eastern Europe?". Paper presented at the Arne Ryde Symposium on the "Transition Problem", Rungsted Kyst, Denmark, 11–12 June.

Wyzan, M. L., 1989, "The Recent Performance of the Bulgarian Economy", in Joint Economic Committee, US Congress, *Pressures for Reform in the East European Economies*, Vol. 2. Washington, DC: US Government Printing Office, pp. 169–185.

_____, 1991, "The Bulgarian Economy in the Immediate Post-Zhivkov Era", in Sjöberg, Ö. and M. L. Wyzan (eds), *Economic Change in the Balkan States: Albania, Bulgaria, Romania and Yugoslavia.* London: Pinter Publishers, pp. 83–100.

8

Some Issues on Macro-Economic Stabilisation Policy in the Economies in Transition

*Dragomir Vojnic**

Introduction

The first thing that I would like to emphasise at the beginning of my discussion concerns some of the inevitable problems and limitations surrounding macro-economic stabilisation in the economic and political transition in the ex-socialist countries. These problems are wellknown, but it seems useful to review them here. Essentially there is no theory that would define the scientific foundations of the 'Economies and Politics of Transition'. Likewise, there is no practical experience that could be used in outlining a corresponding economic policy. In actual practice we are witnessing only the first uncertain steps in an attempt to define such a theory and to acquire the relevant practical experience.

Despite a lot of discussion of these problems in the past two years we are still far from a theoretically verified synthesis. Since we are actually only at the very beginning of the transition processes in the ex-socialist countries, such expectations would be highly unrealistic. In the search for the appropriate methods, trials and errors are unavoidable. This will of course contribute to the increasing price of the transition processes. However, they are a historical necessity.

---

* Zagreb University, Institute of Economics-Zagreb.

Some Theoretical Limitations

The second thing I would like to underline is the fact that in defining various aspects of the macro-economic policy of transition, we are actually using certain segments of traditional economic theory. A justification for this approach may be found in the interpretation of the main causes of the overall crisis of socialism and the bankruptcy of the bolshevik option.

In this respect, I have in mind in the first place that from the first day socialism has broken with some of the historical trends of our civilisation. Three of these trends may be mentioned, each connected with a corresponding pluralistic feature:

(1) pluralism of markets in the sense of an integral market,
(2) pluralism of ownership with the dominance of private ownership, and
(3) pluralism of political structure in the sense of the multi-party parliamentary democracy ensuring the function of the corresponding legal system.

The fundamental task of the economics and politics of transition is to restore these broken trends and thereby to stimulate the development of the ex-socialist countries of Central and Eastern Europe so as to achieve the model of the market democracy (Macesich, 1991).

This may be taken as a justification for the use of classical or traditional economic theory as a basis for creating the macro-economic policy of transition and stabilisation. It is however hardly necessary to emphasise that the application of this theory, particularly in the first stage of transition, was met by a number of limitations. The main source of these limitations lies in the essentially different macro-economic environment in which the ex-socialist countries start their transition processes in comparison with the environment that prevailed at the time when contemporary macro-economic theory was shaped.

Pluralisation of the Market and Ownership in the Light of Some Historical Controversies

The third element that I would like to discuss is related to the problems that have to be solved by the economics and politics of transition.

The basic task of economic transition is the enhancement of economic efficiency through the pluralisation of markets and ownership. The main task of political transition is to increase political democratisation and human freedoms through multi-party parliamentary democracy which ensures the functioning of the legal system itself.

Both theory and practice demonstrate a high degree of interdependence of these phenomena. Without market and ownership pluralism, there is no economic efficiency nor political democratisation. In the history of our civilisation, the pluralism of ownership with the dominance of private ownership has been a basic obstacle to monopolies of any kind. This is true both of the market monopoly and of the monopoly of the political power.

In the ex-socialist countries, only one of these interrupted historical trends has been restored: parliamentary democracy. The market and ownership pluralisms are therefore the main objectives of the economics and politics of transition.

In this respect it is important to underline a historical contradiction. New democratic governments in the ex-socialist countries, through their own initiatives, legislature and political decisions directed at the privatisation of ownership, must create a natural barrier to any monopoly including that of their own political power. This is a new phenomenon and a historical challenge.

All these elements, which are otherwise well known, are mentioned here in order to attract attention to the great differences in the macro-economic environment which existed when classical macro-economic theory came into being and which now exist in the ex-socialist countries that are attempting to achieve economic and political transition. It is therefore also clear that the behaviour of the relevant factors in the society and economy in the ex-socialist countries is very different from the behaviour of contemporary developed countries of the market economies. This is true of the behaviour of the population, of the workers and managers, and of the producers and consumers, as well as of the government and its agencies.

It is therefore self-evident that the same or similar measures of the macro-economic policy will not have the same effect on both groups of countries.

Such problems and controversies must, however, be taken into account, because at the present stage they are unavoidable. In consequence the transition costs will be increased.

Some Limitations Caused by the Tradition of the 'Soft Budget Constraint'

The fourth element that I wish to stress is concerned with the characteristics, problems and difficulties common to all ex-socialist countries and expressed in the form of low economic efficiency. The other side of the medal in the pretransitional period was the unsatisfactory political democratisation and the lack of human rights and freedoms. The main cause of the low economic efficiency was the dominance of state (or social) ownership and the non-existence of factor markets for labour and capital. Even the market for commodities and services was relatively underdeveloped. It is quite evident that in a situation of centrally-planned allocation of investments and capital, the role of the central and business banks and of the whole financial system was fundamentally different from that of the classical market economy. Especially marked were those differences in the monetary and fiscal spheres which were closely interrelated. Through selective and concessional credits, monetary policy assumed the role played by fiscal policy in the market economy.

All this, and especially the state distribution of investments and capital, was a negation of the motivation system based on profit. The losses incurred by enterprises were socialised. The responsibility for losses was taken over, directly or indirectly (through prices, credits and subsidies) by the state. A prominent theoretician of transition, Janos Kornai, used the concept of the 'Soft Budget Constraint' to describe this situation. His generally accepted recommendation for the macro-economic policy of transition is to transform the 'soft budget constraint' into the 'hard budget constraint' (Kornai, 1986, and 1989).

Transition Crisis and Problems of Crisis Management

My fifth remark is related to a number of specific scenarios used by the countries in transition in their macro-economic policy.

All ex-socialist countries have created the essential legal conditions for the transition. The legal framework is similar to that of the market democracies. However, the non-existence of the sufficiently developed factor markets, especially for capital, is a great obstacle.

Being unable to go simultaneously into privatisation and to establish and develop labour and capital market institutions, the majority of ex-socialist countries have decided to undertake simpler measures which amount to classical measures of liberalisation, primarily involving the liberalisation of prices and imports, or foreign trade in general.

As a rule, the liberalisation of foreign trade is based on a radical devaluation of the currency and on pegging a fixed exchange rate for the German mark in terms of the US dollar. This has a preventive influence on inflationary expectations. However, at the same time it is a major challenge (and test) for macro-economic stabilisation policy. But, owing to the large structural deformations, especially in terms of price relations, the movement towards a general liberalisation has actually intensified all aspects of the transitional crisis (Dubravski and Duj, 1992). In addition, major problems of indebtedness in most countries in transition must also be taken into account. The worsening of the transitional crisis expressed itself especially in declining production and investments and in increasing inflation and inflationary pressures. This is caused by the increasing number of loss-making enterprises as well as those that have to be liquidated as a result of investment failures.

In these circumstances, a fall in salaries and living standards is inescapable. Hence liberalisation is inevitably accompanied by a large number of economic and social problems which require political agreements and a political consensus.

Aware of this, all governments of ex-socialist countries are trying to achieve their transition policy on the basis of a political consensus. The experiences discussed at several international conferences have illustrated the overwhelming importance of political agreements and of political consensus in overcoming problems of the transitional crisis and social tensions.

In this connection I would like to refer to several international conferences which have dealt with the topic of the 'Economics and Politics of Transition' and where I myself have also taken part. They were held under the auspices of the Vienna Institute for Comparative Economic Studies in Tübingen (Germany) and in Marianske Lazni (CSFR),[1] and also by the Hoover Institution (Stanford University). Such conferences were also held in London and Frankfurt under the auspices of the International Centre for the Study of the Transformation of Central and Eastern Europe in Zagreb.[2] These conferences were concerned with the common characteristics of the transitional crisis and, at the same time, with the issues concerning macro-economic policy measures, in particular monetary, fiscal and exchange rate policies, as well as income policies.

Generally, there was a high degree of unanimity regarding the key role of the restrictive monetary and, in a sense, competitive fiscal policy. It was frequently pointed out that monetary policy should not only be restrictive and hard, but also 'merciless'. It should, however, also be mentioned that a wide

---

1. Vienna Institute for Comparative Economic Studies. The International Workshop on European Economic Interaction and Integration, sponsored by the Vienna Institute for Comparative Economic Studies, has been run for more than twenty years. The materials and proceedings of the conferences of this workshop which are held each year in another country, are issued in special books by the Publishing House MacMillan, London.

2. More detailed information on this Centre can be found in Vojnic and Puhovski (1992), "Economic and Political Dimensions of Transition", *Ekonomski pregled* 3–4, Zagreb.

range of views and opinions, in favour of and against the prevailing strategy of the macro-economic stabilisation policy had been expressed at these conferences.

The essential segments of this policy, also favoured by the IMF, are as follows:

(1) radical suppression of inflation,
(2) balanced state budget and the elimination of the budget deficits,
(3) balanced and competitive exchange rate policy.

As is wellknown both from the theoretical and practical viewpoints, these are the means used to lay the foundations of the market economy with respect to providing an efficient allocation of resources (investments and capital) and the basis of future development. This was also at the heart of the stabilisation programme adopted in 1989 in former Yugoslavia and, on more or less the same basis, immediately after that in Poland and Hungary, and somewhat later in the CSFR. Similar programmes have also been prepared in the former USSR, in Bulgaria and in Romania.

The execution of the programmes in these countries in the course of 1990 and 1991 was, in addition to the high degree of liberalisation of prices and imports, primarily directed at a radical reduction in inflation. In different countries, the results were different. However, a high price had to be paid for them which consisted in a drastic fall in production and employment. The average rate of the fall in production in the countries of Central and Eastern Europe in 1990 amounted to more than 8 per cent and in 1991 to more than 16 per cent. In other words, production in these countries had been reduced to 75 per cent of the level attained two years before.

The situation in the countries of transition is actually still worse because in the last decade they were seriously lagging behind in their economic and technical development. Only in the course of the last six years the gap between the CSFR, Hungary and Poland on the one side, and Austria on the other, measured in per capita GDP, has increased by nearly one-third. Large devaluations of national currencies in order to strengthen external liquidity and to accomplish the stabilisation programmes have given rise to these differences in per capita GDP, measured at existing exchange rates and purchasing power parities. According to the existing exchange rates, per capita GDP in 1990 in relation to Austria was only about 8 per cent in Poland, 14 per cent in the CSFR and 15 per cent in Hungary (Laski, 1992). Such a drastic fall in production has only previously been recorded during the great crisis in 1929–33. Let me mention only in passing that the stabilisation programme in Israel, 1985–89, did not cause any fall in GDP. Similar stabilisation programmes were also carried out at the same time in Mexico and Argentina.

As for the former Yugoslavia, the inflation rate in the first half of 1990 was reduced from more than 50 per cent per month (December 1989) to practically nil. Foreign currency reserves increased to more than $US8 billion. Because it was tied to the D-Mark at a fixed relationship of 1:7 a limited convertibility of the dinar was achieved. GDP fell about 10 per cent. The fall in employment was less than GDP, which means that labour productivity fell. During the second half of 1990, major problems in the execution of the programme arose because of disruption to the political consensus. At the beginning of 1991 the programme collapsed altogether and the limited convertibility of the dinar was abandoned.

Had the stabilisation programme been continued, it is very likely that the same or similar problems would have arisen as in other ex-socialist countries which are now in the process of transition. Let us take the example of Poland. In 1991, GDP was about 22 per cent lower than in 1989. The rate of decline of industrial production was still larger. The inflation rate in 1991 was drastically reduced (in 1990 it had reached 250 per cent). A limited convertibility of the zloty (based on $US) was introduced, and was accompanied by highly restrictive monetary and fiscal policies and by a policy of wages and salaries control. A sharp devaluation produced favourable effects on the balance of payments position.

However, as in the case of the former Yugoslavia, the problems were sharpened due to the large pressures to maintain the parity between the existing exchange rate for the zloty and gross labour costs (wages, salaries and taxes). In the absence of adequate labour and capital market institutions, the inertia of the self-management inevitably affects the rise in wages and salaries. As a result, pressure grows to change the fixed relationship of the national currency to the dollar. A new devaluation may establish a new equilibrium, but at a higher price level.

This scenario and the accompanying problems are already 'classical' and not specific only for Poland.

Some Characteristics of the Transitional Crisis in New States

The sixth element that I wish to discuss is related to some special problems of the macro-economic stabilisation policy in the new countries. As an example, I will take my own republic Croatia where the problems are additionally intensified because of the destructive effects of the war. The total war damage of about $US20 billion exceeds by one-quarter pre-war GDP.

Political and monetary independence was achieved at the end of 1991. Attempts were made to formulate the macro-economic stabilisation policy on the same or similar basis as in the former Yugoslavia. The policy of transformation from the soft to the hard budget constraint was also continued as far as the new war conditions allowed.

The new conditions had both positive and negative sides. The positive side was of course political and monetary independence. The obligation to transfer 2 per cent of GDP to the less developed parts of former Yugoslavia was also abolished. Similarly, the withdrawal of 2 per cent of GDP on account of the emission profit (seigniorage) was also eliminated.

The negative aspects stem from the loss of the former Yugoslavian market. It is expected that the GDP in 1992 will reach around 60 per cent of the pre-war level in 1989. Simulation analyses have shown that about 50 per cent of this loss was caused by war destruction, and the remaining 50 per cent by lost markets, both in former Yugoslavia and in other ex-socialist countries.[3]

In such circumstances, Croatia is faced with great problems in pursuing its macro-economic policy which, on the other side, is a precondition for receiving the financial support from the international financial institutions, in the first place from the IMF and the World Bank. But without this support, it is not possible to carry the through the stabilisation programme, having in mind the especially large costs of the war that was imposed on the country.

A large rise in public spending could only be covered by a large increase in taxes. Before the war in Bosnia and Hercegovina, there were more than 300,000 refugees in Croatia. The war in Bosnia and Hercegovina has led to a substantial increase in this number. The humanitarian aid covers only one part of this cost. The monthly rate of inflation is around 15 per cent. In such circumstances, a recent devaluation of the dinar with the introduction of the floating rate was decided.

Similar problems are also encountered in neighbouring Slovenia, albeit in a better environment, since there is no war there. They actually expect to attain a limited convertibility of their new currency (tolar).

Macro-Economic Stabilisation Policy and Development

The seventh point, I wish to raise is the question whether it is possible to attain on this basis the level of stabilisation that would give rise to more efficient

3. See Rohatinski, 1992 (ed.), *Current Economic Developments and Economic Policy* 10, Narodna banka (National Bank) and Economic Institute-Zagreb.

growth and development.

In all ex-socialist countries, the trend of falling production is still predominant. There is no answer as to when and on what conditions this trend could be reversed and a new growth cycle started. The experience of some countries (Mexico and Chile) point to a multi-year gap between stabilisation and growth. Even the experience of Israel is not much better. These rather pessimistic considerations require a constant critical evaluation of the existing standard segments of the macro-economic stabilisation policy, carried out especially by the IMF.

Without calling into question the validity of this policy it seems advisable to single out and underline the following elements:

(a) in the transition process it is not possible to put into effect the liberalisation of prices and imports without a very active economic policy,

(b) in addition to the monetary and fiscal spheres, this policy must comprise in the first place, an income policy which includes the control (even administrative if necessary) of wages and salaries;

(c) the behaviour of both managers and workers in the enterprises of the ex-socialist countries is still fundamentally different from the behaviour of equivalent groups in the market democracies. These differences are rooted in the absence of labour and capital market institutions. Both managers and workers will undertake everything (especially where the traditions and inertia of self-management persist) to increase wages and salaries. In doing so, they are as a rule very insensitive to the price of money and credit, irrespective of whether it is used for the pay of employees or for investments.

In such an environment, the standard measures of macro-economic policy are, to put it mildly, less effective than in market democracies. Nevertheless, such measures must be included in the programme, but at the same time they must be propped up by an active economic policy including direct administrative controls. The stringent need for such economic policy measures will be diminished by the introduction of privatisation and labour and capital market.

All this means that the countries in transition will have to make large efforts to ensure the success of their stabilisation policy.

In spite of the great number of common and similar problems, the cost of the stabilisation policy will differ from country to country. It is already clear that a higher price will be paid by the new independent states as is the case with my own country, Croatia, which was pushed into war against its will.

In any case, the success of the macro-economic stabilisation policy in any country of transition will depend to a decisive extent on the ability of the government to ensure a general national support by means of a political consensus.

Some Problems of Theoretical and Methodological Character

My eighth point concerns questions and dilemmas of a more theoretical and methological nature which are, however, of great importance to the macro-economic policy of stabilisation.

As is well known, the phenomenon of inflation is of a multi dimensional character. The dominant role is sometimes played by cost push inflation, and sometimes by demand pull inflation. In transition, the inflationary processes of the ex-socialist countries are also dominated by structural characteristics. A great number of the structural weaknesses in these countries find expression in low economic efficiency, high production costs and an absence of competitiveness in international markets.

The concept and strategy of the macro-economic stabilisation policy recommended by IMF and the World Bank place the greatest emphasis on demand inflation. Although such an approach may be, on the whole, justified, some other specific moments must also be taken into account.

Stabilisation programmes based on the liberalisation of prices and imports, by their very nature, provoke a cost inflation. Moreover, most of these programmes also include significant rise in the prices of energy and of money and capital. Real interest rates, an active interest rate policy and a real exchange rate policy therefore constitute essential parts of the stabilisation programmes. They have of course an impact on the increase in prices of domestic and imported goods. Furthermore, in most cases, the unit labour costs are also pushed up because the decline in wages and salaries and employment is slower than GDP and, as a consequence, labour productivity weakens.

The purpose of outlining these elements is not to disparage the approach of the IMF and the World Bank, with which in essence I agree, but to attract attention to the other side of the coin as well.

Conclusion

The question must be asked where adequate solutions may be found. According to the transition processes in the ex-socialist countries, as we have known them by now, it seems that the following aspects should be stressed:

1. The success of all macro-economic stabilisation programs depends in the decisive manner in which governments in the countries of transition are prepared to implement resolutely the concept of the 'hard budget constraint'. Monetary policy must be 'ruthless'.

2. In these conditions, the chances of success are greater if continuous financial support is assured. This argument runs also in the reverse direction. The governments will namely receive more financial support if their stabilisation policies are carried through more consistently;

3. In the absence of labour and especially capital market institutions, it cannot be expected that the stabilisation programme in any ex-socialist country will succeed in one round;

4. The influence of cost inflation, particularly in situations of low living standards and large social tensions, given the inertia of self-management workers' rights, will require an iterative procedure to organise and repeat the stabilisation programmes. Even Israel, in much better circumstances, has not succeeded within a single stabilisation programme;

5. The experience of the East German provinces is the only one that deviates from the above pattern. The specific reasons and conditions are well known and they do not fit into the framework envisaged by the IMF and the World Bank;

6. The key question for the countries in transition is not stabilisation as such, but the development and growth of the country. This is particularly important at the present stage of transition in most ex-socialist countries when the level of living standards is lower and social tensions are higher than previously;

7. Economic theory and practice should provide an answer to the question whether the interdependence between stabilisation and development in this transition phase should be treated in the same way as in the developed countries of the market democracies, or should be treated in a more flexible way, for the sake of the successful transition itself.

The answer to this question is of the utmost importance for the countries in transition and for the IMF and the World Bank as well, because the transition processes of restructuring the supply side through the privatisation are slower than expected, except in Hungary;

8. It seems likely that a more flexible approach to the stabilisation programme could only be accepted, or at least justified and tolerated, in cases when increased production within a stringent control of inflation is directed to exports rather than consumption;

9. Concluding considerations suggest a theoretical and practical verification of the view that a given lower inflation rate would be an acceptable price for the increase in production that is devoted totally to exports. According to modern development theory, exports are characterised by the greatest development multiplier;

10. Without glorifying the monetaristic approach it is necessary to accept

the view that a restrictive, hard and ruthless monetary policy must play a key role in the stabilisation programme irrespective of the differences in the macro-economic environment in developed countries or in the countries in transition.

Finally, it should be pointed out that both economic and psychological reasons underline the importance of achieving a maximal success in the stabilisation policy in the first attempt. Nevertheless, the repetition of the process must also be taken into account. Great importance must also be attached to the encouragement of the enthusiasm for a succesful stabilisation policy and to the suppression of an atmosphere of passive resistance and lost perspective. This is highly important because the social costs of transition, particularly in certain countries, are likely to be higher than previously assumed by some theoretical calculations.

References

Dubravski, D. and U. Duj, 1992, *Macroeconomic Policy and Transitional Crisis*. Economic Institute-Zagreb.

Kornai, J., 1986, *The Soft Budget Constraints*. Kyklos, pp. 3–30.

_____, 1989, "The Affinity Between Ownership and Coordination Mechanisms – The Common Experience of Reform in Socialist Countries" in *Problems of the Economic Development and Economic System of Yugo slavia*, Vol. IV. Zagreb: Globus and Economic Institute, pp 120–132.

Laski, K., 1992, "Transition from Command to Market Economies in Central and Eastern Europe: First Experiences and Questions", *The Vienna Institute for Comparative Economic Studies* 183, March, pp. 14–24.

Macesich, G., 1991, *Reform and Market Democracy*, New York: Praeger.

Rohatinski, Z. (ed.), 1992, *Current Economic Developments and Economic Policy* 10, Narodna banka (National Bank) and Economic Institute-Zagreb.

Vojnic, D. and Puhovski, Z., 1992, "Economic and Political Dimensions of Transition", *Ekonomski pregled* 3–4. Zagreb.

9

Private Mechanisms for the Creation of Efficient Institutions for Market Economies

*Paul H. Rubin**

Introduction

Scholars studying the transition from socialism to the free market generally agree that an important requirement for success is the creation of appropriate legal institutions (e.g., Litwack, 1991; Fisher and Gelb, 1991; Svejnar, 1991. See also the articles in Clague and Rausser, 1992). They also agree that this will be quite difficult. I accept both of these premises as a starting point. However, I believe that there are methods of creating efficient institutions which other scholars have neglected, so that the problems may not be quite so difficult as it appears.

One contribution of this paper is to argue that in many cases there is a possibility for the creation of private alternatives to a formal legal system which will make this transition simpler. To the extent that private parties can themselves create efficient legal rules, then there will be less need to wait for the state to pass appropriate legislation. Thus, private creation of efficient institutions can speed up the process of conversion. It can also increase incomes during the time of the transition.

There are two parts to the analysis proposed here. First, there is a discussion of private actions which managers of existing or new firms can take in order to engage in transactions. The second major point in the paper is that there are implications of these mechanisms which go beyond private enforcement. Private mechanisms can develop into formal public mechanisms. The

* Emory University, Atlanta, Georgia.

state can provide proper incentives for private organisations to create efficient legal rules and institutions (Landes and Posner, 1979). It can also adopt mechanisms which make it more likely that the legal system will itself create efficient rules. Indeed, North (1990) argues that the difference between states which are economically developed and those which are not is in the details of the evolutionary process for rules of exchange.

Much of the analysis is based on a study of actions taken by firms in developed countries which have been successful in creating valuable rights (Rubin, 1990). While some managers in developed economies are aware of the nature of these actions, learning about them may be costly for managers in new economies. Moreover, in developed countries the process of establishing efficient institutions has been time consuming and costly. If managers in new economies can learn about successful policies and rules for establishing such institutions, then they can develop more quickly than otherwise. Just as new enterprises can adopt technologies which have been developed elsewhere, so can they profit by adopting mechanisms for reducing transactions costs which have originated in developed economies.

It is also important to note that even in developed countries, explicit enforceable (and enforced) contracts are relatively unimportant. To the extent possible (and it is a large extent) business rely on agreements and do not use enforceable contracts (Macaulay, 1963; Telser, 1980). Thus, the lack of enforceability in many circumstances will present less of a problem and imply less difference between developed and new economies than might appear.

The lessons from developed countries may have additional importance in newly privatized economies. Even under communism, trade and transactions existed. However, many transactions were illegal or semi-legal, and there were benefits to secrecy. Thus, traders developed mechanisms to maintain secrecy, such as reliance on relatives or members of one's own ethnic group for trading (Landa, 1981). In an economy where trade is legal, it will be beneficial for traders to develop more open links and links to additional trading partners. The proposals here will assist in developing such links.

The Problem

In Eastern Europe[1] the legal system is not adapted to problems of free contracts between businesses and others, either other businesses or consumers. There may not be adequate courts and, even if there are, there is not an existing body of precedent aimed at efficient enforcement of agreements. (For a

1. In what follows, I will generally not distinguish particular countries in either the former Soviet Union or the former Satellites. The level of analysis is sufficiently general to cover all economies which lack certain legal institutions.

discussion of the meaning of efficiency in contract enforcement, see Posner, 1986, Chapter 4.) While there are mechanisms which sometimes lead to the evolution of efficient rules in such contexts (Rubin, 1977), these mechanisms may not always work (Rubin, 1982). When the mechanisms do work, they operate by imposing marginal changes on the existing body of law. If we begin with a situation in which there is little or no law, then the operation of unaided evolutionary mechanisms may take longer than is desirable or feasible.

The key class of problems facing potential traders in a world with no contract enforcement are problems of opportunism (Williamson, 1985; Rubin, 1990). In a transaction, one party will have performed his part of the deal before the other, who will then have an incentive to cheat in some way. One key purpose of the law of contracts is then to discourage such opportunism (Muris, 1981). The latter, in its crudest form, may simply refuse to make an agreed-upon payment. More sophisticated forms of cheating include offering high quality goods for sale and delivering low quality (Ackerlof, 1970). A firm may also put a trading partner in a position where the partner is dependent on the firm for some input, and then raise the price, an action called 'holdup'. The general form of opportunism is appropriating the 'quasi-rents' associated with some transaction (Klein, Crawford and Alchian, 1978).

The main cost of opportunism in a context lacking contractual enforcement is not the cost of cheating, or even the cost of precautions taken to avoid being victimised. Rather, it is the lost social value from the deals which would be profitable but which do not get done. To the extent that mechanisms can be designed and adopted which reduce or eliminate such opportunism, then social wealth can be greatly increased.

This paper deals with private mechanisms for solving the problems associated with opportunism in transactions. Private mechanisms are limited in their power. Without efficient government enforcement, it will be impossible to exhaust all potential gains from trade. Thus, in one sense, the proposals here can be viewed as second-best approaches to efficient transacting in a situation in which the state is unable to enforce contracts efficiently.

However, in another sense the proposals may be in some ways superior to state contractual enforcement. This is because the state can err in its enforcement mechanisms. For example, if the governments in Eastern Europe were to try to write a set of contract laws, they would undoubtedly get much of the law wrong from an efficiency perspective. As we will see below, with private contracting, there will be possibilities for competing courts for dispute resolution. This mechanism will allow for quick evolution of efficient law and may ultimately be superior to a rapid adoption of a flawed legal code.[2]

---

2. For example, the current US law is seriously flawed in many dimensions. See, for discussions of some errors, Epstein (1985); Priest (1985); Rubin (1982).

Unilateral Mechanisms

These are mechanisms which one firm by itself can use to commit itself to refrain from cheating. The exact application of unilateral mechanisms will generally be to firms selling consumer goods. Sellers can be manufacturers, who will create reputations in the brand name of their products, or retailers, who will create reputations in the name of their store. The general principle – that reputations can guarantee that the firm will not cheat – will apply in the bilateral and multilateral context as well.

The major mechanism available to a firm to establish its honesty is the creation of a reputation for honest behaviour (Kreps, 1990; Rubin, 1990). A reputation is a valuable asset, and the value of the asset is lost if the firm cheats. In the context of this analysis, a firm wants to be able to credibly commit itself to offering high quality goods for sale. Cheating is claiming to offer high quality goods but actually selling low quality. (In a labour context, cheating might be violating a promise not to discharge a worker to avoid paying a pension.) This can be profitable in the short run for the firm. Unless there is some reason not to do so, then the firm will cheat in this way. However, buyers, knowing that this form of cheating will occur, will not believe the firm's promise to offer high quality goods. Therefore, since some buyers would be willing to pay for high quality, there is a real social loss if the firm cannot credibly promise to offer high quality.

If a firm can invest in creating a reputation for high quality, then there will be a return on this investment. The investment will pay as long as the firm does not cheat. The firm may appear to be earning profits, but these are merely a return on the investment. There are various unilateral mechanisms a firm can use to create a reputation. The key is to create some firm-specific capital which will become worthless if the firm cheats. Then this capital is the investment in reputation which guarantees that the firm will not cheat.

Advertising is one form of investment (Klein and Leffler, 1981). Advertising the brand name of the firm, even if the adverts convey no additional information, indicates that the firm plans to offer high quality. If it does not, then the investment in advertising becomes worthless because consumers will no longer shop at the firm. There are other investments which can serve a similar function. Firms can invest in expensive signs or logos, which again become worthless if the firm cheats. Law firms invest in expensive decor, which serves the same function. Firms can also offer high quality items for sale at the price of low quality items for a time in order to induce consumers to try the product. Consumers will do so because they have nothing to lose even if the firm cheats (since they are paying the price for low quality). Once a reputation has been created, it can be extended to additional products.

Firms can also take advantage of reputations of trading partners. Reputations can be created at either the manufacturing or at the retail level. A retailer can benefit by carrying products of manufacturers which have already established reputations. Conversely, a manufacturer can benefit by selling his product through a retailer who has established a reputation. If there is explicit contracting regarding reputation transfers, then the actions are bilateral (as discussed in the next section), but a firm can also unilaterally benefit from this mechanism.

The key to the use of these mechanisms in a new economy is that *they do not require any government enforcement.* The firm unilaterally creates an investment in its brand name, and this investment is lost if the firm cheats. Firms in Eastern Europe could begin using such mechanisms tomorrow, with no change in legal institutions or rules.

Bilateral Mechanisms

I deal with three issues relating to bilateral arrangements: self-enforcing contracts, vertical relationships between dealers and manufacturers, and the use of 'hostages'. It might appear that contracts including private arbitration clauses would be relevant here but, as we see below, these fit better into the multilateral analysis.

Self-Enforcing Agreements

The most important type of bilateral mechanism is the creation of what has been called a 'self-enforcing agreement' (Telser, 1980). This is an agreement between two firms which contains no external enforcement provisions. The agreement operates as long as it is in the interest of both firms to maintain it. For each firm, the value of the agreement is the value of the expected future business from maintaining the relationship. If a firm cheats, then it gains in the short run but loses the value of the future business.

As long as transactions can be structured correctly, then external enforcement is not needed. Correct structuring requires two major conditions. First, there must be no announced last period for the transaction. If there is a clearly specified last period, then a firm will have an incentive to cheat in that period because there is no future business to lose. But if both sides know that cheating will occur in the last period, then there is an incentive to cheat in the second-to-last period because there will be cheating in the last period anyway. But then in the second-to-last period ... In other words, self-enforcing contracts with specified termination dates 'unravel' and are not stable.

Second, each party must make some return on the transactions which is somewhat greater than a competitive or normal return. The excess return must be large enough so that the present discounted value of the future profits (discounted both for time and for the probability that the sequence of transactions will end) is greater than the one time gain from cheating. This means that a firm should not bargain so hard with a trading partner that there is no profit left in the deal, for if this occurs there is no cost to cheating. If these conditions can be met, then contracts can be self-enforcing with no requirement for external legal enforcement.

Vertical Controls

An interesting class of bilateral transactions is between manufacturers and retailers of the product. There are various policies which manufacturers with brand name capital might want retailers to carry out. Some are: demonstrating the product; certification of quality; maintaining freshness; promoting the product to marginal consumers; maintenance of complete inventories; and refraining from 'switching' customers to alternative product lines when consumers respond to manufacturers' advertisements.

There are numerous mechanisms which can be used to achieve these goals. These include: establishment of maximum or minimum prices at which goods can be sold (resale price maintenance); territorial restrictions; requirements that dealers carry only the brand of the manufacturer (exclusive dealing); and requirements of certain methods of retailing (such as shelf-space requirements). Manufacturers may also integrate directly into retailing, or may establish franchises for selling their product.

It is not my purpose here to discuss the business reasons for these restrictions; such discussions are available elsewhere (e.g., Rubin, 1990, Chapter 6). These restrictions can be carried out as self-enforcing agreements, with the threat of termination as the only sanction. There is no need for state enforcement of these types of arrangements. However, there is a danger of the state banning these practices. For a long time, US antitrust law erroneously believed that such vertical restrictions were anticompetitive, and some are still outlawed. New economies can avoid the errors made in the US and elsewhere and simply decide to leave these agreements alone. They need not enforce them, but certainly should not forbid them.

In new economies, there are particularly strong reasons to allow vertical mechanisms. Certain Western products (Levis, Coca-Cola) may already have established brand name capital in Eastern economies. If so, then the producers of these products are in a position to 'sell' (or lease) part of their reputations to retailers. A manufacturer with a reputation would have an incentive to choose a retailer who will not destroy the reputation of the product. This means that carrying a well-known Western product will create valuable reputation capital for the retailer. That is, a retailer who can become a distributor for a well-known product in a region will himself have some reputation. Retailers may be willing to pay for this acquired reputation by offering better terms for distributing well-known Western goods. Additionally, manufacturers would have incentives to establish vertical mechanisms for policing and monitoring the behaviour of these retailers. If such vertical contracts are forbidden, then an important mechanism for quickly developing reputations of retailers will be lost.

Hostages

One way for a firm to commit itself to not cheating is to offer a hostage to its trading partner. A simple hostage is some cash deposit which will be lost if the firm cheats. Such a hostage requires some outside enforcement, but not by the state. For example, the firms could jointly hire an attorney who would be empowered to decide if cheating had occurred and to award the payment to the victim. Of course, there is a problem in trusting the attorney not to expropriate the hostage. However, firms might exist whose sole value is their reputation capital for enforcing such agreements and who therefore would not have an incentive to cheat in this way as long as their reputation were worth more than any one hostage. Western law firms or investment banking firms might be able to perform this function in new economies.

A more natural method is the creation of bilateral hostages. If firm A is dependent on firm B for some input, then firm A would have an incentive to put firm B in a position of being dependent on firm A as well. Moreover, firm B would have an incentive to be put in this position in order to be able to guarantee not to cheat. For example, in the USA firms making cardboard boxes commonly trade components with each other across geographic areas, and in this case neither firm can 'holdup' the other without also putting itself at risk. As with the case of vertical restraints, the antitrust authorities should be careful not to inefficiently ban or penalise this bilateral trade because it is generally efficient and not anticompetitive.

Multilateral Arrangements

These are the most interesting class of adaptations. A well-defined multilateral arrangement can enforce fair and honest dealing both between members of the group and between members and outsiders. It is generally agreed that the Law Merchant (the medieval body of commercial law) was exactly this sort of private legal system which served to enforce honesty by threats of reputation loss (Benson, 1989; Milgrom, North and Weingast, 1990; Berman, 1983). Similar institutions survive today in advanced countries. The Better Business Bureau, for example, is a reputation-guaranteeing device with properties similar to those of the Law Merchant. Many trade associations have codes which have many of the efficient properties of the Law Merchant.[3] Private

3. For some examples of trade association codes of ethics, see Hill (ed.,1976), Part 4.

contracts requiring arbitration of disputes require similar enforcement mechanisms. Much international commercial law is based on arbitration, with a loss of reputation as the major sanction for breach (Benson, 1992). I begin with a discussion of private arbitration, based on the analysis of Landes and Posner (1979), because this analysis demonstrates the need for multilateral enforcement.

Arbitration

In a contract situation, arbitration may be feasible. The parties to a contract can specify in the contract that, in the event of a dispute, they will settle the issue through arbitration. Moreover, what is equally important, they can specify *ex ante* which arbitrator or forum they will use. Thus, if there are competing 'court' systems, or competing groups of arbitrators, the parties can select the one they desire.

This is an efficient input into evolution towards legal efficiency. Parties to contracts will not expect to breach, and will not plan on breach. Therefore, *ex ante* the parties will desire to select that forum for dispute resolution in which they expect to obtain the most efficient results, so that *ex ante* competition among arbitrators can lead to efficient legal evolution.

There is a limit to purely private arbitration, however. That limit is that the party who loses in a dispute has an incentive to ignore the decision. In developed countries, the solution is that the courts will enforce the decree of the arbitrator. In a society where there is no court enforcement of such decrees, the only remedy is a reputation remedy. In small societies where reputation is common knowledge among all parties, then simple publicising of cheating may work. However, in larger societies, where there are many trading partners, it may be necessary to devise more complex devices for enforcement of arbitration decrees. This is the topic of the next section.

Multilateral Enforcement Devices

Consider a trade association with the following properties:

1. The association collects dues from all members These dues are used to subsidise part of the costs of arbitration proceedings in which disputes among members and between members and customers or suppliers are resolved. Disputants also pay part of the costs.

2. Information is made available to all potential customers and suppliers regarding the list of members, so that it is possible for a potential customer to ascertain at low cost if a potential seller is a member of the trade association.

3. If the decision of the arbitrator goes against a party and the party ignores the decision (e.g., refuses to pay damages as ordered by the arbitrator) then the

party will be expelled from the association.

4. Therefore, if a party has been expelled, then when a new potential trading partner queries the association, he will learn that the seller is not a member, and will accordingly be able to avoid trading with the party.

The structure of this mechanism corresponds to the Law Merchant mechanism, as discussed in Milgrom, North and Weingast (1990). Milgrom et al. analyse this mechanism as a game, and show that the outcome is stable and will lead to efficient trading patterns. It is also the pattern followed by many trade associations (Hill (ed.) 1976) which engage in self-policing. It is also the pattern followed by diamond 'bourses' (diamond exchange markets) such as the New York Diamond Dealers Club, and by the World Federation of Diamond Bourses (Bernstein, 1992). These associations generally have arbitration proceedings, and the ultimate sanction for violation of an arbitrated agreement is expulsion, although sometimes the formal law will be used as well. Better Business Bureau, private reputation enforcing groups in the USA, also follow this procedure, although these organisations also provide information about non-member firms.

Implications

The sort of multilateral reputation enforcement mechanisms discussed here can be privately established and enforced. There is no need for any government involvement. Groups of businesses can immediately establish these sorts of associations and begin advertising that they perform the sort of policing discussed. Of course, it will take some time for reputations of enforcement agencies to be established, but the process can begin and can be done privately.

It seems likely that two sorts of associations might come into being, corresponding to Better Business Bureaus and to trade associations. Better Businesses Bureau are local associations which guarantee reputations of merchants dealing directly with consumers. Some such local mechanism would also seem useful in new economies. It may be that associations would begin on a relatively local level, such as a neighbourhood or even a particular block, and then spread. Trade associations are associations of firms in the same industry. Their value would be in guaranteeing contracts between businesses. While these two types of mechanisms might not in fact turn out to be the most desirable, establishment of them would seem to be a good starting point. Once they were established, natural market forces would determine which types would survive.

Efficient Rules

One advantage of the set of institutions proposed here (and in particular of the multilateral institutions) is that these may actually lead to evolution of more efficient rules than would occur if there were an established legal system. There are mechanisms which might lead a formal legal system to evolve efficient rules, but the power of the mechanisms is limited (Rubin, 1977, 1982; Aranson, 1986). As Landes and Posner (1979), Benson (1989), and Cooter (1983) indicate, competing jurisdictions and competition between judges may be the most efficient method of achieving efficient rules quickly.

When parties are negotiating contracts, then they will consider methods of enforcement. Generally speaking, breach of a contract will occur only in the event of unanticipated events, so parties cannot know *ex ante* the nature of the breach, or the desired remedies. Therefore, the interest of parties in this situation is to choose arbitrators who will maximise the *ex post* joint wealth of the parties – that is, who will choose efficient rules for enforcement. For example, arbitrators are commonly successful businessmen, rather than lawyers, so that they will be familiar with business practice. If these arbitrators then establish rules, the rules will generally be efficient. If they are not, then disputants in the future will choose different arbitrators, so that there will be strong evolutionary pressures for efficient rules.

Will the arbitrators establish rules, or will they only settle disputes? Landes and Posner (1979) argue that there is sometimes an inadequate incentive for arbitration to produce rules (as opposed to decisions) because the creation of rules does not benefit the parties who pay for dispute settlement. That is, they argue that the parties to a dispute will want a settlement of the dispute, but not a rule. The rule is a public good whose private value is less than the cost to the disputants. This has been questioned by Benson (1989) who points out that the Law Merchant did produce rules which were later adopted into the common law. In the diamond example, arbitrators do not generally provide rules, but this is because parties prefer secrecy in this market. More recently, some bourses have begun publishing rules, but omitting the names of the parties to the transactions (Bernstein, 1992).

In fact, Landes and Posner indicate that there are circumstances in which rules will be created. If the arbitration is performed for an association, then rule creation is feasible because the association can collect dues and use these to pay for rules. As Milgrom et al. indicate, the Law Merchant evolved at least in part in connection with trade fairs (their example is the Champagne Fairs) and therefore there was a possibility of creating efficient rules. The scheme proposed here would also apply to various private associations, and so dues could be used to supplement fees paid by disputants and therefore pay for rule creation. The rules would benefit all members of the association, not merely those with a dispute at issue, and so members would be willing to pay dues to obtain such rules. Thus, the proposals in this paper will likely lead to efficient rules, as well as to efficient structures for transactions.

Summary and Implications for Future Research

It is generally agreed that legal institutions in the Eastern European countries which have recently left communism are undeveloped. However, it is also argued that development of these economies cannot proceed until efficient rules are established. This paper argues that this point is often overdrawn. There are many rules which parties can privately create even without the intervention of the state which can lead to efficient transactions.

In this paper, I deal primarily with rules of contract. I show that there are mechanisms which parties can institute by themselves or in conjunction with others which can support trade. Moreover, these private mechanisms can also be the basis of efficient evolution of public law, as was the medieval Law Merchant.

While this paper has dealt with contract, there may also be possibilities for some private establishment of property rights. There are historical analyses of the evolution of property rights which are relevant. (See, e.g., Anderson and Hill, 1975; Libecap, 1981; 1989; North, 1990; Umbeck, 1981. For a recent examination of creation of property rights see DeSoto, 1989). Analysis of this process could be quite useful for new economies. Moreover, there are other institutions which have also provided private enforcement of efficient exchange which have not been discussed here. Financial markets and labour markets have also evolved, but this paper has not explicitly considered such markets. Further research on additional possibilities for development of private institutions would look at the historical record and at mechanisms which have been successful in the past, and attempt to apply insights gained from this literature to the problems of Eastern Europe.

While it is important to create efficient legal structures, businesses in new economies need not wait until these structures are established. The history of legal structures and examples from developed countries indicate that there are private mechanisms which can support trade without the assistance of the state.

References

Ackerlof, G. A., 1970, "The Market For Lemons: Qualitative Uncertainty and the Market Mechanism", *Quarterly Journal of Economics* 84, p. 488.

Anderson, T. L. and P. J. Hill, 1975, "The Evolution of Property Rights: A Study of the American West", *Journal of Law and Economics* 18, pp. 163–180.

Aranson, P., 1986, "Economic Efficiency and the Common Law: A Critical Survey", in Graf von der Schulenberg, J. M. and G. Skogh (eds), *Law and Economics and the Economics of Legal Regulation*. Dordrecht: Kluwer, pp. 51–84.

Benson, B. L., 1989, "The Spontaneous Evolution of Commercial Law", *Southern Economic Journal* 55, pp. 644–661.

Benson, B. L., 1992, "Customary Law as Social Contract: International Commercial Law", *Constitutional Political Economy* 3, pp. 1–27.

Berman, H. J., 1983, *Law and Revolution: The Formation of the Western Legal Tradition*. Cambridge: Harvard University Press.

Bernstein, L., 1992, "Opting Out of the Legal System: Extralegal Contractual Relations in the Diamond Industry", *Journal of Legal Studies* 21, pp. 115–159.

Clague, C. and G. C. Rausser, 1992, *The Emergence of Market Economies in Eastern Europe*. Cambridge, Mass.: Basil Blackwell.

Cooter, R. D., 1983, "The Objectives of Private and Public Judges", *Public Choice* 41, pp. 107–132.

DeSoto, H., 1989, *The Other Path*. New York: Harper and Row.

Epstein, R. A., 1985, "Products Liability as an Insurance Market", *Journal of Legal Studies* 14, pp. 645–670.

Fisher, S. and A. Gelb, 1991, "The Process of Socialist Economic Transformation", *Journal of Economic Perspectives* 5, pp. 91–106.

Hill, I. (ed.), 1976, *The Ethical Basis of Economic Freedom*. Chapel Hill, North Carolina: American Viewpoint.

Klein, B., R. Crawford, and A. Alchian, 1978, "Vertical Integration, Appropriable Rents, and the Competitive Contracting Process", *Journal of Law and Economics* 21, p. 297.

Klein, B. and K. B. Leffler, 1981, "The Role of Market Forces in Assuring Contractual Performance", *Journal of Political Economy* 89, p. 615.

Kreps, D. M., 1990, "Corporate Culture and Economic Theory", in Alt, J. E. and K. A. Shepsle (eds), *Perspectives on Positive Political Economy*. New York: Cambridge University Press.

Landa, J. T., 1981, "A Theory of the Ethnically Homogeneous Middleman Group: An Institutional Alternative to Contract Law", *Journal of Legal Studies* 10, pp. 349–362.

Landes, W. M. and R. A. Posner, 1979, "Adjudication as a Private Good", *Journal of Legal Studies* 8, pp. 235–284.

Libecap, G. D., 1981, *Locking Up The Range*, Cambridge, Mass.: Ballinger.

_____, 1989, *Contracting for Property Rights*. New York: Cambridge University Press.

Litwack, J. M., 1991, "Legality and Market Reform in Soviet-Type Economies", *Journal of Economic Perspectives* 5, pp. 77–90.

Macaulay, S., 1963, "Non-Contractual Relations in Business", *American Sociological Review*, Vol. 28.

Milgrom, P. R., D. C. North and B. W. Weingast, 1990, "The Role of Institutions in the Revival of Trade: The Law Merchant, Private Judges, and the Champagne Fairs", *Economics and Politics* 2, pp. 1–23.

Muris, T. J., 1981, "Opportunistic Behavior and the Law of Contracts", *Minnesota Law Review* 65, p. 527.

North, D., 1990, *Institutions, Institutional Change, and Economic Performance.* New York: Cambridge University Press.

Posner, R. A., 1986, *Economic Analysis of Law.* Boston: Little, Brown. (Third Edition.)

Priest, G. L., 1985, "The Invention of Enterprise Liability: A Critical History of the Intellectual Foundations of Modern Tort Law", *Journal of Legal Studies* 14, pp. 461–528.

Rubin, P. H., 1977, "Why is the Common Law Efficient?" *Journal of Legal Studies* 6, pp. 51–63.

_____, 1982, "Common Law and Statute Law", *Journal of Legal Studies* 11, pp. 205–223.

_____, 1990, *Managing Business Transactions: Controlling the Costs of Co ordinating, Communicating and Decision Making*. New York: Free Press.

Svejnar, J., 1991, "Microeconomic Issues in the Transition to a Market Economy", *Journal of Economic Perspectives* 5, pp. 123–138.

Telser, L., 1980, "A Theory of Self Enforcing Agreements", *Journal of Business* 53, p. 27.

Umbeck, J. R., 1981, *A Theory of Property Rights.* Ames Iowa: Iowa State University Press.

Williamson, O. E., 1985, *The Economic Institutions of Capitalism.* New York: Free Press.

10

Employment Issues in a Period of Systemic Mutation

*Dominique Redor**

Introduction

During the systemic changes at the beginning of the nineties, unemployment grew rapidly in the economies of the former Soviet system. Until the fall of this system, unemployment was very low, and most enterprises suffered from labour shortages. However, within two years (1990 and 1991), unemployment reached the level of Western Europe (the National labour centre in Hungary at the end of 1991 registered 6 per cent of the active population, a figure which is certainly well below the actual facts; in Poland at the same date, the rate of unemployment was estimated at 11.4 per cent). In addition it can be feared that in most economies of the former Soviet system, the rate of unemployment will exceed Western economies in the near future.

Indeed in Western economic theory, the debates concern neo-Keynesian as opposed to neo-liberal explanations of the present unemployment. Although they differ on the measures of economic policy which must be applied, the models refer to stable institutional and structural frameworks.

For example fixed price theory (Barro and Grossman, 1976; Malinvaud, 1977) models disequilibria which rule out structural or systemic changes. In addition we must bear in mind that the sophisticated instruments of economic policy which are used by Western governments (monetary policy using open

---

* University of Lille 1 and Réforme et Ouverture des Systèmes Economique Socialistes.
I am very grateful to P. Ronnås (University of Stockholm) discussant of the first version of this paper, M. Gora (Warsaw School of Economics), J. Kiss (University of UN Geneva), A. Leijonhufvud (University of California LA) participants to the Arne Ryde Symposium, for their comments, remarks and criticisms.

market mechanisms, some elements of fiscal policy) are not yet available for the governments in power in Eastern countries.

Nevertheless it must not be said that Western economic theory and policies are not useful to Eastern countries. Indeed from an empirical point of view most Western economies experienced major changes in their productive structures under pressure from their opening up to international trade (I am referring particularly to the economic integration of the less developed EC members). These changes, and the conquences of 'structural policies' carried out by governments, have been studied by Western economists (Auer, Maruani and Reynaud, 1990; Commission of the European Community, 1990, Bassi and Crawford, 1990).

At the micro-economic level, the theory of labour market segmentation (Doeringer and Piore, 1971) emphasises that the labour market is structured by its institutional framework. More recently neoclassical theory has developed new models of the labour market and labour relations inside the firm under the hypothesis of imperfect competition (implicit contracts theory, efficiency wage theory, insider-outsider models for example) and has introduced a new approach to employment and structural policies (Bulow and Summers, 1986; Jones, 1987).

The aim of this paper is to offer an interpretation of present unemployment in Eastern Europe in the light of economic theory (Part 1). Employment policies in these countries will then be assessed, and finally I consider whether some of the experiences and lessons (positive or negative) of the West may be of some help to Central and East European Countries (CEEC) (Part 2).

Although our approach is more theoretical than empirical, I shall refer particularly to Hungary and Poland, the two economies where economic mutation has progressed most. So it can be assumed that my analysis can be applied to the future situation of the other countries according to the pace of their own economic mutation.

Economic Analysis of Unemployment in Eastern Europe

First of all I shall draw a very rapid picture of the structure of the labour market under the Soviet Type System (STS). Then I shall explain the present changes from a theoretical point of view. Particular attention will be paid to the rapidly growing unemployment.

Structural and Systemic Mutation of Employment

If we consider employment, the STS which prevailed until the end of the eighties in the CEEC can be characterised by two main features.

Firstly budget constraint imposed by the State on firms were 'soft' (Kornai, 1980) i.e. many firms were subsidised to develop 'priority sectors' (heavy industries) or to cover deficits: no firm went bankrupt. These subsidies had different forms and different objectives. One of these objectives was to avoid laying off workers and creating unemployment considered to be a 'capitalist disease'. Traditional and declining activities which were suppressed in the West were maintained through State intervention, while new ones suffered from shortages of productive resources, including manpower.

This system proved to be extremely rigid. Economic structures evolved very slowly under the STS. This rigidity was the result of the administrative 'planning' of the economy and possibly of political options (to create the basis of a 'socialist society' through the development of heavy industries).

The gap between the structure of production on the one hand and social demand on the other hand (which changed rapidly during the last decades) is one of the most important economic reasons underlying the fall of the STS.

It is no wonder that at the beginning of the nineties, the systemic mutation is closely linked with a mutation of productive structures.

The decentralisation of economic mechanisms means that State intervention in the management of firms and the provision of subsidies are progressively suppressed. This systemic mutation can lead to privatisation of most of the previously state-owned firms. It can also lead to a basic change in the management of state-owned firms following the model of some Western countries (Austria, France, Scandinavia, for example).

In both cases, the main management criterion is profit in a competitive environment which may be characterised by the suppression of administrated prices, the introduction of competition on the national market, the opening to World trade to varying degrees according to the country considered.

What is the impact of such a dramatic systemic shock on employment? Two main factors of change may be singled out.

1. The reduction of the gap between the structure of the final demand and the production of firms requires the suppression of many 'old' activities and firms. These mainly include energy (coal mines), the steel industry, metal manufacturing, shipbuilding. On the other hand some activities will be developed to satisfy the new economic needs e.g. consumer industries (electronics, cars, building industries) and tertiary activities (banking, insurance, private services to enterprises and households, and so on).

Thus CEEC are usually confronted with structural unemployment. This kind of unemployment is the result of a mismatch between the actual skills of the manpower and the skills needed by firms. These countries will be obliged to retrain part of their manpower.

But there is also a geographical mismatch which is linked to the concentration of activities during the Soviet period. Large urban districts were built in the fifties and sixties and were founded on mining and steel industries. At the same time geographical mobility was low because of the housing shortage, especially in diversified industrial centres (for example in Warsaw and Budapest, see Gora, 1991, p. 171).

The decline of the heavy industry districts is going to increase the geographical imbalances. In Hungary (Hárs, Kövári and Nagy, 1991, pp. 184–186) these districts as well as the rural areas are badly hit by unemployment. However, labour mobility towards diversified industrial centres is still hindered by housing shortages.

2. It is true that other sectors will not be hit by the structural shock, as they supply goods and services which satisfy a growing demand. Nevertheless in these sectors employment will be marked by the changes in the regulation of the economy. This will be the result of the suppression of State subsidies (for firms which are still State owned) or of privatisation.

This latter kind of unemployment is clearly different from the former. For example, for the people who are laid off, it is easier than in the case of structural unemployment to find a job that corresponds to their actual skills. We shall call this kind of unemployment which is linked to change in the regulation of the economy 'unemployment of systemic mutation'.

Although these two kinds of unemployment are undoubtedly interconnected, we find it useful to distinguish between them in analysing the present situation. Indeed they can evolve differently and may require different measures of economic policy.

For example when declining enterprises are replaced by new or expanding ones, skill and geographical mismatches can involve a rapid increase of structural unemployment. On the other hand, retraining of manpower and geographical mobility will not curb the rise of unemployment if the new systemic regulation does not involve the creation of new firms and activities.

Actually structural unemployment concerns the supply side of the labour market, whereas systemic mutation unemployment concerns the demand side. Both of them require a large range of measures at the micro- as well as at the macro-level.

If we consider the demand side of the labour market, State decisions influence the speed of the employment mutation. Thus manpower transfers from declining sectors to expanding ones depend mainly on two factors:

1. The tightness of the budget constraint imposed on State-owned enterprises.

2. The speed of wage increases (which are still regulated in Poland and Czechoslovakia for example, see Part 2 below) which is a regulator of the intensity of manpower transfers.

New Approaches to the Labour Market in the CEEC

We shall turn toward two important theoretical issues. First, changes in the skills needed by firms raises the question of manpower training and retraining.

Secondly institutional rules and social divisions on the labour market are now changing. This requires the analysis of the evolution of the 'segmentation' of this market.

The mutation of the structure of production will entail manpower transfers from declining to developing sectors. This corresponds to a very big shift in the skills required by enterprises.

It is out of the scope of the present study to determine what skills must be promoted and developed. My purpose is rather to outline the theoretical implications of such a shift.

It can be useful to start with human capital theory. According to Becker 'general skills' can be transferred from one firm to another without a reduction of individual labour productivity. They can be exchanged in theory on a market which is supposed to be competitive. On the contrary 'specific skills' are attached to a particular firm and require specific training which cannot be transferred to other firms. So the cost of general training must be paid by the trainee (even if he is trained by his firm) because it increases the wage he can obtain on the outside labour market. On the contrary specific training costs are paid for by the firm.

In addition 'efficiency wage' theory states that if a firm invests in the specific skills of its manpower, it is in its interest to pay a higher wage rate than on the external labour market. Hence it prevents trained employees from leaving and profits from its training investments.

Two other important arguments against the competitive hypotheses concern the collective nature of general education and training (corresponding to 'general skills') and the uncertainty which weighs on education and training investments.

Indeed expenses in education and training are very long-term and uncertain investments. Thus it is very likely that individuals will underinvest especially if they are constrained in their financial resources (Eicher, 1990).

Nor do firms have the incentive to invest in training since they are also faced by uncertainty in their long-term investments. A 'free rider' behaviour of firms wanting to benefit from the investments of the other firms is rational from an individual point of view, but is collectively inefficient as it leads to the neglect of investments in education and training. In CEEC this behaviour is all the more likely as the financial resources of enterprises are now severely constrained.

This analysis may explain why in all Western countries education and training are partly financed by State or regional public authorities. But it is noteworthy that collective financing of education and training varies very much from one country to another. For example, the gap between the United States and Western continental Europe must be outlined.

During the seventies and the eighties, Western Europe and the United States experienced rapid structural changes under the pressure of technological progress and international competition. In other words, during this period when uncertainty regarding the labour skills required by the production mutations was growing, individuals and enterprises tended to underinvest in education and training. From this point of view, the American experience is very interesting. At the beginning of the nineties, several studies (Bassi and Crawford, 1990) pointed out that the United States was lagging behind its main competitors (Japan, Germany) in terms of the skill level of manpower. These studies recommend the more collective financing of education and training and (or) fiscal incentives for firms and individuals to invest in that field.

If we now consider the present situation of the CEEC, there are very strong theoretical and empirical arguments in favour of the collective financing of education and training, especially in this period of rapid structural changes.

It is also important to know how these principles could be implemented in these countries. This point will be studied in the second part which deals with economic policy.

Labour market segmentation theory (Doeringer and Piore, 1971) is a fundamentally different approach since it does not refer to a perfect or imperfect labour market. On the contrary, it starts from the study of the institutions and social relations at the national level.

It is noteworthy that this theory which was born and was first developed in the United States was also applied to the STS, especially to Hungary, and to a lesser degree to the USSR (Redor, 1992, Part 2, Chapter 2). Indeed each country has a different segmentation of its labour market since it depends on its national institutions. Nevertheless from a very general point of view one can draw the following conclusions from these studies.

The 'segments' of the labour market are 'mobility chains' for manpower: they make up a hierarchical structure. The movements and mobility of workers are channelled and constrained by this structure. At the origin is the 'duality' of the labour market which is the result of the shaping of the labour market by firms.

In the eighties, some of the divisions of the labour market could be encountered in both Eastern and Western economies. The lower ('secondary') part of the labour market is occupied particularly by non-skilled workers with a high turnover. They are employed by firms whose activity is subject to fluctuation. The lower segments of the labour market also contain a majority of women or country people, who have recently settled in towns. On the contrary, the 'primary' labour market is made up of enterprises which employ a relatively stable labour force which benefits from higher wages and training programmes. This division is related to the cost of uncontrolled turnover. This cost is higher when the skills of workers are specific and (or) are difficult to find on the external labour market.

In the eighties there were also 'systemic' differences between East and West in terms of labour market segmentation. The main difference hinges on the role of the State in the former case. In fact 'planning authorities' played an important role in channelling manpower toward the 'priority sectors' (heavy industry) (Kollo and Redor, 1990). First they differentiated wages in favour of these sectors, and secondly they encouraged young people leaving the education and training systems to take up work in these sectors. In the STS, heavy industry comprised a particularly important segment in the primary part of the labour market.

Undoubtedly the present systemic changes reshape the morphology of the labour market in the CEEC. What can be said about the main present and future transformations of the segmentation of the labour market in these countries?

New divisions are going to appear. The first one concerns (or will concern) the new private sector which is expanding through the privatisation of State firms and also through the creation of new activities. Along with this private sector, the State sector will remain important for a long time. In so far as the old 'priority sectors' will still be owned by the State, relations between the private sector and the State sector will be progressively reversed. More specifically, State-owned declining firms will lose their favourable positions and will be progressively integrated within the secondary segments of the labour market (indeed the pace of this integration will vary according to the countries considered). On the contrary some of the new private enterprises will make up the 'primary' part of the labour market.

However it is certain that the private sector will not be homogeneous. As is the case in Western countries, different segments will arise. For example, it is likely that national firms and foreign-owned firms will follow different patterns. The latter will use a more efficient technology, have access to the international financial markets, and eventually will profit from favourable legal rules for their investments.

These differences will have consequences for the level of wages and training of employees. New segments of the labour market are going to appear in connection with the labour management of these firms.

The most important message of segmentation theory for economic policy is that the labour market is a locus of dynamic forces which continually create new structures and destroy old ones. From this point of view, the aim of economic policy cannot be to create or to recreate the conditions of pure competition, an aim which is fundamentally irrelevant. It is rather to reduce unemployment, taking into account the labour market structures shaped by firms.

This theoretical and empirical analysis must be kept in mind if we want to assess the employment challenge with which the CEEC are now faced and the policies which are being implemented concerning wage, training and social benefits.

Employment Policies

First of all we shall very briefly introduce the employment and wage policies which have been followed since the fall of the STS in the countries which are the most advanced in systemic mutation (Hungary and Poland). Then we shall try to draw some lessons, for the future, from the experience of Western economies.

Wage Policies and Unemployment Compensation in the CEEC

The term 'wage policy' is not common to Western economic literature. Its place in economic policy after the fall of the STS can be explained by the objective of the new economic authorities to curb inflationary forces.

Indeed in the STS, the administrative control of wage increases was very strict extending to the wage bill of each firm (Redor, 1992, Part 2, Chapter 1). After the fall of the centrally-regulated system, a very high open inflation was to be feared especially in economies which suffered from major imbalances on the goods market. This inflation could have been strengthened by wage claims after the suppression of central controls over the wage bills of firms, especially in the light of the development of the private sector.

These are some of the arguments which have led the new economic authorities to implement highly restrictive wage policies.[1]

The most typical example is Poland (Chilosi, 1992). The 'popiwek' is a 'punitive tax' which has been imposed since the beginning of 1990, on increases in the overall wage bill of each firm above the norm set each month by the government. In its first version the rate of the tax ranges from 200 per cent to 500 per cent. The norm is fixed each month on the basis of the rate of inflation of the previous month but indexation is only partial. As a result, the real wage rate decreased in 1990 and 1991. It is noteworthy that foreign firms and joint ventures are exempted from the tax.

In Poland and Hungary, the official objective of the highly restrictive monetary policies (reduction of the money supply in real terms) was also to control the rise of the average real wage rate and the inflationary forces.

How can one assess the impact of this wage policy on employment and on the evolution of the structure of the labour market?

There is no doubt that taxing wage increases curbs the forces acting on the labour market. Indeed all firms are practically constrained to increase their wages at the same pace. This contributes to keeping non-profitable firms in operation and holding back the development of firms in the sectors where demand is expanding.

---

1. Regarding labour market regulation in the CEEC a very good collection of articles is presented by the *International Labour Review* 2, 1991 (see especially Gora (1991), Hárs, Kövári and Nagy (1991), Kapl, Sojka and Tepper (1991), Jones (1991)).

Monetary restrictions also seek to constrain wage increases. The official policy is to curb final demand and thereby the capacity of firms to increase wages. However, the structure of this demand changes, as does the structure of supply. If no tax is imposed on wage growth, the profitability and ability of firms to increase wages differs.

If we consider international trade, it can be assumed that monetary and wage restrictions have a positive effect on the price of exports in the world market. But this is only true if we consider 'comparative costs' between the CEEC countries and the rest of the world. However, at the present time it is very likely that the other factors of international competitiveness are more effective. They are linked to the restructuring of the economy, i.e. the adaptation of national supply to world demand, the upgrading of products, and of the commercial services.

Thus the restrictive tax on wages and the control of the supply of money are very powerful instruments of economic policy in controlling the speed of restructuring. Indeed, since 1990, the relatively slow pace of structural changes in the CEEC is linked to these measures which have prevented the market forces from being fully operative.

Another policy, which has often been used in Western countries, loosens the monetary and fiscal constraints and allows market forces to play in order to reallocate the labour force in expanding firms and sectors. The possible negative effects on unemployment can be reduced through financial incentives. For example firms which hire the unemployed are exempted from social contributions (the legislation operating in the EC countries can be found in: Commission of the EC, 1990, p. 129). If we refer to the above analysis (part one), there is no doubt that this mechanism would favour the transfer of manpower from declining enterprises to the expanding ones. The employment of the former is untouched by the contribution cuts (as they are constrained by the demand for their production), whereas the latter would be induced to produce more to satisfy the growing demand for their production.

I think that this kind of incentive would be more effective for increasing employment than 'employment subsidies' which are paid by the Polish Administration (Chilosi, 1992). This latter administrative device means that 'the cost of maintaining employment would be shared between firms, workers and the State'. In other words the employment subsidies would be granted to those enterprises which would expect to reduce wages to protect the level of employment. From a dynamic point of view, this kind of administrative measure is certainly inferior to those which favour hirings (through a reduction of social contributions for example). Indeed in the former case, the level and structure of employment remains unchanged, whereas in the latter manpower transfers towards expanding firms are favoured.

If we then consider labour market segmentation, it could be thought that the restrictive regulation on wages or money supply might reduce the differences between the segments which make up the labour market (the imposition of a minimum wage which reduces market segmentation is analysed by Zajdela (1990) and Jones (1987)). Indeed the wage level is one of the basic factors behind market segmentation. However we must qualify this statement.

First of all, inequalities on the labour market are not only a function of wage levels but also of fringe benefits, training programmes, promotion opportunities etc. It must also be noted that State constraints do not weigh equally on all firms. For example in Poland, 'popiwek' is not applied to foreign firms and joint ventures. In addition all firms are not subject to monetary restrictions to the same degree. For example foreign firms may find financial resources in the international financial and monetary markets. Even inside each country, firms do not have equal access to the banking system (especially as long as this system remains State owned).

Finally the trade-off between constraints (on wage and money supply) and incentives (founded on market mechanisms) depends on many factors rooted in each national economy. Among these factors one can cite: inflationary forces and the deficit in the State budget, the possibility of creating and developing new firms, the level of unemployment which can be politically and socially borne, the capacity of the education and training system (public and private) to cope with the retraining of dismissed people.

In all of these cases, the rapid growth of unemployment raises the question of social protection of the unemployed.

In a critical review of unemployment compensation, Atkinson and Micklewright (1991) point to the wide range of institutional rules which can be found in OECD countries. First of all they distinguish between unemployment insurance (UI) and unemployment assistance (UA) schemes. In the former scheme, eligibility for unemployment benefits is subject to several conditions:

1. They are refused to anybody who enters unemployment voluntarily.
2. Eligibility depends on the time worked before the claim.
3. The unemployed must make genuine efforts to seek new employment and be available for work.
4. Anybody who refuses suitable job offers, beyond some specified number, is no longer eligible.
5. Benefits are contributory, and the contribution is paid by employers and employees.
6. The amount of benefits may depend on past earnings.
7. Benefits are paid for a limited period and may be reduced over time.

On the contrary, the Unemployment Assistance (UA) scheme is non-contributory and eligibility is independent of employment history. In some cases there is no time limit.

The main OECD countries can be classified in three groups:

1. The group where the UI scheme prevails: Belgium, Denmark, Italy, Japan, United States.

2. The group where UI and UA are mixed: Austria, France, Germany, United Kingdom, Sweden.
3. Countries which only have the UA scheme: Australia, New Zealand.

But it must be pointed out that each group is not homogeneous: for example in the second group, the duration of benefits may be limited (France, Sweden), whereas in the first one it may be indefinite (Belgium). Thus institutional considerations make the economic analysis of unemployment diversified and multidimensional.

If unemployment benefits are considered as a wage paid independently of the seven conditions set above, there is no doubt that they increase the level of unemployment and constitute a disincentive to work (this point of view is defended by Johnson and Layard (1986) in the *Handbook of Labor Economics*).

However the theoretical and empirical analysis of unemployment insurance schemes leads to rather different conclusions.

If we refer to labour market segmentation, only the upper part of the market (primary sector) is entirely covered by UI. But in this sector an employee runs the risk of being laid off without unemployment compensation if he shirks. Atkinson (1990) has shown that, in this context, a rise in the benefits level makes employment more attractive in the primary sector thus reducing the equilibrium wage rate and hence increasing the level of employment in this sector. On the contrary, the queue for primary sector jobs grows as it attracts more workers from the secondary sector (where there is less advantageous or no UI).

The statistical tests between the duration of unemployment and the level of compensation rely heavily on the availability of statistical data (for example on the kind of 'unemployment' which is studied) and on national institutional rules. More specifically most studies consider the behaviour of those categories of unemployed people who receive unemployment benefits whereas they are a minority among all unemployed. In addition if the variation of benefits payments over a period of unemployment is taken into account, the link between the payments and the unemployment duration is weak for the UK, but higher for the United States (Atkinson and Micklewright, 1991, pp. 1711–1712).

Moreover, in France it seems that the level of unemployment benefits is negatively linked to hirings in 'precarious jobs' (seasonal, temporary, fixed-term works) (Gerard Varet, 1990) but has no connection to hirings in 'regular jobs'.

The North American example is very particular if the reasons for entry into unemployment are investigated. In the United States, temporary lay-off unemployment is widespread (it touches about 50 per cent of the unemployed). In Canada half of all recipients of unemployment insurance in 1984 returned to their pre-unemployment employer (Atkinson and Micklewright, 1991, p.

1684). In addition in North America, UI reduces the cost of lay-offs for firms (there is then no experience rating) and this explains why there is a close relation between UI and temporary lay-offs (research on the 'implicit contract' between employers and employees provides a theoretical interpretation of this phenomenon).

This very brief overview shows that we must study very carefully the implementation of an unemployment benefits scheme in the CEEC. The analysis must thereby take into account institutional and administrative rules as well as the situation and structure (segmentation) of the labour market.

In Hungary a first unemployment compensation scheme was in operation between January 1989 and March 1991 (Micklewright, 1991). In terms of the above-mentioned classification, it was a 'mixed' scheme. Indeed it was financed by the State budget. Eligibility was based on an employment period of 18 months during the 3 years prior to the claim. The duration of benefits was limited to 12 months in a three-year period. The benefit rate was 70 per cent of previous gross earnings for the first six months and then 60 per cent.

The new employment compensation adopted in March 1991 comes closer to the pure UI scheme. Benefits are paid by employers' (1.5 per cent of earnings) and employees' contributions (0.5 per cent of earnings). Eligibility is restricted to people who are employed for at least 12 months in the 4 years prior to the claim. The duration of benefits is fixed at a maximum of 24 months (6 months for career beginners). Unemployment insurance amounts to 70 per cent of previous gross earning for the first half of the entitlement period and 50 per cent in the second half. It must be emphasised that in Hungary at the end of 1990, coverage of the registered unemployed by unemployment benefits was exceptionally high (73.5 per cent according to the data cited by Micklewright, 1991, p. 29). This high figure may be explained by the fact that there was little long-term unemployment at that time. Consequently, most registered unemployed were eligible for unemployment benefits. In addition it must be taken into account that not all the unemployed were registered because of the inadequacy of the unemployment administration which was in a phase of rapid growth.

In Poland in 1989, the act 'on employment' (Chilosi, 1992) set up an unemployment scheme which was amended and on some points was replaced by the act of October 1991 'on employment and unemployment'.

The 1989 Act was based on the assistance principle for all categories of involuntary unemployed. Special provisions were established for those who were affected by collective lay-offs. The main restrictions concerned the refusal to accept an offer for an adequate job (corresponding to the qualification of the unemployed).

This first legislation was very extensive and many non active or employed signed up to receive unemployment benefits (students, young people working on their parents' farm, housewives and so on). This is why, in July 1990, the first restrictive measures were taken. The payment of unemployment benefits hinged on a period of 180 days work in the previous twelve months. The October 1991 Act has further restricted eligibility and the amount of unemployment benefits. This act also provided four types of intervention in favour of those laid off:

1. Access of the redundant to a programme of professional training.
2. Financing self-employment.
3. Participation of the unemployed in local community works.
4. Participation in public works. Only when none of these solutions are possible, do the unemployed receive benefits.

What can be concluded after two years of unemployment schemes in Hungary and Poland?

It is sometimes argued that these schemes reduce incentives to work (this is particularly the case in Poland (Chilosi, 1992)). However, it must be noted that from an institutional point of view, these schemes are now similar to those of Western Europe. It seems that the initial mismanagement (especially in Poland) has been gradually corrected.

The above developments tend to show that the disincentive effect does not apply if we refer to the experience of Western Europe.

Another point which must be kept in mind is that in the period of economic depression which follows the fall of the centrally-planned system, unemployment benefits may help to maintain final demand and prevent its dramatic fall. In this way unemployment benefits indirectly contribute to diminishing 'Keynesian unemployment'. It is true that this kind of unemployment probably does not exist at the very beginning of the mutation period, but does increase when restrictive monetary policies become effective.

The question of the financing of unemployment benefits must also be raised. At present in Western countries, the financing of unemployment benefits is very varied. In North America it is based on private insurance schemes. In Western Europe the schemes are largely State regulated. In the latter case, financing can be made via the State budget (Denmark) or from contributions made by employers and employees (France, Italy, Germany).

If we consider the CEEC we once again encounter the dilemma between State intervention and decentralisation of economic mechanisms which could increase the pace of the restructuring of the economy.

State budget financing of unemployment benefit is in keeping with the centrally-planned system where most social benefits came from public resources. Such financing maintains the former situation and keeps wage costs fairly low. This corresponds to a slow restructuring of the economy.

On the other hand if unemployment contributions are paid by firms (and to a lesser extent by employees), this will increase labour costs and speed up restructuring. Only expanding enterprises will be able to pay higher wages and contributions.

As previously mentioned (see wage policy), variations of unemployment contributions may become an instrument of economic policy. For example firms which increase their employment could be partially exempt from part of their contributions.

'Active' and 'Passive' Policies

We shall now turn to the other factors behind employment policies. First of all the analysis will draw on the experience of Western countries. Then we shall try to draw some conclusions from this experience for the CEEC.

Most publications about employment policies distinguish between 'active programmes' to improve employment and 'passive programmes' (Commission of the EC, 1990, Chapter 9). These two kinds of programmes have been applied in all Western countries in different periods to varying degrees.

In the active programmes we find:

1. Improved services carried out by the public employment agencies (information on available jobs, advice to make the search more efficient).
2. Training of young and adult unemployed people.
3. Subsidies (tax cuts) for hiring the unemployed (this point is studied above).

The passive programmes consist for example of:

1. Paying benefits to the unemployed.
2. Promoting early retirement.
3. Reducing labour time or developing part time employment.
4. Creating public jobs.

In the late 1980s and early 1990s passive programmes declined to the advantage of active programmes.

Most of the time, passive programmes proved to be costly and inefficient: they reduced unemployment in the very short term but had no long-term effect on the labour market. This is the case for example for early retirement which was extensively implemented in France and Belgium in the eighties.

The present policy, especially in the EC, consists of creating incentives to reduce the gap between the skills of the unemployed, (young or adult), and the skills required by firms. These incentives concern firms as well as individuals.

In the EC, professional training institutions differ greatly (Hellier and Redor, 1992, Chapter 5). The 'dual' system in Germany links apprenticeship in the firm for young people and general and professional training in public schools. In addition the training system is open to people seeking to increase their skills, be they employed or unemployed.

In Spain, Italy and France the training system depends on the State (Ministry of Education or Labour). Training is free of charge for trainees who receive special allowances if they are unemployed. Firms which take part in the professional retraining programmes receive special subsidies.

It is noteworthy that in the United Kingdom, State intervention has increased in the eighties through the Employment Training Programmes (for unemployed) and the Youth Training Scheme replaced in 1988 by the Training and Vocational Education Initiative. Most training takes place in firms and trainees receive benefits paid by the State.

From a general point of view, there is a gap in Western Europe between Northern countries which have a fairly low rate of unemployment (Scandinavia, the Netherlands and Germany) on the one hand, and the other countries (Mediterranean countries, including France, and the United Kingdom and Ireland) on the other hand where unemployment rate remains high.

Obviously this gap has many causes. One of these is certainly that education and training in the first group are treated at a very decentralised level by firms and local authorities. In the second group centralised procedures and the non-participation of firms are an obstacle to a rapid adaptation of skills to the changes brought on by technical progress.

It must be pointed out, however, that if the role of firms is undoubtedly fundamental, their intervention is quite diversified in the countries which have effectively fought against unemployment: Sweden, Japan (Nohara, 1988) and Germany. In Sweden the role of local organisations (for example firms, unions and public administration), is fundamental. In Japan professional training and retraining are carried out by big firms where people are employed during most of their professional life, so these firms do not risk losing the benefits of their training investments. In the 'dual' German system, professional training is organised on a sectoral basis and apprentices are trained by firms which do not necessarily hire them at the end of their apprenticeship.

Special training programmes were implemented in countries where youth unemployment is high, for example: Italy, France, and Great Britain (Auer, Maruani and Reynaud, 1990, pp. 27–31). National rules instituted 'employment training contracts' according to which private firms receive subsidies if they take the responsibility for part of the training of young people including on-the-job training.

How can this short analysis shed light on the present training situation in the CEEC?

First of all it must be noted that most firms are now subject to stricter budget constraints and are faced with slackening demand so it is very likely that most of them will reduce or suppress their training programmes. Hence, they may try to rely on public education and training systems or hire workers who have been trained by other firms. For example, there is evidence to show that in Poland in 1990 and 1991, State-owned enterprises have drastically reduced their training programmes.

This is all the more negative given that structural unemployment is developing rapidly and the participation of firms is vital as:

– To complement to public education and professional training system. It can help to diminish the deficiencies of this system.

– To train or retrain people laid off by declining industries.

At the present time, participation can only be based on financial incentives.

It would be advisable to institute tax exemptions for training investments which could be assimilated with research and development investments. Firms could also be encouraged to create joint professional schools on a sectoral basis. In so doing the profit of the 'external effects' drawn from training investments could be shared by all the firms of the sector (Bassi and Crawford, 1990).

Finally subsidies could support apprenticeships in countries where this system has been traditionally developed.

Conclusion

Unemployment is one of the most important challenges facing the CEEC. In the first theoretical part of this paper, we singled out the two main kinds of unemployment, 'structural' and 'systemic mutation', which can be found in these countries. This distinction serves to assess the present economic and employment policies in the CEEC (essentially in Hungary and Poland).

Then we investigated the conditions for the substitution of central regulations (which are still important in these countries) for indirect, decentralised economic mechanisms. We also studied the impact thereof on the speed of economic restructuring.

In addition, the empirical analysis shows that labour market institutions and education and training systems differ between Western countries where they play various roles in the struggle against unemployment.

In this period of rapid institutional change in the CEEC, the Western experience reminds us that economic policy cannot be regarded as an abstract science which can make the economy move toward a single 'optimal equilibrium'. Its role is rather to propose courses of actions based on rational economic principles, and which must also be consistent with the rest of the economic and social system.

References

Atkinson, A. B., 1990, "Institutional Features of Unemployment Insurance and the Working of the Labor Market", *Welfare State Programme*. Discussion Paper No. 50. London: London School of Economics.

Atkinson, A. B. and J. Micklewright, 1991, "Unemployment Compensation and Labor Market Transitions: A Critical Review", *Journal of Economic Literature*, Vol. 29, December, pp. 1679–1727.

Auer, P., M. Maruani, and E. Reynaud, 1990, *Chroniques internationales du marché travail et des politiques de l'emploi, 1986–1989*. Paris: MIRE.

Barro, R. J. and H. I. Grossman, 1976, *Money, Employment and Inflation*. Cambridge: Cambridge University Press.

Bassi, L. J. and D. L. Crawford, 1990, "Labor Economics and Public Policy" in Ehrenberg, R., *Research in Labor Economics: Labor Economics and Public Policy*,Vol. 11, pp. 1–11. New York: JAI Press.

Bulow, J. and L. Summers, 1986, "A Theory of Dual Labor Market with Applications to Industrial Policy, Discrimination and Keynesian Unemployment", *Journal of Labor Economics* 3, Vol. 4, pp. 376–414.

Chilosi, A., 1992, "The Impact on Employment of Institutional Transformation in Eastern Europe and the Task of Social Policy: The Polish Case", *Working Paper of the IRSES*, Maison des Sciences de l'homme, Paris.

Commission of the European Community, 1990, *Employment in Europe*. Office of the Official Publications of the European Community, Brussels.

Doeringer, P. B. and M. J. Piore, 1971, *Internal Labor Markets and Manpower Analysis*. Lexington Mass.:Heath Lexington Books.

Eicher, J. C., 1990, in Greffe, X., et al.

Gerard Varet, L. A., 1990, *Durée du chomage et trajectoires individuelles vis à vis des marchés du travail*. Marseille: Greque.

Gora, M., 1991, "Thérapie de choch sur le marché du travail polonais", *Revue internationale du travail* 2, pp. 161–178.

Greffe, X., J. Mairesse, and J. L. Reiffers (eds) *Encyclopédie Economique*, pp. 1307–1335. Paris: Economica.

Hárs, A., G. Kövári, and G. Nagy, 1991, "La Hongrie face au chomage", *Revue Internationale du travail* 2, pp. 183–191.

Hellier, J., and D. Redor, 1992, *Le travail en Europe*. Paris: Masson.

Johnson, G. and R. Layard, 1986, "The Natural Rate of Unemployment: Explanations and Policies" in Ashenfelter, O. and R. Layard (eds) *Handbook of Labor Economics*. Amsterdam: North Holland.

Jones, D. C., 1991, "Le marché du travail Bulgare en transition", *Revue Internationale du Travail* 2, pp. 231–249.

Jones, S., 1987, "Minimum Wage Legislation in a Dual Labor Market", *European Economic Review*, Vol. 31, pp. 1229–1246.

Kapl, M., M. Sojka and T. Tepper, 1991, "Chomage et économie de marché en Tchécoslovaquie", *Revue International du Travail* 2, pp. 217–231.

Kollo, J. and D. Redor, 1990, "Marché du travail et restructuration de l'emploi en France et en Hongrie" in Dubois, P., J. Koltay, C. Mako and X. Rihet, *Innovation et emploi à l'est et à l'Ouest*, pp. 267-293. Paris: L'Harmattan.

Kornai, J., 1980, *Economics of Shortage*, Vol. 2. Amsterdam: North Holland.

Malinvaud, E., 1977, *The Theory of Unemployment Reconsidered.* Oxford: Basil Blackwell.

Micklewright, J., 1991, "Income Support for the Unemployed in Hungary", Working paper of the European University Institute, Florence.

Nohara, H., 1988, "Formes d'insertion professionnelle des jeunes: le cas du Japon", in Commissariat au plan (ed.) *Structures du marché du travail et politiques de l'emploi*, pp. 341–355. Paris: Syros.

Nuti, M., 1990, "Stabilisation and Reform Sequencing in the Soviet Economy" in *Recherches économiques de Lauvain* 56 (2), pp. 169–179.

Redor, D., 1992, *Wage Inequalities in East and West.* Cambridge: Cambridge University Press.

Zajdela, H., 1990, "Le dualisme du marché du travail: enjeux et fondements théoriques", *Economie et prévision* 92–93, pp. 31–42.

11

The Political Economy of Privatisation

Alastair McAuley[*]

Introduction

It is a truism to observe that in the state-socialist societies of Eastern Europe the vast bulk of productive capital was owned by the state; and further, this is one of the major ways in which centrally-planned economies differed from the market economies of Western Europe. But this feature presents the new governments of the region with one of their most difficult tasks: the substantial privatisation of the state sector.

Privatisation is widely regarded as one of the essential pre-conditions for the introduction of a market economy. A successful programme can increase economic efficiency, lay the foundations for future growth and reinforce political support for the new regime – and, not least, for the government in office. A badly conceived and executed programme, on the other hand, will preserve too much of the old structure, leading to persistent inefficiency, to continuing inflation and relative stagnation. Alternatively, it might result in very high rates of unemployment and a collapse in popular living standards.

So seldom, however, have economies been converted from plan to market that there is little by way of foreign experience for policy makers to draw upon. Each of the programmes adopted in Eastern and Central Europe, in the member republics of the CIS, can be thought of as a social experiment. Some of these programmes have already produced results which can act as examples – or warnings – to those about to embark on the privatisation project. Furthermore, economic theory provides certain guidelines; and the experience of recent privatisation programmes in market economies also yields insights. In

[*] University of Essex.

this paper I use all of these to construct a framework for the assessment of the programmes that have recently been adopted in Russia.

The paper consists of three substantive sections and a conclusion: the first contains a discussion of the gains that economic theory suggests will follow from privatisation – and the necessary conditions for these gains to be realised. The next one examines the Russian privatisation programme to discover how far it will allow the realisation of theoretical gains – and avoid major costs. This section is followed by comments on the main differences between the Russian programme and those that have been adopted elsewhere in Eastern Europe. The final section consists of a summary of the argument and a statement of conclusions.

Privatisation in Economic Theory

In this section, I first spell out what is meant by privatisation and what categories of assets I will be concerned with. Then I describe the objectives that are conventionally ascribed to privatisation programmes. The rest of the section consists of a discussion of the ways in which privatisation can contribute to the attainment of these objectives. In particular, I explore how far a change in ownership alone can result in improvements in economic efficiency and consider when policy makers might also make use of regulation and the encouragement of competition. Finally, I explore some of the subsidiary goals of privatisation: revenue raising and the search for political support.

The Objectives of Privatisation

The term privatisation can refer to a variety of different processes or procedures for the transfer of control over assets from the public to the private sector. In former state-socialist societies, it is usually used to describe the transfer of control over the following four categories of assets. First, there is the sale of small shops, and small-scale service outlets – so-called petty privatisation; the term is sometimes used to include small factories, and even peasant proprietorships. These are usually small enough to be purchased by a single family.

Second, there is the privatisation of the bulk of state enterprises. These are usually too large to be bought outright by any one individual. For analytical purposes, it is often worth distinguishing between the sale of those enterprises that operate in competitive – or at least contestable – markets on the one hand and, on the other, those which enjoy substantial market power. Among these latter, one can distinguish again between natural monopolies and those whose market power derives from previous investment and location policies of the state or from trade protection. Privatisation in this sense may also involve the 'contracting out' of services and/or the deregulation of others.

Then there is the sale or transfer of land and the privatisation of the housing stock. The second of these may well be a precondition for the increased mobility needed to facilitate large-scale structural change. The first may be needed to create a degree of positive supply response in the housing market. I shall not deal with the privatisation of either of these types of asset in this paper.

Privatisation is intended to improve the working of the economy; it may also provide political advantages. As far as the economic benefits of privatisation are concerned, many economists argue that private markets are more likely than public enterprise to achieve economic efficiency. In ex-socialist economies, the switch is also likely to increase consumers' sovereignty.

Furthermore, the disposal of state enterprises contributes to the budget in two ways: it reduces budgetary expenditure by removing candidates for public subsidy. This presupposes that privatisation is accompanied by an attempt to 'harden' enterprise budget constraints. It may also add to budgetary revenue – if enterprises are not given away. Finally, governments that carry out privatisation programmes can look forward to the political support of those who acquire the state's assets. After all, the new capitalists would not welcome the re-nationalisation of their companies. This political support is likely to increase if the assets were secured at a discount – so that their new owners will have made immediate capital gains.

Ownership, Regulation and Competition

Economists identify two concepts of efficiency. First, there is x-efficiency which involves the choice of technologies that minimise costs at all levels of output (Hare, 1992, p. 4); then there is allocative efficiency which, as its name implies, refers to the choice of input proportions and the structure of output. This is sometimes known as Pareto efficiency. It is claimed that private enterprises do better than public ones in respect of each of these types of efficiency, because in a market economy, their owners have the incentive to concentrate on the right aspects of their performance.

X-efficiency requires enterprises to use technologies that minimise the use of resources; it requires them to be aware of new developments and to adopt them where appropriate. It is a necessary condition for profit maximisation. Economists have suggested that, even if public enterprises are set profit maximisation as a goal, their managers are likely to enjoy greater discretion about how to achieve it than are those in the private sector. Firms in the public sector are supervised by politicians and civil servants who often have little experience of business; they may well have even less detailed knowledge of production possibilities in the industries for which they are responsible. The owners of private firms – their shareholders – are directly interested in profits; this is what determines the size of their dividends and the value of their shares. Many of them have detailed knowledge of business in general and can devote a great deal of attention to the performance of *their* firms. Such firms are more likely to achieve high levels of x-efficiency.

Allocative efficiency requires that firms not only employ best-practice technologies but also choose input proportions that reflect the relative scarcities of factors. It also requires that the structure of production corresponds to the pattern of demand. Neoclassical economic theory asserts that such an outcome will be achieved by profit-maximising firms operating on competitive markets. As I pointed out above, economists have argued that privately-owned firms are more likely than public ones to concentrate on profit maximisation – and thus ensure the attainment of an efficient allocation of resources.

The 'case' for privatisation thus involves two implicit assumptions: that both factor and product markets are competitive and that private owners do, indeed, exercise better corporate governance than politicians and civil servants. It is also assumed that market outcomes are not distorted by so-called externalities. Let us consider each of these issues in more detail.

It is true that many civil servants have little detailed knowledge of management. As a result, public sector managers may have scope to pursue their own objectives – to the detriment of economic efficiency. It is also true that politicians may pursue objectives other than economic efficiency; they may even use taxpayers' money to buy the necessary discretion. This is one of the things that is meant by the soft budget constraint. To some extent, however, politicians are only responding to the pressures upon them: they are reflecting the preferences of their electors. Thus, the governance of public enterprises may be lax and this is likely to lead to economic inefficiency.

There is another feature of the public sector that may result in a certain amount of economic inefficiency. It is not possible for publicly-owned enterprises to go bankrupt; rather, where they make losses, an explicit political decision has to be taken to reorganise them or to close them down. And, as pointed out above, governments can often think of good reasons for not doing so. This is what is meant by the claim that the public sector faces a soft budget constraint: governments will underwrite the losses they make. Thus, publicly-owned firms lack what is sometimes called the discipline of the market. This may deprive managers of the power to resist wage claims or demands for excessive employment.

It is not only the public sector, however, that enjoys a soft budget constraint. In practice '... government [in a market economy] has many ways to loosen the budget constraints for private firms.' (Vickers and Yarrow, 1991, p. 116). Furthermore, as Mrs Thatcher showed in the early 1980s, governments can harden the budget constraint facing public sector enterprises too.

Moreover, even when they face hard budget constraints, there are circumstances when the governance of private corporations fails. First, where there is a large number of shareholders and the holding of each is small, the company is likely to suffer from the so-called free-rider problem. No shareholder will be willing to invest the time and effort needed to supervise management. Managers will enjoy substantial discretion.

In such circumstances, the most likely response for an owner dissatisfied with performance is to sell his shares in the company concerned. This is what Hirschman referred to as 'exit'. (He contrasted exit with 'voice' where shareowners intervened directly in the running of their companies, replacing unsatisfactory managers and so forth.) Exit will affect the value of a company's shares and thus serve as a signal that not all is well with its management. But capital markets must be efficient if they are to provide the necessary discipline for managers. There are both empirical and theoretical grounds for doubting whether the so-called efficient markets hypothesis holds in such cases (Vickers and Yarrow, 1991, p. 115). Thus, it may only be in those circumstances when share ownership is sufficiently concentrated to secure 'voice' that good corporate governance can be assured.

It is often assumed that it is impossible to organise competitive markets in the absence of private ownership and that therefore the one implies the other. This is not true. It is possible to have private ownership without competition – as the existence of private monopolies demonstrates. It is also possible to organise competition between state-owned enterprises – although it is true that this was not done either in Britain or throughout most of socialist Eastern Europe. Moreover, there is some evidence to suggest that in competitive conditions, public enterprises are no less efficient than private ones (Vickers and Yarrow, 1991, pp. 116–117). Thus competition and privatisation are conceptually distinct.

Formally, economists define a competitive market as one in which no single firm can determine the price. This normally requires the participation of a large number of firms. The same outcome can be achieved with as few as two firms if there are no sunk costs; such markets are defined as contestable (Filatotchev, 1991, pp. 488–489). The existence of several firms in competition with each other can provide regulators with valuable information about costs and technical alternatives. More important, as basic neoclassical theory demonstrates, competitive markets ensure allocative efficiency. Further, rivalry can constitute a valuable spur to innovation.

The experience of Western Europe suggests that private ownership is not sufficient to ensure an adequate degree of competition. The authorities need to take explicit actions to limit the growth of monopoly and other barriers to entry. Indeed as even Adam Smith was aware, they must fight a continuous battle against restrictive practices. This is likely to be true in the ex-socialist states of Eastern Europe as well.

One relatively straightforward way for the governments of the region to encourage competition is through the removal or reduction of tariffs and non-tariff barriers. But the scope for opening up their economies is limited by concern for the balance of payments. There is another justification for protection in the short run. Just like so-called infant industries, some sectors of these economies are in principle capable of competing successfully. But to do so they require extensive investment and reconstruction. This will take time. If tariffs were removed immediately, firms in such branches would be unable to compete against their Western rivals and would be forced into liquidation (Hare, 1992, pp. 6–7).

The pursuit of competition in addition to privatisation – or indeed without it – should result in increased efficiency. But competitive markets will fail to achieve socially efficient outcomes in the presence of significant externalities. And a suitable policy-response has also to be found to the problem of so-called natural monopolies.

These problems with the regulation of natural monopolies are part of a wider difficulty faced by neo classical theory; by analogy with market failure, it can be called state failure (McAuley, 1991a). The neoclassical theory of welfare and general equilibrium assumed that the state could avoid the so-called principal-agent problem: it could enjoin its agents to act optimally at no cost. This was also true of the theory of optimal planning and its precursors.[1] This assumption is false; and the distortions introduced by the sub-optimising behaviour of agents can be as significant a source of economic inefficiency as externalities or market power. The possibility of state failure implies that, frequently, a second-best equilibrium is all that can be achieved. It provides additional support for a policy of privatisation.

Political Objectives of Privatisation

It is frequently suggested that a secondary aim of privatisation is the raising of revenue. As Vickers and Yarrow point out, given the problems involved with such a programme in Eastern Europe, it might be simpler for the government to issue bonds (Vickers and Yarrow, 1991, p. 118). Certainly, the costs associated with such an issue would almost certainly be lower than those associated with the valuation of state enterprises, the preparation of prospectuses and so on. Furthermore, potential purchasers would have a far clearer idea of the risk attached to what they were buying.

It is not really an answer to this observation to suggest that the ex-socialist countries do not possess well-organised bond markets on which the government might raise the revenue it needs. They do not possess equity capital markets either; and that is part of the problem involved in privatisation. The

1. For example, economic theorists from Hotelling on saw no difficulty in requiring the managers of nationalised enterprises to price in the public interest – that is to set price equal to marginal cost. Nor did planning theorists from Lange to Arrow and Heal think that such an instruction would be difficult if not impossible to enforce.

implication of this observation is, I think, that the raising of revenue is an inappropriate objective for privatisation in formerly planned economies. As the Chilean experience demonstrates, it may be inappropriate in other circumstances as well.[2]

Finally, there are the political objectives of a privatisation programme. The sale of shares in state enterprises is intended to create an interest group opposed to a return to 'socialism'. The creation of such a group strengthens the new regime's commitment to a market economy and increases the credibility of other components in its economic reform programme. At the same time, the sale or distribution of shares provides an occasion to modify the distribution of wealth – and, consequently – income. This will be achieved, *inter alia*, by under-pricing the assets on sale.[3]

These policy objectives are in conflict with those of greater efficiency. Maximising political support for the new regime implies a wide distribution of share ownership; this may or may not also be implied by the desire to modify the distribution of wealth (McAuley, 1991b and 1992). Similarly, a desire to 'buy off' the potential opposition of workers and managers suggests the distribution of a certain proportion of the shares in any enterprise to the employees of that enterprise. But a widely dispersed pattern of ownership raises the free-rider problem: the new owners are unlikely to exercise close supervision over the management of their property; corporate governance will depend upon the operation of capital markets of doubtful efficiency. Furthermore, workers and managers are likely to use their position as owners to oppose radical restructuring – especially where this involves the closing of plants and large-scale redundancies.

To summarise this discussion: economic theory suggests that privatisation programmes should concentrate on enterprises which face potential competition. This justifies the priority that almost all the new regimes have attached to so-called petty privatisation. But it also has implications for the order in which large-scale industry is reorganised. Second, in the short run, the privatisation procedure should concentrate shareholdings sufficiently to ensure that the new owners exercise 'voice'. Third, privatisation is not a complete policy. It must be accompanied by measures to maintain or increase competition. This will ensure that the economy receives the full benefit from the greater

2. In Chile after the fall of Allende, the government's objective was to sell off as much of the state sector as quickly as possible. Since a subsidiary objective was to raise revenue, many of the sales involved partial payment with the balance financed through loans from the state; this created relatively highly-geared enterprises. During subsequent recessions, many of these failed and had to be re-nationalised. As two specialists have remarked the Chilean experience suggests '... privatisation per se is not always an effective way to establish credible commitments to new incentive structures' (Vickers and Yarrow, 1991, p. 127). The method of privatisation may well be of fundamental importance for the attainment of this objective.

3. This was a procedure favoured by the Thatcher government in Britain in the 1980s.

efficiency of the newly privatised firms; it will also improve the performance of those enterprises which remain in the hands of the state. These will include monopolies, particularly natural monopolies. Economic theory gives contradictory prescriptions about how these should be handled. It is also unclear about the practical response to other cases of market failure. Finally, there is a conflict between the objective of greater economic efficiency and that of ensuring political support for the transition to a market economy through the redistribution of wealth. In the light of these propositions, what are the key features of the new Russian privatisation programme and how does it compare with those that have already been introduced in Central Europe?

Privatisation: the Russian Programme

At the same time as it launched its price liberalisation programme, in early January 1992, the Russian government embarked upon a far-reaching programme of privatisation. This is described here. First, I set out what the government has said that it hopes to achieve through the programme; then I outline the procedures that it has adopted.

The Objectives of Privatisation

The Basic Principles state that this programme is supposed to contribute to the overall objective of economic stabilisation in two ways (*Ekonomika i zhizn'* 2, 1992, p. 18). First, since it is expected that private trade outlets will exhibit greater flexibility in price-setting than state-owned ones, privatisation will facilitate the shift to free prices. The authorities are aware that private stores might be more willing to increase prices in the face of excess demand; but they also believe that such stores will be more willing to reduce prices in the face of excess supply. And it is this response they wish to encourage. Also, they hope that the sale of assets will mop up part of the monetary overhang – and thus reduce the scale of increase of consumer-goods prices.

Second, privatisation is supposed to reduce the level of budgetary expenditure by relieving the authorities of their responsibility for large numbers of loss-making enterprises. This, too will contribute to macro-economic stabilisation by reducing the budget deficit. This objective is, I fear, somewhat disingenuous: loss-making enterprises transferred to the private sector are likely to make a proportion of their workforces redundant – in time they may shut down altogether. The resulting increase in unemployment – and thus in unemployment pay – will result in an increase in budgetary expenditure which may equal the original subsidy.

In addition to these indirect contributions to macro-economic stabilisation, the Basic Principles state that the privatisation programme is supposed to con-

TABLE 11.1 Criteria for Determining Privatisation Procedures

Enterprise Type	*Privatisation Procedure* Auction	Competitive tendering	Sale of Shares after conversion to joint-stock company
Trade, catering, services, retail newsagents; road haulage	remaining enterprises	not more than 40% of enterprises by decision of appropiate Soviet.	book value greater than 1 million roubles
Woodworking, forestry, printing, light, food, metalworking, engineering, construction	employing less than 200 persons on approval of Committee for Management of State Property		employing more than 200 persons or book value above 2 mill. roubles
Sea and river transport	individual vessels	–	–
Hotels	–	up to 100 beds	above 100 beds
Agricultural PTOs, building materials	–	book value less than 1 million roubles	book value above 1 million rubles
Other branches	by decision of the relevant Committee for the Management of State Property		book value above 1 million roubles

Source: Ekonomika i zhizn' 2, 1992, p. 20.

tribute to budgetary income. Most important, it is intended to raise the level of economic efficiency.

The privatisation programme distinguishes between two broad categories of state assets: those which are intended for privatisation in 1992; those whose immediate privatisation is forbidden or restricted. The programme lists the following seven categories of establishment as intended for immediate privatisation:

1. wholesale and retail trade establishments, public catering enterprises, household service outlets;
2. state agricultural establishments – not including *sovkhozy*;
3. unfinished construction projects which are seriously behind schedule;
4. road-haulage establishments;
5. construction organisations and factories producing building materials;
6. factories in the food and light industries;
7. loss-making enterprises in various sectors of the economy.

The first three of these should be privatised before the end of September 1992; the privatisation of the next three categories should start in the second half of the year. In the first instance, light and food industry enterprises employing less than 200 employees will be disposed of.

The Basic Principles contain a list of twenty-three categories of state or municipal asset that it is forbidden to privatise in 1992; some of them are unlikely ever to be privatised. The list includes such items as mineral deposits, water resources, forests etc., nature reserves, elements of the country's historical and cultural heritage; the state treasury – including foreign currency holdings, the pension fund etc.; banks – especially those responsible for currency circulation; the armed forces and their weapons and so on. Among the items that can be privatised only with the express consent of the Russian government the Basic Principles list enterprises which occupy a dominant position in their branch or market; large state enterprises – those with a book value of more than 200 million roubles or more than 10,000 employees on 1 January 1992,[4] enterprises in the armaments industry and in atomic power; enterprises in extractive industry and elements of the so-called energy complex; enterprises in rail, water and air transport. It also singles out higher educational establishments, printing firms, telegraphic agencies and last but not least factories producing spirits and tobacco.

Privatisation Procedures

All local government units in the RSFSR have been given targets for the amount of privatisation that they are expected to achieve in 1992. For example, Arkhangelskaia *oblast* is expected to privatise the following percentages of enterprises by branch (ibid., p. 20):

Light industry	60	Food industry	50
Construction	50	Construction materials	45
Road haulage	60	Agricultural PTOs	60
Retail stores	60	Wholesale bases	50
Service outlets	60	Catering establishments	35

The figures for other *oblasti* and for Moscow and St. Petersburg are very similar.

The Basic Principles envisage that privatisation will be effected by different methods depending on the branch and the size of the enterprise in question. Basically, small enterprises will be auctioned off as going concerns. Large ones will be converted into joint stock companies; a part of their shares will then be distributed to managers and employees; the remainder will be sold at auction. The various criteria laid down by the Russian government are set out in Table 11.1. The book value of the enterprise will provide the opening bid price; there will be no attempt to value individual enterprises (*The*

4. These enterprises account for the following shares in the total in industry (per cent): of all enterprises 1.3, of production 25.7, of employment, 19.4 of book value of capital, 47.2, (Terplukhin, 1992, p. 15.)

Economist, 15 February 1992, p. 94). In addition, the Basic Principles state that non-commercial tendering (that is not making use of an auction to establish price or scale of investment) will not be allowed in 1992. Nor will the conclusion of leases be allowed which give the lessee an option to purchase the asset at a later date. Finally, the holding of an auction with less than two bidders is also forbidden.

The Basic Principles also state that, at least in 1992, purchasers of state assets will not be able to pay by instalments. The one exception to this rule relates to the shares purchased by the workforces of newly privatised enterprises; even here, however, full payment must be made within twelve months. Lastly, neither foreigners nor enterprises that remain in state hands are to be allowed to take part in auctions (ibid., p. 94).

When enterprises are converted into joint-stock companies prior to privatisation, the employees are to receive an allocation of the shares. This will take the form of preferential non-voting stock. Employees will be entitled to 25 per cent of the issued capital of the enterprise or to an allocation per person equivalent to 20 times the minimum monthly wage – whichever is the less. The distribution of these shares between employees will be decided by a general meeting of the enterprise's labour collective. Employees will be entitled to purchase ordinary shares worth 10 per cent of the issued capital of the enterprise at a discount of 30 per cent; these shares will have to be fully paid for within twelve months. Managers, too, will receive options on 5 per cent of the issued capital of the firm. Proceeds from sale of enterprises are to be distributed as shown in Table 11.2.

The authors of this Russian privatisation programme have decided to use very Soviet methods to achieve their objectives. But Anatolii Chubais, the minister responsible, is reported as saying that this is deliberate; he argues that the new government is forced to rely upon the existing regional administrative structure and that structure only understands the language of plans and targets (ibid., p. 94). In this respect, the programme might even be an improvement on those that have been adopted in Central Europe (see below).

Second, the plan emphasises speed rather than equity in the privatisation of state assets. This may be inevitable since the Russian state does not have access to the armies of accountants, lawyers and valuation experts needed to proceed with privatisation along Western lines. Even if it did, it is doubtful whether such methods could be applied: in the absence of active markets it is conceptually difficult to establish the value of potential asset and liability streams – and hence establish profitability. But such an approach risks leaving some workers owning a share of nothing while others will receive a real addition to their wealth. This will almost certainly lead to bitterness and resentment in the future.

Finally, the attempt to buy off potential opposition to privatisation with shares may backfire. Under the plan, management and employees will own up

TABLE 11.2 Distribution of the Receipts from Privatisation

Recipient	*Share of Proceeds from Privatisation (per cent)*		
	From municipal property	*From oblast property*	*From federal property*
Employees of privatised firms	10	10	10
Local budgets	50	10	10
Oblast/ASSR budgets	10	50	10
RSFSR budget	20	20	60
State privatisation agencies:			
Property funds (all)	5	5	5
Committees for property management	4.5	4.5	4.5
RSFSR committee for property	0.5	0.5	0.5

Source: Ekonomika i zhizn' 2, 1992, p. 20.

to 40 per cent of the issued capital of newly privatised enterprises. There is no reason to believe that the remainder will be concentrated in the hands of a few shareholders. This is likely to result in relatively weak supervision of managerial decision making; it may also provide the basis for effective opposition to radical restructuring or closure.

Privatisation: Alternative Approaches

All the new regimes in Central and Eastern Europe have stated their intention to replace central planning with a market economy. Most of them have also embarked upon programmes of privatisation. Those adopted by the countries of Central Europe are reasonably wellknown and will not be described in detail. But it is worth commenting on ways in which they overlap with and differ from the Russian programme – and with each other. It is also worth describing briefly the German approach.

The Central European Experience

The three Central European countries, Poland, Czechoslovakia (CSFR) and Hungary adopted radically different solutions to the problem of disposing of state property.

In Poland, the privatisation programme was included in the so-called Balcerowicz plan. It involved the following steps. First, all Poles were to be given vouchers representing their share of the nation's assets; they were required to deposit their vouchers with one or more privatisation funds. The privatisation funds were to use their pledged vouchers to acquire equity in a number of state enterprises. The funds might also 'manage' the state's holdings in enterprise equity. The 'funds' were to reconstruct and sell the enterprises that they acquire. At a later date, citizens were to be able to buy and sell shares in the 'funds' – thus exposing them to market discipline themselves (*The Economist*, 11 May 1991, p. 84; Thomas, 1992, p. 282). This plan was designed to combine a 'big bang' approach to the alienation of state ownership with a mechanism for minimising inequity in the distribution of wealth. It made little attempt to generate revenue for the state budget. Furthermore, it emphasised 'voice' rather than 'exit' as the mechanism for ensuring corporate governance.

With the fall of the Mazowiecki government and the abandonment of the Balcerowicz plan, it is not clear how much of this programme will be – or has been – implemented (*The Economist*, 22 February 1992, p. 45). But despite problems with privatisation, the Polish private sector continues to grow rapidly through the establishment of new private enterprises. At the end of the day, these new firms may well constitute the growth of a more competitive and efficient manufacturing sector than will the reconstruction of existing enterprises.

The privatisation programme contained in the CSFR government's marketisation plan includes the following elements. First, all citizens were to receive a package of vouchers – for a nominal sum; they would be able to use their vouchers to bid for shares in regular auctions of state enterprises. To do so, however, they would have to 'register' their vouchers and pay about two weeks wages for the privilege. Foreigners, of course, were not to be permitted to take part in these auctions – at least at the beginning (*The Economist*, 11 May 1991, p. 83; Thomas, 1992, p. 289).

At the auctions, citizens would be able to buy shares in specific ex-state companies. Since many state enterprises are technically bankrupt, many citizens will end up buying a piece of nothing; but it was argued that those enterprises which survived would feel the impress of personal ownership from the start. Further, the only way to discover what enterprises are worth is to create a market: formal or bureaucratic valuation procedures are both too time-consuming and too inaccurate. This so-called voucher scheme was to be accompanied by the sale at auction of up to 50,000 small enterprises (Begg, 1991, p. 254). The Czech programme was less concerned with equity in the distribution of wealth than the Polish one. As befits an ardent supporter of Mrs Thatcher, the Finance Minister was keen to ensure both a wide distribution of share ownership and the fastest possible development of a capital market.

The scheme is now under way. In the Czech lands, it has generated a certain amount of enthusiasm; in Slovakia, it is treated with rather more suspicion. Apparently, in the absence of real information about the value of different companies, or about the sectors in which the economy might possess a comparative advantage, citizens have expressed a preference for plants producing chocolate, beer and glass – goods for which the country was known before 1939 (*Independent*, 22 January 1992).

TABLE 11.3 The Status of Treuhand Firms: end November 1991

	Number	*Per cent of total*
Firms disposed of in their entirety	4,125	38.0
Sold to the private sector	2,467	22.7
Management buyouts	602	5.5
Sold to foreigners	223	2.1
Returned to previous owners	463	4.3
Transferred to local authorities	250	2.3
Being closed	636	5.8
Other – wound up through closure, merger or subdivision	241	2.2
Enterprises still to be disposed of	6,744	62.0
Majority-owned by private sector	557	5.1
Majority-owned by Treuhand	6,187	56.9
Total	10,869	100.0

Source: *The Economist,* 21 March 1992, p. 95; quoting Wendy Carlin and Colin Mayer "East German Economic Reconstruction". Paper delivered to an NBER Conference, February 1992. (Unpublished).

The programme has been criticised as an election ploy by the Finance Minister Vaclav Klaus. It has also generated resentment at the possibilities it creates for 'insider dealing' by former managers and communist party officials; after all, they have more information than ordinary citizens about the relative profitability of different state enterprises. There is also evidence of foreign – or dirty – money being used at various auctions (*The Economist,* 9 November 1992, p. 140). The government rejects these criticisms and it is fair to say that critics have not produced evidence to suggest that abuse is widespread. At the present time, there is more hope that the Czech privatisation plan will be implemented than that the Polish one will. But the situation may change after the general election due in the summer of 1992.

The Hungarian privatisation programme avoided the use of vouchers altogether. As in the CSFR, small enterprises were sold off – or are in the process of being sold – to local entrepreneurs for 'real' money. The larger enterprises were to be sold either to foreign firms or, also, to local businessmen (*The Economist*, 11 May 1991, p. 84; Thomas, 1992, p. 286). This programme emphasised 'due process' and the raising of revenue at the expense of either the rapid creation of a capital market or a substantial modification in the distribution of wealth. The difference in emphasis between Hungary and the other two Central European countries may have been due to a belief that there was already a protocapitalist bourgoisie in the country.

I have no recent information on the success or otherwise of the programme. But despite a deep recession, new business formation continues at a substantial rate. The number of firms in November 1991 was more than 60 per cent greater than a year earlier (PlanEcon Report 7–8, 1992, p. 26). Here too, perhaps, new businesses will prove more viable in the long run than privatised state enterprises.

The Treuhandanstalt Approach

Following the unification of the two Germanies, the bulk of state enterprises in the DDR were transferred to the Treuhandanstalt, an agency of the Bonn government, to be 'reconstituted' and sold – for real money. The so-called Treuhand agency has been staffed by civil servants and management consultants recruited from the Western part of Germany; the enterprises for which it has been responsible have received substantial subsidies from German taxpayers. The Treuhand's strategy appears to have been to reconstitute its enterprises in accordance with the requirements of the West German social market economy; it has then sought 'purchasers' who were willing to commit themselves to invest in the new entities. In the meantime, it has kept most enterprises open – and most of the labour force in employment, even if on short time or zero time. Given the experience with market economies of those running the Treuhand, and the resources that they have had at their disposal to facilitate the reconstruction of East German enterprises, the German approach to privatisation was bound to be different from that elsewhere in the region.

Recent evidence, reported in Table 11.3, suggests that Treuhand has disposed of about 40 per cent of the firms which were transferred to it. But only 2 per cent have been sold to foreigners – suggesting a degree of protection or discrimination. Also, only 6 per cent of enterprises have been closed down; this is far less than the share of enterprises thought to be technically bankrupt. The Treuhand may be softening the contraction to allow the labour market more time to absorb those made redundant; it may be wasting resources prolonging the life of no-hope plants. Dornbusch has argued that these resources may be better spent in retraining and investment in totally new firms (*The Economist,* 21 March 1992, p. 95). In addition, it appears that the population of the former DDR will receive little additional wealth from the Treuhand's privatisation programme.

Conclusion

In this paper I first examined the lessons that could be drawn from neoclassical theory for the design of privatisation programmes in ex-socialist economies. The discussion can be summarised as follows. First, private firms are more likely to respond to the tastes and preferences of individual consumers than are publicly-owned ones. This is especially true where the public sector enterprises are subject to the constraints of central planning.

Privatisation – particularly what I have referred to as petty privatisation – will result in a significant increase in consumers' sovereignty (Fischer, 1992, pp. 232ff).

Privatisation, however, will not in itself ensure economic efficiency. What I have called x-efficiency will result only if an adequate framework of corporate governance is secured. Allocative efficiency requires competitive – or at least contestable – markets. Corporate governance and hence the reduction of managerial discretion requires either the existence of efficient capital markets or a sufficient concentration of shareholdings to ensure adequate supervision. Of these, the latter is probably preferable: control through the capital market encourages an unhealthy preoccupation with short-term results. Further, to secure the efficient allocation of resources, governments must supplement privatisation programmes with policies to promote and maintain competition. Also, monopolies will require divestment or regulation.

Finally, privatisation programmes frequently contain political objectives in addition to goals of increased efficiency. For example, they may be intended to raise revenue, to secure support for the government in power, to achieve a significant redistribution of the nation's wealth. The pursuit of such objectives will often if not always conflict with the aim of increased efficiency.

In subsequent sections I explored how far the privatisation programmes adopted in Russia and a number of Central European countries conformed to these prescriptions. By implication, I also raised the question of their likely success or failure.

As an aside, it is worth noting that privatisation will be accompanied by radical restructuring of the ex-socialist economies. This will inevitably result in an increase in unemployment. Unemployment has also resulted from the collapse of central planning in the former USSR and the collapse of trade between former members of the CMEA. Since all ex-socialist countries have difficulty in absorbing a rapid rise in the level of unemployment, the deepening recession has led to a slowdown in the pace of privatisation.

This leads on to a second observation. Even if the privatisation programme envisages a rapid transfer of control from state to private hands, it will not happen instantaneously. Further, as I pointed out in the last paragraph, transfer may be slowed down in response to changing macro-economic conditions. This creates a new task for the bodies charged with promoting and maintaining competition: supervision of those enterprises that remain in state ownership. The objective must be to ensure that budget constraints are hardened; and, second, that opportunities to make use of market power (e.g. to take advantage of a monopolistic position) are limited. This issue was not discussed in the paper (but see van Brabant, 1991, p. 518).

Turning to the privatisation programmes themselves: in Czechoslovakia and Russia the emphasis is on the disposal of actual assets in a newly created but real market for capital. If the programme is fully implemented, it should result in the speedy transfer of ownership from the state to individuals. This, in turn, may result in a sharp reduction in the level of budgetary expenditure on subsidies. How far this will be achieved, however, will depend upon the political position of the government and the strength of will of the Finance Minister. A cut in budgetary support will result in a sharp rise in unemployment and considerable pressure to 'bail out' particular firms. In any case, it will lead to an increase in social welfare expenditure.

The sale of shares in real enterprises will result in some buyers being disappointed. Citizens have little previous experience of such transactions; no-one has any real information about the value of different firms. Many firms are technically bankrupt and, as a result, will collapse without state subsidies; others will 'go to the wall' when prices of inputs adjust; this is particularly likely when energy prices are allowed to rise to world market levels. There will be gainers as well as losers from this process; but I doubt that it will be seen as fair. Rather, I suspect, it will engender a great deal of resentment. The government will be blamed by those who lose; those who gain will be suspected of making use of inside knowledge or other corrupt practices. The process will result in an increase in social friction as well as a new social cleavage.

It is not clear, moreover, that the government will be able to deflect this resentment through the distribution of shares to existing employees in state enterprises. Such holdings may slow down or frustrate attempts to restructure individual plants; this will reduce levels of efficiency. It may avoid unemployment in the short term but not in the long run.

Finally, the decision to sell real shares will, in all probability, result in a dispersed pattern of share ownership. The owners will be tempted to act as free riders and, at best, to sell their holdings in firms that do badly. Given the likely shortcomings of the newly formed capital market in countries like Russia or Czechoslovakia, managers are unlikely to experience consistent pressure to increase efficiency.

In Poland and Hungary, on the other hand, and even in the former DDR, privatisation procedures are likely to result in more concentrated patterns of ownership; this is likely to lead to more consistent pressure on managers and greater efficiency in the newly privatised firms. But the process of privatisation will take longer to complete. There is thus more opportunity for it to be deflected in response to political pressures. This seems to have happened already in Poland.

A number of the privatisation programmes introduced in ex-socialist economies emphasise the contribution that the sale of state assets can make to the budget. Above I quoted the observation made by Vickers and Yarrow, that such revenue could probably be raised more cheaply through the sale of bonds. But that does not exhaust the issue. Suppose that the programme is successful: should the receipts be considered as part of the ordinary revenue of the state, on a par with the proceeds of the sales tax or the income tax? If so, and if they are used to defray the costs of current government services, then the new regimes would be indulging in capital consumption; they would be guilty of '... selling off the family silver!'

Suppose, on the other hand, that receipts from privatisation are committed to a variety of investment projects. The projects can be in either the public or the private sector. There is no reason to suppose that the new government – or its civil servants – will be any better at identifying appropriate private sector investment projects than were planners under the old regime. *A priori*, one would expect private entrepreneurs to do better. Nor, I believe, is the situation improved, if the government uses the proceeds to finance public-sector projects. There is no reason to believe that revenues raised from the sale of state assets will fund the optimal level of public investment. The optimal level could be greater – in which case, additional funds can be raised either through the budget or the capital market. Equally, it could be less: in which case, funds would need to be returned to the private sector.

Such considerations strengthen the case for not emphasising the revenue side of privatisation programmes. It is possible that the restructuring of the ex-socialist economies, the development of services, of consumer-goods capacity and of those branches in which individual countries have a comparative advantage will proceed most quickly if existing private capital is left in private hands. In this way the growth of new private businesses will be fostered.

References

Begg, D., 1991,"Czechoslovakia", *Economic Policy* 13, pp. 243–286.

Brabant, J. M. van, 1991, "Privatisation in Post-Communist Societies: A Comment", *Communist Economies* 4, pp. 511–519.

Clague, C. and G. Rausser, 1992 (eds), *The Emergence of Market Economies in Eastern Europe*. Oxford: Basil Blackwell.

Corbett, J. and C. Mayer, 1991, "Financial Reform in Eastern Europe: Progress with the Wrong Model", *Oxford Review of Economic Policy* 4, pp. 57–75.

The Economist, 11 May 1991, "Creating the Invisible Hand", pp. 83–90.

______, 15 February 1992, "Privatising Russia", pp. 16, 93–94.

______, 22 February 1992,"Poland Loses Heart", pp. 45–46.

______, 21 March 1992, "Hand of Kindness: is Germany's Treuhandanstalt a Good Thing?", p. 95.

Ekonomika i zhizn' 2, 1992, "Osnovnye polozhenia programmy privatizatsii gosudarstvennykh i munitsipal'nykh predpriatiy v Rossiyskoy Federatsii na 1992 god", pp. 18–20.

Ekonomika i zhizn' 10, 1992, "Vremennoe polozhenie (o privatizatsii gosudarstvennykh i munitsipal'nykh predpriatiy v Rossiyskoy Federatsii po konkursu)", pp. 18–19.

Filatotchev, I., 1991, "Privatisation in the USSR: Economic and Social Problems", *Communist Economies* 4, pp. 481–498.

Fischer, S., 1992, "Privatisation in East European Transformation" in Clague, C. and G. Rausser, *op. cit.*, pp. 227–244.

Hare, P., 1992, Privatisation and Competitiveness in the Transition. Paper delivered at BASSEES Conference, Birmingham, March. Mimeo.

Hirschman, A., 1970, *Exit, Voice and Loyalty.* Cambridge, Mass.: Harvard University Press.

Krueger, A., 1992, "Institutions for the New Private Sector" in Clague, C. and G. Rausser, *op. cit.*, pp. 219–223.

McAuley, A., 1991a, "Market Failure vs State Failure: The Scope for Privatisation in a Planned Economy". Paper prepared for the First EACES Workshop, Trento, Italy, March. Mimeo.

_____, 1991b,"The Economic Transition in Eastern Europe: Employment, Income Distribution and the Social Security Net", *Oxford Review of Eco nomic Policy* 4, pp. 93–105.

_____, 1992, "Economic Justice in Eastern Europe". Paper prepared for the Workshop: Social Responses to Political and Economic Transformations in East-Central Europe, Prague, May. Mimeo.

PlanEcon Report 7–8, 1992.

Terplukhin, P., 1992, *Some Comments on Russian Privatisation.* BASSEES Conference, Birmingham. Mimeo.

Thomas, S., 1992, "The Political Economy of Privatisation: Poland, Hungary and Czechoslovakia" in Clague, C. and G. Rausser, *op. cit.,* pp. 279–296.

Vickers, J. and G. Yarrow, 1991, "Economic Perspectives on Privatisation", *Journal of Economic Perspectives* 2, pp. 111–132.

12

Property Rights, Competition Policy, and Privatisation in the Transition from Socialism to Market Economy

*Laszlo Somogyi and Adam Török**

Introduction

The countries of Central and East Europe have now embarked on the road of transition from some kind of planning to some kind of market economy. The intellectual interest in trying to understand this process has been lively and despite the relatively short time that has passed since the inception of the debate, it is possible to identify four main areas that figure prominently in the transition literature: stabilisation, liberalisation, structural adjustment, and institutional change. The focus of the present paper is on institutional change and liberalisation. More specifically, we examine the complex of property rights (actual, perceived and expected), and their consequences, firstly for competition policy and the access to markets (trade policy), and secondly for privatisation.

The paper seeks to use a triangular-type analytical framework. One has to imagine a triangle with the following edges:

A property rights (or privatisation) policy;
B competition policy (regulation and supervision of the domestic market);
C trade policy (with special emphasis on imports).

* University of Lund and Institute of Industrial Economics of the Hungarian Academy of Sciences, respectively. The authors would like to thank Claes Wihlborg for his detailed comments as well as Yves Bourdet, Ingemar Ståhl and György Szapáry for their helpful remarks. All the remaining errors and omissions are, however, entirely their own.

Each of the edges of the triangle is interlinked with the two others, and our analytical aim is to explore the constraints of each policy imposed by the two others upon it. Our starting assumption is that 'mainstream'-type policies (e.g. accelerated privatisation, the shock liberalisation of imports and anti-monopolistic but 'neutral' competition policies that imply a low level of state intervention in the operation of the market), may very easily contradict each other in the emerging market economies of Eastern Europe.

Let us take a very simple example: a multinational company exporting to an East European (or almost any) country is interested in *low trade barriers* and *anti-monopolistic competition policies*, especially if it has a domestic competitor in the market. If, however, it tries to benefit from *privatisation* and invests there – eventually acquiring its formerly monopolistic domestic competitor together with its market shares – it will become interested in *high barriers to imports* and *a competition policy that is not biased against monopolies*.

The parallel use of different analytical approaches appears fruitful in tackling problems of transition. In the following, use will be made of the tools of both welfare economics and international trade theory. However, the analysis will be conducted within the general framework of the Coasean property rights approach.

The Initial Setting

There is little controversy over the general direction of desired change in Eastern Europe. The transition of these countries should lead them to a market economy. It seems fairly obvious, however, that the target is not that of an ideal *laissez-faire* market system, whatever form such a system might conceivably take. The impediments to the attainment of a textbook-like competitive world order are present both in the actual international economic setting and in the internal structures of the countries concerned. Despite almost half a century of continuous efforts to do away with the obstacles to trade, the international economy is still burdened with considerable barriers to the free exchange of goods and services.

A good negative proof of this fact is the strenuous effort of the European Communities to create the Single European Market. The declaration of free trade within the European Community has not meant trade without barriers – or entirely liberalised trade. Another symptom of the limited success of trade liberalisation efforts is the sluggishness of the current GATT negotiations: even though the Uruguay round is now in its second year of 'overtime'. A settlement on the liberalisation of trade in agricultural products as well as services is still out of sight.

Another indication of the existence of trade barriers is the highly administered and probably highly distorted trade flows between Western Europe and the former COMECON countries.[1]

Apart from technical monopolies that have been transformed into legal ones by many governments, competition has long been restricted in such areas as road transport, telecommunications, civil aviation, financial services and even retail trade.

Deregulation has come a long way since the heyday of Pigovian interventionism. Nevertheless breaking up existing monopolies remains a tricky matter, even in the West. Firstly, technology-linked entry barriers may be substantial whenever sunk costs tend to be high. Secondly, privatisation is not always accompanied by liberalisation, because governments wish to capitalise the existing monopoly profits of the incumbent.

British Telecommunications is a case in point: in addition to its cost advantage because of the ownership of most of the existing trunk lines the company was also assured a dominating position through the licensing system (Swann, 1988, Chapter 8). In other words, the investors who bought the shares of the company also acquired rights of preferential access to the market.

It seems quite clear that the actual international business environment is far from any ideal image of a free market system. If, however, the international environment displays considerable aberrations in comparison with the free trade model, the internal economic structures of the ex-socialist countries are no better. Past trade flows between Eastern and Western Europe were unlikely to reflect specialisation according to comparative advantage.[2]

The situation was probably still worse with intra-COMECON trade where decisions on production and trade patterns were made on an administrative basis, albeit usually preceded by bilateral negotiations between the member countries. The excessively energy- and material-intensive nature of the ex-socialist economies is well documented (cf. Winiecki, 1990). Low prices of energy and other industrial inputs from other COMECON countries gave

1. In an admittedly highly aggregated study, Neven and Röller (1990) find that, with the exception of Germany and the Netherlands, EC and EFTA countries do not seem to use East Europe as a source of labour-intensive commodities. This '... may be the reflection either of highly managed trade or trade barriers' (pp. 104–105). They also find that labour-intensive imports form the ex-COMECON block face a high common tariff wall. A former analysis of the Hungarian export structure and pattern of comparative advantage (Török, 1986, Chapter IV) speaks of a 'Leontief-paradox'-type situation in Hungary's trade with the West. Hungary is a country with a poor physical capital and a good human capital endowment which exports mainly capital-intensive products (iron and steel, petrochemicals and several semi-finished goods belonging to the SITC 6 commodity class) to the West, while its imports from the West include a high percentage of skill-intensive products.

2. Although the problem of measuring and perfectly understanding the comparative advantages of non-market economies has not yet been solved, a solution cannot be expected since there are only a very small number of remaining non-market-type ('unreformed') socialist economies like North Korea or Cuba.

socialist managers the impression that they were using cheap technologies. From this misunderstanding emerged strongly distorted 'revealed comparative advantages' (cf. Balassa, 1977).

Apart from the systematic bias that emanated from the underpricing of energy, numerous distortions were also produced by multiple exchange rates, subsidisation, differential taxation, soft budget constraints and topsy-turvy pricing in general. However, the ample literature on comparative economic systems offers much in-depth information on these problems (for a non-exhaustive list of useful sources on these topics see Kornai, 1986). As of 1 January 1991, tariffs on passenger cars below 1.6 litres of engine capacity were increased from 10 to 18 per cent (and to 13 per cent in the case of cars equipped with catalytic converters). Larger cars were subject to progressively higher import tariffs.

The widespread existence of inefficiencies in the economies in transition makes the assessment of the viability of existing industries very difficult.[3] This is why it is extremely difficult to judge which barriers to imports are justified at least on a transitional basis, and which are not.

The infant industry argument literature might be of considerable help here. According to the Mill–Bastable test, infant industry protection is justifiable on only two grounds. Firstly the industry has subsequently to grow up. Secondly, those who lose during the transition will have to be compensated once production has sufficiently expanded to make such compensation feasible (cf, Södersten, 1978, p. 269). The general approach of the infant industry protection argument and the Mill–Bastable test could eventually provide at least partial guidelines for East European transition. However, substantial modification cannot be omitted: those who might ask for protection may well be the aged rather than infants. Wrong industrial policies in all countries of the region have led to a curious situation in which 'aged' industries in the West European sense seemingly become 'young' industries in Eastern Europe, since most investment funds have been spent on 'smokestack' sectors from the early 1950s.

The Analytical Framework

The neoclassical justification for perfect competition is based on the theoretical finding that under (usually vaguely specified – cf. Coase, 1960, p. 43) ideal

3. Blanchard et al. (1991), estimate that '... what is needed is nothing short of the orderly closing down of most of the existing production structure and the creation of a whole new economy.' (p. xvi). This is an extreme view, but it well reflects the current intellectual confusion as far as the value of productive assets in former socialist industries and the necessary direction of their structural change is concerned.

conditions, competitive equilibrium will result in an optimal state in the Paretian sense.[4]

The theoretical justification for competition policy in general and antitrust policy in particular is that such policies will facilitate the attainment of Paretian optimal states. For example, it is argued that a situation where some parties hold a monopolistic position while free competition prevails in other markets is not optimal from the point of view of the consumer. Therefore, *ceteris paribus*, the breaking up of the monopolies is warranted in such cases.[5]

Modern antitrust policies are designed to defend the consumer on the grounds that the consumer is the weaker party (in contrast with the 'caveat emptor' approach prevailing, for example, in the United States before the Great Depression). Even theory is more concerned with the welfare of the consumer than that of the producer. The tacit assumption here is that factor mobility is assured and that it is immaterial to the factor where it is employed.[6] Actual policies, however, don't necessarily exclusively adopt this approach. The most notable practical exception is the protection afforded to farmers (and to a lesser extent workers in labour-intensive industries) in most industrialised countries.

The interests of the consumer support the necessity of breaking up monopolies, scrapping inefficient industries and restructuring the entire production base in Eastern and Central Europe. According to the 'shock-therapy' approach the immediate introduction of free trade into the monopoly-infested economies of these countries could result, however, in disruptions on such a scale that social losses would outweigh social gains by a considerable margin.[7]

Following some general remarks on the scope of industrial, trade and competition policies for the economies in transition, we propose to look at the problems of Hungarian industry from a different angle. We will use the property rights approach to inquire into the nature of privatisation accompanied by trade liberalisation.

---

4. In other words, it will not be possible to make anyone better off without making someone else worse off.

5. One problem with this approach is that it recommends *changes* with reference to a benchmark that describes the *static* characteristics of a state. In the dynamic context, Paretian welfare economics defines acceptable movements from one state A to another state B if at least one person is better off at B without anyone being worse off. According to another version, albeit with considerably weaker theoretical foundations than the former one, state B is preferable to state A if those who gain from a movement to B could compensate those who lose from the change even though no actual compensation takes place.

6. It is assumed that the factor income is the same or better in the new employment than in the old one,

7. The former German Democratic Republic (DDR) is a case in point, even though it may be an extreme case: unemployment has now grown to proportions that could hardly be tolerated in countries which, unlike it, do not enjoy the backing of the strongest economy in Europe.

Let us start our Coase-inspired analysis with an example. Suppose A and B are two firms and the activity of, say, A results in environmental pollution that causes damage to the business of B. According to the prescriptions of Pigovian welfare theory, a suitable tax on the products of A would result in a socially desirable outcome. In other words, the existence of what are frequently labelled external economies and diseconomies calls for government intervention.

Many of the problems arising from such interdependencies are analysed as well as legally dealt with within the framework of the law of tort as an alternative to economic analysis. The normal approach (or the one based on formal logic) is that the party that causes the damage should be made to pay compensation to the party that is hurt.

Coase (1960), challenges both the legalistic approach and the received wisdom of Pigovian interventionism arguing that:

1. voluntary negotiations between the two parties could lead to efficient solutions without any other government intervention than that which guarantees that the agreement reached between the parties is enforced;
2. in the absence of transaction costs, resource allocation will be the same irrespective of the initial distribution of property rights, i.e., whether A has the right to pollute and B will have to bribe A for not doing so or the other way round (the 'Coase theorem'); and
3. the initial distribution of rights only affects the distribution of income.

Coase goes to great pains to emphasise the reciprocal nature of the problem.[8] His analysis is of great theoretical importance, and is correct in the given framework. Our practical approach requires, however, to see what would happen if there were transaction costs.

The oft-quoted example is that the greater the number of actors, the higher the costs of transacting tend to be. In such cases, liability rules based on the initial distribution of property rights may be preferred to high cost voluntary agreements (cf. Turvey, 1963). However, whether we rely on voluntary agreements or liability rules, the existence of well-defined property rights is essential.

It is possible to reformulate the basic problem presented in the above example and extend its implications to competition policy. Accordingly, pollution will be interpreted as market disturbance or any change that alters the relative strength of market actors (i.e. changes their market shares). If B is the domestic firm, A is the (more efficient) foreign firm and the hitherto protected

8. 'The question is commonly thought as one in which A inflicts harm on B and what has to be decided is: how should we restrain A? But this is wrong. We are dealing with a problem of reciprocal nature. To avoid the harm to B would inflict a harm on A. The real question that has to be decided is: should A be allowed to harm B or should B be allowed to harm A? The problem is to avoid the more serious harm' (Coase, 1960, p. 2).

market is opened up for competition, the following sequence of events may take place:

1. the welfare of domestic consumers increases because the product price falls;
2. the domestic firm collapses and the welfare of the owners of the domestic factors of production decreases (the loss of welfare is assumed to outweigh the gain of welfare by domestic consumers);
3. the owners of foreign factors of production gain.

We should note that the distribution of income – also referred to by Coase – gains added importance from the policy point of view because those who lose are domestic citizens while those who gain are foreigners. In a world of perfect reciprocity such changes could be acceptable as the inevitable price of potential long-term gains. In the real world, resistance is common.

Protection against violent market disturbances is not rejected entirely by the rules that govern international trade. The most famous escape clause is Article XIX of the GATT treaty which allows national legislation to temporarily protect injured industries. Although the article has been subjected to a substantial amount of criticism for being vague as well as frequently misused, it has not been changed. A major reason might be that several countries, and among them the most influential ones, seem to consider it as too valuable an instrument when sudden rescue operations are called for.

Patent legislation is another conspicuous example of temporary protection of industries (or more correctly of commodities and production processes). It seeks to provide incentives for research and development activities. Such protection of intellectual property is especially relevant to the issues discussed here because the market gradually becomes more contestable as well as more contested as the product cycle moves into its mature phase and substitutes that manage to avoid patent legislation appear on the market.

The process of macro-economic transition may be visualised in a certain sense like the product cycle: the initial setting of distorted industrial structure is transformed into a competitive one as protective tariffs and other trade barriers are phased out and industries are gradually exposed to foreign competition.

Both are, in fact, processes by which the exclusive right to a market is attenuated over time, although for different reasons. In the product cycle case (or model), the innovating firm will capitalise on its comparative advantage based on its R and D potential by introducing a new product to the market, thus starting a new product cycle and losing interest in the old one. In the transition case, however, former structural distortions have to be repaired *within the framework of the given transition process*, without any chance of starting a new one, and consequently without any real possibility of reversing import liberalisation.

Property Rights and Competition Policy

Coasean voluntary negotiations may give rise to the following results. The foreign competitor and the domestic incumbent strike a privatisation deal whereby the domestic firm is restructured, slimmed down or closed down. A greater part or all of its employees are laid off while the management conducting the negotiations assures itself continued gainful employment elsewhere in the company or in one of its spinoffs. This type of spontaneous privatisation has taken place in various parts of Central Europe with the perceived result that part of the national wealth was given away to foreigners.

Obviously, we are here encountering another major problem dealt with in the property rights literature, that of principal and agent. Ill-defined rights and lack of relevant information, as well as opportunistic behaviour on the part of the agent, are blamed for the occurrence of known cases.

The possible attitudes of potential buyers of incumbent companies can show a surprising lack of diversity.[9] As it is pointed out by Ábel and Miller (1992, p. 39) a main driving force behind acquisitions is the desire to increase market power.

The strengthening of a firm's market position may take different forms. For instance, raising the competitive threshold for potential entrants may be achieved by the combined effects of increased market share and economies of scale, by demanding outright protection by the state, or by the more subtle method of product differentiation. Privatisation may help the foreign investor combine these tools to set foot in the hitherto protected and eventually monopolised market. It may also raise an interest in reversing the processes of import liberalisation and demonopolisation. The theoretical background for defining the role of market access or market shares in the value of a company is, however, not yet unambiguously available. An analogy from environmental economics might be of some help at this point.

Coase (1960) calls for a new approach to the analytical treatment of harmful effects. A basic element of this new approach would be the substitution of rights for the physical quantities of factors of production. 'If factors of production are thought of as rights, it becomes easier to understand that the right to do something which has a harmful effect (such as the creation of smoke, noise, smells, etc.) is also a factor of production' (p. 44).

We now propose to reformulate the above approach slightly by treating the right of access to a market as a factor of production in exactly the same way as Coase proposes the right to pollute to be one. Consider the following case: A is a domestic producer who has the original and exclusive right to the domestic

9. It was already observed by Adam Smith that the private entrepreneur who in principle is in favour of free enterprise and competition mostly dreams of the quiet life assured by an uncontested position in the market.

market. The exclusive nature of this right produces real income for A as well as for those employed by A. Opening up the market for B may cause harm to A et al. As was argued in the previous section, such changes would probably violate the Pareto criterion and might or might not pass the Mill–Bastable test. From the point of view of competition policy, we may raise the following question: under what conditions would the entrance of B into the market be illegal and thereby liable for sanctions? Law and economics (above all welfare economics) offer different answers to this question.

Law

The right to participate in the market is not dealt with explicitly by the law either in the USA, the EC or Hungary, but each of them guarantee the freedom of competition. This freedom includes, in our view, the right of access to the market. This right, however, can be considered as a special property right as well. The theoretical justification of this statement has been presented in a Coaseian approach. Its practical justification draws upon our experience from privatisation, where a substantial factor of the privatisation value of many Hungarian industrial firms has been its privileged access to the Hungarian or eventually the former Soviet market. The privilege of access to these markets does not necessarily mean technical barriers to other entrants: the familiarity of the consumers with the product or its special parameters highly valued by that market might be decisive factors of its competitiveness.

The freedom of competition and its protection was *first codified in the USA* in 1890 with the adoption of the Sherman Antitrust Act. The Act makes a subtle albeit important distinction between actions to attain and/or preserve a position of monopoly on the one hand and making use of actual monopoly on the other.[10] The attainment or retention of a monopoly can only result from actions directed against parties who could contest such a position. If there are no competitors, i.e., if the market is not only monopolised but also uncontestable, the government has no right to break up the monopoly even if the consumer is hurt. In other words, US legislation distinguishes between behaviour against competitors and against the consumer.

This distinction implicitly means that already existing monopolies (practically mostly those resulting from product differentiation) cannot be broken up legally. Monopolists profiting from their former appearance on markets (market segments) not yet discovered by their eventual competitors can rightfully protect their exclusive right to this market (market segment) as a source of income analogous to income from property.

The main conditions of *competition on the EC market* are defined in Articles 85 and 86 of the Treaty of Rome, while domestic regulations are still

10. '... it is illegal to seek a monopoly or to attempt to keep a monopoly once one is attained, but it is not illegal to have a monopoly' (Davidson et al., 1987, p. 1043).

separated one from another. Articles 87–91 regulate the procedures for implementation while Articles 92–93 deal with government aid to business which also affects the access to markets. The general approach of the EC's competition policy is the fostering of competition and the avoidance of distortions in intra-community trade and production. Restrictive practices such as price discrimination and price fixing are prohibited under Article 85 but practices that '... contribute to the improvement of the production or distribution of goods or to the promotion of technical or economic progress while reserving to users an equitable share in the profit resulting therefrom' are exempted.

This contrasts with antitrust legislation in the USA where agreements with similar consequences have traditionally been viewed with considerably less tolerance. On the other hand, actions which 'take improper advantage of a dominant position' are banned (Article 86). In principle, this rule would exclude the use of existing monopoly power which is tolerated by US legislation. However, the concept of 'dominant position' is rather vague and the rule appears quite flexible.

Direct aid to industry may be the most important source of distortions. Article 92 of the Treaty stipulates that '... any aid granted by a Member State or through State resources in any form whatsoever which distorts or threatens to distort competition by favouring certain undertakings or the production of certain goods shall, insofar as it affects trade between Member States, be incompatible with the common market'. In spite of this, state aid to depressed sectors and depressed regions has been quite common, especially since the mid-1970s.

This is, of course, the case also recognised by Article XIX of GATT which provides for temporary protective measures against import competition when a domestic industry is injured. Most certainly this Article will be referred to on many occasions by one or another of the ex-socialist countries during the years to come (for the discussion on competition policy in the EC, see Bayliss and El-Agraa, 1990; Hitiris, 1988, pp. 229–235; and SPK, 1992).

In general terms, legislation on *competition in Hungary* is as liberal as that in the USA or the EC.[11] The law distinguishes and bans four types of market conduct: unfair competition, the deception of consumers, the restriction of competition and the abuse of market power. From these declarations, it follows that participation in the market is a basic right for everyone.

It is also clear that, in practice, these rights cannot be taken as absolute. Hungary, as most other countries of the world, has tariffs, quotas, and

---

11. According to Article 9 of the Constitution (1) the Hungarian economy is a market economy and (2) the Republic of Hungary recognises the freedom of competition and the rights of entrepreneurship. Also, the law on unfair competition makes it clear that for a precondition the efficient operation of the market is the freedom and transparence of competition.

regulations that restrict access to the market for some actors. In addition, however, problems arise also as a result of two practical considerations: in the first place, the concept of competition itself is getting more and more difficult to operationalise; secondly, competition on an unequal basis is rejected.

The Law on Unfair Competition distinguishes two cases. In the first case the application of the law is conditional upon the degree of competition, i.e., the parties must be direct competitors for the law to be relevant. Thus, legal action can be averted if the parties are found not to be competitors. In the second case there is no such requirement (Vörös, 1991, p. 79).

Economics

The legal explanation quoted above leaves the following question open: who are competitors with each other? The answer depends on whether their products are considered as substitutes by the market. In turn, this product identification problem is closely connected with the definition of the market. If the market is defined as a set of goods with pairwise high positive cross elasticities (for a discussion see Bourdet, 1992, p. 5), it is then clear that two products may not be part of the same market even if they are classified under the same ISIC code or share most technical parameters between them.[12]

Product differentiation reduces substitutability. It also increases the barriers to entry because incumbent firms enjoy an absolute cost advantage (cf. Bourdet, 1992, p. 181). An increasing number of sellers tend to behave according to the rules of monopolistic competition by seeking to provide their products with attributes that are missing in the products of their competitors. The 'market' is thereby transformed into a set of market segments within each of which competition may still prevail but between which it becomes progressively weaker.

---

12. A good illustration to this problem can be found in Török (1992, pp. 81–82.). The Dacia cars assembled in Romania under a licence from Renault are not accepted by the world market as Renault cars (and they can be sold only in Eastern Europe and the Third World), although their technical parameters are the same as those of the Renault 12 model. Opel Astra cars manufactured by General Motors Hungary are, however, internationally considered as perfect substitutes of such cars made in Germany, the UK or Spain. This difference should have psychological reasons as well, although the primary explanation is evident: the multinational company is a co-owner of the plant, and it exerts technological control over the production process only in the Opel case.

A 'mixed' example from the same region and the same industry might shed more light on the problem: Citroën of France participated in the Oltcit joint venture in Romania, producing small-sized Oltcit cars from the early 1980s on. These were initially marketed as the Citroën Axel model in Western Europe, but their bad performance on the market (even as Citroën products) persuaded the French company to withdraw from this marketing operation first, and from the joint venture in Romania afterwards. This car is now sold only in Eastern Europe.

The Hungarian law on unfair competition specifies only two areas in which the presence of competitive conditions is a prerequisite for legal action. These are damage to reputation and imitation. The law recognises that the concept of competition is becoming elusive in a modern economy. On the subject of servile imitation, Vörös points out (ibid., p. 85) that it is not possible to talk of imitation as long as the original product is protected by rights which belong to the realm of patent law, because the issue of servile imitation can only be raised within the framework of competition law.

The servile imitation of a product raises the problem of product identification again, especially if the imitation is a technically perfect one. If the imitation is confused with the original product even by an established expert, and proof is available that the imitation is not a result of business secret violation, the manufacturer of the imitation cannot be prosecuted (such cases are, e.g., those of 'reverse engineering').

We have seen the difficulties of product identification. These problems might make the definition of illegal entry to a market an unsurmountable task. One obvious case is dumping.

Dumping is said to exist when the contract price of a foreign product is found to be lower than the value of the product in terms of its cost. The right to take measures against dumping follows from what Bhagwati calls the cosmopolitan position of free trade. This principle holds that, since only free trade for all will maximise world welfare, countervailing duties and anti-dumping measures are justified in order to maintain competitive trade. It is also this principle of reciprocity that underlies GATT (Bhagwati, 1988, p. 35).

Taking anti-dumping actions might be difficult because relevant legislation is rather vague in most countries (for the cases of the EC and the USA cf. EC, 1992, p. 48 and Bhagwati, 1988, Chapter 3). Cases are handled by the courts of the country of the plaintiff, which could raise the question of impartiality. Furthermore, the plaintiff suffers no damage if the accusation turns out to be unjustified while the defendant is likely to lose his business. Thus, there is an incentive for domestic producers to sue foreign competitors merely on the grounds of harassment and intimidation. The result is a general atmosphere of uncertainty, while the foreign producer will only have vague ideas as to his right of access to the market and trade will be hampered.

Escape clauses or safeguard actions might have a similar impact on market access. Article XIX of the GATT provides for temporary protective measures against import competition when a domestic industry is threatened. The application of the article often means in practice that the industry is bailed out by the government.

Privatisation and Market Access

There is ample experience that one of the main motives of foreign investors in the former socialist countries of Central Eastern Europe is to obtain domestic market shares before the liberalisation of imports is fully accomplished. Their access to these markets is facilitated by their exemption from import duties plus a generous tax treatment offered to foreign investors. Such examples are available from Poland, where the president of the American firm Curtis 'was pleading with the government to raise customs duties on imported televisions to make it easier for its new Mlawa factory to succeed' (*The Economist*, 21 September 1991) or from Hungary where Ford's $US90 million investment was thought to be compensated by the government with the abolition of import duties for just one type of small truck described with highly detailed parameters.

It was not difficult to find out that this description only matched the Ford Transit model. Widespread protest from importers of comparable trucks persuaded the government to extend this duty-free status to all imported models of the same category. Ford Hungary's CEO later denied that his company had been lobbying for these duty-free imports, but he didn't object to the statement that the preferential treatment helped Ford Transit become the leader on the Hungarian market (*Autópiac*, September 1992, pp. 18–21).

The cases mentioned above pinpoint the attitude of the foreign investor who not only welcomes a protected market environment but eventually also eagerly works for it. It is quite simply the changing approach of the foreign exporter to Hungary turned investor in that country which now makes it necessary to inquire into the 'trilateral' relationship between property rights and/or privatisation, competition policy (the domestic competitive environment) and trade policy (with respect to imports).

Our approach is going to become more normative than it was before in the study, although we will avoid direct policy recommendations at this stage of our research. We will tackle within our triangle the two possible 'bilateral' relationships where one element is privatisation. There seems to be no need to discuss the third one (trade policy versus competition policy) in depth, because we feel the government's behaviour is unambiguous in both fields. Trade policy is clearly and very strongly liberal (the average level of customs duties is down to 13 per cent from the pre-1991 16 per cent level, and 93 per cent of imported goods are no longer subject to import licensing) while competition policy is evidently anti-monopolistic. Contradictions may arise between these policies on the one hand, and the objectives and the strategy of privatisation on the other.

Privatisation Strategies

The current Hungarian government's first approach to privatisation (after the elections in March–April 1990) was not accurately defined and it reflected the political intention of sweeping out the remains of the communist economic system as fast as possible. The costs and benefits of different privatisation strategies were not appropriately evaluated, and the tradeoff between the speed and the financial yield of privatisation was not given enough attention.

Two basic approaches may be used for privatisation by the government. The first one can be called the 'throw-away option', in which the state wants to avoid any spending to improve the quality of the assets of the enterprises to be sold. It has to proceed quickly and in a determined fashion, because any delay will probably cause a loss of the enterprise's privatisation value.[13]

The second one might be termed the 'conditioning option', where the government invests in the enterprise to be privatised. This might mean physical capital investment in order to upgrade the company technologically, or just financial 'investment' to ease the firm's debt burden. This option would be chosen if it could be expected that the enterprise's privatisation value would increase by more than the amount spent on it.

There were several highly debated cases in the Hungarian privatisation in 1990 and 1991 when the lack of a clear choice by the government between the two basic options triggered the so-called 'asset-subtraction' process at several firms. 'Asset-subtraction' resulted in considerable financial losses for the government.

There has been at least one famous case in Hungarian privatisation, where an ostensibly 'asset-subtracting' firm had good chances of finding foreign investors due to its privileged access to COMECON markets. When this privileged access evaporated owing to the disappearance of intra-COMECON barter trade, these foreign investors lost their interest in the firm. Thereafter the asset-subtraction process gained speed and bankruptcy became inevitable (cf. Török, 1991).

In such cases, the loss of market access was probably a more important cause of financial collapse than was the depreciation of assets. Owners and management were unable to find the optimal time of privatisation when debts had not yet started to accelerate dangerously and the rapid erosion of market shares had not yet set in. Such examples have shown that market access and/or

13. Two main reasons may be given: 1. the rapid increase of the debt of loss-making and indebted firms due to high nominal (35 to 40 per cent) and real (between 8 and 12 per cent) interest rates in Hungary; 2. other privatisation deals together with the rapid liberalisation of imports, whose combined effect was a decline in the value to the would-be foreign investor of becoming incumbent on the Hungarian market instead of entering it through trade and not through privatisation.

market shares often have a value in privatisation that is not only comparable to the book value of a firm's assets, but superior to it.

Another example on this point is that of a Hungarian computer firm with a fairly weak technological base but excellent positions on the Soviet market. The computers made by this company lagged by about 10 years behind standard products available on the world market, but they were well known by the Soviet users and had been adapted to their special needs. Moreover, these computers had been integrated into country-wide networks (railways, pipeline systems etc.) on an 'overlay' basis, i.e. each year a further chunk of these systems was constructed from the same old brand of Hungarian computers.

A multinational computer firm wanted to acquire this Hungarian company with the purpose of scrapping most of its physical capital and converting it into a trading-house operating on the Soviet market. The offer was rejected by the State Property Agency (SPA) because it requested guarantees for the survival of computer manufacturing in the Hungarian company. The multinational firm couldn't promise such guarantees because it was interested in the Hungarian company's special access to the Soviet market, and not in its physical capital.

The privatisation of the Hungarian electronics industry has suffered from another mistake in trade and industrial policy. The customs duties for most electronic components are above average (i.e. around 20 per cent) in order to protect domestic components manufacturers. The lack of effective protection harmed the domestic and international competitiveness of Hungarian equipment manufacturers. However, it had an even more counterproductive consequence. Namely, most domestic manufacturers of components had disappeared since 1989. As a result, *there was practically no domestic components industry to be protected.*

The problem is that high tariff walls for components make foreign electronics firms interested in either investing only in trade (i.e. setting up subsidiaries for channelling imports of their products to the Hungarian market) or in assembly but together with components manufacturing. Due to the high degree of diversity of components needed plus the high capital intensity of this production no major foreign investor has chosen the second option.

The eventual lack of effective protection of manufacturing in Hungary is just one reason why many prospective foreign investors have chosen to become players on the domestic market as importers instead of becoming local producers. Another reason has been the lack of any sort of protection for the local producers. A good example is the *sugar industry.*

The French, British and Austrian owners of different Hungarian sugar factories jointly urged the government to raise the fixed producer price of sugar by 50 per cent and apply strict quotas against imports (*Világgazdaság,* 22 February 1992). Their assumption seems to have been that with the acquisition of ownership rights, they had also bought *exclusive* rights to the market. Their request was, however, rejected by the government.

This industry, among many others, used to be one where foreign would-be entrants to the market requested the liberalisation of imports. After becoming incumbent players in the domestic market, they started lobbying for protection from imports. This fairly logical change of interests should however be seen in the specific context of the sugar industry: This industry is largely organised along cartel lines abroad, and the firms in question were most probably intent on 'transplanting' that cartel to Hungary.

The case of the sugar industry is one where *the government's liberal approach to privatisation seemed to facilitate the 'imported cartellisation' of the industry, while its liberal trade policy hampered it.* This example is very much to the point if we wish to examine the contrary effects of governmental liberalism in privatisation[14] and trade policy and explore the interactions between privatisation and de-monopolisation. The analysis of these interactions raises the question of the relationship between privatisation aimed at de-nationalising the economy and competition policy aimed at *eliminating existing monopolies*. As we have seen, this would be legally impossible in the American legal system.

At the beginning of this section reference was made to the newly opened Polish television factory whose management immediately demanded restricted access to the market by foreigners. The case of 'perceived' rights to 'inherited' monopolies is still more common and, it could be argued, temporarily justified.

As a result of nationalisations and the establishment of the central planning system, the gradual development of monopolies became common in the industrial sectors of socialist countries. In the Hungarian engineering industry, the share of the dominant domestic company exceeded 95 per cent in the market for buses, railroad equipment, ships, refrigerators, washing machines, electric bulbs, household stoves, turbines, etc. Industries with duopolies were exceptional (consumer electronics, agricultural machinery). All of a sudden, the liberalisation of imports came to pose a threat to the very existence of these domestic monopolists or duopolists, already hard hit by the collapse of the COMECON market.

Whether the companies are sold to domestic producers, foreign investors, or remain in the custody of the state, they will seek to assert their (perceived) original rights to preferential access to the market. They have a powerful incentive to enter the political market to secure protection and demand the classification of competing imports as dumping. The foreign investor's natural objective is to gain access to hitherto closed markets. The objective of the government is to attract as many foreign investors as possible which would

---

14. i.e. when the government doesn't think twice about allowing foreign investors to obtain decisive control over a sector of Hungarian industry. In addition to the sugar industry a number of other industries including lighting equipment, passenger cars, cement and brewing were seen as candidates for privatisation in the summer of 1992. Others such as the rubber industry and/or the paper industry may join them in the near future.

also increase the government's bargaining power. The government wants to secure foreign investments, the foreign investor wants to secure the market and assumes, with or without grounds, that privileged access to the market is an inherited right.

Although, the automobile industry (GM Hungary, Suzuki Hungary and partly Ford Hungary) is a newly established industry with no 'original' rights to market access, it has been successful in securing protection both in the form of higher tariffs, reduced import quotas and – indirectly – preferential tax treatment linked to major foreign direct-investment projects.

The application of the Coase theorem to the theory of markets may unquestionably benefit from a deeper insight into cases where privatisation leads to improved access to formerly strongly protected markets or the acquisition of domestic monopolies. These are special situations where the cost of acquisition of property rights was partly a transaction cost. This transaction cost was linked to the entry to the market.

The existence of such transaction costs means that no voluntary agreement can be reached on the reallocation of market shares, and governmental intervention cannot be avoided. However, this intervention may also take the form of a semi-liberal solution, such as in the case of the sugar industry in Hungary: imports will have free access to the market, but prices will remain fixed by the government.

In any event, the contradictions between 'mainstream'-type (liberal) privatisation and trade policies on the one hand, and the parallel efforts of privatisation and de-monopolisation on the other deserve much more attention by East European governments than they used to get. We hope our study has been able to show that the transition to a market economy is a highly complex process where analogous approaches to different problems may prove counter-productive. In other words, if liberal solutions are the rule, which can and should be accepted theoretically, governments will have to express clearly their priorities (e.g., rapid privatisation or rapid liberalisation).

References

Ábel, I. and R. A. Miller, 1992, "A vállalatokat eladják, ugye?" *Közgazdasági Szemle,* January.

Autópiac, September 1992.

Balassa, B. A., 1977, "'Stages Approach' to Comparative Advantage". Paper prepared for the World Congress of the International Economic Association, Tokyo.

Bayliss, B. T. and A. M. El-Agraa, 1990, 'Competition and Industrial Policies with Emphasis on Competition Policy' in El-Agraa, A. M. (ed.),

Economics of the European Community. New York, London, Toronto, Sydney, Tokyo, Singapore: Philip Allan.

Bhagwati, J., 1988, *Protectionism*. Cambridge, Mass., London, England: MIT Press.

Blanchard, O., R., Dornbusch, P. Krugman, R. Layard and L. Summers, 1991, *Reform In Eastern Europe*. Cambridge, Mass.: The United Nations University; London, England: MIT Press.

Bourdet, Y. (ed.), 1992, *Internationalization, Market Power and Consumer Welfare*. London and New York: Routledge.

_____, 1992, "Competition and Prices in the Passenger Car Market", in Bourdet, Y. (ed.), *Internationalization, Market Power and Consumer Welfare*. London and New York: Routledge.

Coase, R. H., 1960, "The Problem of Social Cost", *Journal of Law and Economics* 3.

Davidson, D. V., B. E. Knowles, L. M. Forsythe and R. R. Jespersen, 1987, *Comprehensive Business Law. Principle and Cases*. Boston, Mass.: Kent Publishing Co.

EC, 1992, *Az Európai Közösségek Jogszabályainak Gyüjteménye*. Budapest: Unió Kiadó.

The Economist, various issues.

El-Agraa, A. M. (ed.), 1990, *Economics of the European Community*. New York, London, Toronto, Sydney, Tokyo, Singapore: Philip Allan.

Hitiris, T., 1988, *European Community Economics. A Modern Introduction*. New York, London, Toronto, Sydney, Tokyo: Harvester Wheatsheaf.

Kornai, J., 1986, "The Hungarian Reform Process: Visions, Hopes and Reality". *Journal of Economic Literature*. Vol. XXIV, pp. 1687–1737.

Magyar Nemzet, 9 March 1990.

McKinnon, R. I., 1991, *The Order of Economic Liberalization. Financial Control in the Transition to Market Economy*. Baltimore and London: The Johns Hopkins University Press.

Neven, D. J. and L.-H. Röller, 1990, "The Structure and Determinants of East-West Trade: A Preliminary Analysis of the Manufacturing Sector" in Winters, L. A. and J. Venables (eds), *European Integration: Trade and Industry*. Cambridge Mass., New York, Port Chester, Melbourne and Sydney: Cambridge University Press.

Södersten, B., 1978, *Internationell ekonomi*. Stockholm: Rabén och Sjögren.

SPK, 1992, *EGs konkurrensregler*. Statens Pris- och Konkurrensverk.

Swann, D., 1988, *The Retreat of the State. Deregulation and Privatization in the UK and US*. New York, London, Toronto, Sydney, Tokyo: Harvester-Wheatsheaf.

Török, Á., 1986, *Komparatív elönyök – nemzetközi példák, hazai tapasztalatok* (Comparative Advantages – International Patterns vs. the Hungarian Experience). Budapest: KJK.

_____, 1991, "'Asset-Subtracting Firms' and their Perspectives: A Case Study from the Hungarian Electronics Industry". Paper prepared for the Annual Conference of the European Association of Research in Industrial Economics, Ferrara, Italy, September.

_____, 1992, "Politique économique des droits de propriété et politique de concurrence. Quelques implications de la privatisation en Hongrie pour la théorie des marchés". *Revue Internationale de Droit Économique* 1, pp. 73–88.

Turvey, R., 1963, "On Divergencies Between Social Cost and Private Cost",. *Economica*, August 1963.

Világgazdaság, 22 February 1992.

Vörös, I., 1991, *Verseny, kartell, ár. Törvények magyarázata.* Budapest: TRIORG.

Winiecki, J., 1990, "Hur det hela började – orsaker till sovjetekonomiernas sammanbrott". *Ekonomisk debatt* 6.

Winters, L. A. and A. J. Venables (eds), 1990, *European Integration: Trade and Industry.* Cambridge Mass., New York, Port Chester, Melbourne, Sydney: Cambridge University Press.

13

Escaping from the State – Escaping to the State Managerial Motivation and Strategies in Changing the Ownership Structure in Hungary

Éva Voszka[*]

Introduction

Managers of state enterprises are often considered as obstacles to privatisation. The reasons are obvious: the state is a weak owner, unable to exercise tight control, dispensing subsidies and thus granting protection against market competition. Why should managers voluntarily give up their comfortable position, without compensation?

In the countries of Central Europe (including Hungary), however, they are accused of the opposite attitude as well: they are too active in the process of transformation and privatisation, wishing to preserve or to convert their former political power into economic power by 'selling off' state assets.

Both contradictory statements may be verified by reasonable arguments and concrete examples. Presumably there is no general rule that may be used to describe the managerial attitudes towards changes in the ownership structure. In order to understand the behaviour of top management, we have to describe a set of criteria that accounts for the differences. A static approach would concentrate on factors such as market and financial position, the prospects confronting various firms, the culture, intellectual capacity and ambitions of the managers etc. This paper tries to provide a dynamic explanation, while still not entering into a systemic comparison. The analysis will be limited to a

* Pénzügykutató Rt, Budapest.

rather specific situation; the post-communist transition period in Hungary from 1988 to 1992.

Depending on the decision-making process involved, three stages may be distinguished within this fairly short period: 'spontaneous privatisation', 'centralised privatisation' and 'decentralised privatisation'. This paper will argue that the dominant form of managerial motivations and strategies have changed. The tendency of escaping from the state has become a tendency to escape to the state. Weighing the experience of the last years, there are three main factors influencing managerial attitudes towards changing the ownership structure. First, the political and financial strength of the state as owner and regulator, second, the formal and informal alternatives available for managers and third, the methods of changing ownership, including the future proprietary structure of the given firm.

'Spontaneous Privatisation': Strengthening the Role of Quasi-Owners

In order to understand managerial motivations, a brief summary of the preconditions and main forms of 'spontaneous privatisation' has to be outlined. (For more details see Móra, 1991; Privatizációs Kutatóintézet, 1991; Tóth, 1991; Voszka, 1991a.)

The process started in 1988, in the last two years of the old political regime. The basis for spontaneity (initiation and decision by the firms themselves) was the introduction of what was called the self-governing enterprise form in 1985. Enterprise councils were established for two-thirds of the economic units. These bodies, which were in practice dominated by enterprise management, received the right to determine the organisational structure, appoint the managing director, make decisions on mergers and de-mergers, and establish joint ventures and companies involving state property.

Hence the enterprise councils – in practice top management – started to found companies on the basis of state assets. In many cases, they took only a minority of the assets into joint stock companies or limited liability companies. Consequently, the remaining state enterprises continued to operate. In several dozen cases, (large) state enterprises founded companies out of each of their factories, plants and even administrative departments one by one. The former enterprise centre simply took on the function of asset (stock) management. Although they called themselves holding companies, they preserved the form of a state-owned enterprise.

It was these 'holdings' that usually held the majority of shares in the new companies. In this type of company, new owners appeared as well; apart from foreign investors, there were state-owned organisations such as banks and other enterprises, that mainly acted as business partners. Thus in most cases 'spontaneous privatisation' did not mean privatisation in the strict sense of the word, since private investors rarely bought shares in the new firms.

What were the motivations of state enterprises in reorganising themselves as (a group of) companies?

The main problem for the firms in the late eighties was insolvency or the lack of additional capital. This was due mainly to the policy of economic austerity which involved cutting back on budgetary subsidies. Hence it was the state as regulator that provided incentives – and at the same time legal opportunities – for its enterprises to choose this way. Traditional methods of survival, such as exercising pressure for more preferences, cancelling or re-scheduling debts did not work any more, and the new constraints on going bankrupt or reducing the size of the organisation seemed to be avoidable. In the case of enterprises in an unstable financial situation, the advantage of transformation was a debt-equity swap with banks or other creditors. Another method of easing the financial burdens was that of assigning all debt to the 'holdings'. If they went bankrupt, their spin-off companies, founded without debts, might survive.

The second type of motivation, which is characteristic not only of units near bankruptcy, is to meet the old desire of the plants for independence. Most of the large enterprises were the products of administrative mergers, mainly from the early sixties. Plants and factories, loosely integrated into the large unit, did not abandon their efforts to achieve organisational autonomy. In the process of transformation into a group of companies, it was the bargaining between the enterprise centre and the factories that determined the organisational frameworks, the distribution of assets and liabilities. The formal independence of the sub-units (i.e. the legal entity in the form of company) was acceptable to the enterprise centres at this time, because of the lack of resources for redistribution and because of an increasing need to find new markets and to change the production structure. They already had the experience of the additional incentives and flexibility that flowed from the increased decision-making rights of internal units. Nevertheless by maintaining majority ownership of the former enterprise centre in the companies, the features of a large enterprise might also be retained. Moreover, as its previous administrative entity was replaced by legitimate owners' rights, this unity has become more difficult to attack from either inside or from outside.

In fact, that was the third important motivation, protection against external, governmental intervention. Such intervention might result, for instance, in a transfer under state control (the suspension of the self-governing bodies), in the splitting up of the enterprise or in a privatisation initiated by state administrative organs. The company form adopted seemed to divert most of these threats by creating shareholders other than any governmental organisation.

To sum up, 'spontaneous privatisation' may be interpreted as a compromise between the state and the top management of large enterprises, and between the latter and the factories. Both the state and the large enterprise centres were weakened in terms of their bargaining position in relation to their subordinates, due to the lack of redistributional resources. In addition, the political background of the government and the large state enterprises was being undermined by that time (Szalai, 1992).

In such a situation, the government understood that opening up possibilities for firms to change their organisational structure could also be of advantage to the state. While in the short run it might help the enterprise to survive (without the problems of re-structuring), it spares the use of central resources and provides an opportunity to change the economic structure. From the point of view of top managers, this possibility might be considered as a last gift from a politically weak and financially strapped government to the state-owned firms. It meant the final stage of decentralisation of proprietary rights from governmental to enterprise level. The managers of the 'holdings' and those of 'normal' firms with majority ownership in several companies, extended their decision-making scope to the buying and selling of stocks and assets. Parallel with that, the former rights of the enterprise centres were obtained by the managers of the factories, i.e. the new companies. Their decision-making power has thus been extended. Hence decentralisation affected a wider and wider circle of managers, who strengthened their 'quasi-owner' role, which is characteristic of the reformed planned economies. Without privatisation in the strict sense of the word, however, they did not achieve the position of a legal owner. As directors of the state-owned 'holdings' or enterprises, they could be discharged by enterprise councils or governmental bodies at any time. This was actually demonstrated by certain precedents during this period.

It is true, however, that managers, like any other citizens, might set up their own private firm, independent from the state enterprise. Moreover, they were able to choose new owners of the state firm – bargaining mainly with state banks and business partners – and did not have to pay any income acquired from these transactions into the central budget. 'Spontaneous privatisation' was criticised in 1989 by certain opposition parties and reform-economists, as well as by civil servants. As one of the last measures of the old regime, a law on protecting state assets was passed and a central organisation, the State Property Agency (SPA), was set up to control transformation and privatisation deals. This was the starting point for the new government to change the decision-making mechanisms after the parliamentary elections of March 1990.

Centralised Privatisation: Towards a 'Real' Managerial Position

The first step of centralisation during the summer of 1991 was the change in the decision-making process on transformation and privatisation. The State Property Agency was taken under government supervision, instead of parliamentary control; its competence was extended to enterprises established by local councils, and to the approval of the transformation of any enterprise into company form (above a relatively low limit). Each deal was subject to the decision of the SPA and the SPA signed the contracts as the seller. The greater part of these incomes was paid into the state budget. These measures sought to protect state property, prevent a 'sell-out', accelerate privatisation and use the increased income for purposes that were important for the economy as a whole rather than for narrow enterprise interests.

How did this new situation affect the options open to the enterprise managers? Firstly, they could try to avoid central control. Here, the basis was the limit set on transactions.

The law allowed the selling or taking into a company assets of under 20, or 30 million forints respectively by the enterprises themselves. According to estimates, in 1991, one-quarter of the companies established with the involvement of state assets were set up under the supervision of the State Property Agency. In the case of companies with foreign investment, the ratio was less than 6 per cent. 70 per cent of incoming foreign capital, however, was concentrated in these deals (Voszka, 1992). The proportions suggest that the majority of transactions avoiding SPA decisions concerned small firms. Nevertheless, it cannot be excluded that even bigger deals successfully managed to avoid central control (Állami Számvevöszék, 1991).

Secondly, centralised privatisation eliminated only the decision, but not the initiatives made by enterprise management.

With the exception of a short period (the third quarter of 1991), more than 90 per cent of the initiatives came from the enterprises (Állami Vagyonügynökség, 1991). This means that they set up their own plans for transformation, tried to find potential investors and entered into negotiations with them. In most cases, proposals from the enterprises were accepted by the SPA. In 1990, 19 applications were rejected (15 per cent of all SPA decisions in that year), but in 1991 there were 9 rejections, 2 per cent of all decisions (Állami Vagyonügynökség, 1990, 1991). Outright rejection had thus become exceptional. The process would be clearer if we knew the proportion of transactions approved without any change. However, here we have only old and incomplete information. According to the report of the State Audit Office on the first year of SPA's operation (Állami Számvevöszék, 1991), in the case of more than half of the decisions, the value of the property concerned, was less than 100 million forints. Of these propositions 85 per cent were simply approved by the SPA, without any detailed examination or interference.

Consequently, apart from formal avoidance of central decisions, a wider group of enterprise managers have found ways to minimise the influence of governmental organs. In the autumn of 1990, the SPA itself stated that even in the period of its operation, the dominant form of privatisation was 'spontaneous privatisation'. The SPA considered that its most important result was not to have disrupted the pace of enterprise-initiated transformations (Állami Vagyonügynökség, 1990).

They stressed, however, that firms were ready to cooperate and often requested state assistance themselves. In assessing the numerical data indicating the limits of the SPA's influence, it has to be taken into account that potential power, even if rarely used, may shift the enterprise plans in a definite direction. This may be confirmed by enterprise experience. In the period of centralisation, the major problem for the management of state-owned enterprises has been to find the relevant person at the SPA, to identify intentions at executive level and, with this knowledge, to work out appropriate arguments and bargaining strategies in order to achieve their particular aims (Csillag, 1991; Voszka, 1991b). In such a situation all elements of transformation and privatisation (form, schedule, selection of owners and managers) may be negotiable. During the actual negotiations, enterprises obtained a strong bargaining position, based on concrete information, business and personal contacts.

The situation did not much differ if the initiation arose at the central level. The SPA started six privatisation programmes in 1990–1991. The first one involved profitable enterprises, the second one, a number of 'holdings' ('shell companies'), while the other four concerned certain branches or activities (retail trade and catering, construction, wine production, the sale of well-located office premises). The firms concerned had a certain influence whether they took part in or kept out of the programmes, and could influence the frameworks of their transformation or privatisation (Csillag, 1992; Voszka, 1992). Due to several factors, including the actual interests of the enterprises, central programmes proceeded slowly. The result, if any, was the transformation into company form, without involving private capital. (The only exception was the small privatisation programme.)

Thus the main consequence of centralised decision making was primarily a change in the orientation of the enterprises, towards government. The main area of bargaining was removed from intra-enterprise connections. It was no longer the factory directors who were the partners of the enterprise top management in seeking compromises, but the state administration.

This was the main reason why transformation into a group of companies was overshadowed by other methods. In this period, the principal feature of the changing ownership structure – initiated by enterprises or some central privatisation programmes – was the establishment of joint stock companies with foreign investors or the sale of a majority stake of the firm as a whole to foreigners. Instead of strengthening the quasi-owners', position in 'holdings', managers of large state enterprises became managers of partially privatised firms.

The transformation of state enterprises into companies without the involvement of private capital did not, however, disappear. Such transformations were not accompanied by decentralisation of the organisation and managerial rights. One enterprise turned into one single company, under the exclusive or majority ownership of the SPA. This type of change became more widespread from the middle of 1991, and was largely characteristic of the next stage of the processes.

The process of centralising all proprietary rights also started in the form of taking several dozen firms under direct state control. The SPA, having received full authorisation to abolish certain enterprise councils, has changed its explanation. In 1990, the main argument in support of direct state control was the excessive activity of the managers in privatising their firms. They were accused of 'selling off the national wealth' to unreliable (foreign) investors at a low price, ensuring managerial positions for the directors. In 1991 the main argument was just the opposite: the old management was an obstacle to privatisation.

Re-nationalisation meant in most cases no more than the replacement of the former management by a ministerial commissary, usually coming directly from state administration. The results of these steps – as several examples show and the State Audit Office pointed out (Állami Számvevöszék, 1991) – proved to be poor. Commissars, not knowing the concrete situation, the internal and external relationships of the given firm, or even being ignorant of micro-economic affairs in general, could do no more than cancel the project prepared by the former management and stop the deal. They were unable, however to come up with new ideas, new privatisation plans or to solve the problems of the firms.

This type of measure was naturally hostile towards the enterprise management. From their point of view, it was an attempt to abolish their position of quasi-ownership and – if not their actual dismissal – to turn them into traditional (bureaucratic and defenceless) state managers again.

Thus centralisation of decisions on transformation and privatisation provided three options for the management: to become real managers in (partially) privatised firms, to be dismissed after turning the enterprise under direct state control or coming into the position of a traditional state firm (without any quasi-owners', rights) after commercialisation. Not surprisingly, they tried to achieve the first version. However, before centralisation became more extensive in late 1991, the government declared a turnover – towards decentralised privatisation. This direction and the intention of the government to centralise all ownership rights at the same time modified the real options of the participants.

Decentralised Privatisation and Centralised Ownership as a New Alternative for Management

As early as the beginning of 1991, the central methods of privatisation and the SPA itself were publicly criticised. The Agency was accused of slowness and bureaucratic administration by ministries, opposition parties and enterprises. As a first reaction, in July, the government started the 'self-privatisation' programme for firms with less than 300 employees.

Self-privatisation (or as it is often called, decentralised privatisation) means the delegation of the SPA's rights to consulting firms. The consulting firms enter into contracts with the Agency and, together with the enterprise concerned, work out and carry on the privatisation programme. The SPA preserves only its supervisory function. The first step in self-privatisation included 300 small enterprises. Several dozen deals were completed by the end of 1991.

The decentralisation of privatisation was declared to be the new approach in the new governmental strategy published in autumn 1991 ("A kormány tulajdonosi és privatizációs stratégiája", 1991). Nevertheless, this move was not nearly as sharp as the official claims for it declared it to be. Firstly, the programme is principally concerned with self-initiation of the enterprises rather than self-privatisation. The State Property Agency, however, is allowed to initiate the privatisation of any enterprise or company. This means that the self-privatisation right of any particular firm may be arbitrarily suspended. Secondly, self-privatisation does not differ much from the methods of the earlier period. As we have seen, enterprise initiative and – especially in the case of small ventures – approval without modification was the general rule. Hence, self-privatisation could be viewed mainly as the legalisation of the former situation. Finally, in other areas (such as taking enterprises and shares under direct state control, selling 'strategic' companies, or small privatisation) the SPA preserved its decision-making rights.

Hence, the easing of centralisation is both partial and ambivalent. In addition, it is also temporary. According to the government strategy, all state enterprises have to transform themselves into companies within one year, or they will be taken under direct state control. The compulsory transformation into company form meant nothing less than the abolition of the self-governing forms, the enterprise councils and the centralisation of all proprietary rights. The owner of the shares, until privatisation, will be the SPA. The firms that were to remain permanently in majority state ownership (roughly with one-third of all assets) will belong to the State Property Company (SPC) (Law LIII and LIV of 1992 on the management, protecting and selling of the state assets, being permanently or temporarily in state ownership).

The rules and mechanisms for the exercising of ownership rights by these two huge state conglomerates are, however, rather obscure. So far the SPA has been unable to exercise control over much smaller assets. Since privatisation of 'temporarily' re-nationalised enterprises may be expected to take many years, if it does in fact happen, a new system of asset-managing contracts is sketched out by the laws. Any private person, group or institution may apply for the position of 'asset manager', including the top management of the firm. The content of the contracts, the relationship between the asset management and the potential owner wishing to buy shares in the company is not fixed. Nor is there any great clarity regarding the methods of controlling permanent state ownership or the relationship between the SPC and the holdings that fall to it. The only thing that is certain in the laws is that it is the right of the government-controlled proprietary and privatisation institutes to appoint the leading bodies of the company (board of directors, managers). Hence, the government may easily get rid of the former directors (the 'preservers of power') who can create well-paid positions for its own cadres. Despite the threat of dismissal, it was not only the SPA but also the managers of state enterprises who initiated the transformation into company form. The process was enlarged to an unprecedented degree, amounting to one-quarter of all the decisions made by the SPA in 1991, and comprised almost two-thirds of the property concerned. From the middle of 1991, a growing number of enterprises transformed themselves into companies.

The motives of the managers are manifold. The first reason was the publication of the draft bills that contained the compulsory transformation within a short period. Managers understood that if transformation had to be carried out within a year, it was better to implement it 'voluntarily' and quickly, until it was possible to submit their own plans.

Secondly, the management of the state firms knows from its own experience that centralisation means something more than just a reduction of their autonomy. It also means a decrease in their responsibilities and in the opportunities to attack them. The SPA is a protective barrier for the management, that helps to divert the flood of external (political) critics. This state protection may extend from acts of transformation to all other fields of operation. If the government again sets its claim to be the 'real' owner, it has to take charge of its property. This could mean providing firms with additional capital (for, let us say, restructuring before privatisation), rescheduling or cancelling debts, introducing export incentives or defending the companies from internal and external competition. All these instruments are familiar from previous decades. Moreover, enterprises and companies (not only state owned, but also privately and foreign owned) have put significant pressure on the government even in recent years. In many cases, this was not a fruitless effort, nor does it seem to be hopeless for the future. Companies belonging to the two huge state conglomerates, SPA and SPC, will – at least at the outset – be the dominant sector of the economy. Hence, their relationships and behaviour will play a key role, and their capacity to exercise pressure on the government will be enhanced by the new institutional forms.

Third, enterprise management also had good reason to presume that the more firms come under the supervision of the SPA, the less the agency could influence the transformation itself. Even in full possession of its ownership rights, the SPA will be unable to exercise tight control over the management. In 1990–91 the possibility of bargaining with the agency and influencing its decisions became clear. As far as management was concerned, centralisation did not have to prove particularly dangerous for any of them.

Indeed, re-nationalisation may even be favourable for the managers. After the ending of political threats by the SPA and after the settlement of the relations of subordination, they might obtain the managerial position for which they and their predecessors struggled during several decades, thereby enforcing their interests against a weak proprietary control. This position might even be strengthened by the new system of asset management. In the competition for this position, the former management is in a good position since it possesses an information monopoly. However, there is presumably a scarcity of other applicants.

Thus, the first task for enterprise management after the formal centralisation of the ownership rights is to preserve or re-establish its informal quasi-ownership position within the framework of state proprietorship. (This position differs from the formal, legal quasi-owners' role, obtained by the managers as directors of state holdings, and is more similar to the position in the reformed planned economy of the seventies and early eighties.) This shift would provide resistance to privatisation. A state, granting protection but hardly able to exercise tight control, may be more convenient for the managers than a strong private ownership. Hence, even sharper interests may rebel against privatisation than before.

Centralisation of ownership rights, however, does not necessarily put an end to privatisation. If dismissals were to become more frequent or strong asset managers were to arrive from outside, then the majority of managers would view an escape from state control to be more favourable.

Thus the second alternative for the managers remains, as before: the attempt to sell the majority of shares to private investors and to preserve their managerial position. There is another form of privatisation, which is becoming increasingly popular: the management buy-out. Several cases of self-privatisation so far completed have resulted in management buy-outs.

This legal conversion of managerial position into an owners' role may be substituted for by an employees' buy-out. This latter form is more acceptable to both internal and external forces (workers and political parties), giving the managers a position very similar to that of the management buy-out. Considering the experiences of self-governing forms (enterprise councils), directors feel that a diffused employee ownership is easy to control. In addition, shares may be concentrated in the hands of the management later on.

Thus, declaration of self-privatisation and centralisation of all ownership rights at the same time offered the management the opportunity to become legal owners of their firm or to preserve a quasi-ownership position in the company bought by the employees. The other alternative opened up by the new legislation is to strengthen the quasi-owner role in another form, namely, in companies remaining in state hands. This option became realistic because the government declared its intention to extend its scope of direct proprietary control to all operations and to all firms. The experience of previous decades tells us that the greater the extent of state decisions, the less is their real influence. Centralisation may be carried out only formally. In other words the aspiration of the government to control economic activity directly modifies the activities of the firms, turning them towards the state. However, it also strengthens the bargaining position of enterprise managers. This feature may be called the pitfall of centralisation.

Summary

Hungarian experiences of changing the ownership structure in the last five years show a tendency towards centralisation. The last government of the old regime followed the main line of previous reforms, that of decentralisation of ownership rights to enterprise management. The state, becoming weaker and weaker both in financial and political terms, has gradually lost its power to control enterprises. Given the lack of resources, redistribution of financial funds and subsidies have been replaced by redistribution of rights and autonomous powers.

After the political turnover, the new government first centralised decisions on selling state assets, and afterwards, the whole range of proprietary rights. The arguments of an economic character which are brought forward in order to support the intention of centralisation, do not seem to be too well founded in the light of the experience gained so far. Centralisation of privatisation and 're-nationalisation' has not so far led to any acceleration of the process of changing ownership structure. Moreover, there are no signs to show that government bodies would become efficient owners, exercising tight control over the management where property remains either permanently or temporarily in the hands of the state. Hungarian economic reforms of the last two decades suggest both historically and logically that the efficient operation of state property is rather hopeless, if it concerns a dominant sector of the economy.

Among the motives for centralisation, the political and power aspects seem to be dominant; replacing former enterprise management and thereby spreading the feeling of being threatened. The aim has also been to fulfil the promises made before the parliamentary election. Among the circles requiring 'radical change' of the system, this would tend to strengthen the voter base, create many new, well-paid positions and also enhance the commitment of the newly appointed persons.

However substantial centralisation of ownership rights (a real and strong proprietary control), is presumably impossible. The changes in legal frameworks and the shifts in governmental aspirations have modified the alternatives and the motivations of enterprise managers. In the period of spontaneous privatisation, they aimed at escaping from governmental influence. Managers had the opportunity to strengthen their formal (legal) quasi-owner position (by transforming the large enterprise into a group of companies, which did not leave the sphere of state property), or were able to choose the position of a real manager in a partially privatised firm constructed by themselves. The latter option also remained available in the period of centralised privatisation. Under the new circumstances, however, managers in large numbers were threatened by dismissal or by transformation of their position into a bureaucratic, defenceless managerial role. Since these dangers remained as only threats and did not turn into reality for the majority, the first phase of centralisation changed the direction rather than the position of state enterprise managers. Government organisations again appeared as the main partners in negotiations, and management regained a strong bargaining power, based on information and personal contacts. Moreover, the second phase of centralisation, that of all ownership rights, paradoxically improved their bargaining position. The extension of the formal rights of state organisation to an increasing number of questions and a growing number of firms meant a weakening of the opportunities for real control. Hence managers may restore their informal quasi-ownership position (or formalise it in the new construction of asset management), bargaining continuously with state organisations.

Although there are two other options, namely to become real managers of privatised firms or real owners through a manager buy-out, both solutions may be relegated to the background. One reason is that most managers may prefer the more comfortable quasi-owner (or asset-manager) position. The other reason is that the government may not intend or may prove to be unable to extend privatisation.

What seems to be certain, however, is that it is impossible to exclude the influence of state enterprise managers on organisational and ownership transformations. Tight and direct control by government bodies is not only inefficient but – in given circumstances – impossible as well. The attempt to centralise privatisation and ownership rights does not eliminate choice for managers; at the very most it modifies the forms of the changes and the options of the managers. The different solutions, of course, have a different impact on the future ownership structure and the prospective economic mechanism. A centralised decision-making system involves the risk of slowing down privatisation or conserving a weak proprietary structure, characterised by dispersed private and/or state bureaucratic institutional ownership forms. This, in turn, may form the basis of a compromise between the managers and the government and could indicate a new intermingling of politics and economics.

References

A Magyar Köztársaság Kormánya (Government of the Republic of Hungary) A kormány tulajdonosi és privatizációs stratégiája 1991, (Strategy of the government on ownership relations and privatisation).

Állami Számvevöszék, 1990, "Jelentés a minisztériumi, illetve tanácsi alapítású vállalatok vagyonkihelyezési és átalakulási tevékenységének ellenörzéséröl", (State Audit Office: Report on the Control of Establishing Companies by and Transformation of State Enterprises).

_____, 1991, "Jelentés az Állami Vagyonügynökség müködéséröl" (State Audit Office: Report on the Activity of the State Property Agency).

Állami Vagyonügynökség, 1990, "Beszámoló az Állami Vagyonügynökség müködéséröl" (State Property Agency: Report on the activity of the State Property Agency).

_____, 1991 "Beszámoló az Állami Vagyonügynökség müködéséröl" (State Property Agency: Report on the Activity of the State Property Agency).

Csillag, I., 1991, "Privatizáció békaperspektívából" (Privatisation from the Perspectives of the Enterprises). Unpublished.

_____, 1992, "Privatizáció 1991" (Privatisation 1991), Pénzügykutató Rt.

Matolcsy, G. (ed.), 1991, Lábadozásunk évei (The Years of Convalescence). Budapest: Privatizációs Kutatóintézet.

Móra, M., 1991, "The (Pseudo)-privatisation of State-owned Enterprises (Changes in Organisational and Proprietary Forms, 1987–1990)", *Acta Oeconomica*, Vol. 43, pp. 1–2.

Szalai, E., 1992, *Perpetuum Mobile*, MTA Közgazdaságtudományi Intézet.

Tóth, I. J., 1991, "A spontán privatizáció mint kormányzati politika" (Spontaneous Privatisation as Governmental Policy), *Külgazdaság* 9.

Voszka, É., 1991a, "From Twilight into Twilight" (Transformation of the Ownership Structure in the Big Industries), *Acta Oeconomica*, Vol. 43, pp. 281–295.

_____, 1991b, "A 'spontaneitástól' a 'központosításig' – és tovább?" (From 'Spontaneity' to 'Centralisation' – and Further On?), *Külgazdaság* 9.

_____, 1992, *Privatizáció 1991* (Privatisation 1991), Pénzügykutató RT.

14

Problems of Decollectivisation with Special Attention to East Germany

*Frederic L. Pryor**

Introduction

In the nations formerly dominated by communist parties (hereafter 'Marxist-regimes'), decollectivisation has raised a number of serious economic problems. These difficulties have been quite different from those occurring in the restructuring of the manufacturing sector that have received so much attention in this volume and elsewhere. In this essay I try to survey the most important issues of decollectivisation in the agricultural sector not just in a general fashion, but also in the context of several specific cases, as the many aspects of these decollectivisation problems differ considerably among the various nations.

I pay particular attention to East Germany for two reasons. First, the special circumstances of its transition have allowed decollectivisation to be carried out under conditions considerably more favourable than in other Marx-ist-regimes. Thus the general problems of decollectivisation are not overwhelmed by the special problems arising from particular national circumstances. Second, since I carried out interviews in a number of collective and state farms in this nation in early 1990, I thought I could gain greater perspective on the changes that have taken place by revisiting the same farms two years later. This procedure raises some obvious problems because the sample is not large;

---

* Department of Economics, Swarthmore College. I would like to thank the Arne Ryde Symposium for encouraging the research for this paper, and also Zora Pryor, who participated in all of the interviews in East Germany on which these remarks are based. I am also grateful to Jed DeVaro for comments on this paper.

on the other hand, little systematic information has been published on the process of transformation and, moreover, such studies are usually outdated when they appear, so that I had few alternatives other than to attempt such a direct approach.[1]

My argument has three steps. First, I try to show that for decollectivisation the importance of conditions at the starting point are important and differ greatly from country to country. Many discussions about the current difficulties of former Marxist-regimes speak of a generic 'country in transition'. Although for some problems of transition to a market this may be useful, for agriculture it is not. Second, I cast a brief glance at macro-economic events since in most countries these have had a more adverse impact on agriculture than on other sectors. Finally, I turn to four general micro-economic problems of decollectivisation:

Restructuring of decision-making rights: In agriculture this involves the decentralisation of the control of decision making from the central and regional governmental and party authorities to the farm level, and the delineation of the rights and responsibilities of the managers and workers of the farm. In industry these problems are more complicated since they raise more serious issues about separation of ownership and control; furthermore, problems of direct government regulations of economic activity are more extensive in the large industrial firms than in the smaller farms.

Repartitioning of the assets: In agriculture this includes the redivision of the fields and the movement from large-scale to small-scale farming, while in industry it refers to the break-up of monopolies and other policies influencing the size distribution of firms. For East Germany, the most surprising development has been the establishment of a new type of cooperative farm.

Privatisation: In agriculture, this means moving from state farms or pseudo-cooperatives to ownership by individuals, corporations, or genuine cooperatives.

Marketisation: In agriculture, this involves a transformation from an administrative system of allocating farm inputs and outputs to a system that is guided primarily by market signals; and the creation of an infrastructure to support these changes. Such a process, however, has been strongly shaped by the different ways in which these functions were institutionalised during the Marxist era.

These four characteristics of transition are logically distinct and can, to a

1. Some of the results of this earlier trip appeared in my essay: "East European Economic Reforms: The Rebirth of the Market", *Hoover Essays in Public Policy,* 1990, Stanford: Hoover Institution and Stanford University. For a more recent period the most useful study I have found of the problems of restructuring agriculture in the former East Germany is by Andreas Kurjo, "Der ostdeutsche Weg der Landwirtschafts-Herausforderung und Chance für das europäische Agrarpolitik", *FS Analysen* 1, 1992, Berlin. (Forschungsstelle für gesamtdeutsche wirtschaftliche und soziale Fragen). This study, however, does not touch on a number of developments that are noted below.

certain extent, be carried out separately. For instance, China restructured property rights, repartitioned the land, and marketised agriculture without privatising it. Land can also be privatised and marketised, without repartitioning. For instance, Guyana has been planning on transferring ownership of the nationalised sugar estates to the previous British owners in exchange for the unredeemed governmental bonds these foreign owners had received for Guyanese lands. In manufacturing, these four characteristics of transition are more closely linked than in agriculture, where the government has the choice of sequencing the changes.

Country Differences

Although the various former Marxist-regimes have experienced many of the same problems, significant differences arise, particularly in agriculture, that deserve attention. Most importantly, the degree of collectivisation was quite different; furthermore, the form of collective farming, particularly the relative importance of cooperative and state farms, varied considerably. Some idea of these differences can be gained from Table 14.1, which presents data on 33 nations identified as Marxist-regimes. The rubric 'collective farm' embraces not only genuine production cooperatives, which were relatively infrequent, but two other forms: *pseudo-cooperatives*, where managers were appointed by the government or party and where the farms were given compulsory targets and treated in a similar manner to state farms, a type of farm found in East Europe; and *nominal cooperatives*, where the collective farm form provided a 'legal front' for many private farming activities. Such nominal cooperatives are found in some third world Marxist-regimes and have been documented most extensively for North Vietnam by Adam Fforde. Clearly, decollectivisation is easier in a system of nominal cooperatives than in state farms and pseudo-cooperatives since it merely legalises those activities that were previously carried out in a covert fashion.

The pre-collectivisation system of agriculture also influenced the division of the land. More specifically, large-scale plantations were an important element in the agricultural sector, especially in third world Marxist-regimes, and in these plantations, few workers have the experience to run an individual farm. In Guyana, where this was the case, there has been surprisingly little political pressure to divide the sugar estates.

The initial path to collectivisation has also been an important element in the decollectivisation process. In those countries where collectivisation was preceded by a land reform which equalised land holdings, returning the land to the beneficiaries of the land reform has been politically easier than in nations which collectivised large estates without such an intermediate step. This factor explains the enormous problems faced by the government of Violeta Barrios de

TABLE 14.1 The Relative Importance of Private and Socialist Agriculture in Marxist-Regimes

Country	Land reform	Form of agricultural organisation Date	Per cent of land in: Private farms	Collective farms	State farms	Definition of land concept and other notes
Africa						
Angola	N	n.a.	n.a.	n.a.	n.a.	
Bénin	N	1981/2	97.2	1.8	1.0	TAL
Cape Verde	Y	1988	96.5	0.4	3.1	Only irrigated land
Congo	N	1973	92.5	0.1	7.4	Cultivated area
Ethiopia	Y	1985/6	92.4	3.9	3.7	Area under crop
Guinea Bissau	Y	1980	95.9	0.3	3.8	Area under crop; estimate very rough
Madagascar	N	1984/5	98.8	0.7	0.5	Cultivated area
Mozambique	Y	1983	94.2	1.3	4.4	Cultivated area
Sao Tomé	N	1987	3.8	0.0	96.2	TAL
Seychelles	N	1988	44.0	6.0	50.0	Only flat agricultural land; estimate very rough
Somalia	Y	1984	88.6	5.0	6.4	Cultivated area
Zimbabwe	N	1984	98.2	0.3	1.5	TAL
America						
Cuba	YS	1987	14.5	12.5	73.0	TAL
Grenada	N	1981	87.0	1.0	12.0	TAL
Nicaragua	N	1986	75.5	11.1	13.4	Total farm land
Guyana	N	1977/8	23.1	– 76.9 –		Cultivated area
Asia						
Afghanistan	Y	1981/2	94.0	4.1	1.9	Cultivated area
China	Y	1980	– 95.6 –		4.5	TAL; private farmland is minuscule
Kampuchea	N	1977	0.0	– 100.0 –		Total farm land
Korea, North	Y	1963	0.0	92.0	8.0	Cultivated area
Laos	N	1986	46.5	53.0	0.5	Cultivated area
Mongolia	Y	1986	0.0	88.6	11.4	TAL
Vietnam	Y	1975	n.a.	85.2	n.a.	Cultivated area; only North Vietnam
	Y	1986	18.2	79.8	2.0	Cultivated area: North and South Vietnam
Yemen, South	N	1986	29.0	2.4	8.6	Cultivated area
Europe						
Albania	Y	1983	0.5	78.4	21.1	Cultivated land
Bulgaria	Y	1987	10.0	0.0	90.0	TAL
Czechoslovakia	Y	1987	6.1	63.5	30.4	TAL
Germany, East	Y	1987	9.7	82.5	7.7	TAL
Hungary	Y	1987	13.7	71.4	14.9	TAL
Poland	Y	1987	78.0	3.6	18.4	TAL
Romania	Y	1987	15.6	54.7	29.8	TAL
USSR	YI	1987	1.8	30.4	67.8	TAL
Yugoslavia	Y	1981	82.3	0.9	16.8	Total farm holdings

Notes for Table 14.1 on page 243 For land reform: N = none; Y = yes; YS = yes, but simultaneous with an important collectivisation drive; YI = yes, but informal (that is, 'from below' and without governmental authorisation); n.a. = not available; TAL = total agricultural land.

For many countries the data on the relative importance of state and collective farms are very uncertain and indicate only general orders of magnitude. Private plots of cooperative and state property are included as part of cooperative or state farms. State farms include 'institutional farms', that is, farms managed by factories (*podkhozy*) and social agencies. The farms of communes are classified as cooperatives since they have been managed according to the same principle. I have tried to eliminate 'pre-cooperatives', although this was not completely possible in all cases.

The classification of the countries and the data come from Frederic L. Pryor, *The Red and the Green* (1992), Chapters 1 and 4.

Chamorro in Nicaragua in trying to return the lands of the former state and collective farms to private individuals.

The length of the period of collectivisation has also made a difference. In the Soviet Union, where collectivisation has lasted over 50 years, or in Albania, China or Vietnam where collectivisation was much shorter but where land records were not carefully kept, it is impossible to return the land to the previous owners. Instead, it has been simplest to divide the land according to the size of the family or the number of family workers on the farm, rather than returning to the *status quo ante*.

A number of technical considerations has also influenced the process of decollectivisation.

Sectoral Self-Containedness

In richer nations, the relative importance of inputs from other sectors into agriculture, for instance, fertilisers, pesticides, machinery, is greater. Furthermore, the relative share of agricultural goods sold to other industries for processing increases and the relative importance of agricultural goods sold without processing directly to the consumer decreases.

It should be evident that decollectivisation is simpler where the agricultural sector is more self-contained than where agriculture is more closely linked with other sectors. In the former case, as exemplified by China, decollectivisation can occur in agriculture without great changes in other sectors; in East Europe, by way of contrast, the government must proceed on a much broader front, especially since the role of monopoly sellers of agricultural inputs and monopsonistic buyers of farm outputs are so much more important in the economic lives of the farmers. Western economists have offered inappropriate advice to East Europe that their economic reforms should start first in the agricultural sector.

Economies of Scale

Although economies of scale are generally not considered to be great in agriculture, they differ considerably according to crop and technical conditions. Wheat (grown in Ukraine) and sugar (grown in Cuba), for quite different reasons, have advantages of large-scale production; viticulture (important in Georgia), vegetables (important in northern Europe and the non-black earth regions in the CIS), or tree crops (Sao Tomé) have few economies of scale. Other things being equal, decollectivisation should, as a result, be easier in Georgia or the non-black earth areas than in Ukraine or the black earth areas.

But confounding these simple considerations of scale is the fact that collectivised agriculture led to a rural infrastructure – farm equipment, marketing, transportation – that was geared to the requirements of large farms. Thus productivity in small-scale farms is much less than its potential, at least until new equipment is purchased and new infrastructure is built.

Human Input and Social Structure

In China the farmers on the collective farms appeared to have a burning desire to become private farmers again; and in other Marxist-regimes such as Vietnam this may also have been the case. But in certain East European nations, the situation appears different. For instance, public opinion polls among farmers in East Germany around March 1990 revealed that more than 90 per cent of them had no desire to become private farmers again. In the former USSR in the late 1980s Tatiana Zaslavkaya wrote: 'I do not know ... of any people who are interested in this [breaking up of the collective farm]. I have been to many kolkhozy and talked to many people and those who would give me that chance, who dream of working individually, they just do not exist'. In February 1992, a *New York Times* (17th February) reporter recorded the following conversation in the village of Koltsove about the possibility of farmers selling food at the railroad station in a regional centre 10 miles away: 'No, never', said Mr. Savitsky. 'Don't ask me to sell. I'd die of shame. I have a conscience still'. Aleksandr Trunin, one of the few staunch reformers in the village, said: 'That's exactly the problem. Those with a conscience won't sell. I could', he added with a smile, 'but I'm too lazy'.

While it is easy to claim that these differences merely reflect 'the values' of the particular rural populations, social and economic factors appear to play important roles in forming these attitudes, and it is useful to list several of the most important:

– *Ageing*. In a number of former Marxist-regimes, such as Bulgaria, the rural population is aged, primarily because of rural flight of young people from the countryside. In some countries, such as China, this type of rural flight was prohibited, while in other third world Marxist nations it was not feasible because of lack of urban employment. In several countries such as East Germany and Czechoslovakia, the rural sector was subsidised to the extent that living standards were little different from urban areas so that economic incentives for rural flight were dampened. Clearly, decollectivisation is more difficult with an aged rural population.

– *Entrepreneurship*. According to a controversial thesis of Gábor Havas, a Hungarian sociologist, entrepreneurially-minded young people were more likely to leave the rural areas than others. Such 'counter-selection' left a rural population less willing and able to go into private farming.

– *Incentives and economic returns*. In a situation where credit is scarce, where farmers are faced with monopolistic input sellers and monopsonistic output buyers, where the agricultural sector is subject to arbitrary governmental measures, and where the government does not have the administrative capacity or fiscal resources to provide the ancillary measures necessary for private farming, the risks of private farming are very great and the foreseeable returns may be low. In such circumstances it should not be surprising that the rural population may prefer to remain on collective farms in order to share such risks. Moreover, as a group they may be more easily able to exercise economic and political influence on the government than as individual farmers.

– *Political factors*. The local collective farm chairmen or the governmental authorities may discourage private farming in many different ways, such as refusing to provide prospective private farmers with the land, equipment, or credit, which would make such an enterprise profitable. This situation appears to have occurred primarily in the Soviet Union and Bulgaria up to 1992.

– *Socialisation of rural workers*. At this point it seems premature to speculate upon the impact of the communist experiment on the psyche and the values of the population in former Marxist-regimes. But in East Germany, many farmers emphasised to me that over the past decades, they have learned how to work together harmoniously; and they contrasted themselves in this respect with rural workers in West Germany. As I argue at greater length below, this has been a particularly important causal element in rural developments in this country. In certain other Marxist-regimes this important change in the rural mentality may have occurred as well.

The message of this brief discussion is simple: in analysing the problems of decollectivisation and in prescribing policies to ease this transition, it is necessary to understand the different starting points for each country. We can not use a cookie-cutter approach – what is useful in Bulgaria may not be useful in Czechoslovakia or Russia.

Macro-Economic Stability and Agriculture

This discussion is brief for I wish to make only one simple argument: for a successful agricultural reform, especially in those nations with important agricultural exports, macro-economic stability should have a high priority. If it does not, then agriculture is usually less able than most other sectors of the economy to obtain the resources necessary for its survival and to adapt to the new economic conditions. This, in turn, imperils the agricultural transformation. Supporting this argument, it is necessary to note several factors.

Most importantly, urban interests are more easily able than rural interests to mobilise large masses of people to prevent cuts in particular governmental programmes affecting them. As a result, expenditures for such purposes as agricultural extension work or rural infrastructure are more likely to be cut back or eliminated. In my book *The Red and the Green*, I provide a number of examples in different countries.

Although it might seem that the rural sector would profit from inflation, a number of offsetting factors must be taken into account. If the government officially sets prices for agricultural products to aid the urban population or if it sets a fixed exchange rate during the transition, agricultural prices inevitably lag the inflation rate so that real prices paid to farmers decline both for agricultural exports and for those products purchased by a monopsonistic state purchasing agency. As Michael Wyzan has pointed out in his paper in this volume, although the state monopolistic/monopsonistic agencies in Bulgaria were broken up in 1991, they were replaced by monopolistic/monopsonistic agencies on a regional level, a phenomenon that also occurred in quite a different context in the agricultural liberalisation efforts in Madagascar. In any case, from the scattered statistics I have been able to locate, the internal terms of trade have turned against agriculture since 1989 in all East European nations with the possible exception of East Germany, which suggests the importance of this industrial organisation question.

Furthermore, although an exchange rate lagging the rate of inflation leads to inexpensive (in domestic currency) imported agricultural inputs such as fertilisers, pesticides, machinery, and spare parts, such imports are in greater competition with inexpensive imports demanded by other sectors. Since the agricultural sector seldom is given the highest priorities for scarce foreign exchange, the volume of these imported agricultural inputs either falls or is allocated to those rural groups with the greatest political influence, namely the state farms. In this scramble for scarce imported agricultural inputs, it should not be surprising that the private farmers are usually at the end of the queue, either because they are unorganised or because their interest groups are weak. Because of its unification with West Germany, East Germany did not have this problem.

A similar situation arises in the case of credit. If credit is scarce and must be rationed, or where credit facilities are not readily available for the rural population, the agricultural sector usually stands at the back of the queue and, as a result, production falls. For instance, in 1991 in Romania, five million hectares went uncultivated for lack of capital; and in the former Soviet Union in the same year it was reported that 40 per cent of the land of independent farmers was not cultivated for the same reason. Moreover, in its April 1992 meeting, the Congress of People's Deputies refused to change the crucial articles on land in the Russian constitution which had the effect of preventing certain classes of farmers from mortgaging their land to obtain credit. Again, East Germany seems particularly favoured in this regard since West German land laws were quickly introduced and West German banks moved rapidly into both urban and rural areas to supply credit. These events, combined with the massive credits provided by the West German government, gave East German agriculture a particular advantage over the rural sector in the rest of the former Marxist-regimes.

Special Micro-Economic Problems of Decollectivisation

After these preliminary remarks, we can now turn to the four crucial micro-economic problems of decollectivisation.

Restructuring Property Rights

The creation of strong property rights in the land may be a more significant reform than changes in ownership. For property rights to be strong, they must be enforceable, carefully delineated, and only slowly changed so that transaction costs can be lowered. Strong property rights also require an effective judiciary to enforce them, as well as the reduction of direct governmental intervention at all levels. In the countries under consideration, the central plans have been dropped, but the administrative tyranny at different levels of government has been more difficult to suppress.

This governmental intervention has been particularly marked in the processes of breaking up the farms, a matter which by necessity must be administered by local governments. Although laws, for instance in Czechoslovakia, provide for the return of property to previous owners, in some places these owners have been forced to pay for 'improvements' without the possibility of counter-charging for depreciation on their old equipment, even though the laws apparently allow for this possibility. Clearly local governments can manipulate these turn-back programmes into a source of revenue, and unless the owners have legal redress, the farming sector becomes decapitalised.

Some governments, especially in the CIS, have been unwilling to loose their grip in other ways. In 1991 in Russia, for instance, land sales by the new private owners were either restricted for ten years or were limited in a manner to comply with a set of special regulations. In the name of 'emergency legislation', some governments have also restricted the sale of farm products. For instance, in Russia in 1991, collective and state farms had to sell to the state at specified prices 25 to 45 per cent of different crops; and private farmers were required to sell 25 per cent of their crop to the state at these prices. In Romania, local officials have prevented farmers from marketing their products outside their district. The same occurred in Madagascar after the demise of the state purchasing organisations.

The creation of strong property rights requires the establishment of institutions for contract enforcement. Many new owners find themselves in the position of having to hire machinery services (for instance, for land preparation) and must have total certainty that these contracts will be honoured. Otherwise, private farming is too risky.

Of all of the countries undergoing decollectivisation, East Germany has been most fortunate because both the laws of West Germany and the accompanying enforcement mechanisms have been adopted. Local governmental interference in farm production or *ad hoc* central governmental interventions have been minimal. Moreover, credit has been available so that these strong property rights can be exercised; and loss-making farms are being liquidated, reorganised, and sold as quickly as possible. For instance, one collective farm I visited in 1990 had huge debts, an antiquated infrastructure and technology, and high costs of production. Since it could not meet its payroll, it limped along with subsidies from the Truehandanstalt for six week and was then closed. All workers on the farm were fired and the land was sold for commercial usage. When I arrived in 1992 I saw that the main administration building had been torn down, a Toyota showroom was being constructed in its place, and the barns were being used as warehouses.

A key to the maintenance of strong property rights is the ready availability of credit; otherwise these rights remain only 'theoretical'. The branches of West German banks that had been set up in the various East German towns employed hard-headed lending rules. Landless labourers who wished to set up as private farmers usually found it difficult to obtain credit since they had little collateral, in contrast to farmers who could use their land for this purpose. Among my interview partners who had collateral, I found that those with feasible and sensible business plans were generally able to obtain credit, while those whose plans were vague and who seemed less able to manage their property were generally denied credit. This has not been the case in other nations of East and Central Europe, where credit has been scarce.

In decollectivisation, the principal-agent problem plays an important role in determining the speed at which property rights are strengthened. If the government does not quickly assign responsibility for management to a single person or group, whose income is tied to the long-term results of the farm, those working on the farm have an incentive to take destructive measures such as mining the soil that might raise their current income at the expense of the long-term value of the enterprise. This problem appears especially acute in situations where farm subsidies have been reduced and where the current farm workers have no claims to the land.

Repartitioning the Land

It is difficult to determine from abstract considerations the appropriate size distribution of farms. In East Europe and other former Marxist nations where individual farm families were technically the owners of the land on the collective farms, two main choices were open. (1) The land could be returned to the former owners or their heirs. Some countries such as Czechoslovakia have limited the amount to be returned in order to equalise the distribution of the land, and have also confined land ownership only to citizens now living in the country. (2) Bonds could be issued to the former owners and the land can continue to be used by the farmers now occupying the land. This approach was used in Hungary where the return of the land to the former owners would leave about 50 per cent of the present rural workers landless, according to a 1991 study by Iván Szelényi.

But division of the equipment and of the other capital stock raises many more problems. If the type of agriculture practiced in the nation is machinery and equipment intensive, some means must be devised in the transition period, not just to divide or share this equipment but also to share the associated risks. For instance, if inclement weather prevents a particular farmer from using the shared tractor during his allotted time-slot, either his losses must somehow be shared by those more fortunate with the weather or the allocation schedule of the equipment must be changed so that the farmer can use the equipment on the first suitable day. Or, if the equipment is leased to a private company, enforceable contracts must be devised to handle the same problems. It is certainly possible to resolve these problems, but considerable negotiation and good-will is required. For certain types of farm infrastructure such as barns, the situation is even more difficult. If a barn houses 2,000 cattle (not uncommon in East Europe), division of the barn raises problems of externalities: if one farmer allows his cattle to become diseased, the other farmers will suffer.

In East Germany, where decollectivisation has occurred in relatively easy conditions, the landscape looks little different from before: the fields are considerably larger than in West Germany and the large-scale farming methods are still evident. A closer look reveals that the repartitioning of land and equipment has resulted in the formation of a new type of cooperative farm.

Around 1980 the original cooperative farms (LPGs or Landwirtschaftliche Produktionsgenossenschaften) were divided into those producing crop products and those producing animal products, a split that led to serious coordination and incentive problems. Quite early in 1990, most of these animal and crop collective farms were combined again. Thereafter, in many cases, the new farm units were divided into much smaller farm units of 1,000 hectares or so that centred around a single village. Many of the auxiliary enterprises, for instance, the building brigades, the cafeteria, and so forth, were sold or leased. Although required to form 'companies', the farmers often took advantage of an 1890s' law still remaining on the books of both East and West Germany to form production cooperatives, renting their land from those receiving title to the land, but farming it collectively. In some cases they formed a limited liability corporation (GmbH) instead, although this was a more complicated procedure.

The shares of the members in either the cooperative or the corporation depended upon the capital they contributed and this, in turn, was drawn from personal savings or the settlement (*Abfindung*) they received at the time of the dissolution of the original collective farm. The settlement was based in part on the inventories of the equipment and buildings that the farm members and their families brought into the LPGs during the collectivisation drive, and in part on the number of years that the person worked for the cooperative. The latter was especially important for those who contributed no land to the collective farm. In the two cooperatives where I requested such information, the members had received about 800 DM for each year of work; this was roughly 7.5 per cent of the annual average wages in 1975, the middle point of the collectivisation period.

All members of the new cooperatives receive a wage (the manager gets roughly twice the wage of a regular worker) and after payment of rent, taxes, and investment expenditures have been made, share in the profits according to their share of the capital. The farms I visited had reorganised themselves in this manner before the Treuhand had time to set up exact rules and regulations for the others to follow; but I was told that the principles that were followed in the farms I visited were roughly similar to those that were officially promulgated later.

In those cooperative farms where the net worth was greater than the sum of the individual settlements, the members had a clear economic advantage to take over the farms; in those cooperatives where this was not the case and where economic prospects were poor, it was advantageous to accept the settlement, work on the farm as long as the Treuhand subsidises the wages or sells the farm, and then hope their job would be continued at high wages. Although the number of collective farms dissolved in this manner is not known, Andreas Kurjo (1992) estimates in a rough fashion the number at about 20 per cent by the end of 1991. By the middle of 1992 the Treuhand has still not sold many of these farms to new owners; the one I visited was in very poor condition and was far different from its bustling state when I had visited it two years previously; the workers had simply allowed the farm to run down, a manifestation of the principal-agent problem previously mentioned.

Although one collective farm I visited in 1991 had tried to keep all the land together, the new cooperative farms I visited in 1992 were much smaller than the original LPGs. The managers emphasised to me that with 20 or 30 workers to manage, they could be in daily contact with all of them and had close oversight as to what was happening; that lazy workers could easily be fired (although they would continue to hold their share of the ownership, if they desired); and that all recognised that the profits received at the end of the year were closely tied to the intensity and quality of their work. These small cooperatives had no need to struggle with the problems of dividing the equipment and buildings; the economies of scale in grain production, which appeared to be the major crop in the areas I visited, could be achieved.

Management of these new cooperatives is hierarchical; the managers with whom I spoke indicated that they made most of the decisions, recommending certain policy decisions to a small board of directors which generally confirmed these decisions. Certain basic financial decisions are discussed in meetings of the entire cooperative, which meets several times a year. The key decision seems to be the relative division of revenues between wages and investment: one cooperative I visited paid its workers 20 DM an hour but had little left over for investment, while another paid its workers half this amount and was undergoing a massive investment programme. The white-collar staffs of these farms are small – generally the manager and a bookkeeper – so that little waste arose from bureaucratisation. The managers spoke knowledgeably about their business problems; they seemed quite aware of the tradeoffs between risk and return, as well as other market phenomena; and they expressed little anxiety about being relieved of their position by the full assembly of members, suggesting to me that the members needed them more than they needed the members.

The motives for the formation of these new cooperatives were complex, but two explanations can be quickly dismissed. The members had not formed the cooperatives out of some sort of political idealism or socialist ideology. When I asked about voting patterns, I learned that most had voted for the Christian Democratic Party and were uninterested in the Party of Democratic Socialism (the successor party to the previous communist party, the Socialist Unity Party). And the members were not creating these cooperatives in order to keep the land for their children; several told me that their sons or daughters were more interested in obtaining work in the city. They have the mentality of commercial farmers, not peasants.

The farmers seemed to recognise that they were overspecialised and unprepared to take on the many different tasks of private farming, which require a variety of skills. As one manager told me, 'I know a great deal about animals, but nothing about fertiliser'. They also seemed to recognise that their possibilities of obtaining credit were greater as a group than as individuals since their joint collateral was greater. They were also following a mode of working together that they had learned during the socialist period, which they believed to be more productive than individual farming in West Germany.

At this point it is difficult to judge whether these new small cooperatives are merely a transitional form to private farming, or whether they will last. In Mecklenburg-Vorpommern I was told that only about 15 per cent of the land is privately farmed. Few of the people I interviewed thought that this percentage would rapidly increase in the foreseeable future; to the contrary, most believed that when the new cooperatives were able to obtain the Western agricultural technology that they desired, they would be more productive than West German private farmers.

In many of the other former Marxist-regimes, large-scale farming has continued for quite different reasons. In a number of these nations members have found it difficult to withdraw from the collective farms because of difficulties in receiving back their land or in obtaining credit to buy equipment. Economic uncertainties are still too great, markets for farm inputs or outputs are still too underdeveloped, and credit is still too scarce to encourage private agriculture. Many agricultural workers lack the skills and the knowledge to become private farmers. Although the East German agricultural sector is still in transition, these uncertainties and problems are present to a lesser degree. In the rest of East Europe, in contrast to East Germany, the decision to remain in large-scale agriculture is more the result of constraints preventing them from exercising other farming options, than a fully free choice.

Privatisation

Many of the issues surrounding privatisation have already been raised. It is noteworthy that in only about one-third of the Marxist-regimes did the government nationalise the land. In East Europe, except for the Soviet Union, the land was never nationalised so that technically, most of it belonged to the original members of the collective farms or their heirs. A considerable asymmetry in the treatment of different types of property exists in East Europe. Property that was managed directly (farms, small stores) has often been returned or will be returned directly to previous owners; property held in the form of ownership shares, for instance, stock in a corporation, has generally not been recognised or recompensed in the form of additional vouchers. This means that a greater portion of the agricultural land will be returned than urban-based property.

A number of legal questions require resolution, for instance competing claims of landless and landowning members of the collective farms, the recognition of claims of land-owners living abroad or with very large pieces of land, and the competing claims of various heirs. Whatever solution is chosen through the political process, the measures must be devised to assign ownership in a quick and unambiguous fashion to reduce uncertainty so that investment can be encouraged. The last issue is crucial: although collectivisation of agriculture in Yugoslavia lasted only about five years in the early 1950s and entailed just one-quarter of the land, Yugoslav authorities told me that lawsuits over ownership lasted for fifteen years after decollectivisation.

If compensation is to be given for land, the problems of valuation of the land must be resolved. Furthermore, the question of farm debts raises additional difficulties. In some countries such as Bulgaria, they were simply written off; in other countries such as East Germany, some were written off; while in still other nations such as Czechoslovakia or Hungary, none were eliminated.

If compensation is to be paid to former owners so that current rural workers can obtain land, then other problems arise. One approach is 'creeping privatisation', where the government merely expands the size of the private plots on all state and collective farms. Problems arise, however, if the farmers do not have proper equipment to farm it. And, moreover, it can be demonstrated using standing indifference curve analysis that under certain conditions this piecemeal approach can result in a considerable loss of labour on the collective plots so that an overall decline in agricultural production takes place.

Finally, the problem of the speed of the process deserves attention. In East Germany the process occurred extremely rapidly, primarily under the pressure of the West Germans. In Czechoslovakia, the process has been much slower, even though the goal has been total decollectivisation, while in still other countries such as Albania, Bulgaria, and Romania there has been a partial decollectivisation in the form of an increase in the size of individual plots, without any timetables for total decollectivisation.

Marketisation

Three aspects of the problem must be noted: a reliable, accessible, and competitive source of agricultural inputs must be assured; a similar system of sale of agricultural outputs must be established; and a widespread system of retail outlets in the countryside to provide consumer goods to farmers must be in place, a problem of considerable importance in the third world former Marxist-regimes.

During the communist period the input suppliers were generally monopolistic enterprises whose sales were oriented toward large-scale buyers. This has raised problems for small-scale farmers. For instance, according to newspaper reports, the land in Albania was relatively easily divided, but a disastrous harvest resulted in 1991 because of lack of appropriate agricultural inputs. A similar problem arose in Romania, especially lack of gasoline for tractors. The problem has been compounded because in most of these countries the factories selling such inputs are located in the cities far removed from the farming area, in contrast to China. The purchase of farm outputs in most countries was generally carried out by monopsonistic purchasers and many of the same problems arose.

The magnitude of the transition problems depends in good measure upon the different ways in which these supply and purchasing functions were institutionalised in the previous years. Four patterns can be readily distinguished.

In East Germany many of these selling and purchasing functions were handled by inter-enterprise units (ZBEs or Zwischenbetriebliche Einheiten) that were jointly owned by a group of collective and state farms. In 1990 these were spun off into independent companies that competed not just against other

ZBEs, but also against West German, Dutch, and Danish purchasing and selling companies that rapidly moved into the region. In my 1992 conversations with East German farmers I heard no complaints about the lack of competition on either the agricultural input or output markets.

In Hungary many of these selling and purchasing functions were handled by special units of particular collective farms. For instance, one farm would undertake to sell a technology package to other farms that would include inputs (seeds, fertilisers, pesticides) and, sometimes, output processing services as well. As in East Germany, a set of units were in place that could provide the nucleus of competition in input supply and output purchasing.

In most of the other former Marxist-regimes, the situation was not so favourable. In the third world nations, many of whom relied heavily on agricultural exports, most of the inputs were sold by a single state import company and most of the farm output was purchased by a single state export company. In this case, competition could be introduced only by widening the scope for other firms to enter the export–import trade, a task more easily recommended than implemented because of the technical difficulties arising in such trade, particularly when the currency was not readily convertible.

In the remaining former Marxist-regimes, the situation was even more difficult because the selling and purchasing functions were handled by monopolistic/monopsonistic firms that were under the direction of particular ministries. While it is possible to break up these firms into their component factors, in several countries such as Bulgaria and Czechoslovakia, they seem to have been replaced by regional monopolies and monopsonies.

The creation of markets for farm inputs and outputs requires institution building about which economic theory tells us little. The process requires the development of information networks, quality standards, exchange markets for staples, publication of price information, packaging regulations, labour laws and regulations for a stable labour market, creation of a social safety network, and a variety of other arrangements which are usually taken for granted in most discussions of the functioning of a market. A number of questions, for instance, the ideal degree of vertical integration in various crops, must somehow be resolved, although Western economics has little of importance to say about these matters.

In this regard East Germany has been particularly fortunate. Through numerous visits to West Germany, East German farmers learned not just about new agricultural technologies and practices, but about marketing channels, sources of price information, and consumer expectations in a free market. West German marketing procedures, product standards, regulations, and other practices were adopted *in toto*. West German agricultural publications flooded the East, and many of the problems of crop quality, packaging, and marketing that occurred in 1990 seemed considerably less important in 1992 as East German farm managers adapted to the new conditions. Furthermore, East German farmers were able to sell their crops all over the European Community. In its speed of institution building to reorganise the links between the farms and consumers and in its ability to export agricultural products, East Germany is certainly unique.

In building the institutions of a functioning market economy, the other Marxist-regimes will have many more serious problems than East Germany. The creation of information networks to disseminate vital news about prices, farm practices, and other topics of concern is particularly important. According to my observation, this problem has not been attacked in a very systematic fashion in most East and Central European nations. As a result, the vital linkages between farm and final consumer are weak. In the former Soviet Union the problem has been particularly serious and a large share of farm produce has been purchased, obtained, or stolen outside of the regular supply system. Liberalisation of prices without structural changes has increased the economic chaos in that country so that, for instance, milk production has fallen because fodder supplies could not be obtained in a timely fashion by cattle farms. The government of Boris Yeltsin has allowed the marketing of agricultural products without licences and some Western observers have noticed the sprouts of capitalism in the form of NEP-men and other forms of small-scale intermediation between the farm and the urban sectors; but a satisfactory marketisation of agriculture seems many years away. The excessively macro-economic focus of the reform programmes in many of these questions has led policy makers to overlook this institution building, which may be equally important for the long-run future of these nations.

Sequencing the Four Steps

In East Germany the creation of strong property rights, repartitioning the land and equipment, privatisation, and marketisation all occurred at the same time. This has required, however, a well-administered government which is not present in many of the former Marxist-regimes. If the four measures must be sequenced, the creation of strong property and marketisation appear to be the logical first steps, while repartitioning and privatisation can be delayed. If the first two steps do not occur close to each other in time, several problems arise.

Strong property, no marketisation. If property is strengthened without increasing the scope of market prices, assortment problems immediately arise because there are no mechanisms to balance supply and demand. The success or failure of the farms depends on arbitrary pricing decisions by the government and the farmers may have few incentives to increase production, a situation which appears to have arisen in the first half of the 1980s in Vietnam, which tried to allow individual agriculture greater scope without significantly increasing the role of market forces. Or else, the governments may find it difficult to set market-clearing agricultural prices centrally to avoid shortages and surpluses so that they must step in again to guide production. Or public agencies, both government and party, may find it difficult to restrain from their old behaviour and from intervening in farm operations so as to 'improve' their own success (Czechoslovakia in 1982).

Marketisation, weak property. On the other hand, if the price reform is carried out before property rights are strengthened (and, of course, before privatisation), then other problems arise. The price reform is almost meaningless if production is still guided by the government; or if the rules of behaviour of government agencies are not changed and if they continue to intervene so as to further their own goals. If the farm managers are unable to respond to market signals and if they are also not held accountable for their actions, which cannot be properly done without strong property rights, the attempted socialist market economy will remain in a limbo and the managers will always have good reasons for appealing for subsidies. The system will end up in some peculiar hybrid, neither plan nor market, with few of the advantages of either.

The phasing of the second two steps, privatisation and the breaking up of the collective and state farms, seems less important. They can, of course, occur at the same time as the first two steps. In Hungary in the early 1990s, however, the government took the first two steps while taking only very preliminary steps toward either privatisation or farm break-up. The four micro-economic reforms intertwined, as they did in China in the late 1970s and early 1980s when a certain degree of marketisation occurred simultaneously with the breaking up of the farms and creation of the lease system, while more important marketisation measures occurred immediately after the new productive units had been consolidated.

This entire discussion about sequencing is, however, predicated on the hidden assumption that the government is relatively strong and that policies set forth from above will be implemented. In some of the third world Marxist countries this is not the case and, as a result, sequencing problems are somewhat different. More specifically, if the government is too weak to prevent state and collective farms, officials from the supervising ministry, or others from plundering the treasury, then decollectivisation, privatisation, and marketisation might precede the strengthening of property rights. The first two measures would put an end to the fiscal drain from the subsidies to the socialist agricultural sector, and the marketisation would merely legalise the extensive second economy. The government could then take its time in carrying out the politically sensitive task of firing the planners and agricultural cadres who would have nothing to do as a result of this wholesale reduction in the functions of the public sector.

Final Remarks

Observation 1: importance of national factors. The decollectivisation problems and processes will be quite different in the various former Marxist-regimes, depending upon the initial degree of collectivisation, the path toward collectivisation, the type of crop, and the social and cultural structures of the countryside.

Observation 2: short-run difficulties and political pressures. Other papers have presented the problem of production shortfalls in much greater detail. The agricultural data are contradictory, but in 1990 gross agricultural production declined in every country – from 1 per cent in Poland to 7 per cent in Hungary and Yugoslavia. In 1991, further production declines appeared in most countries, although we cannot be sure. It is doubtful if production will recover for some time, especially because many of the problems have been resolved in a short-sighted manner. Furthermore, the more that central governments pander to populist pressures to lower the price of food, the more difficult will be agricultural recovery.

Observation 3: tractability. Although agriculture is relatively backward, especially in a number of the nations of the former Soviet Union, the problems of decollectivisation appear more tractable than the restructuring of manufacturing. In both sectors the level of technology plays a critical element. In agriculture, the major problem is the dissemination of the technology and the creation of an infrastructure to support it; in manufacturing, these problems appear more complex.

Observation 4: continuity. The initial impulse of some of the new governments of the former Marxist-regimes to destroy totally the collective farm system seems ill-advised. Group agriculture can provide an important transitional step in the creation of a private farming system; indeed, group farming in a less extreme form than the collective farms of the communist era might well be a viable social form of agricultural production for the future. For this reason the East German experience deserves close monitoring.

References

Fforde, A., 1989, *The Agrarian Question in North Vietnam, 1974-1979.* A Study of Cooperative Resistence to State Policy. Armonk, New York: Myron Sharpe.

Havas, G., 1990. Interview.

Kurjo, A., 1992, "Der Ostdeutsche Weg der Landwirtshafts-Herausforderung und Chance fur das Europäische Agrarpolitik", *FS Analysen*, Forschungsstelle fur gesamtdeutsche wirtschaftliche und soziale Fragen. No. 1, Berlin.

Pryor, F. L., 1990, "East European Economic Reforms: The Rebirth of the Market", *Hoover Essays in Public Policy*. Stanford: Hoover Institution and Stanford University.

_____, 1992, *The Red and the Green: The Rise and Fall of Collectivized Agriculture in Marxist Regimes*. Princeton NJ: Princeton University Press.

Szelényi, I., "The Social Impact of Agrarian Reform: Social and Political Conflicts of the Post-Communist Transformation of Hungarian Agriculture", in Braverman, A., K. Brooks and C. Csaba (eds), *Agricultural Reform in Eastern Europe and the USSR: Dilemmas and Strategies.* Washington DC: World Bank. (Forthcoming.)

Zaslavskaya, T, cited by Stefan Hedlund, 1990, "Private Plot as a System Stabilizer", in Wädekin, K.-E. (ed.), *Communist Agriculture: Farming in the Soviet Union and Eastern Europe*. London: Routledge.

15

The New East, Preferred Trade Regimes, and Designing the Transition

*Jozef M. van Brabant**

Introduction

With the utter collapse of communism over the past three years or so, we have witnessed many dramatic, largely unanticipated, transformations throughout the eastern part of Europe, including Yugoslavia. I collectively refer to this group of old and new planned economies in transition (PETs) – no pun intended – as 'East'. Perhaps the more surprising, if not the most tumultuous, event has been the spectacular disintegration of the old Soviet Union. The former constituent republics, at least in their political posturing, have become unrecognisable. But the 'newly emerging' economic problems of these areas are not. Their old and new trade and payment problems are intrinsically very similar. If evidence were needed, the ample experience since late 1989[1] by the

* Principal Economic Affairs Officer of the Department of Economic and Social Development of the United Nations Secretariat in New York. The opinions expressed here are my own and do not necessarily reflect those that may be held by the United Nations in general and its Secretariat in particular.

1. Certainly, the CMEA was not formally abolished until 28 June 1991, at the 46th Council Session in Budapest and the transferable rouble (TR) mechanisms remained formally intact until the end of 1990. But by then these mutations were only a belated recognition of the decay that had already pervasively tunnelled through the real spheres of trade, payments, and economic cooperation in the East. Note that the formal decision to dissolve the CMEA foresaw a 90-day period for finally resolving the remaining issues of the common organisation, mainly the settlement of common building in Moscow. As far as I know, the latter has not yet been conclusively dealt with. So ironically perhaps, we do not know when precisely the CMEA ceased to exist just as we do not know when the CMEA in fact came

former members[2] of the Council for Mutual Economic Assistance (CMEA)[3] should suffice to buttress that proposition.

This paper dissects the economics of the political posturing behind the wilful destruction of the trade and payment frameworks that were typical for these countries in isolation or in their intragroup contexts. However, the main focus will be on the rouble zone, if only because the TR zone has already been destroyed and cannot be revived for political reasons. Similarly, the ongoing conflicts in Yugoslavia make it simply unacceptable to return to a federalist-type policy dinar zone in the near term. Though the margin for flexibility in the case of the rouble zone is narrow, there is still hope that something can be rescued, provided policy makers in the successor republics can be persuaded that whatever political gain may be obtained from going it their own way may be far outweighed by the economic losses sustained in the process. But some vision is required to come to this seemingly logical conclusion.

I argue here that the analysis of cooperative solutions be examined separately from the hegemony that was formerly exerted by the old Soviet Union in the CMEA or the ambitions that some of the successor republics, notably Russia, may harbour. Abstracting from the high-power politics that all of the new leaderships have recently explored, albeit quite ineffectively, while admittedly somewhat confining the remit of the analysis, nonetheless permits me to focus on the economics of 'common economic areas'. Section 1 briefly sketches the politics of the destruction of the common economic and monetary zones as a prelude to recalling in Section 5 the rationale for earlier having subscribed to these arrangements. Next I present the salient features of the previously existing common areas. The PETs are hoping to implant a very different arrangement as part and parcel of transition policies, and that constitutes the subject of Section 3. The core of what is required for transition from one state to the other forms the next subject. The paper concludes with some pointers to interim measures that, I feel, could usefully be explored by some groups of PETs, if perhaps not all.

---

into being (see Brabant, 1989)!

2. Membership was identical to what is here denoted as East, except Albania, which ceased participation in the CMEA in 1961; Yugoslavia, which became an associate member in 1964, but never assumed full membership; three full non-European members (Cuba, Mongolia, and Vietnam); nine cooperants (Afghanistan, Angola, Ethiopia, Finland, Iraq, Mexico, Nicaragua, Syria, and [Democratic] Yemen); and other developing countries as observers in the CMEA.

3. Here I focus on the European members of the ex-CMEA (Bulgaria, Czechoslovakia, the German Democratic Republic [GDR], Hungary, Poland, Romania, and the Soviet Union). This group is also identified as Eastern Europe, although I shall occasionally use the notion to refer either to the six smaller CMEA members prior to the GDR's absorption into Germany or the areas of the East other than the successor Soviet republics (excepting the Baltics, of course). But the context then makes it clear that I have this smaller group in mind.

The Politics of Economic Disintegration

In view of the precipitous crumbling of the TR, rouble, and dinar zones, in part with the active support of the new-fangled, official as well as self-appointed, policy advisers to the new regimes, it may be useful to briefly recollect the rationale why countries voluntarily pool resources. I shall do so in Section 5 in technical terms after clarifying the environment within which the cited currency regimes have imploded. This is not to deny the importance of politics in international economic relations, particularly when there is a widely felt need for coordination in an environment that has been utterly disrupted, as in the former Soviet Union. Indeed, politics is important in setting the framework within which states coexist and reach their set goals individually or in unison. But the slide in the Soviet polity had started much earlier than the ramblings around the palace revolt (or *coup d'état*) of August 1991.

Perestroika and its associated 'New Thinking' had undeniably salutary effects on world and regional politics, and indeed on the demise of communism, not just its aberration in the old Soviet Union. From an economic point of view, however, it had become an appalling failure well before the disintegration of the Soviet polity. Inflation was rampant, shortages were piling up, the economy was contracting at an alarming rate, unemployment and poverty were coming into the open, productivity was down, the prospect for a decent harvest in 1991 was dim, the budget deficit was well out of control, external imbalances were mounting, and the value of the rouble was declining at an alarming pace. By some measure, rouble printing was running into its own bottleneck of how much paper could be fed to inked presses and for how long the latter could be kept running. Similar conditions have characterised Yugoslavia's disintegration. The rapid erosion of the dollar exchange rates of both the dinar and the rouble reflect only the tip of the icebergs that were rending and melting from within. Any temporary improvement in the exchange rate, as registered in Russia in late February and early March 1992, is likely to stem primarily from the shortage of physical rouble amounts; the need to pay inflated wages in state-owned enterprises, if necessary by mobilising convertible currency holdings; and the tug-of-war between the government and the central bank of Russia, with the latter being under pressure to improve monetary policy by other means than recourse to the printing press, than from a genuine resurgence of confidence in the discredited rouble.

Any reversal of this drift into sheer economic anarchy would have involved stringent demand-management measures aiming at economic stabilisation. In the first instance, it would be directed at eliminating stock disequilibria, or the imbalances built up over the past years because of serious policy mistakes. But it would soon also involve the rudiments of coming to grips in the monetary and fiscal domains with the basic requirements of stabilisation in the flow sense, or managing the economy in such a way that the government either does not run a budget deficit or can finance it out of voluntary savings through financial intermediation, just like other economic agents. That objective should have come to the fore regardless of any contemplated economic transformation in institutions and behavioural patterns.

From about mid-1991 on, the question was increasingly being asked whether with such a loose union it would still make sense to maintain a single currency and indeed whether the rouble as a currency could survive the ongoing seesaw changes at all. With the growing tendency to displace the rouble either with straightforward barter, bilateralism, or convertible currency transactions, one was compelled to inquire into the *raison d'être* of the rouble in any kind of credible reform package. Without it, the rouble would probably have disappeared into oblivion as several other currencies did, following the ravages of war, revolution, or sheer regime mismanagement. All these questions took on even more significance after August 1991, when the three Baltic republics found their way back to formal independence, all other Soviet republics declared economic sovereignty, and only a weak Commonwealth of Independent States (CIS) could be constituted; but the latter's viability is still in doubt.

Managing a union with up to 15 sovereign republics in a single currency zone necessarily raises issues that are familiar from the literature about optimum currency areas. These would not have been confined to external payment problems alone, as experienced in the TR area. Rather, the key issues at stake revolve around meeting the realistic preconditions for harmonising macro-economic policies among the various republics and how this could be ensured without there being any acceptable supranational authority. Even so, these problems of the rouble area are similar to those experienced in the dinar area, and indeed resemble in many respects key obstacles that confronted the Eastern European PETs when they decided to open up their economies to foreign competition in preference to modifying in an orderly manner the intricate CMEA linkages forged within the trade and payment, and indeed pricing, regimes anchored to the TR.[4]

This is not a facetious way of downgrading the convulsions that have gripped the East. Rather, the common thread that unites the erstwhile TR and the more recently emerging 'national' trade and payment problems in the area stem fundamentally from the inability of these countries to switch quickly to, what is euphemistically called, 'world market conditions' if some semblance of normality in trade and economic activity is to be maintained. Of course, a suitably massive devaluation of the exchange rate eventually is bound to engender some equilibrium. But the impoverishment of the country, because of the structures that will thus be destroyed as well as the sheer depreciation of purchasing power in international terms, might be so severe that it is hard to

4. True, the TR was created only in late 1963. Inasmuch as it was, in fact, only a redenomination of the clearing rouble, I will be permitted the shorthand for the more than 42 years of the CMEA's existence.

envisage how even minimal sociopolitical support for such a policy could be mustered, except by default.

The Erstwhile Dinar, Rouble, and TR Zones

Prior to the collapse of the Soviet Union, relations among the various constituent republics devolved more from administrative convenience – and often political imperatives – than any economic rationale. In other words, trade and payment relations between, say, then Belorussia and Ukraine were no different from relations between, say, enterprise *A* in Leningrad and firm *B* in Moscow. All transactions in principle devolved from planning decisions or negotiated contracts at rather inflexible prices with the clearing of transactions ensured through the technical apparatus of the monobank system (Gosbank), backed up by agreed-upon plan priorities, including automatic credits from the banking system. This system had been crumbling for some time prior to the formal collapse of the union as sovereignty claims were being staked out and delivery obligations against rouble accounting were being flouted. But just as the TR regime continued beyond the gradual interruption of contract discipline presumed in bilateral trade and payments agreements (BTPAs), beginning on a more than trivial scale in 1988, the rouble zone and the unionwide technical clearing of settlements were kept intact until the dissolution of Gosbank.[5] The situation was similar for Yugoslavia, although it was much less a centralised than a hypertrophied decentralised nation lacking a firm helm. Furthermore it enjoyed a tattered consensus on how inter-republican economic relations should be dealt with.

Matters among the CMEA member countries were slightly different from those within the rouble and dinar zones proper. For one thing, regardless of aspirations of some key players in the CMEA tug-of-war and the policy framework agreed upon under the label of 'socialist economic integration (SEI)', there never was a unified economic space throughout the CMEA, or even its European components. Whatever the CMEA members aimed at, voluntarily or under Soviet tutelage, it was hardly socialistic, economic, or integrated in the most common meanings of those terms. The essence of the TR pricing, trade, and payment regimes was: market separation through the state monopoly of foreign trade and payments adhered to by each country according to its own rules; artificial trading prices; rather rigid equalisation among domestic, TR, and east–west pricing and trade decision making within each country; and comprehensive interstate BTPAs 'with a few absurd but, in

5. Some formal substitute was created by Russia in early 1992 (Yasiliev, 1992) and subsequently endorsed at the Tashkent meeting of the CIS on 14–15 May 1992. But it is unclear whether this will now function, particularly since agreement on the size and purposes of swing credits has so far remained elusive.

principle, necessary rules: one had to have prices to exchange goods [and] an exchange rate to settle [these transactions]' (Lavigne, 1991, p. 6). For that reason, TR prices and exchange rates were almost pure inventions. In any case, these artificial magnitudes were only remotely linked, if that, to world prices, relative scarcities in the area, or the voluntaristic domestic price policies.

Given the above environment, it is easy to understand that CMEA trade flows did not emanate from genuine natural or strategically elaborated comparative advantages, though they probably became more rationally structured over time than the flows among the various constituent republics; but rationality was not a distinct feature of inter-republican trade in Yugoslavia either. Goods were traded at prices that reflected neither domestic costs, however factored, nor real scarcities in the region or in world markets, and these prices were as a rule not directly passed on to domestic agents. In the CMEA context this was especially so for goods built within the context of inter-governmental specialisation agreements and jointly financed investment projects. The former were mainly in support of machine building and manufacturing more generally. The latter were principally designed to shore up the buoyant exchange of fuels and raw materials, mostly from the Soviet Union, for manufactured products, chiefly from the smaller countries. That is, many goods traded in the CMEA enjoyed 'captive markets'. The same prevailed in the former USSR and Yugoslavia, though there inter-republican trade was not negotiated at the inter-governmental level. Rather, it was set through inter-ministerial negotiations in the USSR and mostly interenterprise negotiations in Yugoslavia. And, of course, there were no visible domestic payment problems within these federations, as distinct from the CMEA. Inter-republican imbalances on trade account, which themselves already introduced a variety of subsidies and taxes, were offset through various income transfers that the plan foresaw or the administrative system simply accommodated.

The resulting patterns of trade were on the whole in support of maintaining economies that were by design without competition from within and sheltered against external competition; that engaged in widespread redistribution of incomes throughout their own economy, but were reluctant to do likewise on a regional level, even among like-minded partners; and that had their economic priorities set by the political and bureaucratic powers in place, rather than through a framework from within which economic decision makers could formulate their own strategies and pursue their own profit motives.

Whatever the considerable defects of SEI through the TR trade, payment, and pricing regimes – and they were very substantial indeed! – these provisions did support buoyant trade for many decades; likewise for trade and payment flows in the former Soviet Union and Yugoslavia. These systems began to totter – and, in the end, faltered abysmally – when one major component (such as the Soviet Union in the CMEA) ran into unanticipated adjustment problems that could not be smoothed in any lasting way short of undertaking radical economic transformation. But that presupposes that resources henceforth be allocated on the basis of more explicit rationality criteria, including perhaps a redirection of trade flows. If the latter is pursued for other than economic reasons, it can only aggravate matters at least for partner economies.

This characterisation in a nutshell suggests that the economic space of the dinar or rouble functioned in a much more integrated, if bureaucratically planned or politicised, way than was the case for the TR's economic space. Nonetheless, if the TR regime suggests solutions for its gradual replacement by more market-oriented criteria, the same applies *a fortiori* to the transformation of the dinar and rouble economic spaces. To identify the common and divergent features, it is useful to have some clarity over what precisely the transformation of the CMEA countries is aiming at as distinct from the objectives embraced by the dissolutions of the Soviet Union (Brabant, 1992b and c) and Yugoslavia.

Aims of the Transition

The dissolution of the TR regime was prompted by the avowed need to obtain 'world market' conditions in economic relations among the former planned economies. In the case of the dinar and rouble regimes, it was more a question of whether and how best to redistribute resources among the constituent republics and who was subsidising whom than moving to conventional market rules *per se* that triggered the fragmentation of the common economic area. But after dissolution of the union, inter-republican trading rules will move closer to world market conditions just the same, and so it is useful to delve somewhat deeper into the meaning thereof.

World conditions in Eastern parlance mean essentially four things: transactions in goods and services are negotiated by micro-economic agents on their own account; market-clearing prices of a sort, given that there are not yet genuine markets in the East, are the terms at which transactions are concluded; imbalances are settled in convertible currency on a current basis or periodically (in the case of clearing); and the usances of world trading, notably on payment conditions (that is, immediate payment for raw materials and fuels and 90 to 120 days supplier credit for many manufactured goods), need to be observed rather closely.

Instituting these 'values' in intra-group trade should, in the end, help to bring about greater rationality in the PETs. This will notably be the case for those PETs bent on organising their domestic economies so that micro-economic agents can play a critical role in resource allocation within an overall arena cordoned off by the institutions and rules of the new political and economic frameworks. But the implications of doing without the former regimes and moving to world conditions should be spelled out clearly. This crucial issue has frequently been misunderstood notably in the Western advisory assistance given to the PETs.

First of all, any switch to some form of market-clearing prices modifies prevailing terms of trade. This will be particularly marked in countries that largely eschewed price reforms during most of the post-war period. In the case of the CMEA, it notably entailed a sharp deterioration for Eastern Europe and a sizeable gain for the exporters of fuels and raw materials, particularly the Soviet Union. Within the unions, some republics are bound to benefit not only from the external price adjustment but also from bringing domestic prices in line with trade prices. These shifts are necessarily the result of the upward drift in prices of raw materials, fuels, and foodstuffs while, at the same time, prices of manufactures are under downward pressure, especially in the medium run, provided economic activity remains buoyant.[6]

Second, demand and supply schedules change because old and new independent agents begin to act in their own interest. Given greater freedom of choice, these economic actors are unlikely to emulate the earlier behaviour of ministerial bureaucrats. Under the circumstances of the CMEA, especially when seen in the short run, the demand of the smaller Eastern countries for shipments from within the area were likely to change more radically than their supply, given that not all countries were reforming at the same pace and there existed considerable asymmetry between the trading patterns of the Soviet Union and the rest of Eastern Europe. In the case of the successor republics, however, demand and supply schedules will change too, but not necessarily in response to micro-economic agents taking over from the erstwhile ministerial bureaucrats. In the successor Soviet republics, at least for now, it is mainly one ministerial bureaucracy taking over from another, rather than the impact of growing concerns on the part of private agents about their own profit-and-loss account, that has so far been modifying demand and supply schedules.

Finally, arguably the most important consequence of moving away from the old regimes is a rise in the demand for convertible currency, particularly in trade-dependent countries; it should not be overlooked that in this category should be included the transformation of inter-republican exchanges into 'ordinary' external trade and payment flows. The demand for reserves rises for both transaction and precautionary reasons. To finance any emerging imbalances, something that is likely to occur with new agents conducting trade, adequate reserves are required. Also the transaction demand for convertible currency rises basically for three reasons. One is the rule of thumb that it is

6. Right after the switch, one can count on a sharp compression of export volumes of some manufactures, given the changes in export and import actors. Export prices of most manufactures will not necessarily change as drastically for two reasons. The existing machine park can be restructured only over the medium run, and so prices for its spare parts and components initially remain about level. Certain products, especially consumer manufactures, also become completely unsaleable in the East, and so volume shifts are likely to be sizeable.

prudent for a country to hold reserves equivalent to about three months' worth of imports. Another is that private trading and related transactions previously all conducted at special bilateral clearing conditions, or in local currency in the case of the former federations, must be financed. Finally, because of the asymmetry in export structures, the countries dependent on imports of fuels and raw materials and exports of finished engineering goods need to grant supplier credit for most of their net exports of manufactures but must pay cash for their net imports of fuels and most raw materials. Even if alternative financing can be explored, the net borrower must, on balance, absorb any borrowing cost differentials. Such stocks of required convertible currency can be built up by running a net current-account surplus now or in the future (if borrowing were feasible). Doing this in the short run would be impossible, given the excess demand for imports, and it would be very costly. Borrowing might help, but only if the funds are appropriated for structural change, which in turn will generate a solid current-account surplus in the near future.

In sum, the switchover to world conditions is bound to exert a profound impact on traditional trade and payment relations. With limited ability to divert exports to other markets, and even then policy makers of some successor republics must reckon with sizeable terms-of-trade and export-revenue losses, there would be a real danger of a massive collapse of the former intra-group trade without adequate gains being made with outside markets. This has been a highly dysfunctional outcome of the arrangements introduced at the outset of effective transition in the former CMEA members. It would seem unavoidable in the dinar and rouble areas, given present and foreseeable policy stances.

Admittedly, the foregoing suggests too stark a picture. Even so, it is worth recalling the weak initial conditions for change in virtually all of these countries, in part owing to *perestroika's* adolescence and its associated follies, which were simply inexcusable, plainly irresponsible policy making. This was particularly so because by the late 1980s virtually all Eastern economies had run into severe growth obstacles. In fact, none had really recovered in a sustainable manner from the blows to the traditional exchange and development patterns brought about by the shifts in the global economy of the late 1970s and early 1980s. Failure to enact adjustments in economic structures nationally or regionally compounded already deeply ingrained economic problems. Incompetence of the political leadership, if only for lack of an historical vision, had a good deal to do with the way in which these barriers were allowed to solidify. In the end they weakened the very sociopolitical fabric of these societies to such an extent that it utterly crumbled when the last supporting pole – the Soviet army – was no longer perceived as a threatening stick.

Debilitating though these events were for trade and domestic economic stability, the malaise in these societies ran far deeper. In the case of the CMEA, the probability of any major change soon being enacted to foster more buoyant relations for the group as a whole quickly evaporated by the effusive weight emanating from the morass stirred up by the vacillations with *perestroika* in the Soviet Union, the emboldened questioning of the very *raison d'être* of the CMEA by the reforming Eastern countries, and the inability to generate sustained growth on the basis of an immobile CMEA and SEI (Brabant, 1990, 1991a and b). Civil war has disrupted the economic ties among the former Yugoslav republics and some of the successor Soviet republics, and widening non-tariff barriers in trade among the republics, notably in the Soviet Union, have created major obstacles to shoring up even moderately buoyant economic activity. But the real crunch of the disintegration of the rouble area in particular is yet to be felt in the successor republics in the course of 1992–93.

Yet concerns about how best to reconfigure intra-group relations in all of the above zones should rank high on the agenda of those managing the transitions. The twin guideline should be how best to maintain some trade flows while restructuring the geographical pattern and commodity composition of trade. This should be part and parcel of the gradual shift to market-based decision making, including putting in place the necessary institutions to underpin these commercialised relations on a sustainable basis. Simply destroying what used to be in place without there being clear-cut alternatives or a sufficiently ambient sociopolitical consensus for absorbing a considerable adjustment burden is dangerous policy making.

Management of the Transition

The transformation of the trade and payment systems of the PETs has been one of the most widely debated questions of designing comprehensive, speedy, and properly sequenced transition policies. There has been little disagreement about the need of these countries to disengage themselves from the inherited TR trade and payment systems; of course, the TR pricing environment was quickly abandoned in the course of 1990 and early 1991, when the last use of that 'currency' was made. Equally unanimous has been the advice on the need to open up the PETs and expose them to international competition. The latter's relative prices, given a proper exchange rate, in principle usher into the PETs the necessary competitive discipline to transform credibly the rules by which economic agents will henceforth be held responsible for their economic performances and mitigate the potentially adverse behaviour of the highly monopolised industrial structure of PETs upon liberalisation. There has been little argument about the desire of these countries to integrate quickly into the world economy by having a quite liberal trade regime with few non-tariff barriers and low, preferably uniform, tariff rates. I shall discuss the core issues revolving around trade liberalisation, exchange rate regime, protectionism, and forcefully disengaging from the erstwhile trade links.

Trade Liberalisation

The case for trade liberalisation has been based on incontestable, if highly theoretical, credentials. The discussions have at times given the impression that a liberal trade regime can do wonders for a country's economy. Most economists involved in proffering advice to the East's policy makers (whether invited or not and regardless of their official affiliation) have not hidden their conviction that trade liberalisation is unambiguously beneficial, although its record is, at best, debatable (Dornbusch, 1992a, pp. 73ff.), notwithstanding some undifferentiated claims (Dollar, 1992) to the contrary.

The theoretical case on which the palpable benefits of trade liberalisation have been predicated is well known. Without going into details, trade liberalisation is expected to improve resource allocation in line with social marginal costs and benefits; to facilitate access to more advanced or better-suited technology, inputs, and intermediate goods; to enable an economy better to take advantage of economies of scale and scope; to bolster competition in domestic markets; and to provide pro-growth externalities, including by shaking up established transformation activities, thereby creating a favourable 'Schumpeterian environment especially conducive to growth' (Dornbusch, 1992a, p. 74). These benefits accrue in a static environment. Arguably even more important can be the beneficial growth-promoting, hence dynamic, effects of trade liberalisation, which should forge a new growth path for the economy as a whole.

Whereas these claimed advantages have impeccable credentials in economic theory, their practical realisation is not self-evident at least until the economy being opened up will have gained an environment conducive to comparatively flexible adjustments to the new demand and supply schedules, that is, an ambient market-oriented environment. Otherwise foreign competition may indeed eliminate domestic production, perhaps inadvertently and inordinately through shifts in demand for 'new' goods, without the freed-up resources being mobilised for growth-promoting activities. The outcome may then be a potentially sharp cutback in aggregate economic activity, which cannot but compress sustainable levels of absorption or welfare. Whether this occurs right away after trade liberalisation, apart from flexibility on the supply side, will be a function of the availability of foreign exchange.

Liberalisation and the Exchange Rate

The orthodox case for trade liberalisation in the PETs has been predicated on relatively low protection with an exchange rate that should help to maintain equilibrium in the current account, at least over the medium run. Because the gap between pre-transition and world prices is considerable, no single devaluation of the currency will suffice to avert palpable adjustments in demand and supply. And because export schedules are unknown it is by no means obvious by how much the home currency should be devalued to enable policy makers to sustain external balances. However, questions of by how much to devalue the home currency and how stable the nominal exchange rate should be thereafter, perhaps to function as a key anchor for the design of transition policies, have arisen.

The answer given to date in the advice proffered by the most market-oriented adherents has been unambiguous: choose the nominal exchange rate as anchor once the home currency has been sufficiently devalued to compensate for unknown, but anticipated corrective inflation, preferably erring on the side of caution by undervaluing the domestic currency, and then hold it stable for a sufficiently long period to impart confidence and credibility to the transition policies. But this may unduly compress the exchange rate if the structural adjustment is of such a nature that target policies are likely to improve matters in a comparatively brief period.[7] If so the devaluation debilitates economic activities that, under more normal conditions of the market, would have been able to survive on their own. In addition, most observers have not given sufficient attention to the potentially destabilising effects of a fluctuating real exchange rate as a result of domestic inflation, which is bound to quickly hollow out the temporary comparative advantage afforded by a marked devaluation of the nominal exchange rate. Yet, an unstable real exchange rate cannot but add to the hazards of restructuring domestic economic activities through an export-led strategy (Fry and Nuti, 1992). This is particularly so since the PETs, given lost CMEA markets and geopolitical realities, are bent on redirecting trade to Western markets.

Regarding the foreign-exchange regime, there can be no doubt that the perplexing multiplicity of exchange rates under planning must be replaced by a single one or, at best, two (one for duly authorised commercial transactions and the other for private trading, as has been the case in Poland for more than three years now). Whether the key commercial rate should be fixed or flexible (and how it is to be linked to any other rate) is one of those 'either–or' choices that many economists and inexperienced policy makers are fond of. In practice, the policy question will be more about what kind of crawling peg should be entertained and at what intervals the exchange rate should be adjusted to avoid imparting adverse credibility effects. The issues at stake are paramount to book progress toward meeting the conditions for current-account convertibility. Only under those circumstances is there a realistic chance of attracting the kind and volume of foreign investment that most PETs are hoping to muster if only

7. One could rationalise the policy stance taken in Western Europe after World War II on that ground. These economies were expected to improve their productivity sharply in a relatively brief period of time. Any sizeable devaluation was bound to interfere with that structural adjustment. It would in fact destroy some structures that could have survived on their own if given a breathing spell prior to the introduction of 'normal' market conditions. Hence the preference for temporarily restricting trade and discriminating against the dollar, including through the arrangements of the European Payments Union.

to confine the costs of the transition and isolate a new growth paradigm.

Unfortunately, there are no unambiguous guidelines about how best to proceed. It is a fact that the majority of PETs have opted for an exchange rate that is undervalued. They have also erred on the side of caution, as compared to the rate that would maintain balance between demand for and supply of foreign exchange for merchandise and related transactions. This choice has been suggested more by concern about infusing some anchored certainty into an exceedingly volatile socio-economic and political situation, than by solid economic arguments. On the latter ground, the choice is probably wrong, but it may be wise political economy provided it does not become a fetish, as was the case in Poland, certainly from January 1990 until May 1991 (Fry and Nuti, 1992). In any case, there are at least two other critical aspects of the design of such a liberal trade regime that bear careful scrutiny. One is convertibility of the currency. The other is the phasing in of the new regime in the context of the more general transition. I do not wish to dwell at great length on the convertibility issue, if only because I have recently had plenty of opportunity to discuss it elsewhere (Brabant, 1991a and c).

Let me emphasise that the PET leadership should promote fast and far-reaching liberalisation of access to foreign exchange. But that objective may be quite distinct from seeking currency convertibility. There may be circumstances in which it is advisable to pursue this generalisation of the foreign-exchange market over some period of time (months rather than years, of course) by organising open auctions for increasing amounts of available foreign exchange accessible to all duly authorised economic agents (such as licensed traders), if only to minimise the danger of capital flight. Critical in advocating such auctions is the flexibility of the nominal exchange rate for liberalised transactions. I certainly would argue that more controlled access to foreign exchange for the procurement of essentials (such as foodstuffs and fuels in countries that, for lack of domestic resources, must necessarily depend on import of these essentials) may be vital. By engaging in such 'monitored' auctions, those managing the transition can obtain a more rounded idea of where the equilibrium exchange rate in the short to medium run may be. That in turn would make the move toward current-account convertibility less hazardous, hence, raise the probability of its being sustainable.

Surely, if all foreign exchange can be appropriated for currency auctions, the authorities may just as well move to a regime with flexible exchange rates for duly authorised agents (capital flight still being forestalled to the extent concrete circumstances permit). However, the experience with flexible exchange rates in recent decades, both in developed and developing countries, has been far from strongly supportive of uncontrolled flexibility. Frequent overshooting has imparted into the economic environment greater uncertainty than is desirable from most points of view. This consideration should apply with full force to the PETs too, and strengthen the case for some measure of foreign-exchange control until two conditions can be met. One is that policy makers must confidently be able to set a reasonable exchange rate and, barring untoward events, maintain it over a period of time (perhaps 6 months) without being pressured to change the rate because of differential price movements. The other is that the authorities must have in place the institutions and policy instruments necessary to manage the exchange regime, preferably according to a crawling peg or an otherwise adjustable exchange rate.

The upshot of this discussion, then, is the desirability of moving to a regime where the nominal and real exchange rates move in tandem, even though they are not necessarily fully synchronised. A managed nominal rate would seem to be preferable to a fixed commitment to a heavily undervalued one, as introduced, for example, in 1990 in Poland and Yugoslavia, 1991 in Czechoslovakia, and possibly in Russia in 1992 (also after a period of free floating, albeit with numerous manipulations).

Trade Liberalisation and Protectionism

On the question of the nature of protection through trade policy, as distinct from foreign-exchange policy and the protection it may afford, I can be brief as well. The clamour for a low uniform tariff (Brada, 1992) has been counterbalanced somewhat by the case made, notably by Ronald I. McKinnon (1991a and b) and John Williamson (1991a and b), for substantial transitional protection. They suggest that very early on in the transition, all barriers to trade should be converted into explicit *ad valorem* tariffs structured into perhaps half a dozen cascading categories. Moreover, such protection should remain rather high, possibly by maintaining the present level that was earlier implicit in the bewildering variety of trade-inhibiting institutions and instruments under planning, assuming such could be assessed with any degree of precision. Furthermore, they argue that the PET should commit itself in a precise time schedule to reducing the level of these tariffs and eventually narrowing their dispersion. The objective of such an exercise would be to forestall the collapse of large segments of industry (especially the so-called 'value-subtracting' or 'negative value-added' enterprises) early in the transition.[8]

I sympathise with the recommendation to translate as many quotas and related non-tariff barriers to straight *ad valorem* tariffs. Whereas some protection of existing economic structures could usefully be entertained under precisely defined conditions, I deem it counterproductive, however, to erect formidable trade barriers for the PETs to safeguard the slow destruction of senile sectors. Certainly, this would permit policy makers to alter gradually the

8. Although I do not doubt that there are such firms in the PETs, I am not as self-assured as most observers to simply assert that perhaps one-fourth to one-third of industry in these countries falls into that category. For one thing, these estimates are generally based on rather shaky data, and a good deal of 'revamping' has already taken place under the force of circumstance. So whatever past measurements might gingerly suggest, should be turned into policy decisions with a considerable grain of salt.

output structure, and hence avoid sudden dislocations of existing production with all attendant adverse consequences. But it would also inhibit competition and the desirable transfer of relative prices for traded goods. Furthermore, in view of the weak central actors in the PETs, credibility for the phasing-out of customs duties, even if a waiver under the GATT rules for all Contracting Parties[9] could be secured, would be rather low.

Rather than aggravate price distortions and introduce levies that may be hard to repeal later on according to a set schedule, if only for want of credibility, the PETs could resort to temporary income transfers. This would permit sectors potentially threatened by bankruptcy to operate below real cost. However, the government would not have to support full unemployment claims. Such a policy choice could also enable valuable assets to survive the rigours of the transition, provided firms will become profitable once this comprehensive policy of change is well advanced. There is, of course, little hope that those managing the transition can neatly separate the potentially profitable firms most deserving of subsidies from others that in any case have to be fundamentally restructured or eliminated. But some guidance can be taken from those able to cover their variable costs under changing circumstances.

As an important footnote, one must, of course, acknowledge that, on the face of it, any government commitment to the phasing out of a subsidy scheme, deserves to be viewed with apprehension. This would be particularly the case if matters were left completely up to the newly installed, rather inexperienced governments of the PETs. However, in my scheme of things, a comprehensive effort should be made to assist the PETs in a number of respects. And the authority of this international assistance should lend credence to the ability of government decision makers to phase out the subsidy scheme fairly and on a timely basis.

Future Linkages and How Policy Should Forge Them

Opinions about the desirable path of disengaging from the erstwhile unions that were either not politically desired or not truly based on economic factors have ranged disturbingly from an advocacy of maintaining the union (for example, Slay, 1991) to the most rapid destruction of the union (for example, Gros, 1991). The latter point of view derives essentially from presumptions

9. All but Albania, Bulgaria, and the successor republics of the Soviet Union and Yugoslavia. Albania approached the GATT in 1990 and may soon lodge a request for full accession. Bulgaria has been an observer in the GATT since 1967 and requested full accession in 1986; it has recently been negotiating this status and will probably soon obtain it. The Soviet Union became an observer in May 1990 and, until its dissolution, appeared keen on requesting full accession if such a move had been favourably reciprocated by the major Contracting Parties (Brabant, 1991c). The Baltic republics and the successor republics of the USSR will probably now wish to pursue this more vigourously. My hunch is that the seceded Yugoslav republics will soon exhibit a similar inclination.

that in the long run – essentially the equilibrium position in a comparative statics perspective – most of the component economies would do better by seceding from the union than from committing themselves to not very credible gradualism. The former position essentially argues that the costs of disengagement are so large (either because of true benefits forgone or because of the opportunities for gradual disengagement) that it would be sheer folly to seek rapid dissolution of the existing unions. Naturally, both positions are suspect. But I would ally myself more readily with the one advocating some gradual unwinding of the union than to the other that propounds shock therapy, evidently relying on the tacit assumption that 'market-based' adaptations will emerge quickly, i.e. the short-term costs of complete destruction will be inferior to the discounted costs of a gradual solution.

Even if such a quick, moderately costly transition were feasible, I am suspicious of arguments that claim to be able to forecast the desirable trading and integration patterns of the PETs. For one thing, I find it all but ludicrous to entertain seriously any eventuality that these countries must return to their trading patterns of the 1920s, either before the Great Depression for Eastern Europe (Bofinger and Gros, 1992, Collins and Rodrik, 1991), including the Baltics and, of course, Albania and Yugoslavia; or before the institutionalisation of administrative planning in the Soviet Union (Bofinger and Gros, 1992; Vavilov and Vyugin, 1992). Even the presumption that the trade orientation registered at that time was in any sense an equilibrium is suspect, if only because of the enormous adjustment difficulties encountered after World War I and the very substantial trade barriers (not necessarily of the tariff kind) erected by the successors to the empires swept away with the conclusion of that war. There simply is no reason to presume that the industrialisation and related structural changes of the past half century have been all for naught, hence, that these countries would be well advised to return to their spuriously imputed pre-war equilibrium.

Similarly suspect are forecasts based on gravity equations constructed for presumptively comparable market economies (Bofinger and Gros, 1992; Brada, 1992; Havrylyshyn and Pritchett, 1991; Rosati, 1991, 1992; Vavilov and Vyugin; 1992; Wang and Winters, 1991). I find it hard to believe that, say, the successor Soviet republics could all be interpolated into the parameter values estimated for one gravity equation using a sample of 'similar' market economies (Bofinger and Gros, 1992). I have my doubts also about the allegation that the current behaviour of Western European economies can be a solid guide to how the Eastern countries will eventually trade (Rosati, 1991, 1992). Arguments that parameter values for gravity equations are stable and almost invariant to the sample are not very persuasive for anyone who has experimented with alternative specifications and samples.[10] And if the invariance

10. I admit that I have not done so since the first half of the 1970s, when I was extensively engaged in forecasting 'normal' trade for the then CMEA members. Some of the

were to prevail, the model itself would be suspect, if only because we know that there are so many countries that cannot be considered 'normal' trading participants. It should be recalled that the gravity model is a specification of general equilibrium, hence only applicable if the sample can be presumed to have been fairly drawn from a global equilibrium. Point estimates based on one-year samples are particularly suspect in this regard.

Measurement problems regarding proper GDP levels in a uniform currency loom large in all of the gravity runs. Little attention appears to be paid to how best to correct for the huge differences between purchasing power and commercial exchange rates, especially those set after the transition, on the one hand, and the measurement of GDP for countries that traditionally adhered to NMP concepts in any case, on the other hand. Perhaps the most difficult problem is the integration of TR and convertible currency trade into one composite measure used in evaluating whether current trade is 'normal' in any meaningful sense.

Even if some invariance were to be observed and justified, it would still be true that the relationship between estimated and observed trade values for many countries tends to be rather different from unity, even once all kinds of dummy variables are introduced. It is for that reason that point forecasts for, say, trade between Denmark and Sweden tend to be rather biased. Once this uncertainty is projected into the future (and parameter values are in any case not very stable over time, hence the presumed base year values are suspect as 'stable' norms for the countries undergoing rapid structural change), the confidence interval is likely to become so wide that any point estimate is going to be just that – pure empiricism with little informative value for policy making. Several observers have admitted the latter (Bofinger and Gros, 1992; Havrylyshyn and Pritchett, 1991), but then contend that what matters is not the biased absolute level of trade but rather the geographical distribution of trade projected therefrom. Well, one cannot have it both ways. If one believes to be able to project geographical partner shares on the basis of the summation of binary absolute trade values, the latter are either 'accurate' or not. If the latter holds then the former cannot. Certainly, shares must lie between zero and 100 per cent, but those are trivial boundaries at best!

However, the greatest uncertainty concerns the proposition that any presumed equilibrium value based on aggregate income (and related) indicators observed shortly prior to or during the transition can be taken as 'normal' magnitudes and thus be used as indicators of what trade should be like once equilibrium is restored. The latter long-term goal is, as a rule, surreptitiously added, but this implicit assumption conceals a great fallacy. In any case, what matters during the transition is not so much a target for long-term equilibrium, but rather how to disengage (if this should be done) from the intricate trading web woven over so many decades to a situation that economic

results with their quirks are reported in Brabant (1973).

magnitudes can fully support.

And, finally, the argument occasionally invoked to the effect that integration among developing countries – read also PETs – is not very likely to emerge because the static and even more the dynamic comparative advantages of these countries are largely with developed markets rather than their fellow developing countries (Gros, 1991) is not persuasive (Brabant, 1992a). To the extent that one believes in path dependency, a good deal of the trade orientation of developing countries emanates from ties built up with colonial powers and subsequently waxed through what is euphemistically referred to as development assistance. Especially in the case of the successor Soviet republics very intimate ties were established over more than half a century. True, if these countries had been able to choose their own development strategy they might now look very different from what emerged under Soviet rule. But that does not necessarily mean that one could overnight embark on such a different development path, as it were, in mid-stream. For one thing, I do not even believe that with 'freedom', economic computations will not warrant completely centrifugal forces. It may well be that, say, Uzbekistan in the year 2000 transacts 70 per cent of its trade with countries other than the former Soviet republics. But I suspect that a good deal of the 70 per cent will be 'new' trade, that is trade creation over and above levels sustained under Soviet rule, once trading patterns have been restored to sensible levels, that is those warranted on economic grounds.

How Best to Ride Out the Transition?

Being sceptical about the alleged forecasts of the directions in which trading patterns of PETs will necessarily adjust is one thing. Quite another is to suggest an alternative that would inspire greater confidence. I for one strongly believe that this can be done for countries that have been intricately interlaced for so long and whose 'natural proclivity', both in terms of proximity and complementarity, argues for there being room for relatively buoyant intra-group trade if accommodated. Under prevailing conditions, this may require policy intervention to enable intra-group trade to be restructured in some orderly environment even if the ultimate sustainable equilibrium level of intra-group trade was to become negligible. Here, the basic elements of 'optimum' currency or economic regimes need to be recalled (Grubel, 1973; Mundell, 1973), albeit in a very rudimentary fashion (but see Brabant, 1992b). The essence of the ideal theory is contrasted with the emerging disarray in the former 'coherent' currency zones. I shall discuss the issue with specific reference to what appears to be required to shift from a common to a ruptured union, while the leaderships of the successor states can nonetheless cope with *de facto* separate reforms.

There is little point in looking for a neat economic rationale to explain the formation of either the Soviet or Yugoslav federation, or the CMEA for that matter. None of them ever explicitly aspired to reaping the economic gains available within an optimum currency area or regional association. Yet, there would be little point in advocating some return to these states without invoking an economic logic. Economics by itself cannot persuade sovereign states – or those aspiring to that status – to engage in constructive collaborative undertakings. However, by pointing out the economic gains and losses of participating in some union of states, one may at least wield a few cogent arguments which may buttress accurate perceptions of the palpable tradeoffs between economic gains and political drawbacks for policy makers.

The case for union depends on the gains available for moving toward an 'optimum' magnitude with an increasingly better-managed union. This applies to economic, monetary, and currency unions, though the specifics in each case differ. An economic union with a single currency, provided there is a common policy stance not only in monetary but also in fiscal affairs, may yield significant economic gains. However, these do not necessarily accrue to all entities of the union, let alone on an equitable basis. There is, therefore, a case to be made for agreeing on redistributing some of these gains, for example, through regional policies (Eichengreen, 1990; Grubel, 1973; Mundell, 1973). This rationale is, of course, very different from advocating the recreation of the CMEA mechanisms within a confederated post-Soviet Union, as László Csaba (1991) has argued. Doing so for any group of PETs cannot be a desirable option. Nor should it be invoked as a means of deriding proposals for temporary payment mechanisms (see Aglietta, 1992a and b; Bofinger and Gros, 1992; Brabant, 1991a; Dornbusch, 1992b; Havrylyshyn, 1992; Havrylyshyn and Williamson, 1991).

The common formula is that gains of scale and organisation can be reaped from having a currency area in which there is only one currency or in which there are multiple currencies that are rigidly and (in the expectational sense) permanently linked through credible exchange rates, but which may periodically adjust in tandem with other currencies. The commitment to a permanently fixed exchange rate requires the harmonisation of aggregate monetary and fiscal policies in order to maintain long-run equilibrium in the current account and to arrange lending facilities to make it possible for members to keep the exchange rate stable in spite of short-run disequilibria. With a single currency, there is, of course, no need to harmonise policies with a view to maintaining the overall current account. However, regional imbalances, including that of employment patterns, must be corrected whenever labour migration is less than perfect. Hence, fiscal policy must be attuned to take over the function that an exchange rate might otherwise play in the adjustment process (Grubel, 1973, p. 101). But even that might not suffice, and it will then be necessary to tackle obstacles to the integration of labour markets (Balassa, 1973).

The above can realistically be pursued only when there is some potent coordination mechanism. This is normally provided through flexible, fully integrated markets. However, that could not prop up the case for the rouble zone or its preferred transformation in the foreseeable future. Nevertheless, there would be little point in fostering a return to intensive inter-republican trade without invoking an economic logic. Not that economics by itself can persuade sovereign states – or those aspiring to that status – to engage in constructive joint undertakings. Nevertheless, by pointing out the economic gains of participating in some union, cogent arguments setting a tangible tradeoff between economic gains and political drawbacks could be formulated for policy makers.

In any restructuring effort, it will be necessary to identify resources, desirable output targets, need for import substitution or export promotion, and other parameters in order to address systematically the core issues at hand if some modicum of order in the transition is to be preserved. It would be all the more important to follow a similar path if some comprehensive recovery programme for the East could realistically be conceived and credibly enacted. It would involve the systematic destruction of specialisation patterns in the CMEA that are not economically justified and the identification of areas in which the PETs can be expected to have a comparative advantage over the near to medium term; the same holds for the narrower dinar and rouble zones, although their domestic specialisation occurred, of course, for other reasons. The instruments through which these modifications should preferably be brought about must themselves be solidly anchored to market indicators, but conceived within an overall programme of bold adjustments in economic structures and institutions. If only for that reason, they deserve outside financial and other support. Seen in that light, the external payment constraints encountered within the 'former national zones' very much resemble the problems that the Eastern European PETs faced soon after their political revolutions. But the adjustment problems of particularly the successor Soviet republics may be even more severe than those of the former CMEA members, owing to the fact that production structures in place were built up on the basis of administrative, military, and political priorities, with only the scantiest of attention paid to economic scarcities. The Yugoslav case falls somewhere in-between the preceding two.

Whatever consensus on restructuring may be gained, it will be necessary to pursue comparatively liberal policies and make as much room as possible for autonomous economic agents to exploit opportunities for profitable trade. For that to work well, policy makers must rectify prevailing domestic and external imbalances and see to it that the new ones which are bound to arise are kept within manageable dimensions. To avoid aggravating external imbalances as a result of sheer economic disarray, I deem it very important for these countries as a group, or several subgroups, to explore joint efforts to avert a total collapse of intra-group relations, whose sociopolitical and economic costs widely exceed the unavoidable. Economically warranted trade should be shored up and new trade opportunities fostered. The rationale of comparative advantage or strategic trade decisions should be self-evident here. However, its desirability also derives from the need to impart credibility to incisive transformation blueprints and indeed to elicit vital foreign support that will not simply dissipate under the impact of the more slippery aspects of weakly anchored policies.

Lessons and Desirable Policy Measures

In pondering what can be done to enhance intra-group cooperation of all or some PETs, it is important to be crystal clear about the complexity of the broad panoply of factors that are impinging on the transition in each PET in isolation. It is even more important to be aware of the reciprocal reinforcements throughout the group of national policies when each is bent on emerging from the transition without heeding what former partners are undertaking. I cannot discuss all of them here (but see Brabant, 1990 and 1991a). In addition to recalling the effect on the demand for convertible currency examined earlier, it is useful to bear in mind three critical features of the transition.

First, because of the sharp devaluation of the exchange rate in nearly all PETs (Hungary being an exception to some degree), effective import demand at world prices becomes curtailed; the same applies to total export revenue in the short run because of the inability to switch markets and the reciprocal compression in intra-group relations. In addition, the undervaluation of the currency destroys otherwise viable activities because of sharply rising import costs and affords domestic monopolies a sizeable protective cushion, thereby blunting the expected benefits of external competition. Furthermore, the policy stance taken by the new decision makers has, in effect, discouraged trade with the former, including 'domestic', partners by economic and often indeed other means (such as tariffs, quotas and other non-tariff barriers, health-inspection regulations, exchange-rate manipulations, barter and bilateral arrangements down to the enterprise level, political invective, and outright export denial). Mostly ill-advised, one-sided demand-management stabilisation measures have sharply compressed import demand and raised export supply, but temporarily more with the West. On balance, real effective protection against former partners has risen sharply while that against the West has been relaxed.

Second, the transitions have invariably proceeded with considerable chaos. It is arguably nowhere more pronounced than in the successor Soviet and Yugoslav republics. Even so, economic turbulence in one country has been reverberating throughout the area. This has been notably the case for the former Soviet Union, given its pivotal role in supplying Eastern Europe with fuels and raw materials and purchasing the latter's custom-made manufactures; the impact on the successor republics is bound to be even more pronounced. All this exerts a multiplier effect larger than one, guaranteeing a downward spiral for some time, although the initial phase of the transition is probably the worst period for this 'imported' depression to manifest itself.

Lastly, political obstacles have inhibited agreement on successor regimes to the dinar, rouble, and TR provisions. The inability to embrace 'world market' conditions and the utter unwillingness to revive some intra-group cooperation have measurably exacerbated the impact of the disintegration of the former zones. Moreover, the startling lack of imagination on the part of otherwise well-intentioned Western donors and assistance agencies has sharply understated the depth and breadth of interdependence among the old and new PETs. The assistance policies formulated under these circumstances have, at best, been poorly designed. They certainly have not effectively supported the structural changes required before the PETs can hope to regain positive growth and carve out for themselves a sustainable niche in world markets.

These aspects of the disarray in the former trading regimes suggest that some of the difficulties encountered during the transition, including intra-group trade, would have been unavoidable. This is a platitude, and the transition could not possibly have been broached without negative implications for short-term economic activity and employment. I contend, however, that a considerable part of the collapse, notably in intra-group trade, can be attributed to chaotic overshooting. This could have been averted, without necessarily crimping the ability of the PETs to explore other markets if effective successor cooperation mechanisms had been in place. Not only would they have slowed down the contraction of intra-group trade, they would also have bolstered the opportunities for trade creation, as detailed elsewhere (Brabant, 1990, 1991a).

How best to come to grips with the collapsed regimes has been the topic of considerable debate among scholars and policy makers. No foreign impulse by itself can revive these economies. The latter must necessarily emanate from domestic policies on the supply side. Countries can do so in isolation or they can try to cushion the blows by cooperating. Just as the intermediate solution to restructuring the former CMEA trade envisaged the creation of a payments union as part and parcel of a broader effort at reforming these countries with international support (Brabant, 1990 and 1991a), I am still convinced that a collaborative effort among the successor republics, and perhaps other PETs, may succeed faster and at a smaller cost than the courses that are now being pursued.

Of course, there are, in principle, solutions other than a payments union that can be usefully entertained. In the end, including the proposal for a free trade area, attention is finally concentrated in one way or another on how to relax the external-payment constraint. I do not want to repeat the pros of such a solution nor come to grips with the myriad of objections that have been launched (Brabant, 1991a). Some are, of course, well taken. But they are incidental in the sense that whatever the international community may wish to launch for these countries short of imposing 'world market conditions' is bound to be discriminatory. My scheme for a payments union forms in fact a small component of a much more comprehensive and bold international effort to buttress the legitimate aspirations of the PETs while averting the dysfunctional repercussions of the remaking of the Eastern part of Europe on other parts of the global economy, notably the developing countries. That is to say, the agency managing the basics (not the technical settlements) of the payments union would have to be fully embedded in this cooperative approach aiming at reconstructing the East.

Rather than exploring the above option, the approach widely advocated and adopted by the international community has been to provide more general financial and other support for the transitions, while not meddling in domestic economic policy making beyond ensuring that policy targets agreed upon in programmes with the Fund are somewhat adhered to. This approach is now also being pursued for the successor Soviet republics for rather odd reasons, given the experiences gathered during the past three years or so.

Policy makers of Russia have repeatedly emphasised the need for a sizeable rouble stabilisation fund. The basic goal is to stabilise the rouble at a realistic exchange rate and have some reserves with which to back up that policy choice. Details of the magnitude of the fund and the conditions for its use are still being debated. A support fund of around $6 billion would now appear to be more or less agreed upon. It would be more of a psychological crutch than a reserve upon which Russia might wish to draw should the initial reaction to monetary stabilisation be adverse (that is, beyond its own reserves). The merits of the scheme would largely derive from bestowing credibility on to Russia's unprecedented liberalisation policies and, one would assume, further ensuring tight macro-economic policies and moving ahead with structural reforms. Moreover the latter will be more critical for domestic liberalisation, notably of prices and trading, than for foreign-trade liberalisation for the reasons noted earlier.

What then should be expected as far as economic transactions are concerned? Well, if the correct exchange rate is chosen and some modicum of confidence is instilled in domestic economic agents, presumably the fund will not be touched as own reserves soak up the short-term excess demand for foreign exchange. The key point is, however, whether a correct exchange rate can be chosen under the prevailing circumstances and defended in the medium run so that current-account balance can be maintained, given the disarray that is likely to be engendered in the process of liberalisation in any case. The first is doubtful. The latter condition depends on whether policy makers will be committed to the nominal rate or the real rate, or at least manage the latter in such a way that it does not get overly eroded by ‘corrective inflation’. The latter may be quite considerable for Russia, owing to the still prevailing imbalances and highly monopolised industrial structures.

Under the nearly chaotic conditions prevailing in Russia and the fact that one can hardly speak of a monetary policy there worthy of that designation, it would seem rather implausible that the authorities could choose *the* correct exchange rate. The dispersion of the plausible range is such that, for the time being at least, there is simply no proper magnitude that can be defended in open foreign-exchange markets. Would the currency fund then be mobilised to defend the chosen rate, whatever its rationale may be?[11]

Even if a more or less defensible rouble exchange rate could be chosen with proper macro-economic stability, the course open for the other republics is either an own currency or remaining within the rouble zone. The latter would require a synchronisation of macro-economic policies so that republican budget deficits will not be financed through recourse, ultimately, to the printing press. There is presently little evidence that such a coincidence of reform policies might prevail anytime soon. Of course, if the ex-Soviet republics were to eschew innovating their own currency, there would be no need for them to have a currency stabilisation fund. But Russia's would then have to be of sufficient size and the other republics of the 'rouble zone' would need to dovetail their transition policies with whatever Russia chooses to pursue; or the successor republics would have to agree on formal policies to permit inter-republican transfers. In any case, remaining within the rouble zone calls for a particular policy on the part of Russia to assist the republics with commercial loans. Thus far, I am unaware of any coherent policy having been intimated in the debate on whether or not to maintain the rouble zone.

Several republics have already taken steps towards an own currency. Hence matters will necessarily have to be resolved in a multiple currency zone. If Russia is going to find it hard to maintain convertibility with economic stability (hopefully at near full employment), it would seem even less plausible that most of the other republics can innovate 'domestic' policies that will be open and based on some modicum of convertibility for merchandise transactions. How, then, will the successor republics conduct their foreign economic relations? Certainly, the IMF could create a stabilisation fund for each of the republics. However, such a move would be even less credible than that for Russia since the other republics have hardly any access to reserves of their own. Moreover, the cost of running the transitions in this way could quickly mount once the stabilisation funds have been eaten into simply to make progress.

Barring sufficient foreign-exchange reserves to weather the initial adversities of the transition and given that a rapid transition to currency convertibility (rouble or new republican ones) is rather implausible, the only alternative would seem to be a cutback in aggregate demand to levels that will permit a sustainable foreign-exchange situation. Such a squeeze of aggregate demand may be very marked indeed, certainly much larger than that experienced thus far in the Central European countries, as well as much larger

11. The latest news is that sometime in July, Russia will adopt a 'floating rate', but that the central bank will attempt to stabilise it within a band of some 7.5 per cent either way around some R80 per dollar (*The New York Times*, 6 May 1992, p. 8) or perhaps R60–80 (*Financial Times*, 15 May 1992, p. 2).

than that ultimately required as present economic activity is squeezed out by the enormous devaluation either for lack of demand or the inability to afford the sharply risen cost of necessary imported inputs.

Is the situation, then, hopeless? Not really for as long as some semblance of trade and payment relations among the former Soviet republics can be maintained. The key would seem to be an orderly transition. Maintaining some semblance of protection may help. But it would almost certainly have to be much larger than existed implicitly prior to the break-up of the union. Moreover, while it might provide protection on average, a devaluation cannot possibly bridge all of the major discrepancies between domestic and world relative prices. Hence corrective inflation will necessarily occur. This would run counter to the aim of the transition which is to infuse these economies with greater economic rationality in resource allocation as dictated by longer-term development imperatives.

If the above assessments are valid, the only feasible solution short of disastrous deflation is the earmarking of some funds for a facility that would ensure current payments within broadly agreed-upon guidelines under external supervision. The latter would be required, in the narrow sense, to reconcile payment requirements with available funding and, in the broad sense, to ensure that foreign-trade adjustment policies are conceived as much as possible within the overall framework of transitional policy making. I have elsewhere argued *ad nauseam* the case for such a facility for all former planned economies committed to broad market-oriented reforms. I had then envisaged it essentially for the Eastern European countries in general and the Central European ones in particular. Now that several ex-Soviet republics are in principle committed to a similar purpose, I deem it even more important than in the case of Eastern Europe to enforce such a facility. Not only would it facilitate payments but also lend a decisive impulse to breaking as quickly as feasible with the inherited consequences of administrative regulation of trade. Instead of this being conducted at the union level, it now consists of bilateral pairs of republics with their respective authorities engaging in all kinds of agreements and interferences in trade decisions of decentralised economic units (including state-owned enterprises). Of course, the facility for the successor republics should be accessible on a voluntary basis to all other PETs, including Albania, the Baltic republics, Eastern Europe traditionally defined, and the old and new Yugoslav states.

As emphasised earlier, I see this approach not in isolation and I do not expect wonders from the creation of a payment facility. A solid breakthrough could conceivably only arise from having such a payment facility as one important component of a broader assistance effort. The latter should be mounted not only by the international community, such as the Group of Twenty-four and the international economic organisations. More important is gaining an understanding on the part of the PETs that cooperative policies are the preferred means to making the transition less painful and faster.

Conclusions

There is an obvious need to invigorate intra-group trade among the PETs. Another conclusion concerns how best to accomplish this task. To do so through all kinds of *ad hoc* arrangements hammered out in a near vacuum, hence unenforceable, since 1990, cannot but hamper proper decisions on restructuring these economies. Enterprise barter is less desirable than enterprise bilateralism, which is itself inferior to inter-governmental bilateralism, which in turn is certainly to be eschewed if solutions within a multilateral environment are feasible. This is particularly the case when it is crucial to emphasise the pivotal role of having micro-economic agents, private or otherwise, decide on how best to allocate their resources at their own risk. Whereas a fully multilateralised environment (such as completely free trade) is not attainable in the short run, there are opportunities for underpinning better solutions than the barter and bilateralism that many observers advocate. This is especially true in the case of the former Soviet republics, where republican bureaucracies have substituted themselves for the federal bureaucracy (Havrylyshyn, 1992).

Now that the remaking of the successor republics to the USSR is a burning issue on the international policy agenda, I deem it even more important to put in place a temporary mechanism that can help sustain viable levels of trade. Once the adjustment phase is over, the existing trade patterns will no longer be economically warranted. The answer of the international community has been to bet on stabilising the rouble and maintaining the rouble regime so that trade among the former Soviet republics can be maintained at a reasonable level. This effort is misguided for two reasons. One is that a rouble stabilisation fund does not make sense unless a firm, enforceable commitment to monetary control and structural reform in Russia can be secured and adhered to. That is not yet on the horizon. Even if the rouble were to be stabilised, it would not solve the newly emerging external trading needs of the other republics that can be expected to run sizeable deficits with Russia, either because of adverse terms-of-trade or export-revenue effects. That would depend on Russia being able and willing to grant credit and indeed to flexibly execute settlements. Rouble stabilisation even with a backup fund provides neither.

Finally, I should like to emphasise that the PETs need all the self-help that can possibly be mustered to maximise the usefulness of Western assistance, however delivered. To avoid artificially obstructing intra-group trade, and at the same time persuade policy makers there to take some risk, I have argued the case for creating a payment facility. Reinforcing mutual commercial ties would be very helpful in shoring up the rebuilding of trade in conjunction with industrial restructuring. Not only would it support the reform trends from within, it would also transfer Western assistance in a form that would least interfere with the emerging economic incentives for micro-economic actors. Finally, it would stave off either the pressure on Western markets to accommodate significant trade diversion or the contraction in levels of domestic economic activity in the PETs during the restructuring process because of built-in supply rigidities in the Eastern economies that are legacies of planning under communism.

References

Aglietta, M., 1992a, "Des mécanismes de paiement pour les échanges entre les républiques de l'ex–URSS-union de paiements ou zone rouble?", *Economie Prospective Internationale* 1, pp. 29–56.

_____, 1992b, "L'Occident face à la crise monétaire dans l'ex–URSS", *Le Monde* 43.

Balassa, B., 1973, "Comment" in Johnson, H. G. and A. K. Swoboda (eds), *The Economics of Common Currencies.* Cambridge, Mass.: Harvard University Press, pp. 173–77.

Bofinger, P. and D. Gros, 1992, "A Soviet payments union: why and how?" Paper prepared for the conference "Eastern European Trade Policy Issues", organised by the European Bank for Reconstruction and Development, London, 25–27 March. Mimeo.

Brabant, J. M. van, 1973, *Bilateralism and Structural Bilateralism in Intra-CMEA Trade.* Rotterdam: Rotterdam University Press.

_____, 1989, *Economic Integration in Eastern Europe – A Handbook.* Hemel Hempstead: Harvester Wheatsheaf and New York: Routledge.

_____, 1990, *Remaking Eastern Europe – on the Political Economy of Transition,* Dordrecht, Boston and London: Klüwer Academic Publishers.

_____, 1991a, *Integrating Eastern Europe Into the Global Economy – Convertibility Through a Payments Union.* Dordrecht, Boston and London: Klüwer Academic Publishers.

_____, 1991b, "The Demise of the CMEA – The Agony of Inaction", *Osteuropa-Wirtschaft* 3, pp. 234–54.

_____, 1991c, *The Planned Economies and International Economic Organizations.* Cambridge and New York: Cambridge University Press.

_____, 1992a, "Economic integration among developing countries – toward a new rationale". Paper prepared for conference on "Regional Integration among Developing Countries", organised by the African Academy of Sciences, Algiers, Algeria, 3–6 June 1992.

_____, 1992b, *The New Commonwealth and the Ruble,* London: Institute of Economic Affairs. (Forthcoming.)

_____, 1992c, *Ruble Convertibility, External and Internal Equilibrium, and Perestroyka* 6. Cologne, Berichte des Bundesinstituts für Ostwissenschaftliche und Internationale Studien.

Brada, J. C., 1992, "Regional Integration in Eastern Europe: Prospects for

Integration within the Region and with the European Community". Paper prepared for the conference "New Dimensions in Regional Integration", organised by the World Bank and CEPR, Washington, DC, 2–3 April.

Collins, S. and D. Rodrik, 1991, *Eastern Europe and the Soviet Union in the World Economy*. Washington, DC: Institute for International Economics.

Csaba, L., 1991, "Post-Comecon Trade in Convertible Currencies", *Est-Ouest* 5, pp. 39–56.

Dollar, D., 1992, "Outward-oriented Developing Countries Really do Grow More Rapidly: Evidence from 95 LDCs, 1976–1985", *Economic Development and Cultural Change* 3, pp. 523–44.

Dornbusch, R., 1992a, "The Case for Trade Liberalization in Developing Countries", *Journal of Economic Perspectives* 1, pp. 69–85.

_____, 1992b, "A Payments Mechanism for the Soviet Union and Eastern Europe" in Gros, D., J. Pisani-Ferry and A. Sapir (eds), *Inter-State Economic Relations in the Former Soviet Union*. Brussels: Centre for European Policy Studies, Working Document No. 63, pp. 31–39.

Eichengreen, B., 1990, "One Money for Europe? Lessons from the US currency union", *Economic Policy* 10, pp. 117–66.

Fry, M. J. and D. M. Nuti, 1992, "Monetary and Exchange-rate Policies During Eastern Europe's Transition: Some Lessons from Further East", *Oxford Review of Economic Policy* 1, pp. 27–43.

Gros, D., 1991, "Regional Disintegration in the Soviet Union: Economic Costs and Benefits", *Intereconomics* 5, pp. 207–13.

Grubel, H. G., 1973, "The Theory of Optimum Regional associations" in Johnson, H. G. and A. K. Swoboda (eds), *The Economics of Common Currencies*. Cambridge, Mass.: Harvard University Press, pp. 99–113.

Havrylyshyn, O., 1992, "Trade and Payments Options for Central and East Europe". Paper prepared for the conference "Eastern European Trade Policy Issues", organised by the European Bank for Reconstruction and Development, London, 25–27 March. Mimeo.

Havrylyshyn, O. and L. Pritchett, 1991, "European Trade Patterns after the Transition". Washington, DC: The World Bank, Working Papers, WPS 748.

Havrylyshyn, O. and J. Williamson, 1991, *From Soviet DisUnion to Eastern Economic Community?* Washington, DC: Institute for International Economics.

Lavigne, M., 1991, "Les pays de l'Est ont besoin de réaménager leurs échanges commerciaux", *Le Monde Diplomatique* 10, pp. 6–7.

McKinnon, R. I., 1991a, "Liberalizing Foreign Trade in a Socialist Economy: the Problem of Negative Value-added" in J. Williamson (ed.), *Currency Convertibility in Eastern Europe*. Washington, DC: Institute for International Economics, pp. 96–115.

_____, 1991b, *The Order of Economic Liberalization – Financial Control in the Transition to a Market Economy*. Baltimore and London: Johns Hopkins University Press.

Mundell, R. A., 1973, "A Plan for a European Currency" in Johnson, H. G. and A. K. Swoboda (eds), *The Economics of Common Currencies*. Cambridge, Mass.: Harvard University Press, pp. 143–72.

Rosati, D., 1991, "The CMEA Demise, Trade Restructuring and Trade Distruction (*sic*!) in Eastern Europe – Initial Assessment". Warsaw: Instytut Koniunktur i Cen. Mimeo.

_____, 1992, "Problems of Post-CMEA Trade and Payments". Paper prepared for the conference "Eastern European Trade Policy Issues", organised by the European Bank for Reconstruction and Development, London, 25–27 March. Mimeo.

Slay, B., 1991, "On the Economics of Interrepublican Trade", *Report on the USSR* 48, pp. 1–8.

Vavilov, A. and O. Vyugin, 1992, "Trade Patterns of Former Soviet Republics after Integration into the World Economic System". Paper prepared for the conference "Economic Consequences of Soviet Disintegration", organised by Österreichische Nationalbank and the Institute for International Economics, Vienna, 20–22 April.

Wang, Z. K. and L. A. Winters, 1991, "The Trading Potential of Eastern Europe". London: Centre for Economic Policy Research, Discussion Paper Series No. 610.

Williamson, J., 1991a, *The Economic Opening of Eastern Europe*. Washington, DC: Institute for International Economics.

_____, 1991b, "Convertibility", in Marer, P. and S. Zecchini (eds), *The Transition to a Market Economy – Special Issues* Vol. II. Paris: Organisation for Economic Co-operation and Development, pp. 252–64.

Yasiliev, S., 1992, "Russia". Paper prepared for the conference "Economic Consequences of Soviet Disintegration", organised by Österreichische Nationalbank and the Institute for International Economics, Vienna, 20–22 April.

16

Problems of Socialist Transformation: Kazakhstan 1991

*Axel Leijonhufvud**

Introduction

The undoing of a totalitarian state does not make a functioning democracy. The undoing of central planning does not make a working market system. Simple truths sometimes make bitter lessons. After the initial euphoria over the undoing of the communist regimes, these lessons have by now sunk in.

The literature on the problems of the socialist transformation is already large and it is growing faster than a reader's eye can follow. Case studies may be more useful than further disquisitions on general principles at this point. The actual reform work has to be carried out under political conditions that vary widely between the various countries and that in almost all instances have been changing very rapidly. In this paper, I will discuss recent reform efforts in the Kazakh Republic and try to put them in their political context. The reader should be warned that Soviet studies has never been my field and that, even though I spent much time on some of the economic reform problems of Kazakhstan last year, I spent only a few weeks in the country and do not by any means consider myself an expert. Much of what follows is personal impressions and opinions based on fragmentary and not always reliable information.

Economic Geography and Demography

Kazakhstan stretches some 1800 miles from the Caspian Sea to the Chinese border. It is more than four times the size of France or six times the size of

* Department of Economics, University of California, Los Angeles.

California. Yet, while the republic is rich in mineral resources, including oil, most of this vast area is poor steppe lands and the total population is only about 17 million. There are as many ethnic Russians as Kazakhs in the republic, about 7 million of each. The remaining 3 million are composed of many ethnic groups with Volga Germans and Koreans the most numerous. The Germans and the Koreans are in Kazakhstan as a result of two of Stalin's pre-World War II mass deportations.

Such simple facts of geography and demography do much to dictate the policies of the present government. Kazakhstan's main trade-routes to the rest of the world will go north and west, to and through Russia. Long-term economic interests will tie it to a greater Russian trade area. Ethnic tensions are not severe at present, but if the Kazakhs, who are politically in control, were either to overdo their emerging nationalism or to orient themselves altogether towards the Muslim-dominated Central Asian neighbours, a Russian separatist movement would surely result that could split the republic.

Nazarbaev

So far, the policies of the government have very largely meant the policies of President Nazarbaev. For the last two years or more, Nursultan Nazarbaev has played a role in Soviet and now CIS politics out of all proportion to the importance of his republic in the scheme of things. In late 1990 and through 1991, he managed far better than either Gorbachev or Yeltsin to project himself as standing both for political stability and for economic reform. Gorbachev sought above all to ensure constitutional continuity and political stability. For years, he manoeuvred with great skill to prevent the political centre from melting away towards the extremes. But his successive manoeuvres to keep the support now of the moderate conservatives, now of the moderate liberals, set an unsteady, zig-zag course in economic matters that in the end led nowhere. Yeltsin, on the other hand, was impatient for economic reforms to move forward and had come to care little, if at all, for political continuity. Large segments both of the party and the public were fed up with the one and afraid of the other. The Kazakh president gained popularity and influence, also in Russia, as a consequence.

During this period, Nazarbaev devoted all his political skills and much of his time and energy to achieving a Union Treaty. His main objective was for Kazakhstan to escape the stifling economic control of the Moscow ministries and, above all, to gain ownership of its own natural resources. The Gosplan-imposed terms of trade, whereby Kazakhstan exported raw materials at prices far below world market and had to import consumer goods at Russian retail prices, had short-changed the republic for decades in the President's view. His campaign to extricate the republic from this situation began with a series of bilateral agreements with other republics, notably Yeltsin's Russia, the Ukraine, and Kazakstan's four Central Asian neighbours. These agreements were to be a prelude to a Union Treaty. They were directed against the Centre and at this stage therefore against Gorbachev. Nazarbaev at one point went so far as to suggest that a treaty might be reached among the republics that could exclude the central government.

The objective, however, was for Kazakhstan to gain a measure of control over its own economic fate, not to dissolve the USSR. From the perspective of Alma-Ata, whether the distant Baltic republics or Moldavia were to secede or not was hardly worth bothering about. But it was not in Kazakhstan's interest to have the core republics break apart. When, after the August 1991 coup, Nazarbaev continued to strive for his 9 + 1 Union concept, this distanced him from Yeltsin and Kravchuk. Having conceived this policy in opposition to Gorbachev, he ended up Gorbachev's last ally of significance. When Russia, Bielorussia and Ukraine met in Minsk to torpedo the Union and form the improvised Commonwealth, Nazarbaev was left out. But his hand had been forced and he had no alternative but to join the CIS.

Economic Reform

Back in mid-1990, it appeared that Gorbachev, after five years of irresolute economic policies, was finally going to back genuine market reform. Shatalin's protegé, Grigor Yavlinsky, who became the main architect of the '500-day Plan', spent half of his time in Gorbachev's Kremlin and half in Yeltsin's White House and expected the joint support of them both. But at the crucial juncture, Gorbachev again compromised with the conservatives, withdrew his support from the Shatalin plan, and backed the alternative proposed by his prime minister, Ryskov. Ryskov's plan was itself a non-starter. Aganbegyan was called in to craft yet another compromise, more palatable to reformers, but to little avail. By the end of the year, it was obvious that the stalemate in Moscow on the economic front would not soon be resolved.

President Nazarbaev had a keen sense of the dangers of marking time in a situation where the command economy no longer worked and a market economy did not yet work. Following the defeat of the Shatalin plan, he decided that Kazakhstan would have to move ahead on its own. It should be made clear that his goal is not a socio-economic system on a West European or North American pattern. Nazarbaev is not looking West for his models, but to the East, to South Korea, Taiwan, Singapore, that is to countries that have combined fairly autocratic regimes with rapid economic growth.

In January 1991, he created a new High Economic Council consisting of top-level representatives from various sectors of the economy and also an Economic Expert Committee with himself as chairman and with two vice-chairmen: Dauton Sembayev, subsequently Vice-Premier for Economic

Affairs, and Chan Young Bang, a Korean-American economist, who had already been an informal advisor to the President for some time. I became a member of this committee and so, for a time, did Yavlinsky.

The Economic Expert Committee of the President (informally often referred to as the Economic Reform Committee) was an *ad hoc* creation. It fitted nowhere in the organisation chart of either government or Party. Initially, this seemed to be an advantage. The President used the committee to make the coming of reform seem credible both to the citizenry and to foreign media and diplomats, leaving the impression that the committee's proposals were very likely to become policy. The various staged appearances of the committee or its members attracted a great deal of attention, therefore, particularly from the government and Party bureaucracies. But this was not a sustainable situation. The committee was not subordinate to the Prime Minister and when it started to produce proposals 'out of the blue', the Council of Ministers and the higher-level bureaucracy (still Red at that time) must, I imagine, have found it a loose cannon on the deck. Apart from the President's personal backing, it had no legitimacy whatsoever. As toward mid-year Nazarbaev's energies became increasingly absorbed by the power-politics of the disintegrating Union, he had correspondingly less time to push the implementation of reforms. By late fall, the government 'couldn't find' the hard currency for the committee's travel expenses. By the end of the year, although not officially abolished, it had for all practical purposes ceased working. The structural problem was regularised by moving Mr. Sembayev into the cabinet with the rank of Vice Premier.[1]

February 1991

I first visited Kazakhstan in February. The main question put to the Committee at that time was straightforward: 'What in the way of economic reform could be undertaken in Kazakhstan as long as there was stalemate in Moscow?' A great many desirable things were indeed not possible at that time (without a break with the Union). The main reasons were two: (1) the strong inflationary pressures, and (2) the uncertainties surrounding the rights of the republics to control the economic resources on their territories.

Inflation Issue

At this time, the republics were of course in no position to have macro-

1. Dr Bang's official position is now that of Director of the newly created Kazakhstan Institute of Management and Economics (KIME) while, unofficially, he continues as a personal economic advisor to the President. KIME, which has inherited the physical facilities of the Institute of the Central Committee of the Kazakh Communist Party, will use teachers from the West to teach management, business law, and economics courses to Kazakh officials and students. The plans for the Institute were drawn up by the Expert Committee and it is partly funded by the European Community.

economic policies of their own.[2] The high and mounting inflationary pressures created a number of problems that the Kazakh government could do nothing about. But they also posed policy issues, such as what stand to take on revenue sharing with the Union.

The Union government was still suppressing inflation by means of comprehensive price controls and did not dare to lift them in the face of the monetary overhang. With price mechanisms thus disabled, not only was the scope for market reforms limited, but it was even difficult to design small-scale measures that had some promise of demonstrating to the public the advantages of market-regulated resource allocation. The suppression of inflation produced thriving black markets and almost universally 'empty shelves' in the legal retail sector. Normally, retailing would be the most natural place to begin privatisation. But most people would prefer being a salaried state employee of a store with empty shelves to being the proud owner of it. Privatisation of shops, therefore, had to be largely confined to certain, not very numerous service establishments. Privately run barbershops are not a very long step towards a free market system, however.

The growth of black markets was of course the result of six years of dithering and inaction over market reform. They nonetheless became a threat to the legitimacy of market reform. At the inconsistent planned prices, huge profits could be made with the greatest of ease by those able to command supplies. Organised 'mafias', using strong-arm tactics, were increasingly controlling the black markets, and the consumption of their members was blatantly conspicuous whereas the bosses of the communist era had done theirs in the discreet isolation of guarded government compounds. Many Soviet citizens took these black market phenomena as a foretaste of what a system of free markets would be like: Capitalism pretty much as portrayed by 70 years of traditional communist propaganda! It is an open question whether market reform would really be backed by a democratic majority today.

The dangers of inflation were little understood in the Soviet Union. In part, policy makers and their economists simply underestimated the inflationary pressures being created (and also overestimated the chances of keeping them contained by traditional methods of suppression). It was a commonly expressed apprehension at the beginning of the year that inflation might be in the double digits, and perhaps over 20 per cent, for the year. But the deficit of the Central government was running at a rate that made *double digits per month* the more realistic fear.

Very few people in the entire USSR had any idea of what a double digit monthly inflation would entail either for the (hopefully) emerging private

2. For an early 1991 view of the Soviet inflation from a Union perspective, cf. the attached appendix "Inflation and Reform in the USSR", originally published (in Russian) in *The Manager*, May 1991. Moscow.

sector or for the government itself. Experience elsewhere has shown that such high inflations tend to eliminate the contract forms and destroy the intertemporal markets that the Soviets were hoping soon to establish. Even with decades of experience in coping with inflations, Latin American populations have not been able to 'neutralise' the disorganising forces of high inflations. The Soviet citizenry had had no such experience.

The government in a market economy appropriates resources by *paying* for them, preferably out of tax proceeds. This is a simple point but not on that account an intuitive idea to officials whose whole careers have been in the command economy. Consequently, they did not (and do not) really understand how very powerless the government will be, once its ability to 'command' is gone, if it renders money worthless through hyperinflation. To avoid hyperinflation, however, the republics would have had to share sufficient revenues with the Central government to enable it to finance remaining Union functions. A stable and enforceable agreement to do so would have been difficult to reach under the best of circumstances. In this instance, as became evident later in the year, Yeltsin's Russia and Kravchuk's Ukraine in particular were bent on starving Gorbachev's Union of taxes – even at the cost of hyperinflation.[3]

Who Owned the Command Economy?

About three-fourths of the economy of Kazakhstan had been controlled by the central planning apparatus in Moscow. Yet, Soviet law did not make clear whether the Central government or the government of the Republic 'owned' the natural resources and industrial capital stock located in Kazakhstan and there appeared to be almost complete uncertainty concerning which property rights would be accorded the Republics and which retained by the Union. It was the main objective of Nazarbaev's Union Treaty policy to achieve a settlement of these issues. But, in the meantime, it was for the most part not yet possible to move toward privatisation of the manufacturing and extractive industries. It was not within the power of the Republic to create secure private property rights to the *kombinate* that are the industrial legacy of 70 years of central planning.

Privatisation Proposals

President Nazarbaev wanted a significant move toward privatisation that would signal the intention of the Kazakh SSR to move decisively on market reform. The main proposal of the committee became to *privatise housing* throughout the Republic. Under the conditions of the moment, this was the biggest chunk

3. In the last months of the USSR, Ukraine was persistently complaining that Moscow was not printing roubles fast enough for the needs of Ukraine. The response from the Centre was that the mints were running around the clock.

of wealth that could be moved from the State into private hands. We also saw it as a big step towards improved labour mobility and, to the extent that it would ease the State out of subsidising housing, as a small step towards budget balance. As the proposal was worked out, it came to involve also the introduction of *mortgages,* and various measures designed to make it possible for private firms to operate in *residential construction.* Other proposals concerned limited privatisation of retail and service establishments and doubling the size of private plots in agriculture.

Criteria for the Distribution of State Property

Kazakhstan was pretty close to the communist ideal of the State owning everything and the people nothing. Privatisation by sale, therefore, was basically out of the question. Auctions, stock-markets, or mutual funds managed by European investment bankers are not likely to come to Central Asia very soon. Clearly, State property had to be distributed directly and the problem was finding a practical means of doing so that would be accepted as legitimate and fair by a substantial majority of the population.

Dr Bang had already been arguing for privatisation by *vouchers* before the Committee was formed.[4] We sought to provide a suitable ideological basis for the voucher scheme by pointing out that 'under socialism, the worker is not paid his product' (sic!) but that the State takes a substantial portion of it as a tax-in-kind. The means of production in the possession of the State have been accumulated from past taxes of this sort. If they were now to be privatised, therefore, the distribution should bear some relation to the efforts that present citizens have expended in the past to achieve this accumulation of capital. The size of individual vouchers, it was proposed, should be based on two factors: (i) age or number of years in the labour force, and (ii) average salary over a number of past years. The weights were of course left for the relevant political bodies to determine.

Privatisation of Housing

In the case of housing, we recommended a variant of the voucher scheme *based solely on age*. In brief outline, the following was proposed:

i) *All* residential housing presently belonging to the State, with the exception of State residences for officials, was to be transferred to current residents. The terms of this transfer would, however, vary with the age of the head of household.

ii) Heads of household above a certain age, to include in particular all

4. One of the problems we encountered was that some well-known Soviet economists had argued that the issue of privatisation vouchers would be inflationary!

persons already on pensions, were to receive full title to the apartment or house without payment being required or financial obligation incurred.[5] Full title was to entail the right to bequeath the apartment to heirs or to sell it for whatever price the free market might pay.

iii) Younger residents with fewer years in the labour force would have to assume a financial obligation in the form of a mortgage in exchange for the property right. The size of the mortgage as a proportion of the property's value should decline with the age of the prospective owner. Thus the equity share of the citizen would increase with age, becoming 100 per cent at or near retirement age.

iv) Ownership of houses or apartments should be encumbered by property taxes payable to the municipality. These should be set at a level sufficient to maintain streets, waterlines, and sewers provided (where provided) by the municipality. In addition, apartment owners would have to contribute to their respective apartment house cooperatives for the maintenance and repair of collective facilities.

Both the State and the public in Kazakhstan face what theorists are pleased to call 'imperfect capital markets'. It was the Committee's intention not only to transfer a large block of wealth into private hands, but at the same time to improve (however marginally) the budget position of the Republic, by letting maintenance expenses fall on private owners and by levying a modest amount of property taxes. Rents were however often set at such a low level as not to cover minimal maintenance. The staff of the High Economic Council feared, therefore, that housing privatisation might be unpopular with many people. In the early stages, it was made voluntary, which became one of the factors slowing down the process.[6]

Introduction of Mortgage Financing

The Committee wanted the government of the Republic to get out of subsidising housing. Newly constructed housing, therefore, would have to be sold at prices covering the cost of construction. Few people, other than black market dealers, would be able to pay cash for housing. Thus the State Savings Bank should get into the entirely novel business of providing mortgages for buyers of new residential housing.

To create and put into operation this system of housing financing would be a start on a more modern financial sector. It would give bank officers experience in appraisals of real estate and in evaluating loan applications. The banks would have to create computerised systems of accounting and bill col-

---

5. Actually, no other obligation than property taxes and possible condominium fees. See below.

6. At this time, however, it is the declared policy of the government that the privatisation of 'all' housing will be completed before the end of 1992.

lecting, and so on. With perhaps a few exceptions, banking officials in Alma-Ata had practically no experience with any other banking function than the transmittal of money to and from Moscow. In this sector, as in most, there was much talk of needed training programmes. Such programmes certainly were needed,[7] but some of us came to regard the demand for training as a tactic for postponing change of any kind. The mortgages created as a result of the distribution of apartments and houses to not yet retired citizens would add large sums of assets to the State banking system. The learning-by-doing that this would force on the banks would, we hoped, accomplish much of the required training of the personnel of the new financial system.

Two sets of problems were foreseen to complicate the modernisation of the financial sector:

(i) The inflation then under way – and, more particularly, the much higher inflation that was waiting to happen – was bound to reduce the real value of simple rouble-denominated mortgages quite rapidly. More of the housing stock would end up being simply given away than the privatisation plan intended. Since Kazakhstan could do nothing about the inflation rate, these mortgages ought to be indexed. For obvious reasons, we proposed indexing to the taxable money income of the individual household, rather than to the consumer price index.

(ii) Many families lacked sufficient money income to be able to shoulder the payments on a substantial mortgage. To the extent that Kazakhstan might succeed in creating a large private sector, however, wage and salary incomes would rise so that the ability to service debt would rise in the future. This problem could be dealt with by initially setting mortgage payments quite low and letting them rise more than in proportion to the real income of the household until a reasonable rate of interest and amortisation is reached.

At this time, I do not have any information on how these problems were eventually handled.

Residential Construction

There had been previous episodes of liberalising private construction. But these had been rescinded as soon as it became clear (a) that private builders made money, and (b) that in one way or another they succeeded in siphoning off building supplies from the State sector. The Committee wanted to open up this sector to private activity not only because this would 'fit' with the privatisation of housing but also because this was one sector where it should be possible to see a substantial expansion of employment even as employment in a number of other sectors inevitably started to decline.

---

7. The Kazakhstan Institute of Management and Economics is being created to conduct such programmes on a fairly large scale.

The proposals made here are not of much general interest except for one point: economists usually preach reliance on the division of labour and are not used to finding themselves recommending self-sufficiency. But in the economy that Gosplan has bequeathed to the people, it is likely that, say, all faucets come from Novosibirsk, and all electrical wall outlets from Odessa – and that each is controlled by some horrendous Ministry in Moscow. In that setting, local diversification and smaller production units have much to recommend them.

Agriculture

The committee did not have an agricultural economist. But we were well aware that a good many ambitious land reforms in various parts of the world have been fiascos. A good many people were calling for the breaking up of collective farms in Eastern Europe and the USSR. The incentive structure of family farms, the high productivity of private plots in Russia, and the success of Chinese agricultural reforms were constantly cited as conclusive arguments or evidence for dismantling Soviet *kolchozes*.

But these commonplace observations do not give much guidance in practice. The new Chinese 'private' farms require neither tractors nor other purchased inputs for their economical operation. It is not obvious, therefore, what lessons they provide for the reform of agriculture in the former Soviet Union. In much of Kazakhstan, economies of scale may preclude family farms. Historically, the steppe had supported not family farms but nomadic herders. The comparative advantage of most of Kazakhstan in agriculture should lie in large-scale sheep and cattle (and perhaps camel!) ranches.[8] Admittedly, today's large Kazakh *kolchozes* are not grazing large herds over extensive areas. Instead, they have pursued an ideal of 'industrialised' production, whereby the feed is trucked in to animals crowded into feedlots. With this pattern of production the argument for maintaining large units (in terms of acreage) is not strong, but it is probably the wrong technology for Kazakhstan.[9] The present *kolchozes* are also horrendously overmanned by Western standards, but that is true of the Republic's industries as well, and it is in any case not obvious that parcelling out the land to all those now living on it is the proper solution.

In sum, we were (as you can see) too ignorant in this field to make sweeping recommendations. Just as well, as we quickly learned, because one recommendation was made. Already in early 1991, concern was widespread over the provisioning of the cities next winter. With that concern in mind, we

8. It is worth noting that Western investors are interested in East German state farms today because agricultural units of that size can hardly be assembled in the West any longer.

9. The collectivisation of agriculture in Kazakhstan in the 1930s had been one of this century's more horrible tragedies, with a loss of life in the millions. It seems that, even fifty years later, the communist regime was not willing to let these erstwhile nomads loose to herd their animals on the steppe where the Party might not be able to keep an eye on them!

recommended quite simply that the size of private plots on the *kolchozes* should be doubled. (The private plots are a vanishing small proportion of the land.) This recommendation, I learned later, was simply 'politically impossible'. This little incident was a lesson in the political realities of Kazakhstan to which I will return below.

June–July 1991

By mid-June, there were some reasons for optimism. A very comprehensive 'Privatisation and Destatisation Bill' had just been enacted. The morale of the High Economic Council staff was very high at this time. They had done an enormous amount of work in a short span of time inventorying the housing stock and implementing the voucher system.[10] The privatisation of housing was to begin in mid-September. In addition, some privatisation of retail establishments and small- and medium-size manufacturing plants through employee buy-outs was beginning.

The political assumptions for the reform work had changed a great deal since February. The main question put to the Committee now was how to proceed with the privatisation of the big manufacturing enterprises. Their legal status was still not clear but it was assumed that a Union Treaty would be achieved and that it would put most of the manufacturing and extractive industries under the control of the Republic. Moscow had previously insisted on Union control of transportation and energy, but at this time the Union Oil Ministry withdrew from the Tenghiz field negotiations, leaving Kazakhstan to deal with Chevron on its own.[11]

Large Manufacturing Enterprises

On this issue, there was not a consensus within the Committee and what follows should be understood therefore as giving my own position.[12]

---

10. In the meantime, the voucher system had got a bit more complicated than I would have liked. The usufruct rights to the existing stock of housing were of course not equitably distributed at all. The voucher scheme was modified in an attempt to make the property rights distribution resulting from privatisation more equitable than the pre-existing usufruct distribution. At this time I do not know the actual outcome.

11. This oversimplifies the situation, but I cannot go into it further.

12. In Roman Frydman and Andrzej Rapaczynski, "Evolution and Design in the East European Transition", July 1991. Mimeo. I have found some support that was particularly welcome since I had found the previous papers by Frydman and Rapaczynski for my purposes the most insightful contributions to this literature that I have come across. Cf., their "Markets and Institutions in Large-Scale Privatizations" and "Privatization and Corporate

Obstacles to Immediate Privatisation

The manufacturing sector built up under central planning relied to a dysfunctional extent on very large plants. Individually, these plants tend to be technologically inflexible and so is the entire system consisting of such plants. The *gigantomania* of the planners has left a very vulnerable legacy: many large plants depend on a single or at least dominant supplier for raw materials or intermediate goods and, similarly, have one dominant customer. If one of these gigantic plants ceases operations, others are left without customers or without supplies. Failure in one part of the system, therefore, can cascade through a large part of it.

Failures in this system constitute the most intractable part of the current crisis of the Soviet economy and the aspect of it, moreover, that is not at all amenable to macro-economic stabilisation measures of the type traditional in capitalist systems. The collapse of CMEA trade had already shown how vulnerable the system was. During 1991, the Soviet economy became increasingly susceptible to such failures by the new tensions among the republics; cessation of deliveries from one republic would interrupt production in others.[13] These problems were already multiplying half a year before the break-up of the USSR and the creation of CIS.

In this sector, privatisation and economic reform in the East European countries were not going well. The East European countries have advantages that Kazakhstan lacks: proximity to alternative markets for both inputs and outputs, and somewhat better access (so far) to foreign capital and foreign technical expertise. The cascading collapse of the East German manufacturing sector, considered by many to have been the technologically most advanced among the command economies, was particularly alarming. Kazakhstan had no West Kazakh big brother. Privatisation was proving not to be an easy panacea. It is not only state ownership that ails the command economies, it is also the way in which their manufacturing sectors have been built up.

The centrally-planned manufacturing sector may be likened to the assembly lines of a single plant.[14] For a single line, we have the following propositions:

1) If any one workstation breaks down or fails to receive necessary inter-

---

Governance in Eastern Europe". (Both forthcoming.)

13. A large furniture manufacturing plant in Kazakhstan was not producing at this time because all the furniture glue originated in Azerbaijan and the Azeris were not delivering. A year later, lumber from Russia was not forthcoming, although the Kazakhs kept up their own deliveries.

14. For further discussion of production systems of this type, cf. A. Leijonhufvud, 1986, "Capitalism and the Factory System", in Langlois, R. (ed.), *Economics as a Process*. Cambridge: Cambridge University Press, and also my "Information Costs and the Division of Labor", *International Social Science Journal*, May 1989.

mediate inputs, the whole assembly line comes to a halt – output becomes zero. This is the extreme case of the vulnerability discussed above.

2) The assembly line is the simplest example of *vertically integrated production*. The workstations on an assembly line cannot be made into individual firms, each one selling its output to the next, because no determinate set of equilibrium prices can be found for such a chain of bilateral monopolies.

3) The physical assets that together make up the assembly line have little market value separately. The *liquidation value* of the machinery is only some small fraction of the value of the going concern. The whole is worth more than the sum of the parts.

Obviously, the analogy is hard drawn and the applicability of the propositions derived from it is easily exaggerated. Nevertheless, the inherited manufacturing structure could hardly be more vulnerable to supply interruptions if it had been designed by the US Strategic Bomber Command in the worst days of the Cold War. Privatising the large Soviet manufacturing plants would in many cases surely have the same consequences as would the breaking up of a vertically integrated multi-plant conglomerate. In many instances, bilateral monopoly situations would be created with two firms facing each other, one without alternative suppliers for one of its inputs, the other without alternative customers for most of its output. In some of these cases, moreover, the bargaining situation is inflamed from the start when the relationship between the two plants spans the boundary between two republics one of which (and sometimes both of which!) feels historically exploited by the other.

My own conclusions from the above were as follows:

i) The so-called *valuation problem* is not just due to having operated at arbitrary plan prices in the past. Simply deregulating prices will not reveal the 'true' value of plants that are elements in a vertically integrated production chain.

ii) For plants of this description, net current revenues (or losses, mostly) will *not* provide a reliable indicator of their social value, even if all prices have been liberalised. Note, in particular, that forcing such a plant into bankruptcy may, by the 'cascading effects', cause social losses that vastly exceed the losses recorded at the plant.

iii) If the plants in a vertically integrated chain were to be privatised individually, the productive assets may fetch no more than *liquidation sale values*.

Large Manufacturing Enterprises: Approach to Market Reform

It is true enough that the arbitrary price systems of centrally-planned economies do not give us much of a clue to what enterprises are socially efficient or inefficient. The already conventional wisdom on this subject is that rationalisation of these economies can only be achieved by (a) privatising all enterprises and (b) letting the market weed out the inefficient ones through bankruptcy. And it is also conventional wisdom that it is best to get this all over with quickly – the quicker the better – so that the emerging market economy can take off from as clean a slate as possible.

The points made above are meant to throw doubt on this conventional wisdom. They do not mean, however, that one should be satisfied to make permanent either the inherited manufacturing structure or the State ownership of the manufacturing sector. They must not become the excuse to keep truly inefficient plants in operation indefinitely with the help of state subsidies that drain the budget of the Republic. They do mean that one should look for more gradual, less destructive strategies to accomplish the transition to a market economy – but not so gradual so as to postpone the transition indefinitely. In my opinion, the immediate steps to be taken were the following:

1) To convert all large enterprises to corporations partially owned by their employees but with the State retaining a large majority interest. The State should exercise control through boards with the power to hire and fire management and composed of representatives of the State Committee on Management of State Property and of the State Banks. The objective of control should be the enforcement of 'hard' budget constraints on these enterprises. Legislation changing the conditions under which workers could be laid off or fired was also needed if overmanning was not to become a permanent condition. This in turn required some overhaul of social legislation dealing with unemployment.

2) To pursue a consistent policy of reducing the vulnerability of the inherited manufacturing structure to supply disruptions. A number of concrete measures could easily be taken, such as having the big metal working *kombinate* spin off their machine and repair shops and allow these to diversify. The objective of this should, of course, not be self-sufficiency but a degree of diversification normal to an economy of Kazakhstan's size.

After August

The August coup and the process of political disintegration that followed became a considerable set-back to the reform process. Nonetheless, in September President Nazarbaev signed the High Economic Council's three-stage plan and timetable for privatisation. It envisaged the privatisation of 50 per cent of small- and medium-size industrial and agro-business enterprises, of the great majority of small retail and service establishments, and of all housing by the end of 1992(!). By the year 2000, the entire privatisation process should be completed.

Implementation got under way only slowly, however. With the President otherwise occupied, the Alma-Ata bureaucracy was not pushing the reforms effectively and local authorities in many areas were clearly dragging their heels. In late fall, Nazarbaev dismissed the Prime Minister and reshaped the Council of Ministers and, in December, replaced all *oblast* leaders with his own appointees. The pace of privatisation is now picking up. A couple of months ago, the *New York Times* reported that 16 per cent of housing had been privatised and that the proportion was 40 per cent in Alma-Ata.[15] A recent IMF report notes that 400 small to medium industrial establishments have been privatised. This number is now growing rapidly.

As previously mentioned, a third working trip to Alma-Ata was cancelled. The intention had been to bring a small team out that would concentrate on fiscal and financial issues. But Kazakhstan has in fact done pretty well – ending the first quarter of 1992 with a small budget surplus(!)[16] – and now has the assistance of IMF and World Bank teams.

The Tenghiz field negotiations have finally produced a signed contract and the Chevron Overseas Corporation will begin the multi-billion dollar investment project that will bring Kazakh oil to world markets. Meanwhile, there are reports of a new strike in a different region of the Republic that may be of a size similar to Tenghiz (estimated at 25 bn barrels).

Obviously, I have left a number of important policy issues out of this narrative. In addition to those having to do with the utilisation of Kazakhstan's oil riches, there is, for example, the question of an independent currency. But I will confine myself to one more point.

The Old Economy and the New: the Legal Framework

Up to this point, I have written in 'transformation' terms of how to change the socialist economy into a free market system. But it is sometimes useful to think of the problem differently, in two parts. One set of questions concerns what to do with the *old economy*, what can and cannot be salvaged, and so on. The other set of questions has to do with how to make the *new economy* grow. There is a tendency, I think, to get so preoccupied with the many difficult and technical problems of how to convert the old economy that we do not give enough attention to the relatively simple matter of establishing the right conditions under which private sector activity will thrive.[17]

---

15. I have not been able to confirm these numbers. I am told that, by spring 1992, housing privatisation is proceeding considerably faster *outside* Alma-Ata than in the capital. This may reflect the fairly unchecked executive powers of Nazarbaev's new *oblast* 'prefects'

16. Under current conditions in the CIS, this is quite an achievement. It is hardly possible that it will last, however. Russia will determine the rate of inflation for the rouble area and it will be high. Kazakhstan is bound to see the real value of tax revenues seriously reduced by the Oliveira–Tanzi lag effect.

17. To take the example most to the point: China has done remarkably well in making the 'new economy' grow but has not even attempted to tackle the 'old economy'. China is

Kazakhstan passed a rather revolutionary 'Privatisation and Destatisation Act' in June, 1991. 'Privatisation' carries the connotation of putting assets in private hands and (implicitly) under the protection of property and contract law. 'Destatisation' is, of course, a curious term that probably has no legitimate existence in English. What it suggests is the removal of assets from state control. It is much the better word for describing what is actually going on. 'Destatised' assets are not taken out of the command economy to be put into the legal and institutional context of a free market economy. Rather, they end up in a legally indeterminate or less than determinate status.

There has been a spate of important acts of this sort. One does not need to be a lawyer to realise that, as a body of law, all this recent legislation has many holes, much ambiguity and not a few contradictions. The new laws assert rights of private property – but it is not clear that the agents of the State are giving up the corresponding powers to intervene, to permit or prohibit, or to take control. The omissions and ambiguities of the new laws (and the lack of independent judicial power backing them) provide the ecological niches where officialdom can and will continue to thrive.

It is too much to ask that a legislature consisting almost entirely of former communist apparatchiks, with no experience and little understanding of free economic systems, should be able in a few sessions to develop a civil code as consistent and comprehensive as the bodies of law that have evolved over centuries in the West. It is obviously not just unlikely, but simply impossible. Nothing remotely like it is going to be accomplished.

It would be far better if Kazakhstan were to import the entire body of property and contract law from a Western country and let its legislature work on modifying and adapting it to local conditions and traditions. I am told, for example, that the old German *Handelsrecht* forms the core of the commercial law of some 80 countries. It would be a good idea[18] for Kazakhstan to join the eighty and to start training the judges and lawyers it will need in that well-developed body of law.

Nothing is more important for the new economy to grow and prosper than well-defined and secure economic rights, enforced by 'impartial arbiters' and protected also against the agents of the State.

Prospects

If political stability can be maintained and conflicts with neighbouring Republics be avoided, the medium-term economic prospects for Kazakhstan look

growing rapidly *despite* the drag put on the economy by the completely unreformed system of state enterprises.

18. It is of course an 'academic' idea. The signs are unmistakable that it will share the fate of most other recommendations from the ivory tower.

rather good to me. The Republic's natural resource endowments are really very impressive. But even as they constitute the Republic's best hope for the near future, they also constitute a clear threat to Nazarbaev's dream of emulating the socio-economic systems of resource-starved South Korea, Hong Kong, Taiwan or Singapore. The danger is that the erstwhile *nomenklatura* will transform itself into an oligarchy commanding much of the oil revenues and other resource rents for its own purposes and that, rather than the alert, innovative and always hardworking businessmen of the 'Tigers', the future elite of Kazakhstan might bear a closer resemblance to Latin-American rent-seekers or the sheiks of Kuwait.

Nazarbaev will try to avoid this, but it will not be easy. His present widespread popularity does not translate into the effective support of a broad-based, organised political movement. There has been very little turnover among the ruling strata of the Republic. The communist party is gone but all the same people are in much the same powerful positions. Without the party's authority over them, moreover, many may now have a degree of independent power that they did not have before. Consider, for example, the chairmen and party secretaries of the *kolchozes*. A friend once characterised them as 'feudal rulers lording it with almost absolute power in the countryside'. These people, running the collective farms that were established with such a terrible toll among the Kazakhs, now find support in their opposition to any kind of land reform from Kazakh traditionalists who abhor private property in land as alien to the culture of the nomads that once ruled the steppe. Will Nazarbaev be able to govern without the support of these people?

Appendix

Inflation and Reform in the USSR[19]

The impressions of an economist visiting the Soviet Union today are dominated by two acute dangers: the danger of the reform movement coming to a standstill and the danger of inflation.

The current economic situation is not one where it is possible to remain for any appreciable length of time. The command economy system has been undermined. The minimal institutional requirements for a private sector market economy have not been met. The State has yet to create for itself the public finance system of the mixed economy. It is, of course, possible *not to act* in the present situation, but it is not possible to sustain it. The current economy is in

---

19. The views expressed pertain to the economic situation of the Soviet Union in February and March 1991. Published in *The Manager* (in Russian), May 1991, Moscow.

several respects an unworkable system and a stalemate in economic policy will, by default, make it increasingly so.

If this is a bad place to stand still, should you move back or go ahead? Western observers take it for granted that moving back is not an option. But in the Soviet Union it is not only conservatives, anxious to repair the military-industrial complex, who are talking retreat. There are also those who, professing a desire for market reform, think that the only cautious and responsible strategy at this point is to 'take one step back' with the intention of then going 'two steps forward'. The supply of food and other basic consumer goods has to be made to recover, they argue, before one can proceed with market reforms.

Reculer pour mieux sauter? A foreign visitor is hardly in a position to pronounce on the chances that 'discipline' can be restored in the command economy without also returning to other aspects of the Stalinist system that *glasnost* and *perestroika* have left behind. What is obvious, however, is that retreat now will undermine the public confidence in the very possibility of reform, just as the continuation of the current situation is undermining the faith of many ordinary people in the desirability of moving towards a market economy. They do not much like what they see: shops with empty shelves, farmers that do not harvest for lack of goods to buy, miners on strike for lack of affordable food, and black market dealers making tons of roubles the easy way – and they tend to associate it all with the new economic policy of moving toward a market economy.

In fact, of course, all these phenomena are the result of not permitting market mechanisms to work. Prices must be allowed to respond to supply and demand if markets are to regulate economic activities. But they are not allowed to move and so the market mechanisms do not function. Prices fixed at a level below the free market level will keep the shelves empty indefinitely. And it is the discrepancies between controlled prices and market prices that create the black market profits. In an operating market economy, competition eliminates the easy profits of black markets. The black marketeers that so preoccupy Soviet thinking are the product not of free markets, but of government-imposed price controls.

Price and wage controls are maintained for the purpose of *suppressing inflation*. The failure to contain inflationary pressures and the decision, instead, to keep the lids on legal prices have put a stop to the creation of a private sector. You cannot privatise shops with empty shelves. You may not even be able to give them away. However low the salary, people are better off working for the State in an empty store than owning it.

So inflation is the key to the major policy dilemmas at present. Economists and policy makers in the USSR express great alarm over the danger of inflation, yet they underestimate it. The error is rife in Soviet circles of focusing on the measured rate of inflation rather than on the underlying determinants of inflation. The official price index has only the most tenuous links to economic realities. This is most obvious in so far as it includes the legal prices of goods that are simply unavailable at those prices. But, even apart from this point, it is a serious mistake to think that a slowdown in the rise of controlled prices is a policy success and an acceleration necessarily a failure. If policy making were to be guided by such feedback, it would end up out of touch with realities.

Soviet economists express alarm that the inflation rate this year might be 'in double digits'. But the inflation rate that people should think about is not that at which the controlled prices rise but the rate at which prices would rise, if they were liberalised and hence were market determined. Policy should focus, therefore, on the *determinants* of inflation not on the measured inflation. The main determinant of inflation in the Soviet Union today is simply the combined government sector deficit which, in the absence of a market for Soviet public debt, has to be monetised. The figures for this deficit are unreliable – no two Soviet economists will give you the same number – but few dispute that it is running at a rate at least equal to 10–12 per cent of annual GNP. A deficit of that magnitude, we know from experience in other countries, will generate an inflation not in the double digits per year, but in the *double digits per month*!

The market economy cannot function under suppressed inflation. Nor can it function well under open inflation. And an open inflation on the order, say, of 30 per cent per month is a tremendous disorganising force that will destroy the financial structures that a private enterprise economy requires in order to function efficiently and in order to mobilise the capital for growth. The USSR has yet to develop these financial institutions. It cannot hope to create them under the kind of inflationary conditions that have destroyed them elsewhere in the world.

The government has concluded that to liberalise prices and let inflation rip is out of the question. It is realised that the current deficit is highly inflationary and, more terrifying yet, that the so-called 'monetary overhang' might trigger immediate price rises of such magnitude as to send the economy into a hyperinflationary spiral that could be nearly impossible to bring under control later. Recent policy, therefore, has sought on the one hand to reduce the monetary overhang by measures that, it was hoped, would succeed in expropriating the profits of black market operators and, on the other hand, to suppress price rises as far as possible but to allow the controlled prices to be adjusted from time to time when the inflationary pressures become impossible to contain.

There is no hope in such a policy. It does not try to to cope with the causes of inflation but only to delay its consequences. Although the controlled prices are revised upward periodically, they remain far below the time-path that market prices would follow, if they were freed. Unless the underlying inflationary pressures are dealt with, such fitful price adjustments will *never* catch up with the level of free market prices that the monetary situation would dictate. The use of the market mechanism to call forth supplies will then be postponed indefinitely. The very fact that the consumer price increases that will take effect in early April were announced many weeks in advance proves how far out of touch with market determinants current prices were. To announce 'we will not raise prices now, but we are going to do so in a few weeks' is an elementary mistake that would normally cause chaos in markets anywhere in the world. That the Soviet authorities can do so without 'life teaching' them never to do so again shows how fantastically large excess demands in these markets already are.

What kind of policy ought then to be pursued in this situation? The basic strategy should be to *bring the free market price level down* to the general neighbourhood of the current price level, to get the *determinants of inflation under control*, and to *liberalise prices* – in order then to start on the tasks of *privatisation.*

The first step in this strategy requires dealing with the so-called 'monetary overhang'. The second requires the elimination of the current Union budget deficit. The first task is far easier than the second, but it would be a serious mistake to do the easy one and not undertake the difficult one.

The budget deficit problem is far more important than the monetary overhang. It is important to understand why this is so. In a system of free prices, the fundamental determinant of the price level is the money supply, but the determinant of inflation is the rate at which the money supply is growing. In an economy lacking a well-developed financial market in which the government can borrow, the government budget deficit determines the rate at which money is being created. Reducing the size of the money supply at a particular point in time may provide a *pause* in the inflation, but, if the deficit is not cured, the money supply will soon grow back to its former size and then grow beyond that. At best, all that has then been achieved is that inflation has been postponed a bit. At worst, this kind of policy can produce a sharp contraction of activity without significant anti-inflationary impact. The experience of Brazil in 1990 is an example.

By the monetary overhang, one means the difference between the money stock actually in existence and the money stock that would just suffice to transact the nation's business at the present, controlled prices. Since the latter is a hypothetical magnitude, the monetary overhang is not easily measured. Past data give little guidance in trying to estimate a money demand function for the Soviet Union. So the size of the overhang is to some extent a matter of guesswork. It may amount to 50 per cent of the present money supply. In any case, an overestimate is safer than an underestimate, since the policies designed to eliminate the overhang are easily relaxed, but cannot be costlessly tightened, in a second round.

The objective of eliminating the overhang should be to make possible the liberalisation of all consumer goods prices without causing a large immediate rise in the consumer price level. It can be done in the following manner:

1) *Forced conversion of large bank deposits.* Bank deposits above certain values (to be determined) are converted into *privatisation bonds.* These bonds should be of fairly long maturity, perhaps 10 years, but carry an interest rate somewhat higher than currently paid on bank deposits.

Privatisation bonds can be used in payment for State assets being privatised and will be accepted at face value for that purpose. Owners will have the alternative of holding the bonds to maturity or of selling them to other parties for cash at whatever price the market provides.

2) *Currency reform.* All old rouble notes are to be withdrawn from circulation and no longer be legal tender beyond some specified date. Individuals can exchange a certain amount (to be determined) of old notes for the same amount in newly issued notes. It is much to be preferred that there be no further attempt to expropriate money balances from private parties in connection with this currency conversion. People should be allowed, therefore, to exchange any amount of currency exceeding that which can be converted into new money for privatisation bonds and to do so with no questions asked.

It is important to note that dealing with the overhang in this manner will *not be worth doing unless the Soyuz budget deficit is also corrected.* If the deficit cannot be tackled now, these currency reform measures should be postponed until it can be done.

The most common error in attempts to stabilise is to design a programme with no tolerance for miscalculation or unanticipated disturbance. An unanticipated rise in consumer prices will force the government to compensate low-and-fixed income groups; this would put a just-balanced budget back into deficit, renew the printing of money, and thus start a fresh inflationary spiral. Ideally, therefore, one should – if at all possible – *aim for a slight budget surplus* so as to provide a margin of error.

Whether the Soyuz government will be able to master the deficit is now in doubt. The purely economic and technical difficulties would be formidable, even were there no challenges to the central government's authority.

Cutting subsidies while raising taxes is not a programme designed to court popularity. The suggestion that the deficit must be brought under control meets with immediate warnings in Soviet circles: eliminating subsidies will cause the productive sector to collapse and raising taxes would cause most of the household sector to fall below the poverty level. Yet, look behind the 'veil of money' for a moment: it cannot be true that *all* of the productive activities in an economy are unprofitable; nor can it be true that total income is insufficient to buy the national product. At the bottom of the fiscal problem, therefore, lies a structural one, that is, one of relative prices and income shares. And such a problem is not to be solved, or in any degree ameliorated, by printing more roubles.

One of the legacies of socialist planning is its almost completely arbitrary system of prices. When some industries are taxed in order to subsidise others, we cannot conclude that the former should be allowed to expand and the others made to contract for the profits of the first category and the losses of the second are calculated at prices that provide little in the way of reliable guidance to the allocation of resources. That planning on the basis of a too low (or even a zero) rate of interest causes much waste of capital has been pointed out innumerable times. But wages that are too low is an equally pervasive problem.

Labour is not paid the value of its product under socialism. Instead, most of it enters into the command economy to be physically allocated to various uses; some of it is eventually returned to labour in the form of goods and services (health care, education, housing) provided by the government more or less 'for free'.

Labour is paid its product under (competitive) capitalism – and then much of it is taxed away. Some of the things that the worker received free of charge under socialism, the capitalist worker pays for with his taxes and others he pays for privately out of a larger after-tax income.

In moving from a command economy towards a market economy, the public sector has to change from commanding the uses of physical products to the taxing and spending of money. This will require, among many other things, a *substantial rise in the level of real pre-tax personal income* throughout the economy. It is now far too low. Fear of wage-push inflation makes the government keep a lid on wages – and then refrain from raising income taxes because wages are so low. If the government were to double all wages (and pensions) paid by the State and then tax half of them away, neither the finances of the citizens nor those of the State would improve *at first*. But it would make the public finances look a good deal more like those of a market economy with a sizeable public sector and it would make State enterprises calculate with a higher, and more realistic, cost of labour. This would make profits and losses better indicators of what activities should be expanded and which curtailed. *Over time*, moreover, any transfer of productive activities and labour from the public to the private sector would improve the fiscal position of the State.

This suggests the general direction in which the finances of the public sector should be moving. But there is also the matter of the relationships between the different levels of government.

On this political front, the threat of mounting inflation should be to the advantage of President Gorbachev in dealing with the republics – or, rather, it is to his advantage to the extent that the main actors understand the economics of the situation (and they might not). Unless the common currency for the union is to be abandoned, it will not be in the interest of the constituent republics *as a group* to deny the union the revenues necessary for defence and other union functions. *Individually*, however, the republics will be tempted to do their utmost to keep all revenues raised on their territories. But such free-riding by individual republics would force the union to rely on inflationary financing. And inflation, whether open or suppressed, will thwart all ambitions for economic development in the republics.

Perhaps the new policies announced in the first week of April will be found effectively to address some of the problems outlined above. It remains to be seen whether a Union–Republics treaty will be reached that makes non-inflationary policies by the central government feasible.

References

Frydman, R. and A. Rapaczynski, 1991, "Evolution and Design in the East European Transition", July. Mimeo.

Leijonhufvud, A., 1986, "Capitalism and the Factory System" in Langlois (ed.), *Economics as a Process*. Cambridge: Cambridge University Press.

_____, 1989, "Information Costs and the Division of Labor", *International Social Science Journal*, May.

The Manager (in Russian), May 1991. Moscow.

17

A Coasean Journey Through Estonia – A Study in Property Rights and Transaction Costs

*Ingemar Ståhl**

Introduction

The Estonian Republic together with the other Baltic republics (Latvia and Lithuania) were the first republics in the Soviet Union to start a movement for political independence during the years of *glasnost* and *perestroika*. Formal independence was secured in August 1991 after the failure of the coup in Moscow and the Baltic republics had been formally recognised not only by a significant number of Western states but also by Russia and other new states in the new federation. There is a proposal for a new constitution that will be approved of in a referendum after which there will be the first free election, probably during 1992.

Tallinn – the capital of Estonia – is the closest foreign capital to Stockholm, scarcely 500 kilometres away. However, since the end of World War II, the iron curtain in this area was very difficult to penetrate since it had a top priority in the Soviet air defence and was (and perhaps still is) an important base and operations area for the *Baltiskij Flot*. The history of the country is mainly a story of occupations and suppression by foreigners. The local population speaking Estonian – a Finno-Ugric language – have been the underdogs for centuries. It is also a history of foreign domination with a base in the few cities and the manor houses of the feudal estates: a succession proceeding in historical order from the Hanseatic league, the German Order, Denmark, Sweden (1564–1710), Russia (1710–1918), and finally the Soviet Union 1940–91 interrupted by a German occupation during World War II. The history of national independence is limited to a short spell of twenty years in

* Department of Economics, University of Lund.

the inter-war period.

Because of its limited size – 1.7 million inhabitants of which 60 per cent are of Estonian nationality and 35 per cent of Russian nationality – and its closeness to Scandinavia and its relative openness, Estonia is a good subject for studies of the transition from a command economy of the Soviet type to a mixed economy more similar to the economies of Western and Central Europe. Its political independence from the new federation centred around Russia might also give some hope for a quicker transition than for some other former Soviet republics.

In this paper, I will take a journey through the Estonian economic landscape. The Baedeker I will use is a book containing the most important articles of Ronald Coase (1988). My choice is in honour of the pioneer in modern analysis of property rights, transaction costs and economic institutions. I could have used any of the modern textbooks or monographs on neo-institutional economics (Eggertsen, 1990; North, 1990; Ricketts, 1987; Williamson, 1985). In a way my travel guide is also the reverse of a Baedeker when it is used for a trip to an economy still dominated by the old Soviet system: many of the most important institutions that we experience in the market economies have not yet developed and the black holes that we may see in the command economy are a sign of some types of politically enforced restrictions (i.e. a kind of property rights exerted by government and the *nomenklatura*) or high transaction costs in the system. However, the main idea of the paper is that modern transaction cost theory and property rights analysis are very powerful tools in explaining and analysing the command economies and the problems that they encounter in the transition phase.

Underdevelopment and the Lack of Market Institutions

After getting used to the general impression of sovietification and russification, the economic traveller will see an enormous number of structures in the economy that can only be explained by government property rights (or just ill-defined property rights), by extremely high transaction costs and institutional black holes. Economic journeys of this type will teach us not only about the command economies but also about many features of the market economy of which we are often not fully conscious.

One conspicuous difference between Stockholm and Tallinn is of course the general standard of living. Estonia had a standard of living before World War II that was a little bit higher than the standard of living in Finland. Nevertheless, the country had a lower standard than Sweden at that time. Today Finland and Sweden are roughly on the same level while Estonia is at a level comparable to South-East Asian countries like Malysia or the Philippines but with some important differences. Most important is probably the lack of all the market institutions that even in an underdeveloped Asian or African economy creates some smoothness in the workings of the economy. The oriental bazaar is not only a charming market place but it will also do all the things that socialist planners, do-gooders or just corrupt bureaucrats can never manage.

It is generally difficult to judge the standard of living in a socialist economy for many reasons. The constant shortage of consumer goods and the queues both outside and inside the shops mean that the consumers spend a considerable part of their non-working time chasing even the simplest kind of goods. Although the formal prices – at least up to a year ago – were very low, the total price of roubles plus time is in a way in an equilibrium. The time constraint might even in many cases be more important than the monetary budget constraint. In addition to the budget constraint and the time constraint there is an extra constraint for some goods rationed through a coupon system. Measuring the queues outside the main supermarket in Tallinn in the autumn of 1991, it seemed to take an hour to perform simple everyday purchases – bread, some margarine, a piece of sub-standard beef or pork, a small sausage and a box of canned fish.

There is always some type of lottery involved with queues waiting for the next delivery to the department store without even knowing what the delivery to the shop may consist of. However it does not really matter if the delivery consists of products that the waiting consumers cannot use immediately for their own consumption. The products may still be valuable as a store of value – in an economy expecting hyperinflation – or as a part of a future barter trade with other consumers. Most families have also adapted themselves to queue behaviour. It is usual for each family member to take his or her queuing week. Some families have rationalised further and use grandparents as queue specialists. Although shops are generally empty, it may pay off for the Estonian consumer to stroll through the shopping area looking out for some random deliveries. In the streets, you will often see potential consumers with empty plastic bags searching through the empty shops hoping for some random delivery or discovery; perhaps the staff in the shop might decide to take out some parts of the stock for immediate selling.

A second problem is the poor quality of the goods. There is no difficulty in explaining why the products are of such low quality: it is a part of the system failure and I will return to that question later. However, the problem is how this quality counts in the standard of living. The actual number of television sets and refrigerators is a bad indicator of the standard of living if the machine breaks down often and there are no spare parts and very few repair shops – and of course no efficient factory warranty giving free repair during the first year.

A third aspect that has become more serious during recent years is the almost complete technical shortage of some commodities due to the break-down of the planning system. Matches, for example, were almost impossible to acquire for months. Distribution of beer was almost completely stopped due to a shortage of bottles that might have been the result of some other technical shortage. If these commodities are complementary products, the value of other products that are possible to acquire might drop substantially.

A fourth aspect that will be treated at some length concerns the lack of variety and diversity in the supply of goods.

What we actually observe are high transaction costs. The smooth matching of consumers and producers that we are accustomed to in the market economies does not work. A market place like the shop is no longer a place where you can guarantee the supply. The producers are generally not interested in finding the customers and the consumers assume enormous pains in their search for commodities including all the primitive barter trade that takes place between consumers. Cheap and subsidised transport is part of this business and probably a large part of all private transport involves journeys to exploit barter opportunities and search for commodities that are more or less randomly distributed over the area.

The corruption, the nepotism and the bribes involved not only in this part of the system but which are characteristic for the whole economy would be a possible theme for a separate paper. If you look in the ordinary shops that occasionally sell meat, you will never see the fillets or the *entrecôtes*. But Estonian or Russian animals are shaped like all other animals. The explanation is that the best parts disappear in complicated processes – special privileges for the *nomenklatura*, thefts and bribes – before they reach the ordinary consumer. The corruption of the system may also have detrimental long-term effects on the transition to a market economy. It is not only legislation regarding property, contract and tort that is lacking, but also all the norms of a market economy that are necessary to prevent or limit opportunistic behaviour.

All the tacit institutions of the market economy like brand names, trade marks, repeated behaviour to create trust and reliable seller–buyer relationships will take time to establish, especially in an environment in which opportunistic behaviour and market behaviour (market economy) for many persons are synonyms. This is a tragic legacy of the command economy in which market transactions by middlemen outside the command system were criminalised and severely punished. There is thus a mental association between the concept of a market economy on one side, and criminal behaviour, black market operations, trading with foreign currency, prostitution and petty criminals ostentatiously drinking Russian champagne, wearing foreign clothes and driving German cars on the other side. Market-like operations have also been limited to the fringes of the economy often close to sectors where some part of the trade can be carried out in foreign currency (without reporting the proceeds to Gosbank). To re-establish the respectability and the moral norms of the market economy will probably take a very long time.

Did God Create All the Goods?

In the thirties we had the long debate between market socialists like Lange and Lerner, and liberal economists – liberal in the classic sense – like von Mises and von Hayek, about the possibility (or rather the impossibility) of market socialism relying on government ownership and on equilibrium prices set by a benevolent and omniscient price control bureau. Most economists will now agree that the liberals won the battle. The arguments against market socialism were mainly based on the problems and the cost of processing information centrally and the advantages of decentralised information and knowledge connected with the proper decision rights. But what was perhaps very little discussed in that context was the poor quality of goods and the low diversity and variety especially of consumer goods in the socialist system. This might have been a minor problem in certain basic industries like the electricity generating industry (a kWh produced in a socialist economy is of course equal to a free market kWh regardless of possible interruptions in the supply) but it is a major problem in the consumer goods' industries. The number of different commodities in a large department store or even in a supermarket in the Western economies is measured in tens or hundreds of thousands. A blue shirt of size 16 is a different commodity from a blue and white striped shirt of size 15 even if both are made of cotton and produced in the same factory.

In the command economies, as in any bureaucratic and administrative structure, there is a strong tendency to limit the number of versions and to standardise. It is then easier to achieve return to scale production and the administrative burden of sending out orders is diminished. The system is much easier to control and consumer complaints can easily be disregarded. There is also almost no threat of competition and the definition of a commodity is determined in an adminstrative process.

A good example may be the production and distribution of compact discs (CDs). Very few persons have CD-players and if they have acquired one it is probably from abroad. (The locally produced players are very few and probably of inferior quality.) Why should the prevailing LP-technology really have a competitor? In the two major record stores in Tallinn you can generally choose between four to six different discs of classical music: they are the production and the deliveries of the week. To build up a CD collection is not only expensive in terms of direct expenditure – the price for a CD is about 3–5 per cent of a monthly salary – but still more in the time and search efforts that have to be spent. There is no competition in the production and no marketing efforts. One can only guess about the true incentives in the Soviet state company, *Melodija*, for selecting the music, the orchestra etc. Are there incentives outside the planning system of a highly personal type inviting nepotism and corruption? Who allocated the CDs to Tallinn instead of to St Petersburg or Moscow? A limited variety of recordings with each recording produced in large quantities will at least minimise efforts in the production unit and provide the appearance of high productivity and scale production.

In most formal models in economics, the number and the character of commodities are given exogenously. This is true for almost all the standard textbooks at undergraduate and graduate level. The only exception is the compulsory chapter on monopolistic and imperfect competition. Even in the West, there is a tradition in the teaching of Economics – but not in the real world firms – to take the commodities as given determined externally. Firms changing the character of the commodities are brought in under a headline containing the word *imperfect.* Except for attempts by Lancaster, Becker and Markowitz, there have been very few attempts to endogenise the commodities. Lancaster tried to define commodities as bundles of basic characteristics, while Becker regarded commodities as an input in the household production function. Markowitz showed that all financial instruments could be described by their expected return and variance of return and constructed a simple algebra for the formation of security portfolios. But outside these attempts economic theory has left the creation of different commodities as a phenomenon outside the market mechanisms.

It is a paradox that the possibilities and the potentials for a market economy to produce new commodities and varieties are treated very superficially in the textbooks. The difference between market economies and command economies when it comes to the supply of a rich variety of commodities is probably one of the the most impressive arguments in favour of the market system but is seldom exploited in modern theory.

The Enterprise

A striking feature of the command economy is the limited number of firms and at the same time, the large size of each firm. Perhaps even the word *firm* is inappropriate because the main idea was to treat the whole country as one hierarchical production unit with production orders and deliveries administered by the central planning unit and the ministries. It is also obvious that the pioneers of the command economy had both the military organisation and the big firms in the USA – e.g. Ford or General Motors – as ideals.

In the modern economic theory of organisation inspired by Coase and followers like Oliver Williamson, the basic question is: markets or hierarchies? A small reformulation would be: should transactions take place between firms (based on voluntary agreements and contracts according to usual commercial law) or should they they take place inside a vertical (or lateral) integrated firm? The solution of the problem emerges from traditional neoclassical marginal analysis but incorporates different types of transaction costs. If the sum of production costs and the costs of transacting through the market, i.e. making contracts with other firms, is larger than the corresponding costs inside an administrative hierarchy, there is an indication for integrating the operations inside the firm.

The limits of the firm and thus also the size of the firm will be determined by the transaction costs (and of course also by the production costs determined by the possibilities of returns to scale). Questions of this type are in a sense not relevant or important for the firm in the command economy as the typical voluntary transaction between firms is ruled out – disregarding black market operations or barter agreements in situations of critical shortages. All important deliveries of raw material are determined centrally and production is finally sent to other firms or distribution units according to centrally-determined 'plans'.

It is important to observe that these plans were never the results of some type of sophisticated mathematical planning performed by a super-brain. I think the best way to describe the planning procedure is to draw an analogy with the budget process in the public sector in the West: bargaining and negotiations – sometimes with exorbitant transaction costs, sometimes with large inefficiencies – are probably the most important ingredients in the allocation process.

The lack of a market environment is met by integration of different activities that are far away from the core production of the firm. Repair shops, construction units and transport units are usually integrated in the firm. The firm normally has its own catering facilities. It might also provide the employees with housing and different leisure activities. An important feature in many firms today is the food shop connected with the firm. In many cases this shop is supplied from nearby *kolchoses* which deliver food on a barter arrangement whereby some of the products of the firm go to the *kolchos*.

Barter arrangements of this type do of course involve enormous transaction costs but the value of having a food shop is obvious: the staff spend more time in the factory instead of cutting down working hours to get food after standing in the long queues outside the food shops. Time is more valuable than the roubles which are close to waste paper. A factory food shop will at least keep the workers in the vicinity of the factory.

The factory is in a way modelled on a miltary hierarchical blueprint. Even in the Western economies, military units and training establishments are run outside the market economy with production orders and physical deliveries of intermediate products and raw materials. In general the colonel of the regiment is not allowed to buy ammunition or rifles in the market but has to accept the commands and deliveries from superiors and the ordnance administration. I think if we want to understand the basis of the Soviet type of firm we have to look at similar organisations in our own neighbourhood.

I will take the large textile factory Krenholm in Narva on the Estonian–Russian border as an example. The factory was founded in the late 19th century and was already in tsarist Russia an important producer of cotton cloth. What is striking to a Western visitor is the sheer size of the enterprise which has about 8,000 employees. This is partly due to a combination of low productivity and probably wide-ranging rent-seeking behaviour. Wages for an unskilled female textile worker may be twice the salary of a female physician or fairly close to the basic salary for a university professor. But the integration into the firm of non-core activities is also important.

The low quality of the products is also striking. However, this may be quite deliberate and a part of the optimising behaviour in full accordance with the incentives. As there are no external private owners and the management can regard the production orders and raw material deliveries mostly as exogenous restrictions, the easy way of describing the incentive structure is to rely on the economic theory of bureaucracy as it has been developed by Niskanen and other public choice economists. Combinations of size maximisation (employment maximisation) or effort minimisation (with given production orders) are good candidates for the preference function of the enterprise.

The production target of the firm has been formulated in metres of cotton cloth. There are two main widths: 90 cm or 150 cm. The latter width now predominates in Western economies as it provides greater flexibility for the next step in the production: the manufacturing of clothes, curtains, bed sheets etc. In the Krenholm factory, the 90 cm machine predominates as it facilitates the fulfilment of the plan. The cloth is also stretched and thin but this is compensated for by the addition of starch, which at least gives it a more attractive appearance before the first wash.

The enterprise is also dominated by production engineers. The feed-back from consumers is very low as most of the production is just sent to final distribution according to centrally-determined 'plans' or orders. As the products are in short supply in the retail stage and the consumer prices are far below the equilibrium prices for the given supply, everything that is produced can also be sold. There is no need to use a trademark or market the Krenholm name. Design and marketing departments inside the firm are almost non-existent and there are a lot of internal complaints from more market-oriented engineers about the difficulties of introducing new designs and patterns.

The accounting system is from our point of view very primitive. It is at present impossible to construct a balance sheet and a profit and loss account for the Krenholm firm. But we must also ask the question why this is not possible – perhaps not even desirable. In a system based on quantitative production orders and physical deliveries, the firm needs other types of control instruments, mainly forms for checking all the quantities. The aggregation of the result in monetary terms is pointless when prices have very little meaning. It should be remembered that accounting in the Western economies is based on the equity capital of the firm, i.e. the aim of the accounting is to estimate the wealth of the firm to the shareholders. The principal-agency problem that modern accounting partly solves in the capitalist firms has to be solved by quantitative controls in the socialist firm.

The Currency Problem and the Collapse of the Rouble

At a seminar in September 1991 at Timbro – a market-oriented think-tank in Sweden – arranged with Gorbachev's two main economic advisors, academicians Shatalin and Petrakov, I asked them the following question: in the West, we have been very interested to know who has got the finger on the button to the nuclear missiles. But for economists a question of equal importance may be: whose finger is pressing the button on the printing presses for bank notes at Gosbank, the Soviet national bank? Their reply was that they had some vague idea about the answer to the first question about the responsibility for the nuclear weapons, but they did not really have an adequate answer to the second question about who is in charge of printing rouble bank notes.

However the answer may be that the rouble printing presses and the nuclear missiles are run by the same power structure. During 1990 and 1991, the Soviet Union was in great difficulties in collecting the taxes from the republics and had to resort to the printing presses. The result was an ever increasing inflation rate – probably somewhere between 60–100 per cent during 1990. From May 1991 to May 1992 there are indications of a hyperinflation of more than 1,000 per cent price increases. The problems of measuring inflation rates become more complicated because at the same time there is an ongoing process of increasing administered prices or in some cases liberating prices in order to decrease excess demand. After the coup, tax administration has been taken over by the republics. In the Estonian case, this means that all expenditures that were earlier financed from Moscow have now been taken over by the republic. The big exceptions are military expenditures, costs for still operating units of KGB and the pensions to former military and KGB staff.

As far as is known there is no agreement on how to finance the Soviet military forces through contributions from the republics and a good guess is that printing new roubles is a main source for financing the Red Army and its closest friends. The present budget deficit seems to be somewhere around 25 per cent of GDP in the former USSR. As the banking system is underdeveloped and there are virtually no financial markets and traditional financial instruments such as bonds, the deficit will mainly be financed by printing new rouble notes. The credibility of the monetary system received an extra blow in February 1991 when all higher nominations were declared non-valid and only a limited number of old banknotes could be exchanged for new ones.

Interest rates on savings accounts were around 3 per cent at the end of 1991 and it is difficult to explain why people still keep these accounts as they run a higher risk of direct confiscation of accounts than of banknotes.

Withdrawals from bank accounts were limited to around 1,000 roubles a month, i.e. slightly more than one month's salary for a well-qualified person. Three per cent seems to be a very low premium for the lack of liquidity and the political risks connected with the savings accounts.

The effects of the increasing inflation and the expected monetary collapse are dramatic. Everybody tries to get out of roubles and buy foreign currency, capital goods or consumer durables. This can be seen mainly through the price structure. Salaries at the end of 1991 were generally between 500 and 1,000 roubles a month. The price of an owner-occupied house in the suburbs of Tallinn was then about one million roubles, i.e. equal to the total of salaries for 100 years. Of course the only buyers are those who have made their incomes in the black market sector or have had incomes from abroad. Prices for second-hand cars were equally high – perhaps around 100,000 roubles In most cases these transactions were conducted in foreign currency. In Estonia this often means Finnish marks, in the Soviet Union, US dollars or German marks.

The changes that have occurred in the exchange rates between the rouble and foreign currencies are also an indication of the problems of the monetary system. The official rate was for a long time 10 Swedish crowns to a rouble. (One US dollar is equal to six Swedish crowns.) This exchange rate has been used for recalculating Soviet GDP in official comparisons. A couple of years ago an official commercial rate was introduced with three Swedish crowns to the rouble. But this was above the black market rate that was one Swedish crown for a rouble. In 1990 this black rate was made official as a tourist rate. When currency auctions started in 1990 the exchange dropped further and in October 1991, the exchange rate was six roubles for a Swedish crown. Since then a further drop in the exchange rate has occurred and in December 1991 there have been auctions with exchange rates of more than 12 roubles for a Swedish crown.

This exchange rate, however, undervalues the rouble from a purchasing power parity (PPP) point of view. One should of course be careful when talking about purchasing power parity in relation to a system partly in chaos but we wish nevertheless to make some rough comparisons. My personal and partly intuitive feeling is that a purchasing power parity could be established around one Swedish crown equal to one Soviet rouble, or six roubles to the US dollar in 1991. This would have meant a monthly salary for a university professor of about 150 US dollars a month and a wage rate in industry perhaps around 50 cents an hour, but not a full dollar. Observations from Poland and Czechoslovakia with floating exchange rates and almost convertible currencies would give similar indications of PPP-wages in the former command economies.

These figures seem at first glance to be very low but should then immediately be compared to the prevailing exchange rate as it is determined at currency auctions and in the black market. This exchange rate is of course highly influenced by the attempted flights out of roubles. At these exchange rates prevailing in 1991, the monthly salary of the professor would be around 30 US dollars and the hourly wage rate less than a dime. Of course you could ask yourself the rhetorical question how much you are willing to pay a professor who all his life has been lecturing economics students Marxist-Leninism or how to fill in the forms from Gosplan and was not allowed to speak about supply and demand and market pricing until a few years ago and certainly knows very little about modern economic theory.

The constant shortage of goods is thus the result of an escape from the increasingly valueless rouble into durable commodities, the inadequate price structure and 'real' shortages created by the break-down of the production system. A more anecdotal piece of evidence is to see what happened to the billions of cigarettes that Phillip Morris delivered almost as a gift in 1990 and 1991.Very few Soviet citizens would smoke these cigarettes as they have become a store of value that could even be smuggled to Finland and sold at a profit.

The failure of the monetary system increases the already exorbitant transaction costs in the Soviet economy. But it is also a basis for widespread corruption especially in the cases when people can make arbitrage between the regulated market and the free market.

Property Rights

If an economist takes a walk through an old city and a brick falls down on the pavement in front of him, his immediate reaction might differ substantially from what we expect from a scientist or an engineer. They will probably talk about the strength of materials and try to explain the incident in statistical terms, perhaps even putting forward claims for increased government intervention with regard to safety regulations and control. The true economist would probably exclaim: I am obviously walking in an area under rent control! The economist will try to explain reality in terms of property rights, prices and regulations.

Except for consumer durables and a very limited number of owner occupied dwellings, there has been no private property. All enterprises – with the exception of recently formed cooperatives or joint ventures with foreign firms – are owned by the government. The lack of private property rights, including the transferability of rights, is of course one main explanation of the deterioration that is so characteristic of both urban and rural areas. The tenant has almost no incentive to repair and maintain his house or flat. But it is not only the low rent that does not even cover expenditure on heating and maintenance that is the main problem. A tenant could carry out some improvements at his own expense. But the problem is that he can never get back the value of the improvements. He has a protected right of tenure but he can never transfer this right in a legal way.

Ownership of the firms has until recently been divided between Moscow and Tallinn. Although Estonia has attained formal political independence, there are still disputes to settle. Some of the firms belonging to the union and not the local republic have been controlled by the Department of Defence and their position is thus still unclear. The present state seems to be that firms are still controlled politically in the same way as public service or public utilities are controlled in the West but that the control has been transferred from Moscow to Tallinn. As has already been discussed, these firms should theoretically be treated as government bureaucracies that have a monopoly position and in which the employees and management have some property rights or privileges that cannot be transferred.

A special problem with property rights in Estonia concerns the major environment problems from e.g. the shale-fired electricity-generating stations. The question whether the polluter shall pay or the polluted shall bribe the polluter is in a sense meaningless in a situation where property rights in this context are undefined and where compensation or tort procedures are almost unknown. It is also of some interest to observe that internalisation with one owner has not solved the problem.

The Transition Problem

Can an economy like that in Estonia be transformed into a market economy? It is obviously not sufficient for the parliament to declare that the country should have private property rights and a market economy. In this final section, I will discuss some of the priorities.

The most important problem is to get out of the chaos created by the collapse of the rouble. An independent, national currency or a switch to a foreign currency, Finnish marks or US dollars are the main options which I had the opportunity to discuss at a recent seminar in Tallinn. The main proposal from the government and the Bank of Estonia is to create a national but not convertible currency (Estonian crown) by exchanging rouble assets for crowns up to a certain limit at a fixed exchange rate between roubles and the new crown. The authorities refer to the introduction of the D-Mark in the former DDR and will use that as a model.

However, the problem is of course much more complicated. The new crown lacks all the attractive features of the D-Mark. There is no Bundesbank. In addition – is it really possible to exchange only a small part of all the roubles floating around in what used to be the Soviet Union? Are there any guarantees that a new democratic government will not use the printing presses to finance popular expenditures and thus continue to create inflation. The most realistic alternative seems to be to create a *currency board* with foreign aid providing a guarantee for the convertibility. The new currency would then have a fixed exchange rate in relation to some basket of European currencies. The rouble assets will not be involved and will not be exchanged officially but each individual is of course free to buy foreign currency in the black market or go to St Petersburg and try to buy consumer durables for his roubles. Here a small country has a possibility to get out of a declining currency that is not open to the currency area as a whole.

A *currency reform* and the introduction of a *convertible* currency can be regarded as a prerequisite for all other reforms. One important effect of a convertible currency is that large parts of corruption and rent-seeking connected with the rouble and the currency regulations will disappear immediately.

Personally I am very sceptical about the possibilities for large-scale *privatisation.* The large firms are at best organised as military units or public utilities. It is also typical for the economy that politicians have a very vague idea about what we see as natural borderlines between public activities and market activities. There is now a tendency that the management will buy out some of the firms. However, as the financial markets are rudimentary, it is not easy to finance MBOs and there is a major risk that the present management will buy out without competitors. Management looting the firms seems to be a possible course of events in many of the transition economies. It is also difficult to get foreign firms as buyers as long as the currency is not convertible.

A prediction would rather be that with freer markets – which require some important infrastructural legislation – the establishment of new domestic firms mainly in the service sectors will be the first step towards the market economy. In the command economy the service sectors were not only underdeveloped, there was also a prejudice against many of these activities as being unproductive. The break-down of the centralised command coordination leaves the economy in a sort of vacuum. In a market economy there are a lot of middlemen in the retail and in the wholesale sectors who perform some of the most important functions of the invisible hand. Private lorry owners in the market combined with other middlemen will even out shortages – and hopefully make some money out of these arbitrage operations. The lack of middlemen and service industry has thus reinforced the shortages in the present situation. But free entry and establishment in these sectors could not only make the invisible hand visible and functioning but will also absorb a considerable part of the unemployment that will occur when the large production firms are rationalised.

Another step may be the establishment of foreign firms which will use the low wage level for subcontracting operations. In a final step we will see more privatisation of the existing and over-manned firms. Even here, however, it may be necessary as a first step to break up the firms and allow for limited MBOs of the non-core activities. Only subsequently will it be possible to privatise or sell the remaining big firms to foreign investors.

It is also obvious that the future of the companies depends on the switch from the relative price system of the Soviet Union to world market prices. Today it is virtually impossible to judge whether a firm is viable or not in a price system based on world market prices. However, the introduction of world market prices is closely connected with the implemention of a currency reform.

Post Scriptum

This paper was written in early 1992. Many changes have occurred during the last year. Price reforms took place and some of the queues disappeared. The first democratic election has taken place and Estonia carried through a currency reform in June 1992 with an Estonian currency with a fixed exchange rate in relation to the German mark (8 Estonian crowns equal to 1 D-Mark). The currency is almost convertible for commercial purposes and inflation is down to perhaps 10 per cent a month. The exchange rate actually meant an undervalued Estonian currency but production is still decreasing and disorganisation is taking place in the industrial sector. However, Estonia and to some extent, Latvia have become centres for trade – partly illegal or involving violations of customs rules etc. between Russia and the West. The present picture is one of some improvements in living standards for groups in the growing commercial sector and an access to most domestic and foreign consumer commodities in the shops but without most of the subsidies. The black market has ceased to exist for consumer goods. Ethnical problems between the Estonian and Russian sectors of the population are becoming increasingly more serious. I have preferred not to include these changes in my paper but will let it stand as an eye witness report from an early phase of the transition.

References

Coase, R. H., 1988, *The Firm, the Market and the Law.* Chicago: Chicago University Press.

Eggertsen, T, 1990, *Economic Behaviour and Institutions.* Cambridge: Cambridge University Press.

North, D., 1990, *Institutions, Institutional Change and Economic Performance.* Cambridge: Cambridge University Press.

Rajasalu, T., 1990, *Estonian Economy and its Development Problems.* Tallinn: Estonian Academy of Science.

Ricketts, M., 1987, *The Economics of Business Enterprise, New Approaches to the Firm.* New York, London, Toronto, Sydney, Tokyo and Singapore: Wheatsheaf.

Sandström, P., 1991, *Baltiskt dilemma.* Stockholm: SNS.
Williamson, O., 1985, *The Economic Institutions of Capitalism.* New York: Free Press.

Data and observations from Estonia are based on personal communications and the above references.

18

Ethnic Nationalism and Post-Communist Transition Problems

*Christopher Lingle**

Ethnic Nationalism in Post-Communist East and Central Europe

Perhaps the most difficult issue in the post-communist transition process in East and Central Europe involves the emerging demands and evident tensions associated with ethnic nationalism. This paper shall seek to identify a causal role for authoritarian socialism in the maintenance and extension of this post-communist force.[1] Ethnic nationalism in East and Central Europe can be seen to be a type of institutional schizophrenia wherein demands for protection and fair treatment of one's own ethnic group (which often leads to favouritism or nepotism) occurs simultaneously with xenophobia and the persecution of other ethnic groups.

Optimism for the success of progressive, democratic forces in the post-communist transition process has been dampened by the revival of nationalistic tensions and rivalries, which were either forgotten or unknown to those less familiar with the history of these regions. The resurfacing of ethnic divisions as a vital and vibrant force has occurred despite theoretical expectations emerging from socio-economic models whether based upon liberal democracy or Marxism. Both models were purported to exhibit their own internal forces which would lead to a dilution rather than a strengthening of ethnic nationalism. Under capitalism and liberal democracy, economic prosperity combined with a political system based upon tolerance and multi-party politics were

* Visiting Professor of Economics, Loyola University, New Orleans.

1. Authoritarian socialism shall be applied as a descriptive term used interchangeably with communism.

meant to erase or mitigate many of the sources of nationalist tensions. Nonetheless, nominally capitalist systems presently show strains of ethnic and cultural divisions despite continual economic growth and development. Marxian theory asserted that internationalism and the solidarity of the proletariat would arise from elimination of the class system. Quite clearly, the advanced stages of communism were meant to be consistent with the elimination of individualism and nationalism.

This paper shall address several issues. First, there shall be an attempt to identify a model of political economy to explain the sources of the general development of ethnic identity and solidarity. This general model shall then be applied to evaluate the specific role of authoritarian socialism in such group behaviour. A special focus will be placed upon the political mobilisation of ethnic nationalism which has led toward a pattern of (sometime destructive and violent) conflict contributing to the replacement of governments and the probable disintegration of some of the present nation-states in East and Central Europe and their reincarnation in some other form. Second, having offered an explanation of how ethnic-oriented institutions are set into place, their impact upon the post-communist transition process shall be examined. In this present context, the mobilisation of ethnic nationalism as a political force can be seen in terms of its influence upon the allocation of economic and political resources in ways that may reduce economic efficiency. Finally, suggestions shall be offered for policy approach which might mitigate these lingering problems.

Special interest groups arise as rent-seeking coalitions whereby members pursue their own goals and remain active participants within a group as long as the anticipated individual benefits exceed the costs to the individual of maintaining group membership (Olson, 1971). Such groups pose a special problem within representative democracies. The presence of relatively large individual impacts of a policy for members of a particular interest group, and given the small individual impact upon a widely dispersed electorate (e.g., agricultural price support schemes) allow interest groups to capture a disproportionate influence over the development of public policy. Interest coalitions tend to have a much greater incentive to organise and to maintain voting blocs in contrast to the more numerous group of at-large consumers/taxpayers who individually face a low cost of (and thus small pay-off from opposition to) such politically inspired redistributions (Olson, 1971).

Politicians, whether elected within a representative democracy or seeking legitimation within a less responsive regime, will be well aware of how bloc support can be used as an instrument of punishment (reward) by special interest groups for ignoring (supporting) them. In representative democracy, politicians are particularly vulnerable to well-organised pressures since the requirement to attract votes is so strong that it tends to override other considerations, including the interests of the general public (Anderson and Hill, 1980).

There are at least two possible interpretations concerning the role of authoritarian socialism in the present ethnic turmoil in East and Central Europe. The first argument is in fact trivial and suggests that ethnic nationalism was simply held in a form of suspended animation, cryogenically frozen by authoritarian socialism in the midst of the Cold War. If one accepts this argument, the current conflicts appear as an historical inevitability, a bizarre twist of Marxian historical materialism. There is no surprise in a suggestion that the force and suppression which was characteristic of the Soviet regime restrained the settling of some old scores which might have been based upon ethnic differences. Yet this argument assigns a *passive*, *ex post*, role to authoritarian socialism, failing to explain the immediate availability of nationalism.

What shall be investigated here is the more complex issue of an *active* train of causality between East and Central European experiments with socialism in relation to the survival and the recent resurgence of ethnic nationalism. The hypothesis offered points to a variety of causal links between ethnic nationalism and the institutions of authoritarian socialism. In this context, authoritarian socialism can be seen not only to have contributed to the maintenance of residual ethnic claims but it might be seen as being responsible for the promotion, persistence, and virulence of new movements.

Although (authoritarian) socialism is not purported to be the primary cause, its institutional structure can be interpreted to have contributed to at least four conditions linked to the survival and rise of ethnic nationalism:

(1) the encouragement of a collectivist mentality;
(2) the presence of systematic political compulsion;
(3) systemic shortages and economic insecurity characteristic of authoritarian socialist regimes; and
(4) the purposeful repression or neglect of the role of the entrepreneur.

It is argued here that these conditions promoted the formation of interest groups based upon national, ethnic, racial or cultural characteristics. The following arguments do not deny the importance of spontaneous preferences of individuals for persons with shared attributes as an important factor contributing to ethnic selectivity. While historical bonds and belief structures are undoubtedly important, the consequence, even the intent, of socialist policies is seen to have significantly reinforced and strengthened group preferences. It is also possible to interpret much of the ethnic activity as the result of a politically unsophisticated electorate which is easy prey to the populist appeals of politicians relying upon a nationalistic rhetoric. In all events, contrary to the international aims of socialism and its goal of producing a conflict-free society, collectivism as an end and interventionism by the state as a set of defining tools tended to inspire nationalistic identity.[2]

---

2. An interesting question arises concerning why these collective pressures might have

Socialism and the Collectivist Impetus of Ethnic Identity

While ethnic nationalism is unquestionably a universal phenomenon, the exaggerated expressions in post-communist East and Central Europe are of considerable international concern. A common thread in the recent history of these countries lies within the failed application of a socialist project which involved a consistent set of institutional features designed to instil a collectivistic consciousness in the population. The principal intent of this *social engineering* was to develop institutions which supplant or curtail individualism. Secondly, specific ethnic attributes were to be redirected toward a different sort of homogeneous collectivity, to be expressed principally in terms of class. Under communism, individualism was considered to be either counter-revolutionary or an inconvenience condemned as social heresy. Ethnicity was tolerated since it would pose a short-term problem of the bourgeois stage of communal evolution eventually resolved in the socialist stage (Seton-Watson, 1977). Socialist institutions aimed to promote the conceptualisation of class whereby individuals adopt a group-identity, along class lines, and to validate the collectivisation of property. In such manner, the basis and legitimation for a group mentality served as a necessary, though not sufficient, component of ethnic nationalism.

Without claiming a victory for social engineering, it might be suggested that the group mentality arising from or perpetuated by the institutions of socialism simply operates as a habit of thought which emphasises, as a matter of principle, the collective over the individual. Actions directed toward individual betterment without regard for the collective would tend to be considered as anti-social, unlikely to be judged on merit alone.[3] In conclusion, moral and practical pressures resulting from socialist development encourage a group mentality and discourage the sort of individuality which might otherwise frustrate attempts to promote ethnic identity.

Political Economy, Politics, and Ethnic Nationalism

The use of compulsion, directives, and central economic planning under authoritarian socialism may also be seen to provide a political stimulus for ethnic nationalism. Ethnic nationalists can be expected to behave much like other interest groups, attempting to influence policies concerning the dispersal

---

evolved into ethnic or nationalist expressions rather than class. For extended ruminations on this point, see Lingle (1992). Another question not dealt with in this paper concerns why nationalism might become xenophobic rather than patriotic.

3. Intentions to serve society might be considered to be more important than unintended consequences which may in turn generate collective benefits, as in competitive market transactions. For a detailed discussion of these different 'visions' of behaviour, see Sowell (1987).

of national, international or inter-ethnic income or wealth. While changes in or maintenance of such policies require expenditures of real economic resources by the individual members of the overall group, these groups tend to survive as long as the individual pay-offs exceed the costs of the groups' self-seeking actions (Olson, 1971).

Politics and the Formation of Economic Interest Groups

Membership within or identification with an ethnic group becomes a form of 'collective capital' in terms of the expected pay-offs or protections associated with such affiliations (Breton, 1964). When implemented through governing parties or some power structure, payments out of this 'collective capital' are disbursed in both monetary and non-monetary rewards. Monetary rewards to members of groups or political parties are most often in the form of relatively high-income jobs. Thus, programmes and policies can be diverted through nationalist pressures on the basis of the preferential treatment for members of these groups.

Access to political privilege and patronage, largesse and special favours are likely to be a strong incentive to the establishment and maintenance of group membership. Likewise, systematic deprivation, prejudice or persecution may also encourage group identity. First, individual security may be enhanced by becoming a member of an identified group, especially in the case of inalienable attributes (e.g., race). Second, the higher political visibility and cohesive economic clout of a group enhances the probability of changing social policies or attitudes which work against individual members.

Anti-Colonialism and East European Ethnic Nationalism

It might be argued that qualitative differences exist between the nationalist movements in developed and less-developed countries (Spanier, 1972). Nationalism in the developed nations has tended to serve as a centralising force, while in developing countries it tends to reflect an anti-colonial statement. However, these distinctions in the nature of nationalist movements may reveal more similarities than differences by recognising that the essence of nationalism in either setting is found in the struggle for self-determination (Snyder, 1990, p. 245). In East and Central Europe, in the casting off of the burden of 'Soviet imperialism' or the disposal of their own suffocating centralist governments, ethnic nationalist movements might be seen to share much with historical anti-colonial independence movements in Africa and Asia. As it is now well accepted that the Soviet bloc was effectively a socialist empire, nationalist movements there can also be understood to be, at least in part, an anti-colonial reaction.

Demagogues, Populists, and Ethnic Nationalists

Candidates for post-communist governments have found that populist appeals to nationalist sentiments can serve as an effective binding element among their supporters. Freedom from externally-imposed authoritarian socialism might result in an extension of existing governmental organs to serve nationalist autonomy. If the centralised institutions and existing collectivistic and interventionist policies survive intact, as a remnant of the previous regime, diversions from pluralistic democracy and the marketisation of the economies are likely, especially in those countries with ethnically diverse populations. Initially, opposition to the ideological pressures from the Soviet centre provided a mobilising element for nationalists and regionalists which could then be offered up in a populist/traditionalist, post-communist political cocktail. In its heyday, socialism was seen to be a technique whereby historical have-nots (e.g. Slovaks) might expect to be able to narrow the gap with more advanced regions or ethnic groups (e.g. Czechs) by holding back more progressive and productive regions. Rather than diminish the historical tensions, an extension of existing or a new imposition of centralised redistributions of income and/or wealth would draw even clearer lines between winners and losers in the disbursement of state income and assets. Cohesion of (ethnic or regional) interest groups is promoted by the large individual benefits/costs which may arise from an individual's affiliation with a readily identifiable community in response to the continuation or implementation of a redistributive economic policy.

Ethnic Interest Groups and the Economic Failures of Communism

As suggested above, most of the political means of ethnic nationalism are directed toward reaching limited, group-specific economic or political goals. The centralised authority and the presence of a necessarily discriminatory rationing system under authoritarian socialism may have facilitated the pursuit of such objectives. Regardless of the political structure of regimes, interest group formation/cohesion is encouraged by increased opportunities for large politically-directed and determined pay-offs.

Replacement of the non-arbitrary market mechanism by arbitrary state *diktat* under authoritarian socialism did not eliminate the need for a rationing system. In fact, the absence of a price system combined with systemic shortages of many consumer goods simply transformed the rationing system allowing it to rely upon more explicit discrimination to resolve the problem of the allocation of scarce resources (Sowell, 1981; Becker, 1971). In the presence of the systemic problems of the 'shortage economy' (Kornai, 1985), determination of who would hold the best jobs, receive housing, and have access to income or goods would necessarily be politicised and based upon arbitrary judgements. Decisions on the distribution of these 'goods' were readily based upon some special characteristics which might include political party membership or identity with a (ethnic) group. Once allocation and distribution decisions are no longer based upon willingness or ability to pay, rationing necessarily depends upon personal contacts, individual characteristics, ethnic or regional origin or merely the chance of being at the head of the queue. In the latter instance, one's position in the queue is likely to depend upon some feature such as party membership, racial identity, religion or ethnic characteristics. In the absence of the sort of neutral rationing mechanism as in the market, discrimination, favouritism and nepotism based upon familial ties, ethnicity or tribal links are likely to become decisive.

Shortages, Discrimination, and Rationing

Rationing based upon such particularistic or ascriptive criteria provides strong incentives to form, to join or to identify with interest (ethnic) groups whose members might be beneficiaries of institutionalised partiality. At the same time, inter-ethnic rivalries and resentment tends to emerge when ethnic favouritism is used as the discriminating factor. Interestingly, the transformation process which the East and Central European countries are undergoing provided a continuing impetus for support for ethnic nationalism to serve rent-seeking ends. In the light of increased economic deprivation associated with the adjustments required by *perestroika* in the Soviet Union, *glasnost* permitted the advancement of ethnic autonomy as a pay-off for what might have been seen as (temporary) economic dislocations.

Centralised Planning and Regional Underdevelopment

By leading to uneven regional economic development, where such regions might be defined in ethnic terms, central planning or extensive state intervention may have further contributed to ethnic cohesion. Reversing one of the best received critiques of *capitalism* as a principal cause of underdevelopment in third world countries (Baran, 1962; Frank, 1969), the 'underdevelopment thesis' is applied here to explain another failure of authoritarian socialism. In all events, an explanation must be found to explain the extensiveness of poverty and the highly uneven distribution of economic development within and among the former Socialist bloc countries.[4]

It can be argued that central planning and socialist experiments generated, maintained, and deepened underdevelopment in East and Central Europe.[5]

Economic Stimuli for Collective Identity

Policies based upon ethnic nationalism tend to be self-reinforcing since they are neither designed to nor apt to maximise income of a greater community. The consequence is likely to be that as interest group influence in the development of public policy rises, national income will tend to fall below the level which would emerge from the application of more strictly economic criteria (Olson, 1982). Of course, the anticipated redistributional benefits provide the offsetting rationale for this otherwise irrational proposition. For example, apartheid which has been identified elsewhere to be a particularly onerous form of (authoritarian) socialism, furthered cultural and political protectionism and economic redistribution in support of Afrikaner nationalism at the expense of overall economic prosperity.[6] Disproportionately large shares of a growing economy are bad enough. In the end, as has been the case in the socialist economies, the continuing capture of enlarged shares of a stagnant economy by particular interest groups (or fixed allotments of a shrinking economy) is likely to increase envy and hostility between favoured and disfavoured groups.

---

4. There is no intention to challenge the entire corpus of Frank's or Baran's work. However, arguments alleging that capitalism provided sufficient preconditions for the historical impoverishment of Latin America might be seen to be as tenuous as would be an assertion that capitalism caused the current problems of underdevelopment in East and Central Europe. Indeed, in these instances, encounters with capitalism, if at all, were little and late. For example, most of the historical influences described in the use of the model to explain Latin American underdevelopment might be interpreted to relate to mercantilist (i.e., non-private and state-dominated) policies which predated capitalist, private initiatives.

5. It will seem remarkable to many that credible notice is still granted in some quarters to the argument that a socialist revolution is the necessary and appropriate means to correct capitalist-inspired underdevelopment.

6. Within the South African debate over the political economy of apartheid, a radical/Marxian slogan identified apartheid as racial capitalism. A variety of contradictions arise from this expression if one understands that private ownership, freedom of choice in the market, and competition are essential components of capitalism. Indeed, the collectivist/-interventionist aspects of apartheid are more consistent and compatible with socialism. The individualistic claims of the market system are inconsistent with the operation of apartheid which is a group-based dogma. The attenuation of property and political rights associated with apartheid might be described as an outcome of (racial) rent seeking or perhaps as racial socialism. For a more detailed argument, see Lingle (1990b).

Socialist Repression of Entrepreneurs

In the process of altering the production and property relations, authoritarian socialism sought to displace the entrepreneurs' functions. Indeed, one aim of social engineering was to replace the individual entrepreneur by state agencies or planning committees. However, a variety of unanticipated social and economic results might be seen to have emerged from this development.

If one accepts that the entrepreneurial spirit represents, at least in part, an innate human instinct, then suppression of this impulse in one arena would simply divert it to another. Blocked from profiting in legal market activities, natural entrepreneurs might pursue illegal (black market) outlets or might direct their energies to (communist) party politics. In the first instance, the pay-offs from buying low and selling high would have to be reconciled with both the moral and social costs of undertaking a nominally illegal activity, as well as the expected value associated with the risks of being apprehended and punished. A strategy which would minimise these costs and consequences, would be for individuals to operate within groups with whom they were familiar in order to carry out these illegal transactions.[7] This could give rise to particular ethnic groups specialising in carrying out black market activities, such as the reputation enjoyed by the Georgians in the USSR.

Ethnic Nationalism – Alternate Locus of Political Power

Aside from the economic conditions described above, are the political considerations of the recent retreat of the authoritarian socialist state which might explain the ascendancy of (militant) ethnic nationalism. With the simultaneous retreat of the ideology of communism and the demise of its vanguard political parties, these Marxist-Leninist states left disparate nationalities with few alternative political structures. As suggested above, there has been little experience in dealing with political arrangements outside of the communist party structures or ethnically-determined structures. The pressing question is whether these structures shall outlive a transitional period wherein multi-party politics, democratic pluralism, and tolerance eventually become permanent features of the polity.

---

7. In the second instance, in the absence of political competition within a one-party unitary state, two choices emerge. First, one can attempt to rise within the established power structure by jumping through the correct hoops. Failing this approach, one might undertake to overthrow the system. In weaker regimes, such a *coup d'état* might be effective. However, under the discipline of the Warsaw Pact and the Soviet regime, this was too dangerous to attempt.

Transformation of Authoritarian Socialist Institutions

Up to this point, the focus here has been upon the manner in which the incentive structures of authoritarian socialism contributed to a favourable set of conditions for nationalistic propensities to survive, emerge, and expand. Despite the intents of its designers, authoritarian socialism was unable to provide a sufficient mortar to fix the mosaic of cultures into a non-nationalistic, cosmopolitan identity which has been disposed toward an enduring socialist federation. The authoritarian component of socialism simply repressed the most obvious ethnic expressions while reproducing, rather than retarding, nationalistic and ethnic sentiments. Voluntarism, the individualistic focus of the market economy and spontaneous order were supplanted by compulsion, state-compelled collectivism and a false sense of cooperation.[8] These imposed forces have been identified as encouraging a maintenance of a strong sense of ethnic nationalism which may have set the stage for the unpleasant outbursts of ethnic violence observed recently. Restoration of a sense of voluntarism and individual initiative within a market framework may serve to undo the attachment to ethnic structures observed in East and Central Europe.

Interestingly, one of the principal objections to the rapid transformation to market-oriented institutions points to the disruption expected to emerge from the loss of security associated with socialism. However, security in the context of (authoritarian) socialism might best be interpreted to be a destructive social force where gains for one group come at the offsetting expense of others. Protectionism of vested interest, whether to serve the proletariat or industrialists, civil employees or agricultural labourers, professional or unskilled employees, is often proposed as a means to bring about gains in 'social welfare'. However, such protectionist measures are more often likely to provide security to one group at the expense of the rest of the community (Hillman, 1989). On the contrary, the so-called insecurity and economic instability which are seen by some as weaknesses of a market system might be seen as positive and socially beneficial forces. Market transactions, especially under competition and voluntary exchange, allow all participating parties in a transaction to be better off in the end. Voluntarism guarantees that this result is anticipated or the parties would not agree to enter into such an exchange. Such an institutional framework leads to a breaking down of protectionism for special groups and an elimination of the dependencies upon collectives while encouraging greater individual initiative. Full employment under authoritarian socialism often promised little more than a meaningless, degrading job or the necessity of taking several jobs to earn a decent living. Price stability and the absence of inflation were purchased at the cost of quantity adjustments which were observed as shortages, especially of consumer goods.

Following Olson's socio-political model of economic growth (1982),

8. The latter is identified as 'cooperative chaos' by Hayek (1989).

without traditional or explicit restraints on the extent of demands which are made by emerging distributional coalitions, substantial damage can be done to the self-adjusting mechanisms of the economy. Without such restraints, even under representative democracy there is little resistance to such pressures since elected governments resist the pressures to serve these groups at their own peril. Worse, under a one-party populist regime the preferences of a large number of its citizens can be ignored.

Means and Ends of Social Democracy and Authoritarian Socialism

The tragic results of authoritarian socialism might be interpreted as casting a cloud over the acceptability of the model of social democracy in the quest for alternative political and economic institutions to replace authoritarian socialism. Although social democrats remain ambivalent about certain aspects of the socialist projects, they do share a logic and the application of principles of intervention to impose some 'rational' order or to enforce some set of morals. Such reasoning contributes to the formation of government institutions with greater rather than less centralisation of political power. Such centralisation, by extending the distance between citizens and elected representatives, lessens the power of citizens and reduces the accountability of elected or appointed officials. In turn, a situation arises where special interest groups (ethnic or otherwise) are better able to capture a disproportionate share of influence in the formation of policy at the expense of the general public.

A basic problem of social democracy and the social market economy is shared with and was a source of the ultimate failure of authoritarian socialism. An internal contradiction arises from an incapacity of the proposed interventionist means of these systems to achieve their prescribed collectivist goals. One of the principal tools of these various forms of socialism is the application of extensive political intervention into economic processes. However, there are various unintended and undesired results associated with the politicisation of economic activities, most important is that there are reasons to believe that they will systematically fail to reflect the preferences of the masses. On one hand, even under mature representative democracies, special interest groups capture a share of resources which is disproportionate to their numbers. The more intrusive is the state in economic processes, the more extensive will be the occasions for the voter/citizen to be exploited by such groups. On the other hand, the preferences and designs of politicians, technocrats, and bureaucrats are unlikely to be designed to anticipate the wishes of even most of the citizens. Given the dynamic nature of real economic data, it is impossible for a centralised body to make decisions which are consistently correct for any sizeable group. In both instances, attempts to implement policies will undermine the meaning and import of the one-person-one-vote concept of democracy and the voluntary, mutually-beneficial nature of market exchange. Ultimately, the continued widespread presence of institutions which rely upon non-representative distribution of resources might again set the stage and provide the institutional vehicles for a new round of authoritarian repression.

Attempts by 'reform' communists to pose as social democrats and to delay the transformation process should be resisted. The weaknesses and failures of social democracy discussed above suggest that it offers small hope for filling the aspirations of people who wish to free themselves from state oppression and economic deprivation under authoritarian socialism. It may be a hard road to develop a full-blown market economy, but it does not have to be a long one (Lingle, 1990a).

In terms of reducing the divisive and destructive effects of ethnic nationalism, a more complete transformation may require explicit (constitutional) constraints upon state actions which often derive narrowly beneficial results for special interest groups at the expense of the general public. Market-based incentive structures adapted to encourage competition, individualism, and individual effort should diminish the pay-offs as well as the need to identify so strongly with an ethnic group. Operating within market and merit-based institutions will introduce the concept of replacement of the existing order, perhaps leading to a greater sense of tolerance and a better understanding of multi-party politics. Also, the 'marketisation' process will create greater economic interdependencies which will cut across nationalist lines. Importantly, a reduction of the economic and political impact of interest groups will tend to place limits upon the politicisation of the determination of income and wealth while lessening pressures contributing to the emergence and furtherance of the collective spirit conducive to links to ethnic nationalism. Likewise, a 'big bang', accelerationist approach to reform seems to be preferable. Following the logic offered above, the accelerationist approach has the advantage of undermining the ability of new interest groups to form. The sooner the shift toward individualism occurs, the sooner should be the beginning of the difficult road away from dependency upon ethnic nationalist arrangements.

References

Anderson, T. L. and P. J. Hill, 1980, *The Birth of a Transfer Society*. Stanford: Hoover Institute.

Baran, P. A., 1962, *The Political Economy of Growth*. New York: Monthly Review Press.

Becker, G. S., 1971, *The Economics of Discrimination*. Chicago: The University of Chicago Press.

Breton, A., 1964, "The Economics of Nationalism", *Journal of Political Economy* 26.

Frank, A. G., 1969, *Capitalism and Underdevelopment in Latin America: His-*

torical Studies of Chile and Brazil. New York: Monthly Review Press.

Hayek, F. A., 1989, *The Fatal Conceit*. Chicago: The University of Chicago Press.

Hillman, A., 1989, *The Political Economy of Protectionism*. Chur: Harwood Academic Publishers.

Kornai, J., 1985, *The Economics of Shortage*. Amsterdam: Kluwer.

Lingle, C., 1990a, "Apartheid As Racial Socialism", *Kyklos*, Vol. 43, Fasc. 2, pp. 229–247.

_____, 1990b, "Strategies for Structural Reform of Authoritarian Socialism", *Communist Economies* 4, pp. 499–507.

_____, 1992, "Collectivism and Collective Choice: Conflicts Between Class Formation and Ethnic Nationalism", *Ethnic Groups*, Vol. 9, pp. 191–201.

Olson, M., 1971, *The Logic of Collective Action: Public Goods and the Theory of Groups*. New York: Schocken Books.

_____, 1982, *The Rise and Decline of Nations: Economic Growth, Stagflation, and Social Rigidities*. New Haven: Yale University Press.

Seton-Watson, H., 1977, *Nations and States: An Enquiry into the Origins of Nations and the Politics of Nationalism*. London: Methuen.

Snyder, L. L., 1990, *Encyclopedia of Nationalism*. London: St James Press.

Sowell, T., 1981, *Markets and Minorities*. New York: Basic Books.

_____, 1987, *A Conflict of Visions*. New York: William Morrow and Company.

Spanier, J. W., 1972, *Games Nations Play*. London: Thomas Nelson and Sons, Ltd.

Stern, G., 1990, *The Rise and Decline of International Communism*. Aldershot, England: Edward Elgar.

19

Sustainable Transition

*Hans Aage**

Transition

At the summit in Paris of the Conference on Security and Co-operation in Europe (CSCE) on 19–21 November 1990 the so-called Paris Charter was signed as the proposed foundation or constitution for the new European order. The 34 heads of state or government pledged allegiance to the four principles of democracy, rule of law, values of freedom, and the market economy,[1] thus elevating the market, which is currently the fashionable euphemism for capitalism, to a place among the lofty ideals of European culture emanating from 18th century Enlightenment and the Revolution of 1789.

Nevertheless, the following discussion will proceed with the assumption that marketisation and privatisation are just means among others and that the ultimate aim of the revolutions of 1989 was to achieve democracy and prosperity. Democratisation implies liberation from the hegemony of the communist parties as well as national liberation. Prosperity means improving living standards to the levels of the most affluent (regions in) Western countries, to which the populations of Eastern Europe and the former Soviet Union aspire.

The economic tasks facing the transition economies can be separated into different types according to the time perspective of problems and policy actions:

1) short-term stabilisation,
2) medium-term economic growth,
3) long-term sustainability.

---

* Institute of Economics, Copenhagen University.

1. *The Economist,* 24 November 1990, pp. 29–31; *Politiken,* 22 November 1990.

The problem of stabilisation, i.e. to correct imbalances and irrational prices, is the more acute part of the economic crisis in the former Soviet Union and created by the Gorbachev government in the classical way by means of a runaway money printing press. Remedies are well known, although difficult enough to implement, but they do not require system changes. Rather, it is a necessary precondition for transition, which the Gorbachev government was unable to accomplish because of popular and political resistance (CEC, 1990; Nuti, 1990).

Another, much more difficult task is to infuse creativity, entrepreneurship and work effort, dynamism and enthusiasm. In this area of economic growth, ignorance is much more profound. For these purposes, transition to a market economy, profits and unemployment may be the relevant means.

The third, long-term problem of sustainability will be proportionate to the degree of success in raising economic growth during the transition process. This is undoubtedly the most monstrous and difficult problem of all.

Evaluation of the appropriateness of various policy actions, including system reform, privatisation and marketisation, as a means to these ends raises very basic questions concerning the obstacles to democracy and prosperity. It also evokes the problem of forming a coherent picture of the world environment in a few decades' time. Three crucial types of barriers to successful transition, prosperity and democracy will be discussed in some detail:

1) economic systems: institutional barriers,
2) attitudes: ideological barriers,
3) resources: ecological barriers.

The conclusions of this discussion are that the beneficial effects of systemic change are weaker than hoped for by reformers in East and West, that problems of attitudes and resources will endanger sustainable transition, that these problems are remarkably similar in the former planned economies and in other rich countries, and that sustainability is intrinsically related to fundamental problems of democracy.

Prosperity

The current state and accomplishments of the Soviet and Eastern European economies should not be underrated and could very briefly be characterised as follows:

1) they have achieved impressive, although declining growth rates since World War II, cf. Tables 19.1 and 19.2. During the 1970s growth rates declined from 3–5 per cent a year to about 2 per cent, approaching zero in the late 1980s;

TABLE 19.1 Average Annual Growth of GNP for Selected Countries During 1961–1990

	1961 –65	1966 –70	1971 –75	1976 –80	1981 –85	1986 –90
USA	4.8	2.9	2.2	3.2	2.9	3.4
USSR	5.1	5.0	3.0	2.3	1.8	0.6
Poland	4.1	3.8	6.6	0.9	1.2	–1.9
GDR	2.9	3.2	3.5	2.4	1.8	1.8
Czechoslovakia	2.0	3.5	3.4	2.2	1.4	0.9
Hungary	4.3	3.1	3.4	2.3	0.9	–0.2
Romania	5.2	4.6	6.2	3.9	2.0	–2.1
Bulgaria	6.5	4.7	4.5	1.2	0.9	–1.9
West Germany	4.8	4.2	2.1	3.3	1.2	2.9
Norway	4.6	3.7	4.6	4.8	3.3	3.4
Ireland	3.7	4.7	4.9	4.6	2.4	2.4
Denmark	5.3	3.7	2.0	2.5	2.7	1.0

Notes: The numbers are mainly Western recomputations based on official data on the traditional NMP (Net Material Product), which omits 25–40 per cent of GNP, namely depreciation and so-called unproductive sectors like services, education and health. In some cases data for GDP have been used. The low growth figures for the period 1986–90 largely reflect negative rates in 1990.

Sources: OECD (1990b), pp. 90–113; Alton (1989), pp. 80–81; ECE (1990), pp. 82, 87; OECD Economic Outlook 47, June 1990, p. 181; OECD (1992b), pp. 23, 65.

2) they are middle-income countries, and several of them are in fact on a par with the least well off EC member countries;
3) like the rich Western countries they are heavy resource consumers, but inefficiencies in the use of resources are well documented. Energy consumption per unit of output is two or three times Western European levels (Gomulka and Rostowski, 1988; Moroney, 1990), and the amounts of pollution are higher than current Western levels, although they are comparable to Western levels a few decades ago (Hughes, 1991), see Tables 19.1 and 19.2;
4) macro-economic imbalances have increased as well as the excess of consumer purchasing power over the supply of consumer goods at prevailing prices; incentives for management and workers were distorted by unrealistic prices, political infiltration and employment guarantees regardless of productivity. However, unemployment was negligible, and public services like health care and education were provided in high quality and quantity compared to other countries of corresponding economic development.

Difficulties of comparing GNP per capita are tremendous, and for the

USSR/CIS as compared to the USA, a variety of numbers have been presented:

55% in 1987 (Narodnoe Khozjajstvo SSSR, 1988 – no figure is found in the 1989 edition),
53% in 1990 (physical indicators like output of coal, cereals etc., Havlik, 1991),
50% in 1985 (Summers and Heston, 1988, p. 22),
49% in 1986 (CIA, 1987),
37% in 1980 (Marer, 1985),
37% in 1985 (Kirichenko and Martinov, 1991, p. 20),
37% in 1987 (Zoteev, 1991, p. 70),
34% in 1990 (Gorbachev, 1990),
30% in 1986 as a maximum estimate (Åslund, 1990),
30% in 1989 (UNDP, 1992, p. 127).
30% in 1990 (Bolotin, 1991, p. 4),
21% in 1989 (PlanEcon Report, 1990, p. 6),
14% in 1989 (Belkin, 1990, p. 6),
10% in 1989 (IMF et al, 1990), based on a simple conversion of the Soviet GNP in roubles using the exchange rate of 1.8 roubles per dollar.
3% in 1991 (Ståhl, 1992, p. 3), based on an estimate for Estonian GNP evaluated at sales value in the world market.[2]

A realistic estimate could possibly not be much lower than 25 per cent implying military expenditures amounting to 1/4 of GNP, if they are of the same order of magnitude as in the USA where they equal 6 per cent of GNP. A closer look at the Soviet economy is provided in Table 19.2. Taking this evidence into account, it must be concluded that the Eastern European economies are not poor by global standards. It appears that the former planned economies of Eastern Europe and the USSR/CIS, excluding Albania and Romania, belonged to the top 27 per cent of the world population concerning GDP per capita, and to the top 24 per cent concerning the human development index. The economies have in fact been functioning until recently (Murrell, 1990, p. 2). In the USSR/CIS, GNP did not drop until 1990, by 2.4 per cent in 1990 and by 17 per cent in 1991 according to official statistics.[3] The economies through-out Eastern Europe have in 1990 and 1991 experienced sharp declines in production, of 15–30 per cent or more, two or three digit inflation rates and increasing unemployment.

Many possible factors could have contributed to this crisis, and the following appear to be important:

---

2. Narodnoe Khozjajstvo (1988); Marer (1985); CEC (1990); *The Economist,* 10 March 1990, p. 81; Seljunin and Khanin (1987); Ruoho and Eronen (1991); Khanin (1988); US Congress (1982); US Congress (1989); Bolotin, *Moscow News,* 9 June 1991, supplement p. 2; Åslund (1991).

3. *Ekonomika i zhizn'* 5, January 1991, p. 9; 6, February 1992, pp. 13–16.

TABLE 19.2 Soviet Economic Development Since 1960

Annual growth, Per cent	1961 –65	1966 –70	1971 –75	1976 –80	1981 –85	1986 –88	1989	1990	1991
NMP off. figures	6.5	7.8	5.7	4.3	3.2	1.3	2.4	–4.0	–15.0
NMP Seljunin and Khanin	4.4	4.1	3.2	1.0	0.6	–2.0	–4.3	–9.0	..
GNP off. figures	..	..	..	4.8	3.7	2.5	3.0	–2.4	–17.0
GNP est. by CIA	5.1	5.0	3.0	2.3	1.8	0.6	–1.0	–4.0	..
GNP in OECD area	5.3	4.6	3.1	3.4	2.3	3.3	3.4	2.6	1.1
Consumption per capita	3.8	2.9	2.3	2.0	2.5	4.4	2.5	–8.9	..
Investment	6.8	5.4	2.3	2.8	0.6	–1.6	–4.3	–4.0	..
Average wages	..	..	4	3	2	6	9	12	90
Inflation	..	..	0	1	1	2	7	10	150
Labour force	1.1	1.5	1.7	1.5	0.8	0.5	0.6	0.6	..
Grain harvest (mill. tons)	130	168	182	205	180	209	211	215	160
	1965	1970	1975	1980	1985	1988	1989	1990	1991
External debt (bn dollars)	..	2	12	20	29	44	54	56	51
Cars per 100 families (number)	..	2	5	10	15	18	18	..	..
Annual meat consumption (kg per capita)	41	48	57	58	62	66	67	..	..
Employment in agriculture (per cent of total)	29	25	22	20	19	18	18	..	..

Sources: ECE, Economic Survey (various issues); Åslund (1991), p. 29; Ofer (1987), pp. 17–78; Seljunin and Khanin (1987), pp. 194–195; OECD Economic Outlook (various issues); Narodnoe Khozjajstvo (1987), pp. 170, 427; (1988), pp. 6, 454; (1989), pp. 8–9, 46–48, 118, 121, 696; CIA *Handbook of Economic Statistics* (various issues); Aage (1989), pp. 465, 511, 513; US Congress (1987), pp. 194, 202; PlanEcon Report 7–8, (1990); Khanin (1988), (1990), p. 79; Ruoho and Eronen (1990); IMF et al. (1990), p. 4, (1991), p. 87; *Ekonomika i zhizn'* 6, February 1992, pp. 13–16; OECD (1992a); NATO (1992), pp. 31, 22

1) debilitating economic systems;
2) mistaken economic policies. In the USSR/CIS economic policies and a runaway money printing press have in fact destroyed the rouble as a means of payment and made relative prices even more unsuitable for decentralised decisions than they used to be;
3) problems of resources and the environment. The Russian energy crisis and skyrocketing oil-extraction costs have forced hard currency earnings down and contributed to cutting imports by half in 1991. The Eastern European countries are no longer receiving cheap Russian oil, and CMEA trade has collapsed;

4) social disintegration or 'degradation of tissue' (Drewnowski, 1982, pp. 78–82) which are partly caused by reform policies. Soviet enterprises have been widely ignoring plan directives, engaging instead in mutual barter. Due to the so-called war of laws (*voina zakonov*) and the ensuing dissolution of the Soviet Union, republican tax-collecting authorities discontinued payments to union funds. Ownership rights are also increasingly unclear in the Eastern European economies.

Among these contributory factors, the alleged predominance of systemic failure has a surprisingly weak foundation. Apart from the failure of economic policy responses, the real explanations are the social disintegration caused by political liberation and economic reforms coupled with the mounting difficulties of Soviet energy production. The simultaneous decline of Soviet oil production by 20 per cent since 1988 and the decline of the Soviet empire is hardly a coincidence. What has happened is the collapse of a closed CMEA system of production, fuelled by cheap and abundant Soviet oil, which was relatively successful although relatively inefficient by global standards, cf. Tables 19.1 and 19. 2.

How to restore former growth rates under these circumstances is not an easy question, not even in theory. The necessary and sufficient conditions for economic growth are not evident, (cf. World Bank, 1991; Lyttkens and Nalin, 1991; Reynolds, 1983), but the following five conditions appear important:

1) a cultural climate emphasising diligence, work effort and willingness to invest;
2) a strong, uncorrupted state apparatus, especially an efficient system of taxation and a legal framework making contracts enforceable;
3) technical knowledge in a broad sense;
4) availability of resources and capital;
5) external contacts and exchange.

The first two conditions imply a cultural climate, where the need for detailed monitoring is reduced and where economic activity to only a limited extent takes the form of pure rent-seeking behaviour. It is questionable whether this can be achieved by means of any institutional fix. To create viable institutions is difficult and necessary, especially an efficient system of taxation and, according to a study of growth in developing countries, '... the single most important explanatory variable is political organization and the administrative competence of government' (Reynolds, 1983, p. 976; cf. Stern, 1989, p. 614).

Market reforms, while unleashing initiative, actually threaten these important institutions in the short term. Opening the economies towards the world market could spur competition and production, but could also destroy domestic industries.

However, it is not impossible to create growth and prosperity, even at the level of the rich Western economies, as witnessed by the booming economies of South East Asia, e.g. South Korea. In the 1950s economic experts predicted a gloomy future for the country due to its lack of resources, educated labour force and entrepreneurial tradition. What is required is 20–30 years of hard work, low wages, high levels of savings and investment, competent government industrial policy – and a substantial amount of luck concerning external conditions.

Institutions

The faith in marketisation as an unfailing means to spur economic growth is often founded on superficial comparisons with the most affluent (regions in) Western countries. It should be recalled that only five years ago two outstanding American textbooks on comparative economic systems concluded that compared to Western market economies the '... dynamic efficiency of the two systems appears similar. ... The important differences in growth rates appear not between the systems but rather among the nations within the same economic system.' (Pryor, 1985, p. 101; cf. Gregory and Stuart, 1989, p. 414.)

The most striking differences in Table 19.1 are found in the last 5 or 10 years, although the history of nations covers longer periods of time.

The proponents of transition believe in earnest that a 'western type market economy' is a short-cut to wealth. These views are shared with an astonishing degree of consensus in both East and West: 'Free farming and the enterprise economy have come out the winners' (Pinsker and Pijasheva, 1989, p. 194).

Rapid privatisation, even shock-therapy, as applied first in Poland, is vigorously advocated by most Western economists and politicians with only a small although increasing number of sceptical voices (Lipton and Sachs, 1990; Bjukenen, 1990; Blanchard et al., 1990; Kornai, 1990; Tirole, 1991) and *razgosudarstvlenie* (de-statisation) and fast privatisation are on the agenda in the former Soviet republics and throughout Eastern Europe.[4] '... Reformers believe that market economies deliver higher levels of prosperity than planned economies. The evidence in favour of this belief is overwhelming.' (Hanson, 1990, p. 34). '... Mankind has not succeeded in creating anything more efficient than the market economy.' (Shatalin et al., 1990, p. 25). The problem is whether this is true or not.

More specific questions must be considered including the following:

1) Is private or public ownership the more efficient?
2) Which are the crucial differences, especially when ownership is entrusted to large holding companies?
3) What is the optimum number of bankruptcies and the optimum size

4. *Ekonomika i zhizn'* 36, September 1990, Annex p. 1; 7, February 1991, pp. 18–19; Shatalin et al., 1990; *The Economist,* 15 September 1990, pp. 91–92.

of subsidies during transition?

As to the first question, the case for marketisation and privatisation as a means of improving economic growth is founded on rather shaky evidence. Empirical comparisons of private and public enterprises do not give unambiguous conclusions concerning relative efficiencies. A few examples may illustrate: Polish agriculture is predominantly (75 per cent) private, but productivity is low and stagnant, falling progressively behind its Eastern European neighbours. On the other hand, agriculture in the Netherlands is highly efficient and widely based on state-owned lands leased to farmers on long-term contracts. There are two Canadian railroad companies, one privately owned and the other publicly owned. Careful investigations imply the conclusion that '... public ownership is not inherently less efficient than private ownership' (Caves and Christensen, 1980, p. 974). Health care is predominantly private in the USA and almost a state monopoly in Denmark as it is in the Soviet Union, and from an OECD study the conclusion is that the Danish system is far more cost-efficient than the American (OECD, 1990a, p. 10).

A review of empirical findings suggests that 'privately owned firms tend, on average, to be more internally efficient when competition in product markets is effective',but this tendency is not very striking, and '... when market power is significant, and particularly when company behaviour is subject to detailed regulation, there is little empirical justification for a general presumption in favour of either type of ownership' (Vickers and Yarrow, 1988, p. 40; cf. Grosfeld, 1990; Parker, 1987).

The second question amounts to Alec Nove's classical problem concerning the difference, which is not easy to explain, between the American chemicals corporation DuPont and the Soviet Ministry of Chemical Industry. Their turnovers are of comparable size, they make many of the same things, and their internal organisations are both administered rather than market-determined. It appears that the explanation is not administration or state ownership *per se*, but rather: 1) external competition, and 2) the quality of administration and government (Nove, 1977, p. 117).

In the current noisy phase of transition, the difficulty of selecting competent entrepreneurs is an argument for transferring ownership rights to large holding companies which in turn appoint managers who ought to be given low-powered incentive schemes, because the noisy environment tends to turn profit-based payment schemes into managerial rent rather then efficient incentives (Tirole, 1991, pp. 27–28, 32, 47, 55). Thus the new holding companies face a monitoring problem very similar to that of the ancient branch ministries. Therefore, it is important that the reforms succeed in creating efficient competition, even within the state-owned sector.

The case for privatisation – stimulating entrepreneurial effort and private investment and savings and increasing enterprise responsibility and efficiency

– is particularly strong concerning small- and medium-size enterprises. With respect to sequencing, it may be appropriate to privatise small businesses such as trade and consumer services early in the process and larger firms later when a rational price structure is well established (Nuti, 1990). It is important that new firms are created, especially in the retail trade, which are often local monopolies. The creation of private monopolies could compromise private enterprise and the reform process at large, as witnessed by the earlier waves of popular resentment towards cooperatives in the Soviet Union. Chopping up firms in order to restrain monopolies could endanger efficiency, and in Western-type market economies there is a tendency towards mergers and fusions which prevail even in traditional small business sectors like the retail trade.

State-owned enterprises will remain an important feature of the transition economies for a long time to come, and their deregulation and de-politisation is therefore an essential part of the reform. The aim is to reduce the system of bilaterally bargained, bureaucratic, vertical relationships and transform the production structure (Murrell, 1990). This requires stable legal relationships, efficient taxation, price adjustments and improved central planning and industrial policy. The current trend in Western economies of fusions towards larger units is also an expression of the need for better planning. Apart from the possible consequences for monitoring methods, privatisation first of all implies that maximum profit is established as the pre-eminent goal of enterprises. Profits have the virtue of being fairly well defined, visible and measurable, although they entail problems of their own, especially during transition.

The third question concerning the optimum number of bankruptcies must be addressed politically. In the current situation where substantial parts of manufacturing appear to be value subtractors producing negative value-added at world market prices (24 per cent, 19 per cent and 24 per cent in Poland, Czechoslovakia and Hungary, respectively, according to the study by Hughes and Hare (1991, pp. 105, 106–108)), it is a genuine dilemma whether this should be corrected the hard way by means of free market-determined bankruptcies, or whether more constructive solutions should be explored in order to save parts of several decades of costly investments. Generally, it is easy to demolish and destruct, but difficult to do it creatively and build up new industries.

The lessons from reform policies so far are that they are difficult to implement, that they take time, that long-term beneficial effects are uncertain, and that they cause severe short-term hardships. The outcomes are explained partly by the break-down of CMEA trade and Soviet production, especially energy production, partly by stabilisation and reform policies in the Eastern European countries. The most urgent tasks of reform policy are to restore government institutions and state sector production. This also appears to be a necessary condition for achieving the primary tasks of stabilisation policy, namely to restore the payment system and establish realistic prices and to restore the tax base. Radical reform of the whole economic and social structure simultaneously with stabilisation or even as a means of stabilisation policy is desperate and hazardous, although probably politically inevitable. In Russia in the first quarter of 1992 only 1/3 of estimated turnover taxes were collected. Only 9 billion out of 228 billion roubles of estimated state export revenues were realised. The government can no longer guarantee the value of transfer payments, including pensions.

This paves the way for social disintegration, the withering away of the state, the privatisation of tax collection by organised criminals extorting protection money,[5] the impoverishment of large segments of the population, and the disappearance of any confidence in the institutions of society.

Attitudes

The driving forces of the 1989 revolutions were the popular aspirations for democracy and for higher material living standards, especially the latter, which is a prominent social value shared not only by Western culture but worldwide. The convergence of attitudes towards an increasing obsession with material growth was anticipated in some classic works on social evolution. Tocqueville (1850) noticed the urge to work and make money as a conspicuous feature of American culture, and he even postulated a causal relation from democracy to materialism.

Also, according to Marx and Engels consumer materialism was part of the driving force of history. Material consumption is not only deeply ingrained in Western culture and in its ideological legacy. It has also been an important basis for legitimacy of the communist regimes, as well as an overwhelming concern for Soviet and East European citizens according to numerous public opinion polls.[6] The young are especially dissatisfied (and poorly paid)[7] in the Soviet Union, and young respondents in 1990 generally found a post-tax monthly income of 400–500 roubles necessary for a decent living, i.e. approximate average cooperative income at that time, but well above average wages of 240 roubles in the state sector and 196 roubles for *kolkhozniki*.[8]

In the West, the silent revolution towards post-materialist values (Inglehart, 1977, 1981) seems to be superseded by increasing concern for material consumption in recent years. Although general satisfaction with wages seems

5. Cf. Stefan Hedlund in *Dagens Nyheter,* 12 and 13 May 1992.

6. Mason and Sydorenko (1990a), p. 18; Kolarska-Bobinska (1991); Levada (1990), p. 45; AISA (1990), p. 10; *Izvestija,* 25 February 1990, p. 2, and 20 March 1990, p. 2.

7. Mironov (1990), pp. 84–86; *Argumenty i fakty* 16, April 1989, p. 2.

8. M. Ju. Urnov in *Rabochij klass i sovremennyj* 2, mir March–April 1990; cf. VCIOM 15, 1989–91, June 1990, pp. 24–25.

higher in Western Europe than in Poland,[9] there are no signs of saturation of consumer aspirations. In Denmark, the proportion of the population who want to own a motor vehicle (including those who already have one) increased steadily from 65 per cent in 1969 to 83 per cent in 1983. For 'a round the world trip' corresponding numbers were 42 per cent and 59 per cent, and for 'wine for dinner as often as one wants' 63 per cent and 79 per cent (*Observa*, 1985, p. 506). In the USA the share of the population declaring themselves to be satisfied with what their money bought and with their living standards dropped from 82 per cent in 1981 to 62 per cent in 1991, the lowest figure since 1963.[10] An apparent countervailing tendency in the East as well as in the West is the growing concern for the environment, the public's support for environmental programmes appearing stronger than ever.[11] A large majority in Denmark (76 per cent) also favours 'less emphasis on money and material consumption' (Gundelach and Riis, 1990, p. 21). 'People do not always seem willing to act on their preferences, however',[12] especially not when they are expressing socially sanctioned attitudes.

Private property is increasingly positively evaluated in the Soviet Union, by 56 per cent in November 1989, a figure that took even the sociologist Tatjana Zaslavskaja by surprise.[13] In 1990 23 per cent of respondents would prefer that the private sector were dominant in the economy (Bojkov and Toshchenko, 1990, p. 27), and in 1992 72 per cent supported the introduction of private land ownership.[14]

Concerning markets and free prices, there are surprisingly similar and also inconsistent attitudes. Free markets are extremely positively evaluated, but increasing prices are not tolerated, especially in the USSR/CIS where price policy was the main stumbling block for economic reform. In the USSR/CIS 52 per cent supported the transition to a market economy in 1990 (68 per cent among the intelligentsia, 30 per cent among unskilled workers)[15] while 45 per cent approved of the introduction of rationing of butter and washing powder.[16]

9. Stoetzel (1983), pp. 152–153; Jowell and Airey (1984), p. 56; Harding et al. (1986), pp. 171, 184.

10. Gallup published in *Newsweek*, October 1991; quoted from *Information*, 21 November 1991.

11. OECD (1991a), p. 240; OECD (1991b), pp. 50–51; VCIOM 6, 1989–90, November 1989, pp. 7–8; Elklit and Tonsgaard (1989), p. 277; Holmberg and Gilljam (1987), p. 269; Yablokov (1990), pp. 12–13.

12. OECD (1991a), p. 240; cf. the interesting warnings against misuse of public opinion polls by V. Jadov in *Izvestija*, 22 February 1991.

13. VCIOM 7, 1989–90, November 1989, p. 12; *Izvestija*, 25 February 1990, p. 2; *Moscow News* 11, 18 March 1990, p. 10; Mason and Sydorenko (1990a, and b).

14. *Moscow News* 25, 21 June 1992, p. 2

15. *Voprosy Ekonomiki* 7, July 1990, p. 57; *Izvestija*, 24 May 1990, p. 1; Aage (1991), pp. 9–10.

16. VCIOM 9, 1989–90, April 1990, p. 13; cf. Grazhdankin et al., 1990, pp. 34–38.

Surprisingly, there was also widespread scepticism concerning market clearing prices in the West, as documented by the parallel questionnaire survey by Shiller, Boycko and Korobov in New York and Moscow (Shiller, Boycko and Korobov, 1991, p. 389).

Against this background, the reactions to the price liberalisation of 2 January 1992 have been remarkably positive. In November 1990 50 per cent were against free prices,[17] but after that the reform attitudes became less hostile. In August, 73 per cent mentioned increasing prices among the greatest problems of society. In February 1992 it still topped the list, although the figure had dropped to 62 per cent. The number of 'categorical opponents' of price reform in St. Petersburg decreased from 33 per cent in January to 22 per cent in February 1992.[18]

However, growing popular impatience has materialised in Eastern Europe and may soon endanger the sustainability of transition, if its social consequences are not controlled and do not deliver rapid results in terms of higher living standards.

Resources

In relation to consumption of resources, the countries of Eastern Europe and the CIS are characterised by a heavy ideological legacy and a pronounced similarity with Western countries in their performance. Contrary to most of their contemporary fellow economists Marx and Engels cherished strongly optimistic views on future growth possibilities.

In 1979 it was still possible to read in the journal *Social Sciences*, edited by the Soviet Academy of Sciences, that 'There has not been a single case of science not being able to solve a pressing problem facing mankind ...', (Fyodorov, 1979, p. 221) which is of course nonsense, but not very different from the assertions of ill-founded optimism by many Western economists like this very recent one by Lawrence H. Summers: '... our grandchildren will in all likelihood be much better off than we are. ... raising the spectre of our impoverished grandchildren if we fail to address global environmental problems is demagoguery'.[19]

Lenin and the bolsheviks adopted some laws on conservation, including the establishment of national parks (Feshbach and Friendly, 1992, pp. 40–43), but later on the pursuit of economic growth became all-dominant just as in Western countries, expressed in the well-known slogan of 'Communism is Soviet power plus the electrification of the whole country'.[20] Figures 19.1 and

17. *Moscow News* 44, 3 November 1991, p. 1; *Argumenty i fakty* 42, October 1991, p. 1.
18. *Nezavisimaja Gazeta,* 21 February 1992.
19. *The Economist*, 30 May 1992, p. 71; cf. Aage (1984) for further examples.
20. Which was transformed by popular wit into: Soviet power = communism +

19.2 show that with respect to consumption of resources, Eastern Europe and the Soviet Union have achieved a level which is on a par with that of the rich Western economies. Energy consumption is relatively high, consumption of fertiliser and pesticides closer to the average. The main differences are that they use resources relatively inefficiently, progress has been minimal since 1973, while pollution is at a level approximately equivalent to that of Western countries 20–30 years ago i.e. much higher than present-day Western levels. Moreover, pollution is more concentrated in a few heavily polluted areas (Hughes, 1991; Gomulka and Rostowski, 1988; French, 1990; Goskompriroda, 1990; Goskomstat, 1989). Concerning the more global, less visible and more serious types of pollution, e.g. the emission of greenhouse gases, Eastern Europe and the CIS do not contribute more than average.

To describe these facts as 'No other great industrial civilisation so systematically and so long poisoned its land, air, water and people.' 'A society long given to the use of self-descriptive superlatives came to see itself not as the world's best but as the most polluted, most incapacitated ...' 'Ecocide in the USSR stems from the force, not the failure, of utopian ambitions.' 'The Soviet economic and political system, in any case, ensured a low level of priority for environmental protection.'[21]

– is nothing less than a monumental failure. The similarities between industrial countries in the East and in the West are much more striking than the differences. Although this book by Feshbach and Friendly is an undoubtedly useful source of documented information, it is open to an oversimplified interpretation of the 'us/them' type – the CIS has substantial environmental problems while we have solved ours.

A scientific account requires not only documentation, but also a well-defined problem (e.g. what kind of environmental problem, local or global, short term or long term) together with relevant and exhaustive information (especially comparative evidence). The Feshbach and Friendly book, as well as most current newspaper treatments, presents a host of cases of pollution in excess of norms, but little about the content of the norms; much information about the Chernobyl catastrophe of 26 April 1986, but nothing about Three Mile Island or Windscale; very much about the Aral disaster, but nothing about the problems of water resources in other parts of the world, including the American South West; much on forest mismanagement due to planning, but nothing about Brazil, Costa Rica or Malaysia.[22] The analysis of causes

---

electrification of the whole country. V. I. Lenin at a party conference in November 1920, speaking on the GOELRO plan for the electrification of Russia; quoted from Carr (1952), Vol. 2, p. 373.

21. Feshbach and Friendly (1992), pp. 1, 11, 29, 44. This book was reviewed in *The Economist*, 25 April 1992, pp. 93–94 under the heading: 'Rubbishing of a superpower'.

22. Feshbach and Friendly (1992), pp. 73–76, 86–88; *The Economist*, 21 September 1991, p. 31; El-Ashry and Gibbons (1988).

FIGURE 19.1 Energy Consumption Per Capita 1987 (ENECAP) and GDP Per Capita 1985 (GDPCAP)

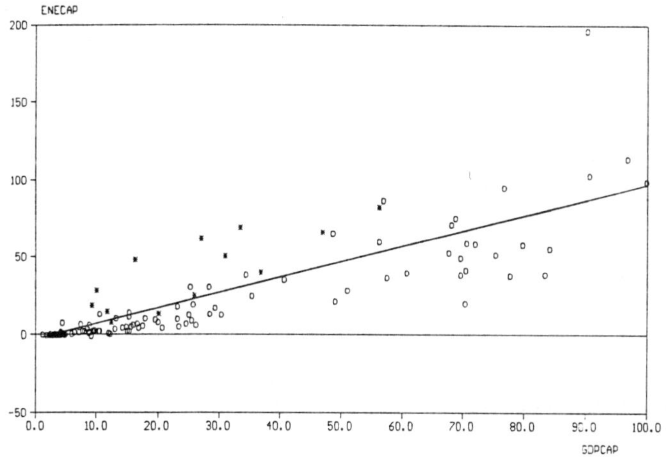

FIGURE 19.2 Greenhouse Effect Per Capita 1987 (GRECAP) and GDP Per Capita 1985 (GDPCAP)

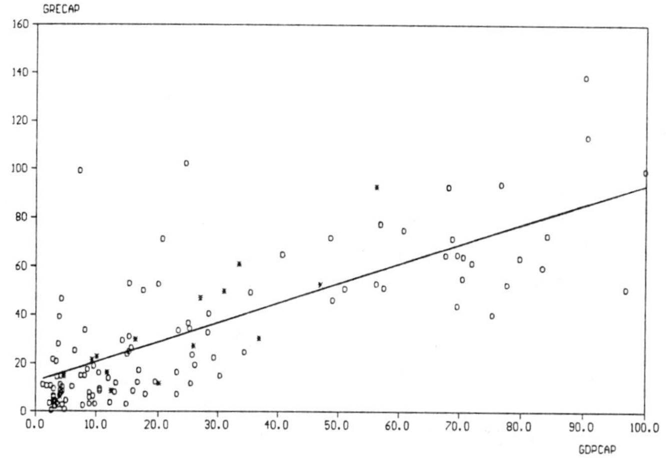

Notes and Sources: All data are expressed relative to the numbers for the USA which are set equal to 100. GDP per capita (Summers and Heston, 1988, pp. 18–21); Havlik (1991, pp. 6, 37); UNDP (1992, pp. 127–129. Energy consumption per capita: World Resources, 1990–91, pp. 316–317; World Bank, 1991, pp. 212–213. Only commercial energy is included. Greenhouse effect: World Resources, 1990–91, pp. 348–349. Net additions to atmospheric concentration: carbon dioxide emissions from fossil fuels use, cement production, and land use changes; methane emissions; CFE use. For more details, please communicate directly with the author.

becomes correspondingly primitive.

Concerning the very important issue of energy production and efficiency a number of studies are available, showing that Eastern Europe and the CIS use 50–150 per cent more energy per unit output than the OECD average (Gomulka and Rostowski, 1988; Moe, 1991; OECD and IEA, 1990). This is only partly explained by differences in production structure and climatic conditions. The comparison between the Soviet Union and Canada is particularly interesting because of climatic as well as certain structural similarities, as both countries export energy corresponding to some 20 per cent of total energy output (OECD and IEA, 1990). Soviet overall energy intensity was about 50 per cent higher than the Canadian in 1988. This is only partly due to structural differences and mainly to higher energy intensities in most sectors, especially in energy production itself. The marginal costs of oil extraction have soared and probably increased 1,500 per cent during 1970–88, even to a point where increasing oil extraction produces a negative net energy output.[23] The reason is first of all increasing transport distances and depletion of high quality deposits.

Therefore investment in energy conservation is extremely profitable. The Energy Research Institute of the Soviet Academy of Sciences has estimated that annual savings of 266 MTOE up to the year 2005 could be obtained for a cost of 38 billion roubles, approximately corresponding to a cost of 34.7 billion roubles needed in 1989 only to maintain current production. To create capacities for additional annual production of 266 MTOE would cost 61 billion roubles (OECD and IEA, 1990, p. 8). It is difficult to understand why opportunities like these have not been exploited.

The ever recurring explanation is a lack of market institutions, which are also regarded as the panacea for all ecological problems (Sätre-Åhlander, 1992, p. 129; Waeterloos, 1992; Feshbach and Friendly, 1992; OECD and IEA, 1990). This could possibly be relevant for minimising costs of oil production, but it nevertheless presents a paradox for everybody trained in the economic theory of externalities. At least it requires the assistance of a very visible and firm hand. Among the first consequences of marketisation in Eastern Europe were imports of hazardous waste in Poland and the USSR (Zylich, 1990, p. 364; Yablokov, 1990, p. 11), logging in Russian national parks and even development for dacha construction in the historical battlefield of Borodino outside Moscow,[24] increasing commitment towards nuclear energy in Latvia,[25] and the signing of the European Energy Charter 17 December 1991 in The Hague, by 31 European countries, 9 former Soviet republics (followed later by the last six) and USA, Japan, Canada and Australia, with the

23. According to D. Aksenov in *Ekonomicheskaja Gazeta* 16, April 1989, p. 5; cf. L. Dienes in *Report on the USSR*, 1 December 1989.

24. *Moscow News* 16, March 1992, p. 14.

25. Vera Rich in *New Scientist*, 25 April 1992, pp. 12–13.

one and only purpose of establishing free market conditions in the energy market throughout Europe.[26]

This kind of arrangement could prove dangerous to Russia. One proposed oil deal has already been described as 'the robbery of the century'.[27] The combination of privatisation and liberalisation of external trade opens the door for foreign dominance which poor and middle-income countries do not possess the economic strength to resist without political control.

Russia has brought herself into the same position as the USA. Both have used up most of their energy reserves. Russia produces about 20 per cent of world oil output, but has only 6 per cent of proven reserves, and Russia has not the economic and military strength of the USA to obtain alternative sources of energy. The Soviet Union and Eastern Europe have ruined themselves trying to imitate the West, and now they will probably ruin their future in the same way. From now on Eastern Europe and increasingly the CIS as well will have to compete in the world market by means of cheap and educated manpower against strong competitors in Asia and Latin America (cf. Cohen, 1991).

Political intervention in the market involves not only the correction of various externalities including environmental effects which call for central planning to assist the market mechanism with a firm and very visible hand. It also involves the much deeper issue of democracy for future generations which the market is incapable of handling. In the current mood of making a fetish of the market, it is often asserted that the market takes care of the needs of future generations because, for example, a profit-maximising owner of an oil deposit will leave the oil in the ground for future exploitation if the price of oil is expected to increase sufficiently. But this does not eliminate the problem of discounting the utility of future generations at a rate of for example 5 per cent. It may be true that the utility for us of one barrel of oil now is 148 times greater than the utility of one barrel to be delivered in 100 years and 22,000 times greater than the utility of one barrel to be delivered in 200 years. But our great-grandchildren will probably think differently. Whether or not a hundred years is a long time, depends, as is well known, upon the end from which they are regarded (Aage, 1984).

It is true that market equilibria over long time spans are theoretically possible and that in theory there is no difference between people living in, say Denmark, and people living 100 years from now. In practice, however, markets only work in the short run, and there is also a more cardinal problem. The equilibrium actually realised among the many possible equilibria with widely differing distributions of final consumption, is largely determined by the initial distribution of ownership rights when the market opens, which means now. The problem for future generations is that they own nothing.

The mix of decentralised market decisions and centralised political

26. According to Waeterloss, 1992.

27. *Moscow News* 16, April 1992, p. 11; *The Economist,* 2 May 1992, p. 86.

decisions depends on external economic conditions. In the long perspective which is relevant for that aimed at fundamental reform and restructuring, it is necessary to form a coherent picture of economic conditions some decades hence, rather than leaving all decisions to market forces which have their potency in relation to short-term efficiency but are notoriously myopic. The present strategy of joining the current boom in (some of) the Western-type market economies raises the questions of the time horizon for the persistence of the boom and the time horizon for the process of catching up.

The affluent Western societies are presently experiencing an explosion of wealth, production, consumption and exploitation of resources. As a matter of fact this is also the situation in the Eastern European countries although on a less excessive scale. The explosion has been protracted, but it is certain that it will draw towards a close. The remaining questions are simply when and especially how? For Western Europe, the process of catching up with the USA after World War II required about 30 years under extremely favourable conditions. It is unlikely that this amount of time will be available for Eastern Europe before a mounting multitude of problems will fundamentally change the economic outlook, especially environmental damage, scarcity of clean energy resources and the need to cut CO_2 emissions (United Nations, 1987). Therefore, it must now seriously be considered that the objective of catching up with Western Europe by imitating its market economies is most likely a mistaken problem in Eastern Europe and elsewhere, the relevant problem is to adapt to a future of difficult and deteriorating conditions.

The arguments for state intervention in this market madness are overwhelming, and it has been recognised by prominent researchers, including Nobel-prize laureates Jan Tinbergen and Trygve Haavelmo in a recent report from the World Bank recommending limits to growth in rich countries and political interventions (Goodland, et al., 1991).

The revolutions of 1989 have endorsed the ideal of liberty and its manifestation as freedom of the market together with the current world-wide obsession with material growth. However, other ideals of 1789 and later revolutions have figured less prominently, namely equality and fraternity. This is highly regrettable as both will soon be badly needed in the future of economic hardship and escalating conflicts.

References

Aage, H., 1984, "Economic Arguments on the Sufficiency of Natural Resources", *Cambridge Journal of Economics* 8, No. 1, pp. 105–113.

_____, 1989, "Inequality, Incentives, and Income". A review article and seven-teen papers in comparative and Soviet studies. *Studier* 32. Københavns Universitets Økonomiske Institut.

_____, 1991, "Popular Attitudes and Perestroika", *Soviet Studies* 43, No. 1, pp. 3–25.

AISA, "Czechoslovakia – November 1990. Survey Report". Praha: Association for Independent Social Analysis 1990.

Alton, T. P., 1989, "East European GNP's, Domestic Final Uses of Gross Product, Rates of Growth, and International Comparisons". Vol. 1, pp. 77–96 in US Congress, Joint Economic Committee (ed.): *Pressures for Reform in the East European Economies*. Washington, DC: US Government Printing Office.

Åslund, A., 1990, "How Small is the Soviet National Income?" in Rowen, H. S. and C. Wolf (eds), *The Impoverished Superpower*. San Francisco: ICS Press.

_____, 1991, "Gorbachev, Perestroika, and Economic Crisis". *Problems of Communism* 40, No. 1–2, pp. 18–41.

Belkin, V.,(1990), *Moscow News*, 27 May.

Bjukenen, D. M. (D. M. Bukanan), 1990, "Minimal'naja politika rynochnoj sistemy", *Voprosy Ekonomiki* 12, December, pp. 7–15.

Blanchard, O., R. Dornbusch, P. Krugman, R. Layard, and L. Summers, 1990, "Reform in Eastern Europe". 1990 Report of the WIDER World Economy Group. Washington, DC.: WIDER.

Bojkov, V. and Zh. Toshchenko, 1990, "V zerkale sociologii", *Partijnaja zhizn'* 18, September, pp. 23–28.

Bolotin, B., (1991), *Argumenty i Fakty,* October, No. 39.

Carr, E. H., 1952, *A History of Soviet Russia 2. The Bolshevik Revolution 1917–1923*. London: Macmillan.

Caves, D. W. and L. R. Christensen, 1980, "The Relative Efficiency of Public and Private Firms in a Competitve Environment: The Case of Canadian Railroads", *Journal of Political Economy* 88, 1980, No. 5, pp. 958–976.

CEC (Commission of the European Communities), 1990, "Stabilization, Liberalization and Devolution: Assessment of the Economic Situation and Reform Process in the Soviet Union", *European Economy* 45.

CIA, 1987, *Handbook of Economic Statistics 1987*. Washington, DC: US Government Printing Office.

Cohen, D., 1991, "The Solvency of Eastern Europe" in *The Path of Reform in Central and Eastern Europe. European Economy.* (Special Edition No. 2, 1991), pp. 263–303. Brussels: CEC (Commission of the European Communities).

Drewnowski, J., 1982, "The Anatomy of Economic Failure in Soviet-type Systems" in Drewnowski, J. (ed.), *Crisis in the East European Economy,* pp 72–86. Beckenham: Croom Helm.

ECE (Economic Commission for Europe), 1990, *Economic Survey of Europe in 1989–1990*. New York: UN.

El-Ashry, M. T. and D.C. Gibbons (eds), 1988, *Water and Arid Lands of the Western United States.* Cambridge: Cambridge University Press.

Elklit, J. and O. Tonsgaard (eds), 1989, *To folketingsvalg*. (Two General Elections). Aarhus: Politica.

Feshbach, M. and A. Friendly, 1992, *Ecocide in the USSR*. New York: Basic Books.

French, H. F., 1990, "Green Revolutions: Environmental Reconstruction in Eastern Europe and the Soviet Union", *Worldwatch Paper* 99. Washington DC: Worldwatch Institute.

Fyodorov, E, 1979, "Relations with Nature Optimised", *Social Sciences* 10, No. 1, pp. 205–221.

Gomulka, S. and J. Rostowski, 1988, "An International Comparison of Material Intensity", *Journal of Comparative Economics,* 12 December, No. 4, pp. 475–501.

Goodland, R., H. Daly, S. El Serafy and B. von Droste, B. (eds), 1991, *Environmentally Sustainable Economic Development: Building on Brundtland.* Paris: UNESCO.

Gorbachev, M., 1990, *Pravda* 26 October.

Goskompriroda: 1990, Sostojanie prirodnoj sredy v SSSR v 1988 godu: Mezhvedomstvennij doklad. Moskva: Lesnaja Promyshlennost'.

Goskomstat: 1989, Okhrana okruzhajushchei sredy i ratsional'noe ispol'zovanie prirodnykh resursov v SSSR. Statisticheskij sbornik. Moskva: Goskomstat.

Grazhdankin, A. I. et al., 1990, "Otnoshenie naselenija g. Moskvy k uzlovym problemam perekhoda k rynochnoj ekonomike". Moskva: VCIOM.

Gregory, P. R. and R. C. Stuart, 1989, *Comparative Economic Systems.* Boston: Houghton Mifflin. (Third Edition).

Grosfeld, I., 1990, "Reform Economics and Western Economic Theory: Unexploited Opportunities", *Economics of Planning* 23, No. 1, pp. 1–19.

Gundelach, P. and O. Riis, 1990, "Værdiforandringer i Danmark 1981–1990" (Value changes in Denmark 1981–1990). *Working paper.* Institute of Political Science, University of Aarhus.

Hanson, P., 1990, "The Baltic States. The Economic and Political Implications of the Secession of Estonia, Latvia and Lithuania from the USSR". Special report No. 2033, March 1990. London: The Economist Intelligence Unit.

Harding, S., D. Phillips and M. Fogarty, 1986, *Contrasting Values in Western Europe*. London: Macmillan.

Havlik, P., 1991, "East–West GDP Comparisons: Problems, Methods and Results" *Forschungsberichte* No. 174. Wien: Wiener Institut für Internationale Wirtsschaftsvergleiche.

Hoeller, P., A. Dean and J. Nicolaisen, 1991, "Macro-economic Implications of Reducing Greenhouse Gas Emissions: A Survey of Empirical Studies", *Economic Studies* 16, pp. 45–78. Paris: OECD.

Holmberg, S. and M. Gilljam, 1987, *Väljare och val i Sverige*. (Voters and Elections in Sweden). Stockholm: Bonniers.

Hughes, G., 1991, "Are the Costs of Cleaning up Eastern Europe Exaggerated? Economic Reform and the Environment", *Oxford Review of Economic Policy* 7, No. 4, pp. 106–136.

Hughes, G. and P. Hare, 1991, "Competitiveness and Industrial Restructuring in Czechoslovakia, Hungary and Poland", *European Economy,* Special Edition No. 2, pp. 83–110.

IMF, IBRD, OECD and EBRD, 1990, *The Economy of the USSR*. A study undertaken in response to a request by the Houston summit. Summary and Recommendations. Washington, DC: IMF December.

IMF, IBRD, OECD and EBRD (eds), 1991, *A Study of the Soviet Economy*. Paris: OECD.

Inglehart, R., 1977, *The Silent Revolution. Changing Values and Political Styles Among Western Publics*. Princeton: Princeton University Press.

_____, 1981, "Post-Materialism in an Environment of Insecurity", *American Political Science Review* 75, December, No. 4, pp. 880–900.

Jacobs, M., 1991, *The Green Economy*. London: Pluto Press.

Jowell, R. and C. Airey, 1984, *British Social Attitudes. The 1984 Report*. Aldershot: Gower.

Khanin, G., 1988, "Ekonomicheskij rost: Alternativnaja otsenka", *Kommunist* 17, pp. 83–90.

_____, 1990, "Krizis uglubljaetsja", *Ekonomika i organizatsiia promyshlennogo proizvodstva* 1, pp. 73–87.

Kirichenko, V. and Martinov, V., (1991), *Ekonomika i zhizn'* February, No. 6.

Kolarska-Bobinska, L., 1991, "Civil Society and Social Anomy in Poland", *Acta Sociologica* 34. (Forthcoming.)

Kornai, J., 1990, *The Road to a Free Economy. Shifting from a Socialist System: The Example of Hungary*. New York: Norton.

Levada, Ju.A. (ed.), 1990, *Est' mnenie!*. Moskva: Progress.

Lipton, D. and J. Sachs, 1990, "Creating a Market Economy in Eastern Europe: The Case of Poland", *Brookings Papers on Economic Activity* 1, pp. 75–147.

Lyttkens, C. H. and C. Nalin, 1991, "Varför är rika länder rika och fattiga länder fattiga?" (Why are Rich Countries Rich and Poor Countries Poor?), *Ekonomisk Debatt* 2, pp. 108–118.

Marer, P., 1985, *Dollar GNPs of the USSR and Eastern Europe*. Baltimore: Johns Hopkins University Press and The World Bank.

Marx, K. and F. Engels, 1848, *Manifest der kommunistischen Partei*. Berlin: Dietz Verlag 1968. English Edition by D. A. Drennen, Woodbury, New York: Barron's Educational Series 1972.

Mason, D. S. and S. Sydorenko, 1990a, "Perestroyka, Social Justice, and Public Opinion". Paper presented at the 6th World Congress for Soviet and East European Studies, Harrogate, 24–27 July 1990a.

_____, 1990b, "Perestroyka, Social Justice, and Soviet Public Opinion". *Pro-*

blems of Communism 39, No. 6, pp. 34–43b.

Meek, R. L., 1956, *Marx und Engels über Malthus*. Berlin: Dietz Verlag.

Mironov, A. A., 1990, "Ot zarplaty do zarplaty", *Sociologicheskie issledovanija* 1, pp. 84–86.

Moe, A., 1991, "The Soviet Oil Industry: Where do we go from here?" in Weichhardt, R. (ed.), *The Soviet Economy under Gorbachev*. (NATO Colloquium 1991). Brussels: NATO Economics Directorate.

Moroney, J. R., 1990, "Energy Consumption, Capital and Real Output: A Comparison of Market and Planned Economies", *Journal of Comparative Economics* 14, pp. 199–220.

Murrell, P., 1990, "'Big Bang' versus Evolution: East European Economic Reforms in the Light of Recent Economic History". PlanEcon Report 29 June 1990, No. 26, pp. 2–11.

Narodnoe Khozjajstvo SSSR, 1987, 1988, 1989. Moskva: Finansy i Statistika.

NATO Economic Committee, 1992, *Soviet Economic Performance in 1991. A Weak Foundation for a New Beginning*. Brussels: NATO.

Nicolaisen, J., A. Dean and P. Hoeller, 1991, "Economics and the Environment: A Survey of Issues and Policy Options", *Economic Studies* 16, pp. 7–43. Paris: OECD.

Nove, A., 1977, *The Soviet Economic System*. London: Allen and Unwin.

Nuti, D. M., 1990, "Stabilisation and Reform Sequencing in the Soviet Economy", *Recherches Economiques de Louvain* 56, No. 2, pp. 169–180.

_____ , 1992, "Lessons from the Stabilisation Programmes of Central and Eastern European Countries, 1989–1991". Paper presented at the Arne Ryde Symposium on 'The Problem of Transition'. University of Lund, Rungsted Kyst, 11–12 June.

Observa, 1977, 1981, 1985, *Danskerne – meninger, holdninger, vaner*. (The Danes – Opinions, Attitudes, Habits.) Three Vols: 1967–77, 1977–80, 1981–84. Copenhagen: Observa.

OECD, 1990a, "Health Care Systems in Transition. The Search for Efficiency". *Social Policy Studies* 7. Paris: OECD.

_____ , 1990b, *National Accounts 1960–1988*. Paris: OECD.

_____ , 1991a, *The State of the Environment*. Paris: OECD.

_____ , 1991b, *Environmental Indicators. A Preliminary Set*. Paris: OECD.

_____ , 1992a, *Centre for Cooperation with European Economies in Transition* (ed.): *The Transition to a Market Economy*. (Two Vol.) Paris: OECD.

_____ 1992b, *Reforming the Economies of Central and Eastern Europe*. Paris: OECD.

OECD Economic Outlook (various issues).

OECD and IEA, 1990, "Energy Efficiency in the USSR". Note by the Secre-tariat of the Ad Hoc Group on International Energy Relations. Paris: OECD.

Ofer, G., 1987, "Soviet Economic Growth: 1928-1985", *Journal of Economic*

Literature 25, No. 4, pp. 1767–1833.

Parker, D., 1987, "Private vs. Public: A Critique of the New Right", *Economia Aziendale* 6, No. 1, pp. 35–57.

Pinsker, B. and L. Pijasheva, 1989, "Sobstvennost' i svoboda", *Novyj Mir* 11, pp. 184–199.

PlanEcon Report (Various issues) New York.

Pryor, F. L., 1985, *A Guidebook to the Comparative Study of Economic Systems*. Englewood Cliffs, NJ: Prentice-Hall.

Reynolds, L. G., 1983, "The Spread of Economic Growth to the Third World: 1850–1980", *Journal of Economic Literature* 21, No. 3, pp. 941–980.

Ruoho, S. and J. Eronen, 1991, "Poor Man's Index and Soviet Economic Growth in 1960–1989". Paper presented at the Nordic Conference on Soviet and East European Studies, Uppsala, 23–25 November.

Sätre-Åhlander, A.–M., 1992, "The Effect of the Soviet Shortage Economy on the Environment and Natural Resources". Doctoral thesis. University of Stockholm: Department of Economics. (Unpublished.)

Seljunin, V. and G. Khanin, 1987, "Lukavaja cifra", *Novyj Mir* 63, No. 2, pp. 181–201.

Shatalin, S. S. et al., 1990, *Perekhod k rynku. Koncepcija i programma*. Moskva: Arkhangel'skoe.

Shiller, R. J., M. Boycko and V. Korobov, 1991, "Popular Attitudes Toward Free Markets: The Soviet Union and The United States Compared", *American Economic Review* 81, No. 3, pp. 385–400.

Ståhl, I., 1992, "Valutareform i Estland". Paper presented at the Nordic Economic Research Council's Workshop on 'The Baltic States'. Copenhagen, 25–26 May.

Stern, N., 1989, "The Economics of Development: A Survey", *Economic Journal* 99, No. 397, pp. 597–685.

Stevens, C. and J. Kennan (eds), 1992, *Reform in Eastern Europe and the Developing Country Dimension*. London: Overseas Development Institute.

Stoetzel, J., 1983, *Les valeurs du temps présent*. Paris: Presses Universitaires de France.

Summers, R. and A. Heston, 1988, "A New Set of International Comparisons of Real Products and Price Levels Estimates for 130 Countries, 1950–1985", *Review of Income and Wealth* 34, No. 1, pp. 1–25.

Thalberg, B., 1992, "Should the East-European Countries Aim, in the First One or Two Decades of their Transition, at a Kind of System Similar to Those Employed by Certain Western Social Democracies in the Early Afterwar Years?". Paper presented at the Nordic Economic Research Council's Workshop on "The Baltic States". Copenhagen, 25–26 May.

Tirole, J., 1991, "Ownership and Incentives in a Transition Economy". Working paper. Cambridge, Mass.: MIT Press.

Tocqueville, A. de, 1850, *De la démocratie en Amérique*. (Treizième édition, tome deuxième). Paris: Pagnerre.

Turnbull, M., 1991, *Soviet Environmental Policies and Policies*. Aldershot: Dartmouth.

UNDP, 1992, *Human Development Report 1992*. Oxford: Oxford University Press.

United Nations' World Commission on Environment and Development, 1987, *Our Common Future*. Oxford: Oxford University Press.

US Congress, Joint Economic Committee (ed.), 1982, *USSR: Measures of Economic Growth and Development, 1950–1980*. Washington, DC: US Government Printing Office.

_____, 1987, *Gorbachev's Economic Plans*. Washington, DC: US Government Printing Office.

_____, 1989, *Pressures for Reform in the East Europen Economies*. Washington, DC: US Government Printing Office.

VCIOM (Vsesojuznij centr izuchenija obshchestvennogo mnenija po social'no-ekonomicheskim voprosam): "Obshchestvennoe mnenie v cifrach", (various issues), 1989–91.

Vickers, J. and G. Yarrow, 1988, *Privatization: An Economic Analysis*. Cambridge, Mass.: The MIT Press.

von Weizsäcker, E. U. and J. Jesinghaus, 1992, *Ecological Tax Reform. A Policy Proposal for Sustainable Development*. London: Zed Books.

Waeterloos, C., 1992, "The European Energy Charter. Progress to Date and Priorities for the Future". Paper presented at the NATO Economics Colloquium, "External Economic Relations of the Central and East European Countries". Brussels, 8–10 April.

Wirl, F., 1991, "Impact of the Political and Economic Restructuring in Eastern Europe on the Availability of Net Energy Exports – An Empirical Framework", *Economics of Planning* 24, No. 3, pp. 181–202.

World Bank, 1991, *World Development Report 1991: The Challenge of Development*. New York: Oxford University Press.

_____, 1992, *World Development Report* 1992: *Development and the Environment*. New York: Oxford University Press.

World Resources, 1990–91. *A Report by the World Resources Institute*. Oxford: Oxford University Press 1990.

Yablokov, A., 1990, "The Current State of the Soviet Environment", *Environmental Policy Review* 4, No. 1, pp. 1–14.

Zoteev, G. N., 1991, "The National Product and Income in the Soviet Economic System", *Most* 1, pp. 61–76.

Zylich, T., 1990, "Miljöpolitik för före detta centralplanerade ekonomier – ett polskt perspektiv", *Ekonomisk Debatt* 4, pp. 361–368.

Name Index

Subject Index